Order, Conflict, and Violence

There might appear to be little that binds the study of order and the study of violence and conflict. Bloodshed in its multiple forms is often seen as something separate from and unrelated to the domains of "normal" politics that constitute what we think of as order. But violence is used to create order, to maintain it, and to uphold it in the face of challenges. This volume demonstrates the myriad ways in which order and violence are inextricably intertwined. The chapters embrace such varied disciplines as political science, economics, history, sociology, philosophy, and law; employ different methodologies, from game theory to statistical modeling to in-depth historical narrative to anthropological ethnography; and focus on different units of analysis and levels of aggregation, from the state to the individual to the world system. All are essential reading for anyone who seeks to understand current trends in global conflict.

Stathis N. Kalyvas is Arnold Wolfers Professor of Political Science at Yale University, where he directs the Program on Order, Conflict, and Violence. He is the author of *The Logic of Violence in Civil War* (2006) and *The Rise of Christian Democracy in Europe* (1996).

Ian Shapiro is Sterling Professor of Political Science at Yale University, where he also serves as Henry R. Luce Director of the MacMillan Center for International and Area Studies. His most recent books are *Containment: Rebuilding a Strategy against Global Terror* (2007), *The Flight from Reality in the Human Sciences* (2005), and *Death by a Thousand Cuts: The Fight over Taxing Inherited Wealth* (with Michael Graetz, 2006).

Tarek Masoud is a doctoral candidate in Political Science at Yale University. He is the editor of *Problems and Methods in the Study of Politics* (with Ian Shapiro and Rogers M. Smith, 2004).

Order, Conflict, and Violence

Edited by

Stathis N. Kalyvas, Ian Shapiro,
and Tarek Masoud

CAMBRIDGE
UNIVERSITY PRESS

CAMBRIDGE UNIVERSITY PRESS
Cambridge, New York, Melbourne, Madrid, Cape Town,
Singapore, São Paulo, Delhi, Tokyo, Mexico City

Cambridge University Press
The Edinburgh Building, Cambridge CB2 8RU, UK

Published in the United States of America by
Cambridge University Press, New York

www.cambridge.org
Information on this title: www.cambridge.org/9780521722391

© Cambridge University Press 2008

First published 2008

A catalogue record for this publication is available from the British Library

Library of Congress Cataloguing in Publication data

ISBN 978-0-521-89768-6 Hardback
ISBN 978-0-521-72239-1 Paperback

Contents

Part 2 Challenging, transforming, and destroying order

Figures

Tables

Contributors

Robert H. Bates Department of Government, Harvard University

Carles Boix Department of Politics and the Woodrow Wilson School of Public and International Affairs, Princeton University

Lars-Erik Cederman Center for Comparative and International Studies, Swiss Federal Institute of Technology, Zurich

Lucy Chester Department of History, University of Colorado at Boulder

Francisco Gutiérrez Sanín Institute for Political Studies and International Relations, Colombia National University, Bogotá.

Michael Hechter School of Global Studies, Arizona State University

Isabel V. Hull Department of History, Cornell University

Courtney Jung Department of Political Science, New School University

Nika Kabiri Department of Sociology, University of Washington

Stathis N. Kalyvas Department of Political Science, Yale University

Ellen Lust-Okar Department of Political Science, Yale University

Tarek Masoud Department of Political Science, Yale University

Karma Nabulsi St. Edmund Hall, University of Oxford

Robert J. Sampson Department of Sociology, Harvard University

Ian Shapiro Department of Political Science and the Whitney and Betty MacMillan Center for International and Area Studies, Yale University

Jack L. Snyder Department of Political Science, Columbia University

Scott Straus Department of Political Science, University of Wisconsin, Madison

Leslie Vinjamuri Edmund A. Walsh School of Foreign Service and Department of Government, Georgetown University

Per-Olof H. Wikström University of Cambridge

Steven I. Wilkinson Department of Political Science, University of Chicago

Elisabeth Jean Wood Department of Political Science, Yale University

Preface

This volume emerged from a conference on "Order, Conflict, and Violence" held at Yale in May of 2004. It is one of a series of books to come out of the Yale Political Science Initiative on "Rethinking Political Order." Other volumes resulting from the Initiative are *Problems and Methods in the Study of Politics*, edited by Ian Shapiro, Rogers Smith, and Tarek Masoud (Cambridge University Press 2004); *Rethinking Political Institutions: The Art of the State*, edited by Ian Shapiro, Stephen Skowronek, and Daniel Galvin (New York University Press 2006); *Identities, Affiliations, and Allegiances*, edited by Seyla Benhabib, Ian Shapiro, and Danilo Petranovich (Cambridge University Press 2007); *Political Contingency: Studying the Unexpected, the Accidental, and the Unforeseen*, edited by Ian Shapiro and Sonu Bedi (New York University Press 2007); *Divide and Deal: The Politics of Distribution in Democracies*, edited by Ian Shapiro, Peter Swenson, and Daniela Donno (New York University Press 2008); and *Representation and Popular Rule*, edited by Ian Shapiro, Susan Stokes, Elisabeth Wood, and Alexander Kirshner (in press).

We are pleased to record our gratitude to Yale University for the financial support that has made this initiative possible. Thanks are due to Sage Publications for permission to reprint Courtney Jung, Ellen Lust-Okar, and Ian Shapiro's essay, "Problems and Prospects for Democratic Settlements: South Africa as a Model for the Middle East and Northern Ireland?" which first appeared in *Politics and Society* 33:2 (June 2005), in the present volume. Pamela Bosward, Alice Kustenbauder, Anne Nguyen, and Sandra Nuhn all deserve recognition for invaluable organizational and editorial assistance. Finally, we owe special thanks to the two anonymous reviewers for their excellent feedback, and to John Haslam and Carrie Cheek, our editors at Cambridge University Press, for helping to bring this volume to completion.

1 Introduction: integrating the study of order, conflict, and violence

Stathis N. Kalyvas, Ian Shapiro, and Tarek Masoud

There might appear to be little that binds the study of order and the study of violence and conflict. Bloodshed in its multiple forms – interstate war, civil conflict, crime – is often seen as something separate from, and almost unrelated to, the domains of "normal" politics that constitute what we think of as order. Students of political, social, and economic institutions simply assume that violence is absent and order established, never considering that the maintenance of such institutions might involve the ongoing management of conflict and the more or less direct threat of violence. Likewise, students of violence and conflict tend to focus on places and periods in which order has collapsed, rarely considering how violence is used to create order at the national and local levels, maintain it, and uphold it in the face of challenges. In Charles Tilly's (1975, 42) famous formulation: war makes states. Clearly, order is necessary for managing violence as much as the threat of violence is crucial in cementing order.

Yet the question of how order emerges and how it is sustained is but the flip side of understanding the dynamics of conflict. On the one hand, order requires the active taming of conflict. However, this is often impossible without an actual or threatened recourse to violence. In game-theoretic language, violence is off the equilibrium path of order.[1] On the other hand, violent conflict entails the successful contestation of existing order, and its collapse. Put otherwise, violence is employed both by those who wish to upend an existing order and by those who want to sustain it.

The lack of integration between the study of order and the study of conflict and violence is in part a natural consequence of disciplinary and

---

[1] One is reminded of the famous example (related to us by John Ferejohn) of the two thieves: one mangles his victims before relieving them of their wealth; the other presents his quarry with a choice: "your money or your life?" Though no blood is spilled in the latter scenario – which might even be labeled a voluntary transaction – it is dripping with violence nonetheless. Likewise, much of what we identify as order is simply violence in disguise. Political institutions are often erected on violent foundations, and maintained through implicit and explicit threats of bloodshed should obedience be withheld.

sub-disciplinary barriers that have long separated the various ways of studying human behavior and institutions. Different disciplines operate at different levels of analysis, and focus on different variables and aspects of these phenomena. Sociologists emphasize social control and the deviation from it – crime and *anomie* – while economists point to economic forces under secure and protected property rights. Anthropologists study the lived experiences of individuals and communities primarily under conditions of peace, while psychologists try to uncover the properties of a universal "human mind" under similar conditions. Historical sociologists examine instances of major breakdown (such as revolutions), economists have turned their attention to terrorism and civil wars, as have political scientists who are also exploring medium-range phenomena such as riots and pogroms, while criminologists study "everyday" forms of collapse of order such as crime and "interpersonal violence." Within political science, international relations scholars study cooperation and conflict between states, while comparativists highlight similar processes at the domestic level. The first have made a specialty of the study of interstate war while the latter have focused on the study of civil wars and revolutions.

Differences of focus are reinforced by methodological ones. Some scholars work at the macro level, others at the micro level. Some scholars rely on interviews and archives of historical documents, while others employ statistical analyses or reason deductively from abstract formal models. Furthermore, scholarship on violence and conflict and political order is splintered not just by differences in their substantive focuses, disciplinary boundaries, and the methodological predilections of researchers, but by what appear to be fundamentally different assumptions about the nature of the individual. Studies of violent conflict seem to be populated with individuals who are easily swayed by irrational passions and genocidal ideologies, while studies of order are peopled by reasonable, calculating maximizers of material interests. There are important exceptions to this characterization, of course,[2] but for the most part, students of phenomena like the 1994 Rwandan genocide offer us a very different view of human motivations than those who study such processes as the building and development of democratic institutions. Of course, it is difficult to say whether this divergence in the ontology of the individual is a cause of the divide between studies of order and violence or a result of it, but it is nonetheless questionable.

Given all of these disciplinary divides and methodological and metaphysical proclivities, it is little wonder that students of order, conflict,

---

[2] See, for instance, De Figueiredo and Weingast (1999).

and violence so rarely speak to each other. This volume is offered as a corrective to this scholarly fragmentation. At first glance, the contributions – which tackle the phenomena of order, conflict, and violence from a set of highly diverse substantive, theoretical, and methodological perspectives – might seem to be impossibly diverse, more a symptom of the fissures we describe than a treatment for them. They raise a dizzying array of questions: How does order emerge and how is it sustained? How are international norms governing violence developed and implemented? How is peaceful interaction maintained and enforced within state borders and among states, and when does it break down? What are the sources of violence? Are they primarily material – found, for example, in perpetrators' economic circumstances and in the institutional structures under which they operate – or can ideologies and other nonmaterial factors spawn violence? Are some types of social cleavages – such as class, ethnicity, or religion – more likely than others to erupt in bloodshed? And what determines the forms that such bloodshed will take – from coups, to massacres, to revolutions, to riots, to war, to genocide? How does (and *should*) legitimacy come to be conferred on some uses of violence and not on others? And most importantly, how is conflict tamed and violence averted? These essays could not be more varied – and in this respect, they reflect the state of the current division of labor. But by bringing them into dialogue here, it becomes apparent that all of the questions they raise are in fact facets of a single enduring and fundamental meta-question: how order emerges, is sustained, challenged, destroyed, transformed, and recreated.

The contributions to this volume can be ordered along four axes.

- The first, and most important, axis distinguishes between processes that lead to the creation and sustenance of order (such as Robert H. Bates' examination of how self-interested political leaders choose to cultivate the populations they control instead of expropriating from them) and those that involve the challenging, transformation, and destruction of order (such as Francisco Gutiérrez Sanín's study of the motivations of rural insurgents).
- The second axis differentiates between studies which take place at the domestic level (such as Carles Boix's exploration of class and political violence within states), at the international level (such as Karma Nabulsi's study of the development of legal norms governing conduct in war), or at the intersection of the two, where domestic dynamics are influenced and shaped by external actors (such as Michael Hechter and Nika Kabiri's study of colonial powers' attempts to impose order in Iraq).

- The third axis describes variation in the units of analysis – some contributions focus on highly aggregated units (such as Jack L. Snyder and Leslie Vinjamuri's exploration of the conditions for normative change in the international system), while others address the behaviors and motivations of individuals (such as Elisabeth Jean Wood's investigation of the factors motivating the use of sexual violence), while still others operate at an intermediate level (such as Robert J. Sampson and Per-Olof H. Wikström's study of social order in the neighborhoods of Chicago and Stockholm and Stathis N. Kalyvas' assessment of the "microdynamics of civil war" research program).
- Finally, along the fourth axis we have studies that emphasize the role of material factors (such as the contributions by Boix and Bates), as well as those that emphasize the role of norms, ideas, and culture (such as Lars-Erik Cederman's exploration of the role of nationalist identities in fomenting challenges to order).

This book is divided into two parts, following the first axis described above. The essays in Part 1 consider the foundations of political order: how it emerges, how it is maintained, and how it is restored in the wake of disorder. The essays in Part 2 consider the ways in which violence and conflict serve to challenge political order, transform it, and destroy it altogether.

Part 1: Creating, maintaining, and restoring order

The question of how order is established at the national level is taken up in chapter 2 by Robert H. Bates. Drawing on Mancur Olson's (1993) equation of politics with banditry, Bates attempts to discover the conditions under which those who control a given territory – whom he calls "specialists in violence" – choose to defend rather than prey upon its inhabitants. Reasoning deductively with the aid of a game-theoretic model, Bates argues that political leaders will be more likely to uphold the state when they can derive sufficient wealth through taxation, when they are secure enough in their power that they can focus on long-term growth rather than short-term expropriation, and when there is no easy source of ready cash, such as oil or mineral wealth, outside of taxation. Bates argues that the rash of state failures that plagued the African continent in the late 1980s – characterized by the formation of private militias, signaling the state's loss of its monopoly over violence – was the result of the absence of these three conditions. The global economic recessions of the 1970s eroded Africa's nascent industrial base, immiserating its population; the "Third Wave" of democratic diffusion introduced a measure of political uncertainty among Africa's military and single-party rulers; and the continent's considerable natural resources meant that political leaders were more likely to fight for control of those resources than cultivate a stable tax base. The confluence of these factors allowed leaders to "behave in ways that increase insecurity," resulting in the flourishing of popular militias and a breakdown of the centralized control over the tools of violence.

While Bates considers how national-level attributes figure in the calculations of domestic political elites in choosing whether to uphold or upend order, Michael Hechter and Nika Kabiri in chapter 3 consider the peculiar challenges faced by external powers in imposing order in the territories they occupy. They take up the case of the United States' presence in Iraq, and ask whether the goal of stability in that fractious land is best served by constructing a strong, centralized state apparatus – resurrecting in an admittedly more benign form of the kind of Hobbesian Leviathan once imposed by Saddam Hussein – or by ruling indirectly through local satraps. The authors point out that direct rule, though the most reliable means of quelling civil strife, is enormously costly. It requires the state to expand both the scope of its activities – that is, the range of services it provides – and the penetration of its control and policing apparatus. It also runs the risk of giving rise to counter-movements among minorities who demand control of their own governance. Indirect rule is less costly, in that it delegates some of the functions of the state to local tribal and religious leaders, thus muting demands for independence, but it requires a delicate balancing act. The ruling power must be careful to ensure that it does not systematically advantage or disadvantage any single social group, and that all depend on the central authority for some essential largesse, lest local autonomy breed noncompliance. The authors illustrate how both the Ottoman and British empires learned these lessons during their administrations of Iraq in the nineteenth and twentieth centuries.

Of course, external powers who seek to impose order on fractious territories are not limited to the binary choice of direct or indirect rule. They can also choose to solve the problem of social disorder by cleaving the lands under their control along ethnic or religious lines. In chapter 4, Lucy Chester examines in great historical detail Britain's decisions to divide India in 1945, and its decision not to do so in Palestine during the same period. In each case, she argues, the governing consideration was not what would best achieve order, but what would best serve Britain's long-term interests. In India, partition was adopted because it offered the quickest way for Britain to extricate itself from its colonial entanglements with its dignity reasonably intact. In Palestine, Britain abandoned its early support of partition – expressed in the Balfour Declaration of 1917 offering Palestine as a national home for the Jews – because it feared harming its relations with newly oil-rich Arab states, leaving the matter to the international community. But unlike the decision of whether to enforce direct or indirect rule, which is faced by powers who seek to establish control over a certain territory, the question of whether to impose partition seems to be asked only by powers that have given up trying to control the territories they occupy. For great powers trying to extract themselves from messy situations, order is at best a secondary consideration.

Partition, then, is tantamount to a declaration that order is impossible. In fact, Chester notes that the factors that necessitate partition – ethnic and religious heterogeneity, armed populations, and weak central control – are precisely those that are likely to render it inimical to order. This is illustrated most tragically in the case of the subcontinent's partition, where the waning power of the British empire, coupled with the not-yet-established power of the Indian and Pakistani governments, meant that there was nothing to stop the most ethnically diverse regions of the newly formed states from collapsing into communal violence and ethnic cleansing. The legacy of partition described by Chester appears to render Hechter and Kabiri's prescriptions for indirect rule in Iraq all the more urgent, and emphasizes the high stakes and difficult choices faced by the United States in its attempt to bring stability to that country.

In chapter 5, Robert J. Sampson and Per-Olof H. Wikström turn our attention from the national-level determinants of order to those operating at the level of the city neighborhood. According to the authors, studies of crime and interpersonal violence have tended to focus on the economic and psychological attributes of the perpetrators, ignoring the structural contexts in which they exist, while those that do focus on communities instead of individuals often end up merely identifying "risk factors" for violence, without describing exactly how those risk factors translate into violence. For example, social scientists have long ascribed high rates of interpersonal violence to structural conditions such as poverty, low rates of homeownership, and a lack of economic opportunity. But how these things lead to violence is largely unknown. In an innovative comparison of neighborhoods in Chicago, Illinois and Stockholm, Sweden, Sampson and Wikström attempt to uncover the causal mechanism by which such disadvantage leads to violence. Using survey data collected in both cities, they argue that structural factors like poverty and transience militate against the development of social trust and what they call "collective efficacy," which can be thought of as a willingness to intervene in the neighborhood to prevent violence and antisocial behavior. The absence of collective efficacy, they argue, is the proximate cause of violence in blighted neighborhoods and inner cities.

Sampson and Wikström's careful micro-study of social order on the streets of Chicago and Stockholm, and their elaboration of the role played by ideas and norms in militating against violence, contain important lessons for order at higher levels of aggregation. For example, Bates' analysis of poverty as a factor promoting civil instability is enriched by considering that poor populations not only render political leaders more extractive and more willing to risk instability, but are themselves likely to exhibit a diminished sense of "national" collective efficacy, thus increasing the likelihood that social groups will turn to violence against each other. Likewise, Hechter and Kabiri note that attempts at direct rule necessarily involve the imposition of a "common culture that provides the shared concepts, values and norms ... required for cooperation to emerge and persist." But the success of such an endeavor may depend on pre-existing levels of social trust and community cohesion.

Karma Nabulsi in chapter 6 also attends to the role of norms and ideas in producing order, but moves us from the level of the neighborhood to the international system, offering us a critical account of the historical development of legal norms governing the conduct of states in war. Nabulsi argues that the current legal tradition, inaugurated by Hugo Grotius in the seventeenth century, was designed to serve the interests of states at the expense of those who would resist them. It did this, she argues, in two ways. First, by focusing on conduct in war instead of the justness of war itself, the tradition rendered itself mute on the question of whether any military action (for example, an invasion or an occupation) could be called unjust, essentially conferring legitimacy on whatever states do in this regard. Second, by defining war as the province of states and their armies, the tradition leaves unprotected, and in fact deems as criminals, ordinary citizens who take up arms against occupying powers. Thus, Nabulsi argues, the Grotian legal tradition, ostensibly conceived of as an effort to lessen the horrors of war by imposing standards of conduct upon states and their armies, serves only to arbitrarily legitimate some forms of violence (namely, whatever is deployed by states) while delegitimating others.

In chapter 7, Courtney Jung, Ellen Lust-Okar, and Ian Shapiro address the question of how order is created out of the disorder that often plagues ethnically and religiously divided societies. By comparing the negotiated transition from apartheid to majority rule in South Africa with less successful negotiations between Palestinians and Israelis and between Unionists and Republicans in Northern Ireland, the authors attempt to identify the conditions necessary for the cessation of conflicts and the establishment of democracy. They find that the likelihood of success depends on whether the negotiators are able to consistently claim and cultivate public support for a settlement, thus isolating hard-liners who oppose the negotiations. For example, in 1992 de Klerk neutralized increasingly vicious attacks from rejectionists within his party by holding a "snap referendum" on power-sharing that was approved by a healthy majority throughout the country, thus giving him the political space and clout to continue on the road to transition. But seizing the commanding heights of democratic legitimacy is not a simple matter, and the authors point out it depends in part on the strategic acumen of the players, particularly on their ability to recognize and take advantage of opportunities when they present themselves. For example, the authors suggest that Israeli leader Shimon Peres in 1996 failed to seize the pro-settlement momentum that prevailed in Israel after Prime Minister Yitzhak Rabin's assassination, choosing instead to tack to the right in order to mute attacks from the right-wing Likud Party. According to the authors, if he had held a referendum on the peace process instead of caving to the right, he might have secured a measure of democratic legitimacy that would have allowed him to make progress toward a settlement.

Additionally, Jung, Lust-Okar, and Shapiro demonstrate the complex role of violence in the emergence of order. Violence can sometimes unravel negotiations and send the parties plunging back into chaos, but at other times can serve to stiffen the negotiators' resolve to reach a solution by dramatically illustrating the costs of failure. For example, the authors tell us that the 1992 Bisho massacre in South Africa "made graphic the possibility that escalating violence could spiral out of control, forcing both sides to look into the abyss and resume (secret) negotiations." Though the chapters in this volume have so far tended to equate violence with a lack of order, the authors of this chapter illustrate powerfully that order itself can be born of violence.

Part 2: Challenging, transforming, and destroying order

Some orders are more durable than others, and all come under attacks that can result in their reconfiguration and collapse. The chapters in this half of the volume explore the dynamics of such challenges to order. They investigate the motivations of the challengers, the conditions that make challenges more likely, and the ways in which they can succeed in transforming order. Mirroring Bates' rationalist examination of the conditions under which "specialists in violence" will choose to uphold order, Carles Boix in chapter 8 addresses the "material and organizational conditions under which political actors choose violence as a feasible strategy to shape political outcomes." Boix notes that most current studies of political violence focus either on the presence or absence of opportunities for violence, or on the motives of potential insurgents. Boix aims to offer a unified theory of political violence that gives equal attention to both motive and opportunity.

According to Boix, political actors will engage in violence if they calculate that they have more to gain from trying to overthrow the existing order than from accepting it. The calculation involves two variables: the costs of violence, and the gains from changing the political order compared to the gains from remaining under the status quo. The costs of violence are determined by the kinds of logistical factors discussed by Fearon and Laitin (2003) – such as whether the insurgents have access to remote and hard-to-reach areas from which to stage their attacks, and whether the state has adequate reach. The gains from violence are determined by two factors: the distribution pattern, and relative mobility, of assets in society. If assets are distributed in a vastly unequal manner, potential insurgents have more to gain from violence, since expropriation of the rich will yield a handsome prize. However, if those assets are mobile, then the rich can ferret them out of the country in anticipation of attack, leaving insurgents with nothing. Thus, Boix predicts that violence becomes more likely when assets are immobile.

Boix's framework recognizes the fact that order and violence are but two sides of the same coin. Though he frames his inquiry in terms of the factors that render political groups more likely to engage in violence, he also demonstrates how these same factors contribute to the development of particular political institutions. For example, he tells us that democracy is likely to result when the distribution of assets is not too unequal (such that the poor do not have an incentive to impose confiscatory taxes on the rich), and assets are mobile enough that the taxed have a credible means of escape, thus disciplining the majority's revenue demands.

In chapter 9, Francisco Gutiérrez Sanín takes issue with the notion, which pervades Boix's contribution, that insurgents are motivated solely by mercenary concerns, that their decisions can be reduced to economic calculations. He asks, whether "the political dimensions of armed conflict [can] be reduced to a pretext for individual enrichment." Drawing on examples from the ongoing insurgency in Colombia, he points out that the requisites of economic and political success are often at odds with each other: the single-minded pursuit of economic objectives can lead to the collapse of an insurgency; while politics can "get in the way" of business. Insurgents who pursue their greed often end up evaporating their fund of public support through overtaxation. Additionally, those who are interested solely in rent collection will have short time horizons, rendering them unable to engage in the kind of strategic calculation necessary for political success. Gutiérrez Sanín offers the example of the Revolutionary Armed Forces of Colombia, who lost a great deal of grass-roots support and did violence to their strategic alliances with local elites, in areas when they engaged in predatory taxation. Finally, Gutiérrez Sanín points out that groups that are motivated strictly by economics would never choose to engage in political activities to begin with, since aggressive politicization is too costly for purely economically motivated actors, as it brings the attention of the state – something that criminals studiously avoid. Despite this, Gutiérrez Sanín notes, "the amount and intensity of *direct* criminal participation in politics in the past twenty years is rather amazing," although it is almost always "bad for business." Clearly, then, the motives of insurgency leaders cannot be said to be merely economic.

But what of the rank and file who join such insurgencies? Many existing models that attempt to account for why individuals would join insurgent groups point to the fact that these groups offer members material "selective incentives" as enticements to join (Olson 1965). But, Gutiérrez Sanín notes, such incentives can actually corrode organizational structures. He tells us that Colombian paramilitaries that paid their fighters by giving them control of a small portion of narcotics operations found their organizations torn asunder by internal struggles for control of these rents. Military readiness suffered as well, since officers and troops began to neglect the business of fighting the enemy in order to tend to their own narrow little criminal enterprises. The upshot is that organizations that recruit using greed as their major selling point are unlikely to be successful.

But if political insurgents are not simply mercenary in their aspirations, what are they? Lars-Erik Cederman in chapter 10 attempts to answer this question. Like Boix, he argues that studies of political violence and civil war tend to focus exclusively either on motives or on opportunities. But, like Gutiérrez Sanín, he faults those studies that pay attention to motive for their narrow emphasis on pecuniary incentives. Instead, Cederman offers an alternate account of political insurgency that unifies both motive and opportunity, and retains a place for material and nonmaterial factors. He argues that structural factors – such as geography and state strength – are essential ingredients in the formation of political insurgency, but that these are mediated through cultural and ideational factors. The inhabitants of peripheral areas are more likely to rebel not simply because they exist in areas where the state's control apparatus is weak, but because they are likely to have developed a national identity and sense of self that is markedly different from that which prevails at the center. Using computer simulations, Cederman demonstrates the plausibility of an account of civil wars that begins with material factors, but which are "primarily mediated through geo-cultural mechanisms."

In chapter 11, Steven I. Wilkinson picks up Cederman's focus on the role of identities in producing challenges to the prevailing order. Noting that religious identities are currently thought to be inherently more violence prone than those of class, region, or language, Wilkinson asks where we can make such a claim about any identity. After all, he points out, in the nineteenth century, scholars like John Stuart Mill thought that linguistic identities were the source of intractable conflict, while in the twentieth century, scholars such as Laitin (1999) declare the opposite. Using an original dataset on civil conflict in India, Wilkinson finds that religion is positively correlated with violence, but argues that this is not because religion is fundamentally more bloody than other forms of identity. Instead, he attributes increased rates of Hindu–Muslim violence to the policies of the Indian state, which involve the use of force to quell political mobilization by religious minorities, while tolerating mobilization by the Hindu majority and by regional and linguistic groups. The roots of this policy, Wilkinson argues, can be found in India's struggle for independence, which rendered its leaders hostile to political claims made by Muslims, which they equate with the separatism that led to partition and the formation of Pakistan. Hindu–Muslim violence, then, is in part a function of the Indian state's notions of what order requires.

Wilkinson's contribution is an important antidote to studies of identity-based conflicts which see them as immutable functions of the identities themselves. Nowhere are such views more prevalent than with regard to the 1994 Rwandan genocide, which is often described as the outcome of longstanding inter-ethnic hatred. In chapter 12, Scott Straus examines the microdynamics of the killing in Rwanda and offers further evidence that ethnic differences are in and of themselves insufficient for explaining the collapse of order in ethnically divided societies. According to Straus, not all of Rwanda took to the killing with equal alacrity. And some areas – indistinguishable from the rest of the country ethnically, economically, and socially – managed to escape the violence altogether. According to Straus, the main determinant of violence was the political security of the local leader. Leaders participated in the slaughter of Tutsis when not doing so meant that they could lose their power. According to Straus, the "killing became a basis for authority" in Rwanda, and those who did not participate risked being supplanted by internal challengers more willing to engage in the slaughter. And though we typically view the Rwandan genocide as an instance of the collapse of order, Straus' study emphasizes that the genocide was above all an attempt to erect a new order. Indeed, many of Straus' informants argued that the massacre of Tutsis had become the new "law," suggesting that violence *was* the new order.

We have seen throughout this volume how violence can both create and destroy order, but is there any order in violence? It is difficult to conclude from accounts of mass killings and rapes that there is anything systematic to be said about the tools and technologies of slaughter, but this is precisely what Elisabeth Jean Wood sets out to do in chapter 13. Wood attempts to explore use of sexual violence – which includes rape, sexual slavery, and forced marriages – during conflict. She concludes that existing accounts of sexual violence – which emphasize such things as the promotion of masculine aggression in soldiers and the desire to demoralize the enemy by violating its women – are insufficient to explain regional and temporal variation in the employment of sexual aggression in wartime. Instead, Wood argues that to properly understand the logic of sexual violence in war, we must attend to the "regulatory mechanisms" that govern the "expression of sexual aggression" in peacetime. She urges us to develop an understanding of how these mechanisms work, the peacetime levels of sexual violence they promote, why some of them break down while others persist, and how they are transformed in wartime. She suggests that sexual violence is likely to be restricted during conflict if peacetime norms governing sexual aggression are deeply held by leaders and members, and if the organization depends on civilians for support and resources.

Wood's call to focus on the regulatory mechanisms that govern violence is answered by Isabel V. Hull in chapter 14. Like Nabulsi, Hull focuses on the development of legal norms governing conduct in war during the late nineteenth and early twentieth centuries, and on the ways in which the prerogatives of the powerful end up shaping the norms to render abuses against civilians more likely. Specifically, Hull argues that Imperial Germany's success in obtaining exceptions to international laws of war for cases of "military necessity" meant that Germany's actions during the First World War were restricted only by what its military leaders thought they needed to do to achieve victory. This would not have been alarming if "military necessity" simply implied a "justification for extraordinary actions" in times of war. But in the minds of German strategists, military necessity was actually "a set of basic assumptions about the nature of war" itself. Moderation in war, according to German military thought, was impossible, because all war was total war, necessitating the use of as awesome a destructive force as Germany could muster, against soldiers and civilians alike. Hull describes how, during the First World War, atrocities such as the planned deportation of Belgians to work in German arms factories became the norm (and later figured in the punitive sanctions imposed on Germany after the war). Germany's civilian leaders were helpless to stop the ever widening spiral of uncontrolled bloodshed – they could not question the military's actions, lest they be seen as jeopardizing victory. In the end, argues Hull, "Military necessity, the doctrine which Imperial German military culture had developed to free the army from the fetters of international law, had become Germany's straitjacket." A flawed order contained within itself the seeds of violence.

International order is also the subject of the contribution by Jack L. Snyder and Leslie Vinjamuri in chapter 15. The authors consider the challenges faced by the diverse sets of actors – from states to NGOs – that seek to bring about normative change in the international community – such as the promotion of democracy or the establishment of global legal institutions like the International Criminal Court. Snyder and Vinjamuri argue that "those who seek to transform the culture of contemporary anarchy need to work within an existing material and institutional setting that may enable, derail, or pervert efforts to promote change." In the case of Iraq, for example, efforts to introduce democracy have foundered because of the lack of a "strong reform coalition and useable institutions for the rule of law." Above all, the authors counsel realism and moderation. "Efforts to force the pace of change," they write, "risk unintended consequences that could wind up hindering change and increasing its costs." For example, they point out that a legalistic and uncompromising approach to the implementation of new norms can wreak havoc on the ground. They offer the example of how the zealousness of the International Criminal Tribunal for Yugoslavia in 2001 in investigating war crimes by Albanian guerrillas in Macedonia scuttled a political settlement between the rebels and the Macedonian government, giving hard-line Slavs a pretext to renew the bloodshed. The imposition of international order can destroy a hard-earned domestic one.

The contribution by Stathis N. Kalyvas in chapter 16 offers a methodological assessment of the study of the dynamics of conflict and violence at the subnational level. By focusing on a slew of recent research on Nepal, he aims to highlight the pitfalls of what is otherwise an extremely promising research program, one that can be described as the "microdynamics of civil wars." This research program has emerged as a way out of the current impasse generated by the wave of cross-national econometric research – where it is typically extremely difficult to tell which variables really matter and exactly how they do. He stresses the importance of understanding and measuring territorial control; he

14   *Stathis N. Kalyvas, Ian Shapiro, and Tarek Masoud*

argues that violence is a tricky indicator, as its absence in the context of
an ongoing civil war (or the presence of order) can signal either an
absence of conflict or the presence of intense conflict; he identifies two
key problems, the overaggregation and the omission of key variables, and
demonstrates their potential for bias. As a result, he calls for a deeper
engagement with cases, careful and detailed collection of fine-grained
data, and thorough theorization.

Kalyvas' chapter provides a fitting conclusion to this volume. By
pointing to the perverse and unexpected ways in which order and violence
are related, he reinforces the insight that both phenomena must be
understood with reference to each other. In fact, this is a point that is
driven home by all of the essays in this volume. Though they range widely
over such diverse disciplines as political science, economics, history,
sociology, philosophy, and law; employ different methodologies, from
game theory to statistical modeling to in-depth historical narrative to
anthropological ethnography; and focus on vastly different units of
analysis and levels of aggregation, from the state to the individual to the
world system; all of them demonstrate how order and violence are inextricably intertwined. As we have seen, those who study violence implicitly
attend to the ways in which order is transformed. Those who study the
establishment of order must necessarily attend to the ways in which violence and those with the capacity to use it are tamed. And though we
conceived of the contributions to this volume addressing fundamental
questions of *order*: how it is established, maintained, and destroyed; we
could have just as easily conceived of it as an inquiry into the nature of
violence: how it arises, how it is quelled, and how it is used. In a very real
sense, we are all students of violence, and we are all students of order. Our
hope will be that this volume will demonstrate the benefits to be garnered
by integrating the study of these two facets of human society.

REFERENCES

De Figueiredo, Rui J. P., Jr., and Barry Weingast. 1999. "The Rationality of
    Fear: Political Opportunism and Ethnic Conflict." In *Civil Wars, Insecurity,
    and Intervention,* ed. Barbara Walter and Jack Snyder. New York: Columbia
    University Press.
Olson, Mancur, Jr. 1965. *The Logic of Collective Action: Public Goods and the
    Theory of Groups.* Cambridge, MA: Harvard University Press.
    1993. "Dictatorship, Democracy, and Development." *American Political Sci-
    ence Review* 87: 567–576.
Tilly, Charles. 1975. "Reflections on the History of European State-Making."
    In *The Formation of National States in Western Europe,* ed. Charles Tilly.
    Princeton University Press.

Part 1

Creating, maintaining, and restoring order

2   Probing the sources of political order

Robert H. Bates

Introduction

As stated by Hobbes, without political order

> there is no place for industry, because the fruit thereof is uncertain; and consequently no nurture of the earth; no navigation, nor use of the commodities that may be imported by sea; no commodious buildings ...; no knowledge ... no arts; no letters ... and what is worse of all, continual fear, and danger of violent death. (Hobbes 1961, 368)

Hobbes' argument echoes that put forward by the development programs of contemporary governments, and remains persuasive today: without political order, there can be no development.

Nowhere is development so deeply desired as in Africa, and nowhere has political disorder more forcefully checked its attainment. At the end of the Cold War – 1989–1991 – Africa contained 30% of the world's nations. Roughly 10% of the world's population resided in Africa and roughly 5% of the globe's economic product. However, if marked by the toppling of the Berlin Wall in 1989, the end of the Cold War found 46% of the world's civil wars raging in Africa; if by the collapse of the Soviet Union in 1991, the number rises to 53%. Taking civil war as a measure, then, Africa has oversupplied state failure.

The chapter represents an extension of Bates *et al.* (2002); Bates (2007); and Bates (2008). I wish to thank Paul Collier, Jan Gunning, Benno Ndulu, Stephen O'Connell, Jean-Paul Azam, and David Laitin for comments, plus participants in seminars at the Universities of California in Los Angeles and San Diego, Yale University, ITAM, the annual meetings of the American Political Science Association and Harvard University. Special thanks go to Steven Block for his criticisms and corrections. As ever, Karen Ferree and Smita Singh deserve much of the credit for this work. I also wish to thank Matthew Hindeman, Bela Prasad, Macartan Humphreys, and Marx Alexander for technical assistance. Financing came from the United States Institute for Peace (Grant No. USIP-02597S), the Carnegie Foundation, the National Science Foundation (Grant No. SES-09905568), the Carnegie Corporation, and the Weatherhead Center for International Studies and the Center for International Development, Harvard University. The paper was written while a Moore Distinguished Scholar at the California Institute of Technology. I alone am responsible for the contents.

Table 2.1. *Comparative growth rates*

Region	N	Initial values (1960 or earliest year before 1965)			End-to-end annual growth rates (earliest year before 1965 to latest year between 1995 and 2000)					Ending values (latest year between 1995 and 2000)		
		Real GDP per capita (1996 PPP$)	Gross primary enrollment rate, 1970	Life expectancy (years)	Real GDP		Real GDP per capita			Real GDP per capita (1996 PPP$)	Gross primary enrollment rate	Life expectancy (years)
					Total	Population	Total	Workers per capita	Real GDP per worker			
		(1)	(2)	(3)	(4)	(5)	(6)	(7)	(8)	(9)	(10)	(11)
SSA	35	1263 (14.1)	53.2 (52.2)	40.9 (57.9)	3.17	2.62	0.55	−0.15	0.70	1879 (8.0)	88.8 (85.6)	47.8 (61.0)
LAC	22	3338 (37.2)	99.1 (97.3)	56.4 (79.9)	3.52	2.08	1.45	0.42	1.03	6032 (25.7)	113.0 (109.0)	70.8 (90.4)
SASIA	5	934 (10.4)	58.6 (57.5)	45.3 (64.2)	4.34	2.23	2.10	−0.32	2.42	2049 (8.7)	100.1 (96.5)	63.8 (81.5)
EAP	9	1833 (20.4)	94.0 (92.2)	50.6 (71.7)	5.52	2.07	3.45	0.16	3.29	8314 (35.4)	101.3 (97.7)	69.6 (88.9)
MENAT	9	2809 (31.3)	86.1 (84.5)	54.9 (77.8)	4.84	2.04	2.81	0.16	2.65	8251 (35.1)	104.6 (100.9)	72.0 (92.0)

INDUST	20	8979	101.9	70.6	3.40	0.73	2.67	0.35	2.32	23512	103.7	78.3
Total	100	3443	79.9	52.6	3.71	2.00	1.71	0.12	1.59	8280	100.2	63.9
SSA vs SASIA★		(135.2)	(90.8)	(90.3)						(91.7)	(88.7)	(74.9)

Notes: Except where noted, numbers in parentheses give the relevant developing-country mean as a percentage of the industrial-country mean. The final row [★] shows the SSA mean as a percentage of the SASIA mean.

Source: Stephen A. O'Connell (2004), "Explaining African Economic Growth: Emerging Lessons from the Growth Project," Paper presented at the AERC Plenary Session, Nairobi, May 29, 2004. [www.swarthmore.edu/SocSci/soconne1/aercgrth.html]

Source: PWT6.1 and World Development Indicators.

Regions: SSA = Sub-Saharan Africa, LAC = Latin America and Caribbean, SASIA = South Asia, EAP = East Asia and Pacific, MENAT = Middle East, North Africa and Turkey, INDUST = Industrial countries.

Paralleling the political performance of Africa's states runs the performance of Africa's economies. As demonstrated in Table 2.1, the growth of per-capita incomes in late-century Africa lagged behind that of other regions. In a recent study, the World Bank concludes that civil wars reduced national growth rates by 2.2 percentage points below what they would have been had there been peace (Collier *et al.* 2003). Given the average performance of Africa's economies, the onset of a civil war would be sufficient to render growth rates negative.

Development makes possible the increase of human welfare and political order provides its foundation. To probe the underpinnings of development, this chapter therefore explores the roots of political order. It does so by focusing on state failure in late-century Africa.

Background

The politics of late-century Africa draw us back to Max Weber's definition of the political: that the essential property of politics – the feature that distinguishes it from economic, cultural, or social life – is "physical force" (Weber 1921). Consider, for example, the prominence of the military in Africa. Drawing upon a sample of 1,196 observations drawn from forty-six African countries over a twenty-six-year period (1970–1995) (see Table 2.2), we find that in nearly one-third the armed forces provided the head of state (see Table 2.3). While civilians have increasingly replaced military officers as heads of state in Africa, one need only trace down its eastern coast to appreciate the centrality of the military in its politics: the presidents of Eritrea, Ethiopia, Uganda, Rwanda – the so-called "new generation" of African leaders – commanded military movements that placed them in power. So too did the presidents of Burundi, Zimbabwe, Mozambique, and Namibia.

In keeping with Weber's recognition of the coercive core of the political and the nature of Africa's politics, we shall therefore view governments as specialists in violence. Weber emphasizes not only the importance of physical force, however; he also suggests that a community becomes a state when its government successfully claims a monopoly over its use, defining the state as "a human community that successfully claims the monopoly of the legitimate use of physical force within a given territory" (Weber 1946, 78). Abiding by Weber's counsel, we therefore employ the report of the existence of private militias as an indicator of state failure.[1] The political histories of the forty-six nations in the sample over the sample period (1970–1995) yield reports of private militaries in 20% of

[1] The sources are listed in Table 2.5.

Table 2.2. *The sample set of countries*

1. Angola	24. Madagascar
2. Benin	25. Malawi
3. Botswana	26. Mali
4. Burkina Faso	27. Mauritania
5. Burundi	28. Mauritius
6. Cameroon	29. Mozambique
7. Cape Verde	30. Namibia
8. Central African Republic	31. Niger
9. Chad	32. Nigeria
10. Comoros	33. Rwanda
11. Congo, Republic	34. Sao Tome & Principe
12. Cote d'Ivoire	35. Senegal
13. Djibouti	36. Seychelles
14. Equatorial Guinea	37. Sierra Leone
15. Ethiopia	38. Somalia
16. Gabon	39. Sudan
17. The Gambia	40. Swaziland
18. Ghana	41. Tanzania
19. Guinea	42. Togo
20. Guinea-Bissau	43. Uganda
21. Kenya	44. Democratic Republic of Congo
22. Lesotho	45. Zambia
23. Liberia	46. Zimbabwe

Table 2.3. *Incidences of military heads of state, by time period*

Time period	Military chief executive No	Yes	
1970–74	129	63	192
	67.19	32.81	
1975–79	141	79	220
	64.09	35.91	
1980–84	146	74	220
	66.36	33.64	
1985–89	149	71	220
	67.73	32.27	
1990–95	164	49	213
	77.00	23.00	
Total	729	336	1065
	68.45	31.55	

the country-year observations in the first half of the 1970s and in over 30% in the first half of the 1990s. By this criterion, roughly one-quarter of our data from Africa 1970–1995 provides evidence of state failure.[3]

This interplay between theories of the state and observations from Africa thus frames this analysis. We will represent heads of state as "specialists in violence." And we shall treat political order as problematic. Within this framework, we pose the central question: Under what conditions will states fail – thus undermining the prospects for development?

The logic of political order

While Hobbes provides the motivation for this chapter and Weber its vision of politics, to probe the foundations of state failure we need clearer guidelines than either can provide. We need to develop a line of reasoning that can generate propositions regarding the conditions under which societies will, or will not, achieve political order. We therefore turn from the theory of the state to the theory of games and make use of the model developed by Bates *et al.* (2002).

In this model, there is political order when governments choose to employ force to protect rather than to prey upon their citizens and when citizens choose to disarm, leaving it to the government to protect their lives and property. Political order becomes a "state" when these choices comprise an equilibrium. The conditions that support that equilibrium make possible the existence of the state – and highlight as well the circumstances under which states will fail.

The model[2]

The model is peopled by G, a specialist in violence, and two citizens, each seeking to maximize her utility and each endowed with the capacity to consumer leisure or to secure income, by the use of force if necessary.

Citizens More specifically, each citizen possesses a given amount of resources, denoted by T_i (as in time), that she can allocate between work (w_i), military preparedness (m_i), and leisure (l_i). That is,

$$i \in \{1,2\} \text{ chooses } w_i, m_i, l_i \geq 0 \text{ s.t. } w_i + m_i + m_i + \leq T_i.$$

The resources devoted to work, w_i, are productive; they result in an output of $F(w_i)$ for player i.[3] Those devoted to military activity are

---

[2] For proofs of the claims made in this section, consult Bates *et al.* (2002).
[3] $F(\bullet)$ is assumed to be a twice continuously differentiable, concave function that maps from player i's effort to her income.

unproductive. Rather then creating wealth, force merely redistributes it – or provides a defense against its redistribution.

After allocating their resources, each citizen observes the decision of the other; each then (sequentially) decides whether or not to attempt to raid the other's possessions. To capture this decision, define r_i where $r_i = 1$ if player i raids, and $r_i = 0$ if she does not. The amount the one can gain from raiding depends not only on the quantity of the other's assets but also on the relative strength of the players: if player i attacks and player $-i$ defends, M (m_i, m_{-i}) is the share of player $-i$'s wealth that player i is able to expropriate if she allocates m_i units of effort to perfecting her military capabilities and the other player, $-i$, allocates m_{-i} units.[4]

The citizens derive their utility from income and from leisure, $U(I_i, l_i)$. They can increase their incomes by working or by employing their military capabilities to raid. Player 1's income can thus be written:

$$I_1 = F(w_1) + r_1 (F(w_2)M(m_1, m_2) - k) \\ - r_2[F(w_1) + r_1 (F(w_2)M(m_1, m_2) - k)]M(m_2, m_1)$$

where k is the fixed cost of raiding.

G: The specialist in violence   G seeks to maximize his utility, which, like that of the citizens, derives from income and leisure. As a specialist in violence, however, G does not need earn his income from laboring a farm or factory but from the use of force. He can increase his income by engaging in predation and seizing wealth or earn it by collecting fees for the provision of a valued service: the provision of security for those who create wealth.

In characterizing the military balance between G and private citizens, Bates *et al.* (2002) make three assumptions. Given that private agents are

---

[4] More generally, throughout the paper Bates *et al.* (2002) ignore the possibility that one agent can eradicate the other. Nor do they consider a situation in which one can gain military resources by raiding the other. As in Skaperdas (1992), Grossman (1995), and Muthoo (2000), they attribute the security of property rights to the use of coercive capabilities. Their model puts to the side evolutionary forces and specialization in the use of violence (as in Moselle and Polak [1999]); asymmetries among the agents (as in Grossman and Kim [1995] and Muthoo [2000]); the impact of past conflicts on current military capabilities (as in Fearon [1996]; Fearon and Latin [1996]); uncertainty and loss of potential exchange (as in Skarpedas [1996]); and moral hazard (as in Addison *et al.* [2000]).

By the same token, their framework enables them to extend the analysis beyond that possible in other works. Specifically, it allows them to examine the endogenous determination of prosperity and violence. See the papers cited above as well as Usher (1989). The model in Muthoo (2000) is closest to theirs. While it explores the impact of asymmetries (which Bates *et al.* [2002] do not), it does not enable agents to invest in military capabilities (as do they), to deter raids by consuming leisure, or the welfare implications of the endogenous state.

themselves capable of violence, (i) when G preys upon the economic output of a player i, G succeeds in capturing her wealth only in a probability, denoted by q_i. (ii) G engages in predatory activity only if the expected revenues from its use of violence exceeds its costs of military activity, denoted by C_G, where $C_G > 0$. (iii) And G can dispossess only one agent per period.

G's income therefore can be written:

$$I_G(\bullet) = \{[p_i q_i \sum (F(w_i) + r_i F(w_{-i}) M(m_i, m_{-i})$$
$$- r_{-i} F(w_i) M(m_{-i}, m_i))(1 - t_i i)]$$
$$+ [t_i (F(w_i) + r_i F(w_{-i}) M(m_i, m_{-i})$$
$$- r_{-i} F(w_i) M(m_{-i}, m_i))]\} - C_G(p_i + p_{-i})$$

for $i = 1, 2$.

Should G engage in predation (i.e. should $p_i = 1$, $i \in \{1,2\}$) his income is captured by the first bracketed expression. The revenue he seizes from i equals the probability of successful predation, q_i, multiplied by player i's income from work and raiding, net the amount i has paid in taxes. Should G choose to secure his income from taxes, his income is captured by the second bracketed term, which registers the amount of taxes paid by each private agent who has chosen to do so. Note that – as indicated by the last term of the equation: if G decides to prey upon the wealth of either agent, that is, if $p_i + p_{-i} > 0$, then G has to bear the cost of the predatory activity, $C_G(p_i + p_{-i})$ $i > 0$.

The possibility of the state

Within this framework, Bates *et al.* (2002) characterize political order as the product of choices made by governments and citizens and isolate the conditions that render those choices an equilibrium. The conditions that do so also imply the conditions under which states will fail. The model of Bates *et al.* (2002) therefore highlights the factors that can help us to account for political disorder in late-century Africa.

According to Bates *et al.* (2002), political order prevails when

• G chooses to refrain from predating as long as neither private agent raids or fails to pay taxes. If either agent raids or fails to pay taxes, G then becomes predatory and seizes the wealth of the private agents.[5]

---

[5] Considering a similar equilibrium in which G punishes an agent who raided or failed to pay tax without reverting to the State Failure equilibrium does not change the analysis.

- Each private agent chooses w_i, m_i, l_i optimally (given the strategies of other players); refuses to raid; and pays taxes to G, if the other agent has not raided or if G has refrained from seizing the wealth of a private agent. Otherwise, the private agents refuse to pay taxes and revert to self-defense.

These choices form an equilibrium, Bates *et al.* argue, when no player can gain from deviating after any history.[6] That is:

I.   No private agent should be able to gain by raiding or refusing to pay taxes.
II. Nor should an agent be able to gain by altering the allocation of her resources between work, leisure, and military preparation.
III. G's threat to predate must be credible.
IV. And G must find it optimal *not* to predate if the economic agents adhere to their strategies.

Because Bates *et al.* (2002) cast the interaction between G and the citizens as a repeated game, the prospect of future losses play an important role in generating an equilibrium. The principal threat is that of disorder. In a state of disorder, G engages in predation: rather than earning his income from safeguarding the possessions of others, he seizes them. The citizens, for their part, stop paying taxes and rearm, either so as to raid or to defend themselves against raids by others. Because the citizens reallocate resources from leisure and production to military activities, prosperity declines. Living in disorder, people are insecure and poor. Bates *et al.* (2002) call the equilibrium of this sub-game State Failure (SF) equilibrium. It is the possibility of a reversion to the payoffs of the State Failure (SF) equilibrium that constitutes the threat that promotes – or fails to promote – the decision to adhere to the choices that yield political order (Figure 2.1).

To comprehend the conditions that render nonpredation by governments and the laying aside of arms by citizens as equilibrium choices, it is useful to focus on the incentives that impinge upon G (see Figure 2.2). Doing so also highlights the testable implications of the model, thus proving the logical foundations for an empirical investigation of the sources of state failure.

G's incentives to adhere to the equilibrium choice of strategies derive from the revenues he can secure from taxation. To induce G to refrain from predation, the tax level, τ, needs to be high enough that G finds it optimal, given the private agents' strategies, to refrain from confiscating

---

[6] When deviation results in a reversion to the State Failure (SF) equilibrium (see below).

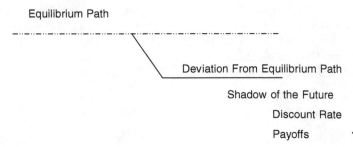

Figure 2.1 The path of play

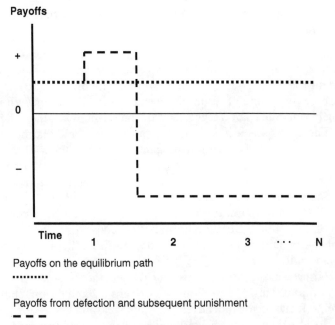

Figure 2.2 Payoffs from strategy choices

the agents' wealth if they pay taxes. But it must also be sufficiently low that private agents prefer to purchase the services of G rather than to incur the costs of providing their own security.

The tax level must also be sufficiently low that G's threat to predate if taxes are not fully paid remains credible. Should taxes not be fully paid, G must choose between punishing and thereby triggering a reversion to the State Failure equilibrium or continuing to play the strategies that define political order. If a receipt of a portion of the revenues accrued when there is political order exceeds the payoffs under the State Failure equilibrium, G's threat to punish will not be credible. For that reason too taxes must not be too high.

The level of revenues that sustains political order, the model thus suggests, is bounded from both above and below.

Adherence to the equilibrium path also depends upon G's payoffs under the State Failure (SF) equilibrium. Should the government have access to sources of income other than the payments it receives from its citizens, it may not fear the loss of tax payments that would result were it to trigger state failure.

Also important is G's discount rate. Should the government place a low value on the losses that would accrue from state failure, it would little fear the consequences that would follow an opportunistic deviation from the equilibrium path. Or should the government consider its future on the equilibrium path to be uncertain or the imperative of present action so powerful that it can pay scant regard for future consequences, then the threat of the low payoffs that accrue when in state failure would be insufficient to compel it to adhere to its choice of strategies.

The model thus yields three propositions:

1. That the likelihood of disorder should be related to the level of public revenues.
2. That as governments face higher levels of risk, the level of political disorder should rise.
3. And that governments in economies that contain valuable resources should provoke political disorder to a greater degree than would governments in economies less blessed by nature.

Bates *et al.* (2002) thus find three variables to be key: public revenues, the ruler's rate of discount, and his prospects were state failure to occur. In absorbing this lesson, it behooves us to return to African materials.

Trends in late-century Africa

A moment's reflection leads to the recognition of magnitude of the changes in these three variables in late-century Africa and of the significance of such changes for political order.

In the 1970s, a sharp increase in the price of oil triggered global recession. Sharp increases in the price of energy led to higher costs of production, laying off of labor, and thus a fall in income. For Africa, the result was a decrease in the demand for exports.

In Africa, as in many other developing regions, taxes on trade constitute one of the most important sources of public revenue. As exports from Africa declined, so too did the taxes collected by Africa's governments. In the latter decades of the twentieth century, then, while Africa's people faced a "growth tragedy" (Easterly and Levine 1997), its states faced a crisis of public revenues. The economic forces at play in late-century Africa thus aligned with those that trigger opportunistic defection by the specialist in violence who preside over the nano-polity depicted in the model of Bates *et al.* (2002).

Not only did the rewards to guardians of the public order decline in the later decades of the twentieth century, but also the rewards for defection continued to loom large, for the economies of Africa are based on natural resources to a degree that exceeds any other region of the world. There is thus a consistent and strong temptation for those who control the coercive power of Africa's states to shift from guardian to predator.

Consider, for example, the Sudan. In 1962, politicians and military from the south rebelled against the central government, protesting its refusal to agree to a federal form of government and its forced incorporation of southern troops into the national army. When Jafar Numeiri seized the presidency in 1969, he negotiated an end to the conflict. But in 1978, oil was discovered in Bentiu, a region lying in the south. Numeiri then redrew the provincial boundaries of Sudan, effectively placing Bentiu in the portion of the country controlled by the central government. The south's perception of Numeiri abruptly changed; once regarded as a guardian, he now appeared as a threat. The south again took up arms and civil war erupted in Sudan.[7]

Consider too the case of the Democratic Republic of Congo. A centralized state under Belgian rule, it fragmented soon after independence. At the forefront of those who sought to dismantle was the Katanga, a region richly endowed with copper, cobalt, and other minerals. Following Katanga's forceful reintegration into Congo, the profits from the mines now accrued to the central government – a government presided over by Joseph-Désiré Mobutu.[8] Succumbing to the temptations offered by these riches of the Congo, Mobutu became one of the richest men in the world – while presiding over the disintegration of Zaire.

For a last example, turn to Angola. In the 1960s, a group of intellectuals, some based in Lisbon and others in Luanda, formed the Popular Movement for the Liberation of Angola (the MPLA). The MPLA was

---

[7] Johnson (1998; 2003); de Waal and Abdel Salam (2004).
[8] Pech (2000); Gould (1980); MacGaffey (1991); Weiss (1995); Blumenthal (1982); Thom (1999); Otunnu (2000).

part political party, part military force. Based close to Luanda, the MPLA was well positioned when the Portuguese retreated from Africa. Its leaders quickly seized the national capital, the central bureaucracy – and Angola's oil fields. As described by Birmingham (2002), Chabal (2002), and others (Dietrich 2000; Meredith 2005), while the MPLA speaks of serving "the needs of the people," it in fact channels little of Angola's oil wealth to them. The president has retreated to his palace, the party elite to their villas, and their Mercedes and Land Cruisers course through streets of Luanda that are strewn with garbage and broken glass and inhabited by maimed soldiers and abandoned children.

Sudan, Congo, Angola: each suggests the manner in which the temptation to defect – i.e. to employ the means of violence to engage in predation – can overpower the incentives to govern prudentially – i.e. to employ the means of violence to safeguard life and property. So great are the riches offered by Africa's natural resources that, in these instances at least, the rewards to be gained by seizing them appear to outweigh the prospects of living in a society consigned to poverty and insecurity because of the breakdown in political order.

In Bates *et al.* (2002), there was a third force at play: the rate at which the elite discounted the future. If the government became impatient or insecure, they argued, the rewards from immediate gratification would grow in value relative to the later losses from political disorder. The "shadow of the future" – the insecurity and poverty that would subsequently ensue – would diminish and so fail to deter the government from behaving opportunistically, thus triggering state failure.

Among the changes that mark late-century Africa, one of the most dramatic was the introduction of organized political competition in the early 1990s. Figure 2.3 classifies the forty-six African states into no-party, single-party or multi-party systems.[9] In the early 1970s, over 80 percent of the observations yielded no- or one-party systems. In the late 1980s, the forces of democratization breached the barriers that separated Eastern Europe from the West and penetrated Africa as well. Incumbents that once faced no opposition now faced an opposition that was legal, and often closely tied to the international community. With the shift from authoritarian to competitive politics, the risks of losing office rose, and thus the level of political insecurity.

---

[9] No-party systems characterize military governments, for example, where political parties have been banned. I also refer to multi-party systems as "competitive" party systems. Where multiple candidates competed for office under the banner of one party, I also classified these cases as "competitive." Such arrangements occur in but 1.7 percent of the 1,196 observations in the sample.

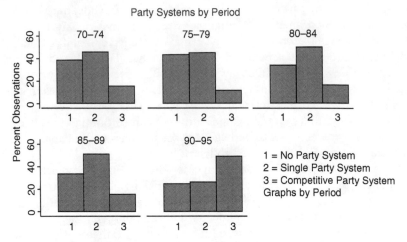

Figure 2.3 Party systems by period

The elements that support the possibility of political order in Bates *et al.* (2002) thus parallel forces that impinged upon political order in late-century Africa at the time of the outbreak of disorder.

Estimation

To test this argument systematically, we move from the use of qualitative materials to the marshaling of quantitative data. The formation of armed militias provides the measure of state failure. Given the imprecision of the available data, we employ reports of the existence of militias rather than of the number of militias. As a result, the dependent variable is either 0 for "no reports" of militias for that country in that year or 1 for the existence of such reports.

Tables 2.6 and 2.7 contain three sets of estimates. In all models, the values of all right-hand side variables are lagged by one year. The standard errors are robust and clustered by country. The first equation reports coefficients estimated from a probit model using a pooled sample; the second, coefficients generated by a conditional logistic model, with country-specific fixed effects; and the third, coefficients generated by a probit model that makes use of instrumental variables. The introduction of fixed effects controls for differences in such time invariant features as colonial heritage, terrain, and geographic location. It thus relaxes the assumption implicitly underlying the pooled estimates that the right-hand side variables will affect the likelihood of reform or disorder in, say, Angola in the same manner as they would affect the likelihood of disorder in, say, Ghana. The introduction of instruments corrects the estimates for the reciprocal impact of political change on several of its possible determinants. Not only may public revenues and growth affect political disorder, for example; but also political disorder may well affect these variables. The introduction of instrumental variables corrects for the possible impact of such reciprocal effects on the estimates of the coefficients.[10]

Particularly in Africa, and especially in countries that are war-torn, the data contain a large number of missing observations. Should cases be dropped because of missing data, then the efficiency of the estimates would decline; in addition, given the long time span of the panels, the dropping of cases could also bias the estimates (Judson and Owen 1996). In addition, because disorder weakens governments, there is every reason to expect the pattern of "missingness" to be related to the phenomenon of greatest concern; dropping observations because of missing data would therefore yield a biased sample. The analysis of multiple, imputed sets of data (Rubin 1996) offers a remedy to this problem and we make use of this procedure.

The theoretical variables

Recall the logic of the argument: public revenues provide incentives for the government to remain on the equilibrium path, i.e. to defend rather than to prey upon the private creation of wealth. If revenues are too few, governments then turn predatory; if too ample, the citizens protest and the government's threats to punish those who raid or fail to pay taxes lose credibility. The implication for testing is that the measure of revenues should enter the equation in quadratic form, with the likelihood of disorder initially falling as revenues rise (i.e. the coefficient on the linear term should be negative) but then rising at higher levels (i.e. the coefficient on the quadratic term should be positive).

The argument also emphasized the significance of forces that affected the government's evaluation of the costs and benefits of deviation. The cost of deviation is entry into a punishment phase, i.e. into state failure. In this period, insecurity rises and incomes fall. Should their future become insecure, incumbents will then discount these future costs more

---

[10] The instruments include lagged values of taxes on trade, primary product exports, and the rate of growth of the advanced industrial nations. We also employed a twice-lagged value of revenues. Regression results confirm that the instruments satisfy the exclusion condition: entered into fixed effects regressions, the instrument is significantly related to the current level of government revenues and income but not to the presence of domestic military groups. That the TR^2 was greater than 30 (where T is the depth of the panel and R^2 is the percentage of total variation "explained") suggests that the instruments are not "weak." See Hausman and Hahn (2002; 2003).

Table 2.4. *Theoretical expectations*

	Coefficient will be significant and:
Public revenues	−
Public revenues^2	+
No-party system	−
Single-party system	−
Value of petroleum exports	+

heavily and fear less the losses that would follow, were they to engage in predation.

The government's rate of discount should therefore relate to the likelihood of political disorder. It is here that political reform becomes relevant: a shift from a no- or one- to a multi-party system should increase the level of insecurity among incumbents. By the logic of the argument, then, party competition should associate with increased disorder in the conditional logit model.

Resource wealth will affect the perceived benefits from deviation: governments assured of access to wealth even in the midst of political disorder – wealth from precious metals, minerals, gemstones, or petroleum deposits, for example – would have less reason to adhere to the equilibrium path. In nations thus endowed, the costs of deviation would be lower for governments – and the temptation to deviate therefore greater – than for those in countries that are less advantaged. Measures of resource wealth should therefore bear a positive relationship with measures of political disorder. The value of total exports that is generated from petroleum provides such a measure.[11]

The reasoning that underlies Bates *et al.* (2002) thus points to a set of "theoretical" variables and suggests the relationship that they should bear with other measures of political disorder (see Table 2.4). As seen in Table 2.5, dummy variables serve as indicators of the nature of the party system – no-, single-, or multi-party – with the dummy for a multi-party system providing the reference category. All the right-hand side variables are entered in lagged form. The negative sign in the cell next to "single-party system" in Table 2.4 thus indicates that we expect a lower likelihood of political disorder in single-party than in multi-party states.

[11] It enters in quadratic form, simply because that specification appears to better fit the data.

Table 2.5. *Variables employed in the analysis*

	Units	Mean	Std. dev.	Source
DEPENDENT VARIABLE				
Formation of domestic military groups?	0 = No 1 = Yes	0.247	0.431	*Keesings Contemporary Archives* *Africa Confidential* *Economist Intelligence Unit* *Africa Research Bulletin* *Africa Contemporary Record*
INDEPENDENT VARIABLES				
CORE MODEL				
Revenues	Central government revenues as percent of GDP	18.106	0.381	*Penn World Tables Mark 5.6*
No-party system	0 = No 1 = Yes	0.349	0.015	*Keesings Contemporary Archives* *Africa Confidential* *Economist Intelligence Unit*
One-party system	0 = No 1 = Yes	0.444	0.015	ditto
Duration				
No-party system	Length of time in years of duration of political system	2.639	4.685	ditto
One-party system	ditto	3.747	5.551	ditto
Multi-party system	ditto	1.395	0.127	ditto
Petroleum	Value of exports per capita in constant US dollars	81.38	14.574	Data collected by research team from commercial sources
CONTROL VARIABLES				
Modernization variables				
Literacy	Percent of adult population that is literate	25.348	0.41	*World Development Indicators*
Urban population	Percent of population living	40.463	0.614	ditto

Table 2.5. (*cont.*)

	Units	Mean	Std. dev.	Source
Income	Log of GDP per capita (PPP)	6.835	0.021	*Penn World Tables Mark 5.6*
Modernization	Factor score derived from principal components analysis of INCOME, LITERACY, and URBAN POPULATION	1.60 E_02	0.024	
Growth	Annual rate of change of INCOME in cities	− 0.15	0.351	*Penn World Tables Mark 5.6*
Drought	Hectares of land per capita	0.388	0.031	*World Development Indicators*
Elections	1 if year before national election 0 otherwise	0.191	0.013	*Keesings Contemporary Archives* *Africa Confidential* *Economist Intelligence Unit*
Neighbors	Total level of conflict in neighboring states (number of coups, domestic military groups, and civil wars)	1.556	0.062	ditto
Cross-border	Percent of population *not* belonging to an ethnic group that spills over national boundary	0.733	0.036	Englebert, *State Legitimacy* and *Development*
Time since last report	Number of years since a domestic military group was last reported	6.292	0.193	*Keesings Contemporary Archives* *Africa Confidential* *Economist Intelligence Unit*

Control variables

Naturally, other variables could also play a role and we seek to control for their impact. There are four sets of control variables. From Deutsch (1961) to Huntington (1968), scholars have emphasized the politically destabilizing impact of modernization, by which they mean (*inter alia*) the growth of urban population, the rise in per-capita income, and the increase in literacy. The first set of control variables (Table 2.5) therefore includes the conventional measures of modernity. These measures enter in two forms: individually and as a composite measure (MODERN-IZATION) derived from a principal components analysis. A second set of variables captures the incidence of shocks: economic (short-term growth), climatic (droughts), and political (elections). Also important is the impact of events in neighboring states, which could spill over directly or through the intermediary of populations that span national borders; time since the last report of the formation of a militia; and population, which provides a time-varying measure of country size – a variable that has been found significant and robust in many other studies (Sambanis and Hegre 2006). A last control variable distinguishes between periods before and after the Cold War.

Discussion

As can be seen in Tables 2.6 and 2.7, the coefficients for the measure of public revenues perform as expected: the linear term is negative in sign and the quadratic term positive. The coefficients derived from the pooled sample are more precisely estimated than those in the model that include fixed effects; it appears that the level rather than changes in the level of public revenues is what matters. Note that controlling for the impact of disorder on public revenues – as is done by introducing instrumental variables – yields a major increase in the magnitude of its coefficients.

Note as well the coefficients on the indicators of party systems. In both Tables 2.6 and 2.7, the negative signs indicate that reports of the presence of domestic militias are less likely to emanate from single- and no-party systems than from multi-party systems. The coefficients generated by the fixed effects model suggest that the movement toward multi-partyism (i.e. within country change) co-varies with increases in the likelihood of militarization. The coefficients are highly significant in all but one equation.

Lest some see in this finding a justification for authoritarian regimes, they should consult the coefficients on the measures of duration. In any given year, a single- or no-party system may be less likely to give rise to

Table 2.6. *Correlates of militia presence: core model*

		Pooled sample (probit estimates) (1)	Conditional logits (fixed effects) (2)	Instrumental variables (probit estimates) (3)
REVENUES		− 0.055**	− 0.055	− 0.151***
		(0.025)	(0.063)	(0.069)
REVENUES SQUARED		0.001	0.001	0.002
		(0.00)	(0.001)	(0.00)***
NO-PARTY		− 0.407***	− 1.110***	− 0.539***
		(0.214)	(0.430)	(0.12)
ONE-PARTY		− 0.691***	− 2.240***	− 0.610***
		(0.258)	(0.470)	(0.09)
DURATION				
	NO-PARTY	0.07***	0.024	0.074***
		(0.021)	(0.037)	(0.00)
	ONE-PARTY	0.045***	0.171***	0.038***
		(0.016)	(0.037)	(0.00)
	MULTI-PARTY	0.001	0.077	0.006***
		(0.025)	(0.065)	(0.00)
PETROLEUM		0.190	0.293	0.295***
		(0.269)	(0.441)	(0.02)
PETROLEUM SQUARED		− 0.031	− 0.047	− 0.041***
		(0.037)	(0.059)	(0.00)
TIME SINCE LAST REPORT		− 0.087***	− 0.019	− 0.082***
		(0.017)	(0.024)	(0.00)
Constant		0.429		1.529
		(0.340)		(6.550)
No. observations		1084	847	1084

Note: Robust standard errors.
Standard errors in parentheses: Significance levels: *** − .01; ** − .05; ** − .01.

reports of militarization than would a multi-party system. But with the passage of time, the coefficients suggest, the likelihood of disorder in such regimes rises, and does so significantly. Given the small number of observations, the rate of increase over time in the likelihood of reports of militias cannot be distinguished from zero in multi-party regimes.

Deviation from the equilibrium path results, Bates *et al.* (2002) suggest, not only when elites apply a high rate of discount to possible future losses but also when the level of temptation is high. The value of oil exports provides a measure of temptation. The coefficient drawn from the pooled sample suggests that higher levels of oil production co-vary with higher likelihoods of observing reports of armed militias. Only in the model that employ instrumental values are the coefficients significant, however.

Turning to the control variables (Table 2.7), we see that differences in the level of modernity bear no systematic relationship to variations in the reporting of militias. Rich countries, such as Congo-Brazzaville, and poor, such as Chad, have succumbed to disorder; and the signs of the coefficients on measures of literacy and urbanization are mixed. Having strife-torn neighbors does indeed affect the likelihood of political disorder. Countries whose neighbors experience higher levels of conflict – more riots, demonstrations, coups, and civil wars – are more likely to generate reports of militias. The coefficients also suggest that larger countries may be more susceptible to political disorder, although the finding is not robust nor the coefficient statistically significant.

Of greater interest, perhaps, are the coefficients on the variables that record shocks: climatic (droughts), economic (short-term growth), and political (elections). The measure of drought is the number of hectares of arable land per capita. That the coefficient is insignificant in equations with fixed effects (equations 3 and 4 in Table 2.7) suggests that within country changes in climate have little bearing on the likelihood of militarization. Rather, the results suggest, the likelihood of political disorder is higher in semi-arid nations. Turning to short-term variations in income (i.e. growth), in equations 5 and 6 in Table 2.7, the coefficient is positive, suggesting that it is positive rather than negative growth shocks that are destabilizing. The magnitude of the coefficient varies depending upon whether MODERNIZATION or its components are included in the equation, however, and in only one of the two estimates is it significant.

Better behaved is the coefficient on the measure of political shocks, which is indexed by the holding of a national election. The coefficient is significant in all models. It does not vary with the inclusion or exclusion of other variables. And everywhere it is *negative*.

One possible interpretation of this finding is that only when citizens have put down their arms do countries hold national elections; by this reasoning, the result is artifactual. Another is that with the prospect of elections, political organizations demobilize, or convert into political parties. No matter the interpretation, the finding suggests that the link between political reform and political disorder does not run through electoral campaigns; the prospect of electoral competition reduces rather than strengthens the incentives to take up arms. The finding thus enables us to rule out an alternative to the explanation offered by Bates *et al.* (2002).

It is useful to return to the discussion of natural resources. In seven of the nine specifications, the value of petroleum production per capita fails to achieve a statistically significant relationship with the likelihood of

Table 2.7. *Correlates of militia presence: core model plus controls*

	Pooled sample (probit estimates)		Conditional logits (fixed effects)		Instrumental variables (probit estimates)	
	(1)	(2)	(3)	(4)	(5)	(6)
REVENUES	−0.047 (0.029)*	−0.049* (0.028)	−0.085 (0.061)	−0.062 (0.065)	−0.245*** (0.051)	−0.248*** (0.052)
REVENUES SQUARED	0.001 (0.00)	0.001 (0.00)	0.001 (0.001)	0.001 (0.001)	0.004*** (0.000)	0.004*** (0.000)
NO-PARTY	−0.542** (0.258)	−0.536** (0.262)	−0.958* (0.523)	−0.969** (0.486)	−0.602*** (0.140)	−0.592 (0.240)**
ONE-PARTY	−0.676*** (0.254)	−0.659** (0.259)	−2.227*** (0.547)	−2.208*** (0.533)	−0.683*** (0.137)	0.265 (0.265)
DURATION NO-PARTY	0.063*** (0.024)	0.065*** (0.024)	0.03*** (0.044)	0.032 (0.04)	0.067 (0.002)***	0.066 (0.004)***
ONE-PARTY	0.037** (0.018)	0.037** (0.019)	0.168*** (0.042)	0.179*** (0.041)	0.036*** (0.001)	0.036 (0.002)**
MULTI-PARTY	0.004 (0.024)	0.004 (0.024)	0.052 (0.066)	0.058 (0.066)	0.002 (0.002)	−0.004 (0.028)
PETROLEUM	0.301 (0.341)	0.314 (0.341)	0.286 (0.528)	0.226 (0.498)	0.357*** (0.029)	0.370 (0.028)***
PETROLEUM SQUARED	−0.039 (0.045)	−0.041 (0.045)	−0.043 (0.080)	−0.036 (0.071)	−0.045*** (0.001)	−0.028 (0.001)***
TIME SINCE LAST REPORT	−0.08*** (0.017)	−0.08*** (0.017)	−0.009 (0.024)	−0.015 (0.024)	−0.075*** (0.001)	−0.077 (0.001)***
INCOME	−0.28 (0.267)		0.155 (0.504)		−0.305 (0.225)	
LITERACY	−0.004 (0.005)		0.052** (0.021)		−0.005 (0.001)****	

	(1)	(2)	(3)	(4)	(5)
URBAN POPULATION	0.006 (0.008)				0.017*** (0.000)
MODERNIZATION	-0.134 (0.188)	-0.054 (0.032)*	0.45 (0.479)	0.000 (0.060)	
GROWTH	-0.017*** (0.006)	-0.024 (0.017)	-0.025 (0.016)	0.069 (0.145)	0.048*** (0.016)
ELECTION	-0.292* (0.156)	-0.698** (0.316)	-0.682** (0.314)	-0.298 (0.113)***	-0.305*** (0.066)
DROUGHT	-0.449** (0.199)	-0.979 (1.048)	-0.918 (1.101)	-0.458 (0.452)	-0.402*** (0.014)
POPULATION	0.121 (0.094)			0.039 (0.062)	0.037*** (0.013)
NEIGHBORHOOD	0.157** (0.08)	0.227 (0.136)*	0.3 (0.132)	0.194*** (0.047)	0.263*** (0.013)
CROSS-BORDER	-0.229 (0.135)*			-0.226 (0.232)	-0.38*** (0.033)
NEIGHBOR* CROSS-BORDER		-0.063 (0.029)**	-0.073 (0.03)		
CONSTANT	0.432 (2.504)			1.96 (31.20)	3.747 (9.087)
No. observations	1084	847	847	1084	1084

Note: Robust standard errors.

Standard errors in parentheses: Significance levels: ***—.01; **—.05; **—.01.

40   *Robert H. Bates*

political disorder. And yet, this measure of natural resource wealth performed better than did others: the total volume of diamond production,[12] the value of minerals production,[13] and resource rents as a percentage of GDP.[14] None of the latter bore a systematic relationship with our measure of state failure.

Empirical measures of resource endowments thus fail to conform to theoretical expectations or to the expectations engendered by qualitative accounts. Not only is this finding of significance for this study; it is of significance for other works as well, most notably the literature on resource wars (Klare 2002; Reno 1998; Collier and Hoeffler 2004).

A possible reason for the disconnect between the statistical and qualitative evidence may be that statistical models offer tests of a theory of the origins of state failure while qualitative accounts document the consequences. The quantitative data indicate that natural resource wealth plays little role in state failure. What the qualitative data confirm is that when states fail, political actors take up arms and seek ways to finance their movements. In countries abundantly endowed with natural resources, they seize control of their extraction in order to generate revenues. The two kinds of data may thus be documenting separate stages in the process of state failure.

Conclusion

This chapter has probed the roots of political disorder. Taking counsel from social theory and observations from contemporary Africa, it turned to the theory of games to determine the conditions under which governments would use force in ways that enhance rather than weaken personal security and under which citizens would set aside arms. The Weberian state, I argued, is not a given. It is the product of choices and prevails when these choices form an equilibrium.

Applying the argument to data drawn from Africa, we find that the poverty of the state, the prospects of wealth from predation, and the fears arising from the potential loss of office increased the likelihood that states would fail and political order break down.

REFERENCES

Addison, Tony, Philippe Le Billon, and S. Mansoob Murshed. 2000. "Conflict in Africa: The Cost of Peaceful Behavior." Working paper, WIDER, Helsinki, Finland.

[12] Data collected by Macartan Humphreys from Baker Library, Harvard University.
[13] Data collected by Anke Hoeffler, Oxford University.   [14] Ibid.

Bates, Robert. 2007. "Political Conflict and State Failure." In *The Political Economy of Economic Growth in Africa, 1960–2000*, ed. B. J. Ndulu, S. A. O'Connell, R. H. Bates, P. Collier, and C. C. Soludo. Cambridge University Press, 249–296.

2008. *When Things Fell Apart: State Failure in Late-Century Africa*. Cambridge University Press.

Bates, Robert H., Avner Greif, and Smita Singh. 2002. "Organizing Violence." *Journal of Conflict Resolution* 46: 599–628.

Birmingham, David. 2002. "Angola." In *A History of Postcolonial Lusophone Africa*, ed. P. Chabal. London: Hurst and Company, 137–184.

Blumenthal, Erwin. 1982. "Zaire: rapport sur sa crédibilité financière internationale." *La Revue Nouvelle* 77: 360–378.

Chabal, Patrick, ed. 2002. *A History of Postcolonial Lusophone Africa*. London: Hurst and Company.

Collier, Paul, V. L. Elliot, Havard Hegre, Anke Hoeffler, Marta Reynal-Querol, and Nicholas Sambanis. 2003. *Breaking the Conflict Trap*. Washington DC: The World Bank and Oxford University Press.

Collier, Paul, and Anke Hoeffler. 2004. "Greed and Grievance in Civil Wars." *Oxford Economic Papers* 56: 563–595.

de Waal, Alex, and A. H. Abdel Salam. 2004. "Islamism, State Power, and *Jihad* in Sudan." In *Islamism and its Enemies in the Horn of Africa*, ed. A. de Waal. Bloomington, IN: Indiana University Press, 71–113.

Deutsch, Karl W. 1961. "Social Mobilization and Political Development." *American Political Science Review* 55: 493–514.

Dietrich, Christian. 2000. "Inventory of Formal Diamond Mining in Angola." In *Angola's War Economy*, ed. J. Cilliers and C. Dietrich. Pretoria: Institute for Security Studies, 141–172.

Easterly, William, and Ross Levine. 1997. "Africa's Growth Tragedy: Policies and Ethnic Divisions." *Quarterly Journal of Economics* 112: 1203–1250.

Fearon, James D. 1996. "Bargaining over Objects that Influence Future Bargaining Power." Paper presented at the Annual Meetings of the American Political Science Association, Washington DC, August 28–31, 1997.

Fearon, James D., and David Latin. 1996. "Explaining Interethnic Cooperation." *American Political Science Review* 90: 715–735.

Gould, David. 1980. *Bureaucratic Corruption and Underdevelopment in the Third World: The Case of Zaire*. London: Pergamon Press.

Grossman, Herschel I. 1995. "The Economics of Revolutions." Department of Economics, Brown University, Providence, RI.

Grossman, Herschel I., and Minseong Kim. 1995. "Swords or Plowshares? A Theory of the Security of Claims to Property." *Journal of Political Economy* 103 (6): 1275–1288.

Hausman, Jerry, and J. Hahn. 2002. "A New Specification Test for the Validity of Instrumental Variables." *Econometrica* 70 (1): 163–189.

2003. "Weak Instruments: Diagnosis and Cures in Empirical Econometrics." *American Economic Review* 93 (2): 118–125.

Hobbes, Thomas. 1961. "Leviathan." In *Great Political Thinkers*, ed. W. Ebenstein. New York: Holt, Reinhart and Winston.

Huntington, Samuel P. 1968. *Political Order in Changing Societies*. New Haven and London: Yale University Press.

Johnson, Douglas H. 1998. "The Sudan People's Liberation Army and the Problem of Factionalism." In *African Guerrillas*, ed. C. Clapham. Oxford: James Currey, 53–72.

  2003. *The Root Causes of Sudan's Civil War*. Bloomington, IN: Indiana University Press.

Judson, Ruth A., and Ann Owen. 1996. "Estimating Dynamic Panel Data Models: A Practical Guide for Macroeconomists." The Federal Reserve Board, Washington DC.

Klare, Michael T. 2002. *Resource Wars*. New York: Henry Holt and Company.

MacGaffey, Janet. 1991. *The Real Economy of Zaire*. Philadelphia: University of Pennsylvania Press.

Meredith, Martin. 2005. *The State of Africa: A History of Fifty Years of Independence*. London: Free Press.

Moselle, Boaz, and Ben Polak. 1999. *A Model of the Predatory State*. Princeton University Press.

Muthoo, Abhinay. 2000. "On the Foundations of Property Rights, Part i: A Model of the State-of-Nature with Two Players." *Economics Discussion Papers* 512. Essex, UK: University of Essex, Department of Economics.

Otunnu, Ogenga. 2000. "An Historical Analysis of the Invasion of the Rwanda Patriotic Army." In *The Path of a Genocide: The Rwanda Crisis from Uganda to Zaire*, ed. H. Adelman and A. Suhrke. London: Transaction Publishers, 31–50.

Pech, Khareen. 2000. "The Hand of War: Mercenaries in the Former Zaire 1996–97." In *Mercenaries: An African Security Dilemma*, ed. A. F. Musah and J. K. Fayemi. London: Pluto Press, 117–154.

Reno, William. 1998. *Warlord Politics and African States*. Boulder, CO: Lynne Rienner.

Rubin, D. B. 1996. "Multiple Imputation after 18+ Years (with Discussion)." *Journal of the American Statistical Association* 91: 473–489.

Sambanis, Nicholas, and Havard Hegre. 2006. "Sensitivity Analysis of Empirical Results on Civil War Onset." *Journal of Conflict Resolution* 50: 508–535.

Skaperdas, Stergios. 1992. "Cooperation, Conflict, and Power in the Absence of Property Rights." *American Economic Review* 82: 720–738.

  1996. "Gangs and the State of Nature." In *The New Palgrave Dictionary of Economics and the Law*, ed. P. Newman. London: Palgrave, 198–201.

Thom, William G. 1999. "Congo-Zaire's 1996–1997 Civil War in the Context of Evolving Patterns of Military Conflict in Africa in the Era of Independence." *Journal of Conflict Studies* 19: 93–123.

Usher, Dan. 1989. "The Dynastic Cycle and the Stationary State." *American Economic Review* 79: 1031–1044.

Weber, Max. 1921. "Politik als Beruf." In *Gesammelte Politische Schriften*. Munich: Duncker & Humboldt, 396–450.

  1946. "Politics as a Vocation." In *From Max Weber: Essays in Sociology*, ed. H. H. Gerth and C. Wright Mills. Oxford University Press.

Weiss, Herbert. 1995. "Zaire: Collapsed Society, Surviving State, Future Policy." In *Collapsed States*, ed. I. W. Zartman. Boulder, CO: Lynne Rienner, 157–170.

3   Attaining social order in Iraq

Michael Hechter and Nika Kabiri

In the year 1918, Arnold Wilson, Acting Civil Commissioner of the
territory now known as Iraq, faced a dilemma. A self-confident British
colonial officer, Wilson was charged with the task of establishing social
order in a well-armed, culturally heterogeneous population that had
been liberated from centuries of Ottoman rule. As is often the case in
the modern world, British governance was made more difficult by the
population's hostility to its new foreign masters. The dilemma, as the
colonial officer later recounted, was this:

Ought we to aim at a "bureaucratic" form of administration, such as that in force
in Turkey and in Egypt, involving *direct control* by a central government, and the
replacement of the powerful tribal confederation by the smaller tribal or sub-
tribal unit, as a prelude to individual in place of communal ownership of land, or
should our aim to be retain, and subject to official safeguards, to strengthen, *the
authority of tribal chiefs*, and to make them the agents and official representatives
of Government, within their respective areas? The latter policy had been already
adopted, in default of a better one, in Basra *wilayat*, and especially in the
Muntafiq division: was it wise to apply it to the Baghdad *wilayat*? Both policies
had their advocates. (Wilson 1931; emphasis added)

After due deliberation, Wilson chose the first option. Two years later
there was a massive rebellion and he was out of a job.

Today, the Iraqi state faces an uncannily similar situation to that of
Britain at the end of World War I. Following the toppling of Saddam
and the establishment of a democratic regime, the Iraqi government
finds itself governing a culturally divided and notably turbulent territory.
Surprisingly, the answer to Wilson's question – is social order in societies
like Iraq best attained by direct or indirect rule? – is as elusive now as it
was at the end of World War I. If anything, the question is even more

Revised version of a paper presented at the conference on "Order, Conflict, and Violence"
at Yale University, April 30–May 1, 2004, New Haven, Connecticut. For comments, we
are grateful to Yoram Barzel, Daniel Chirot, Debra Friedman, Ellis Goldberg, Resat
Kasaba, Tuna Kuyucu, and Nicholas Sambanis. We also thank Devin Kelley and Stefan
Kubicki for their help with the research.

pressing today, for the increasing prevalence of civil war, state failure, and terrorism has sharply underlined the problem of social order in many parts of the world. Critics of the American occupation have lamented that the Bush administration adopted no coherent plan for administering the peace before invading;[1] the result has been a weak interim state that seems unwilling or unable to maintain order at the local level (Ricks 2006).[2] Paul Bremer's solution was to run a highly centralized operation, a strategy that was criticized for fueling sectarian violence (Diamond 2004, 3). Likewise, the constitutionally based Iraqi government has been markedly unsuccessful at fostering peace; it simply does not have the resources to police areas inhabited by Shi'i or Sunni militia. Whatever might be said about these regimes, they did not turn their backs on some received theory of governance. No such tried-and-true theory exists. To promote social order in Iraq, one must understand how different governance structures affect the probability of unrest given the country's specific characteristics and circumstances.

For social engineers intent on attaining order, the choice of a system of governance is a dilemma because evidence supports both of the positions outlined by Wilson. Indirect rule allows the state to pass the high costs of rule on to subgroups. But indirect rule clearly has its downside – ethnofederalism is associated with the fragmentation of the Soviet Union rather than order (Beissinger 2002; Bunce 1999; Roeder 1991), and much the same fate befell Yugoslavia (Woodward 1995). Although direct rule is often a hedge against fragmentation, it is not a sufficient guarantor of social order, either. On the one hand, some stateless societies (like traditional tribal societies in the Arabian peninsula) manifest a good deal of social order. On the other hand, sultanistic regimes (like Duvalier's Haiti) – the *ne plus ultra* of direct rule – are often visited by disorder (Chehabi and Linz 1998).

---

[1] Experts on nation building and Middle Eastern affairs presented the Bush team with possible postwar strategies before the occupation began, but the administration neglected to seriously consider their recommendations. Thus Jay Garner, the initial American official in charge of postwar reconstruction, merely had eight weeks between the announcement of his appointment and the start of hostilities to organize a government in Iraq. As one American ex-general (Barry McCaffree) has pointed out, this is far too little time to set up a new Safeway supermarket, let alone the government of a sizable country (Traub 2004, 62).

[2] Some argue that because US troops did not stop the looting that occurred immediately after Saddam's removal, Iraqis were left with the impression that the United States would tolerate acts of violence. In some cases, US troops encouraged disorder: rather than stop lootings, troops egged the looters on. What was perceived (rightly) as disorder for Iraqis was considered an acceptable byproduct of freedom to US military men and women (Packer 2005).

Evidently, the relationship between social order and these types of governance is complex. In some contexts, an increase in direct rule can instigate resistance in a polity, fostering disorder. But indirect rule is no necessary panacea: it too can hinder social order. Since governance structures are pivotal for attaining social order – in contemporary Iraq as well as elsewhere – this chapter aims to explore their general effects.[3]

Social order and forms of governance

To the degree that a society is ordered, its individual members behave both predictably and cooperatively.[4] Mere predictability is an insufficient condition for social order. The denizens of the state of nature (think of the inhabitants of Rio's *favelas* as portrayed in the recent Brazilian film *City of God*) are quite able to predict that everyone will engage in force and fraud whenever it suits them. Hence they are accustomed to taking the appropriate defensive – and offensive – measures. But none of the fruits of social and economic development can occur in the absence of a cooperative social order. Thus, in a viable social order, individuals must not only act in a mutually predictable fashion; they must also comply with socially encompassing norms and laws – rules that permit and promote cooperation.

Social order is not a constant but a variable; it exists to the degree that individuals in a given territory are free from the depredations of crime, physical injury, and arbitrary justice. Perfect order is an ideal, so it cannot be attained in Iraq, or anywhere else for that matter. By any reckoning, present-day Iraq falls far short of this ideal: Iraqis are facing the perils of gunfire, kidnapping, murder, and bombings on a daily basis. Despite this, there is a greater amount of order in certain Iraqi regions (such as Kurdistan) than others.

How can this woeful amount of social order in today's Iraq be increased? This question is an instantiation of the general problem of social order that has dogged social theorists at least since ancient times. The most popular solution dates from the seventeenth century (Hobbes

---

[3] Proposing an ideal governance structure for Iraq is not our aim here. Nor are we delineating the conditions under which states adopt direct rule, indirect rule, or a hybrid of the two – an interesting question in itself. Rather, we provide a rudimentary analysis of the implications of direct and indirect rule so that we might better understand how greater social order can be attained in post-invasion Iraq.

[4] Hayek (1973, 36), for example, defines order in opposition to entropy. For him it is "a state of affairs in which a multiplicity of elements of various kinds are so related to each other that we may learn from our acquaintance with some spatial or temporal part of the whole to form correct expectations concerning the rest, or at least expectations which have a good chance of proving correct."

[1651] 1996): it implies that social order is the product of direct rule, a multidimensional variable composed of at least two independent dimensions: scope and penetration.[5] The scope of a state refers to the quantity and quality of the collective goods that it provides.[6] Welfare benefits, government jobs, state-sponsored schools and hospitals, and a functioning system of justice are examples of such goods. Socialist states have the highest scope; neo-liberal ones the lowest. Scope induces dependence: where state scope is high, individuals depend primarily on the state for access to collective goods.

In contrast, penetration refers to the central state's control capacity – that is, the proportion of laws and policies that are enacted and enforced by central as against regional or local decision-makers. Penetration is at a maximum in police states in which central rulers seek to monitor and control all subjects within their domain. Polities relying on local agents to exercise control (municipal police forces, for example) have lower penetration. Scope and penetration often co-vary, but not necessarily. For example, federal states with similar scope have less penetration than unitary states.

Just how direct rule may foster social order is a matter of some dispute.[7] On one view, high scope and penetration foster order by instituting a common culture that provides the shared concepts, values, and norms – or in game-theoretic language, the common knowledge (Chwe 2001) – required for cooperation to emerge and persist. Intuitively, cultural homogeneity is essential for social order. However, the stability of culturally heterogeneous societies that have adopted indirect rule – such as Switzerland, the United Kingdom, and Finland – calls this conclusion into question.[8] On another view, social order rests not on cognitive commonality, but rather on the power and authority of central rulers. Indeed, the popular concept of state failure implies the loss of this central authority.[9]

---

[5] For a more extended discussion of direct and indirect rule and their effects on patterns of group formation, see Hechter (2004).

[6] Note that this category includes state regulation of the economy, polity, and civil society, for these too are collective goods.

[7] For a discussion of the major theories of social order and their limits, see Hechter and Horne (2003).

[8] Also consider the attainment of social order in countries of immigration like the United States, Australia, Canada, and New Zealand.

[9] Nearly forty years ago, two eminent comparativists made the same point, albeit a bit differently. Nettl (1968) insisted that the state was hardly to be conceived as an institution carved out of marble and granite but rather a variable that he termed "stateness." And Huntington (1968, 1) assured us that "the most important political distinction among countries concerns not their form of government but their degree of government."

Though rational rulers strive for direct rule because it maximizes their income, revenue, and power,[10] direct rule has two distinct liabilities for the state. First, it engenders the opposition of traditional rulers (and their dependents), whose power is threatened as the state advances. Second, it is costly, for direct rulers must assume the financial responsibility of pervasive policing[11] while simultaneously providing the bulk of their citizenry's collective goods.[12] Moreover, the idea that social order is produced in a top-down fashion by resourceful central authorities leaves a fundamental question begging: Just how can this power ever manage to be concentrated in the first place? To this question, top-down theorists have little in the way of an answer, save for the (often valid) idea that it is imposed exogenously on fragmented territories by more powerful states. Beyond its inability to account for primary state formation, this answer underestimates the difficulty that modern states have had in attempting to impose order on less developed societies.[13]

The nature of this difficulty becomes apparent when we recall that the emergence of the modern bureaucratic state in Western Europe was long-drawn-out and arduous to boot (Elias 1993; Ertman 1997; Gorski 2003). Feudal landholders who managed, against all odds, to secure a preponderance of political power were, for a time, invariably overcome by jealous rivals, rapacious invaders, or intrusive agents of the Church. In consequence, the concentration of power oscillated around a highly decentralized equilibrium. This equilibrium persisted for centuries until new military, communications, and industrial technologies allowed power to be concentrated in the modern centralized state.

At the same time, an increase in state scope and penetration can have perverse effects. Direct rule can fuel the mobilization of both traditional and new groups that carry potential threats to order (as well as the state).

---

[10] Rulers' demand for direct rule is subject to constraints, of course. Due to institutional constraints, rational rulers in democratic regimes are forced to settle for the much more modest goal of reelection.

[11] The costs of policing are political in addition to pecuniary. In present-day Iraq, for example, the Bush administration, unwilling to add more military boots on the ground, has contracted out an increasingly large proportion of the security responsibility to an international mercenary force. Although this adds considerably to the bottom line, it avoids domestic political costs.

[12] Whereas legitimacy reduces the policing costs of direct rule, it does not reduce the cost of providing collective goods. Of course, attaining legitimacy in Iraq and other Arab societies is no easy task: "The central problem of government in the Arab world today is political legitimacy. The shortage of this indispensable political resource largely accounts for the volatile nature of Arab politics and the autocratic, unstable character of all the present Arab governments" (Hudson 1977, 2).

[13] These difficulties are perhaps the single principal concern of historians of the former colonies in Africa and Asia (Beissinger and Young 2002; Cooper and Stoler 1997).

When a state extends its scope – when it becomes the primary provider of collective goods – it increases individuals' dependence on central rulers. Yet state-provided collective goods – like education, welfare benefits, and government jobs – are costly to produce and limited in supply. Not everyone receives as much as they wish, and not everyone gets an equal share. Direct rulers become the principal target of redistributive demands by new or traditional groups that can threaten to disrupt the social order.[14] Moreover, to the degree that state-provided goods are culturally specific, they are likely to dissatisfy groups that have distinctive preferences regarding such goods.

Consider the recent shift from class- to culturally based politics in advanced capitalist societies (Hechter 2004). By providing the bulk of collective goods in society, the direct-rule state reduces dependence on class-based groups (such as trade unions), thereby weakening them. To the degree that state-provided goods are distributed unequally to individuals on the basis of cultural distinctions, however, the legitimacy of the state in the eyes of these constituents is challenged. This provides such individuals with an incentive to mobilize on the basis of factors such as race, ethnicity, and religion. As a result, social disorder may increase. The rise of nationalist violence has been attributed, in part, to just this mechanism (Hechter 2000).

An increase in penetration may also spur disorder. As the state extends its control apparatus, it infringes on the traditional self-determination of social groups, particularly culturally distinctive ones. This imposition of a single set of norms on a culturally diverse population may motivate the leaders of disfavored groups to oppose the state. In pre-invasion Iraq, for example, the Ba'athist regime prevented Kurds from speaking Kurdish in public and pressured them to adopt Arab names and identities in official documents (Human Rights Watch 1995). In addition, throughout Iraq, it implemented a highly invasive system of surveillance by recruiting a network of spies that constantly monitored Iraqis. This Orwellian system of control, coupled with severe punishments marked by physical torture, created a culture of terror that encouraged Iraqis to seek refuge in more protected social spheres such as extended families and religious groups (Makiya 1998). In spite of their relative lack of visibility before the American invasion, such groups likely formed the social bases of the current – and largely sectarian – Iraqi insurgency.

Effective governance need not reside exclusively with central rulers, however. In a system of indirect rule, authority is distributed among a

---

[14] Such preference heterogeneity is one of the principal rationales for the theory of fiscal federalism (Oates 1972).

number of sub-units or social groups. Distributed authority is especially likely to occur in culturally heterogeneous societies. Indirect rulers delegate substantial powers of governance to traditional authorities in return for the promise of tribute, revenue, and military service. Although both direct and indirect rule foster dependence on the state, direct rule results in *individuals'* dependence, whereas indirect rule entails the dependence of *groups*. Since there is no compelling reason to believe that centralized rule is inherently more effective in promoting order than its more decentralized counterpart, bottom-up explanations of social order – which date at least from the time of Althusius ([1614] 1964) – have recently been gaining greater attention. These theories explain how social order is enhanced when a variety of social groups and voluntary associations mediate between individuals and central rulers.

Theories explaining the relationship of indirect rule and social order come in two varieties. In one, *intra-group* relations are critical for the attainment of order. On this view, the internal solidarity of groups contributes to social order either by promoting pro-social norms and orientations to action (Tocqueville [1848] 1969; Putnam 2000), or by subjecting group members to heightened levels of social control (Fearon and Laitin 1996; Hechter *et al.* 1992; Weber [1919–1920] 1958).

The second theory suggests that the key to social order lies in the nature of *intergroup* relations. Societies that foster intergroup relations tend to have groups composed of socially heterogeneous individuals. In such societies, cross-cutting ties attenuate loyalty to any one group by providing individuals with a stake in many different groups (Simmel [1922] 1955). By contrast, socially segregated patterns of group affiliation strengthen group loyalties and foster intergroup competition. The first pattern of group affiliation should produce strong ties, few bridges between groups (Granovetter 1973), and low social order; the second should produce weak social ties, many bridges between groups, and high social order. Whereas there is evidence that cross-cutting ties and network bridges indeed do promote social order (Blau and Schwartz 1984), too little attention has been paid to the difficulty of establishing such bridges in traditional societies characterized by strong ties.[15]

But indirect rule also has its liabilities. Its reliance on solidary groups is only justifiable if these groups do not set out to subvert order or threaten the state. Often solidary groups do subvert social order, however.

[15] For example, Kurdish immigrants in Sweden have been known to employ honor killing as a means of preventing their daughters from having liaisons with Swedish males (Lyall 2002; see, however, Ahmadi 2003). Imagine how difficult it would be to establish social networks composed of Catholics and Protestants in Northern Ireland, Serbs and Croats in Bosnia, Jews and Palestinians in Israel, or Shi'i, Sunni, and Kurds in Iraq at this time.

Consider the large literature on failed states (Kohli 2002), which attributes disorder to a variety of solidary groups that act as hindrances to, and substitutes for, central authority. Moreover, such groups need not be perennially subversive; they can sustain social order at one time and subvert it at another. Since each form of rule has strengths and liabilities, choosing an optimal form of governance is anything but child's play. Direct rule may quell insurgent activity in some contexts, but in others it may stimulate the emergence of social groups that threaten the regime. Under indirect rule, groups may use their autonomy to challenge state authority. Evidently, there is no universally optimal choice of governance structures for the attainment of order.

Nonetheless, insight into the problem of order in today's Iraq can be gained by examining the effect of varying forms of governance on social order in the history of this territory. Since the late Ottoman period, people in this region have experienced varying levels of direct rule and social order. Indirect rule was implemented in some time periods, direct rule at others. Occasionally, the Iraqi state simultaneously adopted different governance structures for different regions. The following discussion of Iraqi history focuses on the relationship between governance structure and order. It suggests that the choice of direct or indirect rule has been crucial for the attainment of order in this troubled land.

The implications of indirect and direct rule for social order in Iraqi history

Iraq under the Ottomans: mamluks and Young Turks

Ottoman Mesopotamia – the territory now known as Iraq – was born of conflict between the Ottoman and Safavid empires during the early seventeenth century.[16] Iraq's strategic position between these two rival empires destined it to be a frontier buffer zone. Due to their limited interest in the territory and its distance from Istanbul, the Ottomans ruled Iraq indirectly.

Centuries of famine, flooding, Mongol invasions, and the collapse of irrigation systems had left much of the land unsuited to agriculture. Two distinct social structures emerged: the urban provinces of Mosul, Baghdad, and Basra; and the outlying territories, which were dominated by tribes (Tripp 2000, 18). Urban and tribal Arabs were so different that they comprised almost separate worlds (Batatu 1978, 13). Istanbul could not exert as much control over rural areas as urban ones (Nieuwenhuis

---

[16] The Ottomans finally took Baghdad in 1639 (Sluglett and Sluglett 1990, 2).

1981, 120). As was customary throughout their empire, in 1702 the Ottomans initially delegated governance in the urban provinces of Iraq to local authorities called *mamluks* – highly educated slaves who were trained specifically as indirect rulers (Hourani 1991, 251; Nieuwenhuis 1981, 14).

Though the mamluks were ostensibly under the Sultan's thumb, Istanbul wielded very little actual control over them. The mamluks recognized the Ottoman Sultan symbolically (in religious services and on coinage, for example) and obtained formal confirmation of their governorships from the Sultan, but they retained considerable autonomy *de facto* (Tripp 2000, 9). Ottoman Janissary troops were dispatched to Baghdad, but the mamluks kept them under their rigid control. The government of Baghdad was largely self-sufficient, consisting of military-administrative financial and judicial branches (Nieuwenhuis 1981, 27). Mamluks provided what collective goods there were and funded their own local armies, enabling them in some cases (as in Mosul) to successfully maintain the Ottoman frontier (Khoury 1997, 188). Mamluks in the Iraqi region were obliged to send tribute to Istanbul, but did so only irregularly. Since Istanbul did not demand much of the mamluks, they had little cause for complaint.

Mamluk power, however, did not extend into the bulk of rural lands, which were arid and unsuited for agriculture. Most rural inhabitants adapted to the desert ecology by embracing pastoralism.[17] Unlike agricultural crops, livestock are easily stolen, and in the absence of a strong state, pastoralists could rely only on their tribal affiliations for protection of their herds and families. Clans forged alliances based on the notion that "anyone who commits an act of aggression against any one of us must expect retaliation from us all, and not only will the aggressor himself be likely to suffer retaliation, but his entire group and all its members will be equally liable" (Gellner 2003, 311). This principle led to a system of strong, self-policing tribal groups that defended themselves by threatening to retaliate, and often retaliating, against individual members of aggressor groups.[18] Because these tribes relied only on

---

[17] That all tribes were nomadic is an overgeneralization. Some tribes settled in small sedentary areas. Nonetheless, these sedentary groups were organized much like their nomadic counterparts, through (fictive) kinship relations (Nieuwenhuis 1981).

[18] Tribes are not necessarily pure kinship groups. "The concept of tribe is unclear and controversial. The word is used to refer to a kinship group, an extended family, or a coalition of related families. It may refer to the elite family from whom some larger confederation gets its name, to a cultural, ethnic, or other non-familial social group, or to conquest movements of pastoral people without regard for the internal basis of cohesion" (Lapidus 1990, 26). Whether blood relations are real or fictive, the bond helps to create group solidarity.

themselves for protection from outside threats, they had to develop effective means for self-defense: they amassed enough weapons and knowledge of warfare to become mini-states (Jabar 2003).[19]

Given their military capacity and acumen, the tribes often attacked settled areas, but they were held in check in two ways. First, the mamluks could rely on their own military strength to resist tribal threats. Strategies of tribal warfare rested primarily on surprise attacks by small groups, as this was the most effective means for engaging in conflict with other tribes. Since their weapons were relatively primitive, the tribes were largely incapable of defeating large provincial armies. Second, Baghdad lured some tribal leaders into the provincial government, providing them with wider-scale governance rights in exchange for their fealty.

But indirect rule came to an abrupt end in the mid-nineteenth century – and with it, the autonomy of the mamluks (Nakash 1994, 32). Reacting to the threat of rising European nation-states and the nationalist secession of Greece in 1828 (McDowall 1992, 14), the Ottomans attempted to increase their authority in Iraq. They consolidated their military forces and sent an army to capture the mamluk leaders in Baghdad, Mosul, and Basra (Tripp 2000, 14). Under the *Tanzimat* reforms initiated by Sultan Abdulmecid, the three provinces fell under the direct rule of Istanbul. The increased presence of the Ottoman army and officials augmented Istanbul's penetration in the Iraqi region.

As direct rule progressed, the Ottomans favored Sunnis over other groups. Government jobs were given primarily to Sunnis, and schools provided by the state were hardly attended by Shi'is, who had their own schools (Sluglett 2003, 8).[20] Meanwhile, Kurdish tribal chieftains, threatened by a loss of autonomy, organized a series of revolts, some hoping for complete independence, others for the control they exercised before direct rule was implemented (McDowall 1992, 14). Ottoman direct rule created resentment along these ethnic and religious lines, foretelling the emergence of contemporary ethnic and religious political cleavages.[21] All told, increased direct rule reduced social order in the urban provinces.

---

[19] "Each strong tribe was a miniature mobile state, with its patriarchal headship usually head by a warrior household; its own military force; its customary law, which was preserved by the 'arfa (literally, 'the knowledgeable', actually tribal jurists or adjudicators); its non-literate culture; its territoriality in the form of *dira* (tribal pastures) or, later, arable lands; and its mode of subsistence economy, i.e. pastoralism, commerce, and conquest" (Jabar 2003, 73).

[20] "In general, religious Shi'is tended to view the state, whether the Ottoman Empire or Qajar Iran, as a sort of necessary evil; for this and other reasons, they were not inclined to press for bureaucratic, educational, or military employment" (Sluglett 2003, 9).

[21] We take the view that although opposition to the state can often be framed in terms of ethnic or religious discourse, organization, and not the mere existence of ethnic or

In addition to encroaching on mamluk rule, for the first time the Ottomans sought to bring the tribes in the countryside under their control. They did so by investing in irrigation,[22] altering the region's ecology and thereby attaching tribesmen to the land.[23] For the most part, Ottoman efforts to domesticate tribal nomads were successful. In southern Iraq, for example, the percentage of nomadic persons decreased from 50% in 1867 to 19% in 1905. Meanwhile, the rural settled population increased from 41 to 72% during these years. New cities emerged as well (Nakash 1994, 35).

At the same time, the Ottoman Land Law of 1858 altered the tribal landscape by creating a new type of relationship between Istanbul and the Iraqi tribes. Although land was deemed the property of the Ottoman state, title deeds, which were handed to anyone who already possessed or occupied parcels of land, granted their holders virtually complete rights of ownership. Since these deeds could be handed only to individuals, tribal shaykhs were the most common recipients (Tripp 2000, 15–16). By offering landownership benefits only to shaykhs, the Ottomans effectively bought their loyalty. The shaykhs became landowners – indirect rulers of their tribesmen who now assumed the status of tenant farmers. Since landownership still resided in the state, the Ottomans could revoke land rights as easily as they could grant them.

The new land laws transformed tribal social structure. Under the new system, the state was no longer just a tax-extracting agency. As differential rights to land created tension and social conflict, landowners relied on the state to enforce their land rights and maintain order.[24] Conflict over land rights aided the regime, for it spurred competition

---

religious diversity, is required for collective action (see Brubaker 2002). Ethnic and religious groups are politically salient only in so far as they are internally solidary (see Hechter 1987).

[22] "Unlike *Mamluk* efforts to break the tribes by occasional blows without providing an alternative way of life, the new Ottoman governors encouraged the tribesmen to settle down and take up agriculture. The governors' effort reflected Istanbul's desire to settle the tribes so as to increase agricultural production and tax revenue to sustain the Empire's growing involvement in world capitalist economy" (Nakash 1994, 32).

[23] "The Ottomans considered settlement the means by which they could 'civilize' the nomads ... In seeking to settle the tribes and bring them under strict government control, the governors attempted to restructure tribal society. They sought to break the great tribal confederations and to undermine the status of their paramount *shaykhs* as 'lords' who controlled large dominions. In this struggle over taxes, and the control of food and trade routes, the governors attempted to reduce the power of the *shaykhs*, partly by conferring their position to others" (Nakash 1994, 33).

[24] Indeed, rebellions against the Ottomans broke out in 1849, 1852, 1863–1866, 1878–1883, and 1899–1905 (Nakash 1994, 34).

between tribal shaykhs.[25] The Ottoman strategy of divide and rule weakened ties between tribes and principal shaykhs as well as those between shaykhs and their tribesmen. A classic form of interdependence – characteristic of indirect rule – resulted between tribe and state. The landowners' stake in state law made them complicit in the new political order (Tripp 2000, 17).

But resistance, including widespread revolt, grew among tribesmen who were disadvantaged by the new system. In geographically accessible territories the Ottoman forces crushed the rebellions militarily. Elsewhere, they increased their exploitation of tribal shaykhs, becoming more adept at dividing the tribes. The Ottomans belatedly recognized that tribes were essential for maintaining social order at the local level, and that the indirect rule of tribes was essential for quelling disorder.[26]

The Young Turk movement in the late nineteenth and early twentieth centuries increased direct rule as well as hardship for the majority of the region's rural population. Arab reactions against "Turkification" erupted as the Young Turks augmented state scope by bringing schools and other cultural organizations to Iraq. These were venues where like-minded individuals and intellectuals from different provinces could recognize their common interests. At the same time, the movement created social spaces for individuals dependent on and loyal to Arab cultural institutions to organize against the state. Secret societies emerged to challenge Ottoman hegemony and resist what they deemed to be encroachments on Arab culture. An estimated sixty newspapers and journals appeared in the early twentieth century, as did a number of clubs, groups, and societies. Among the groups that flourished during this time was the National Scientific Club of Baghdad, whose members promoted knowledge of Arab language and culture. This club attracted both Sunni and Shi'i intellectuals. Groups such as the Reform Society of Basra, which organized to regain provincial autonomy, became crucibles of Arab nationalism. Despite Ottoman attempts to suppress them, these secret societies grew stronger (Tripp 2000, 22–28). Direct rule was fomenting social disorder.

---

[25] The Ottoman practice of pitting shaykh against shaykh "so changed the conditions of life in the affected regions as to attenuate the old tribal loyalties or render them by and large ineffectual" (Batatu 1978, 22).

[26] A Baghdad deputy to the Ottoman empire wrote in 1910, "To depend on the tribe is a thousand times safer than depending on the government, for whereas the latter defers or neglects repression, the tribe, no matter how feeble it may be, as soon as it learns that an injustice has been committed against one of its members readies itself to exact vengeance on his behalf" (Batatu 1978, 21).

All told, the Ottoman empire's indirect rule seemed well adapted to the region's social structure. The tribes and mamluks were self-sufficient and self-policing, and neither directly challenged the authority of the state. Low penetration afforded both groups a high degree of autonomy, giving them little reason to resist state authority. Because Istanbul's scope was low, individuals were generally not dependent on the empire for their livelihood. Mamluks supplied the bulk of the collective goods in the urban provinces, and tribal members provided one another with collective goods in the countryside. The Ottomans relied on shaykhs to control the tribes, but no tribe was permanently favored by Istanbul. Uncertainty about the prospect of receiving favored treatment encouraged the shaykhs to toe the Ottomans' line. No tribe was permanently denied the opportunity to receive the few favors the state provided, so in the long run all of them were in the same boat.[27] Neither mamluks nor shaykhs had much reason to challenge Istanbul for a larger share, or a more preferable bundle of collective goods. Indirect rule worked. When the Ottoman empire began to institute direct rule, however, new bases of opposition arose both in the cities and in the countryside. This analysis of the Ottoman period suggests that when indirect rule is maintained by a strong central state it can be cost-effective. To the degree that local groups have high autonomy and are not perpetually disadvantaged by the state, they have little incentive to challenge central authorities. Moreover, when individuals have low dependence on the center, they are unlikely to regard it as a target of collective action. An increase in direct rule, however, carries with it the potential for disorder. As direct rule impinges on previously autonomous groups, they are more likely to become restive.

British hegemony: exercises in direct and indirect rule

World War I brought with it the end of Ottoman governance in Iraq. British troops took Baghdad in March of 1917, and the British occupation of Mosul and Kirkuk followed shortly thereafter (Sluglett and Sluglett 1990, 9; Atiyyah 1973, 151). Interested in controlling a land bridge to India and becoming increasingly aware of the importance of oil, the British initially opted for a sharp increase in direct rule. Considering the Iraqis incapable of managing their own country, they abolished Ottoman

---

[27] With respect to the tribes, the Ottomans employed a strategy of *divide et impera*, which constituted a macrosociological form of intermittent reinforcement. This kind of reinforcement regime – exemplified by Louis XIV's differential allocation of prestige among the nobles at Versailles (Elias 1983) – is notable for its capacity to induce compliance.

governing institutions (such as the elected municipal councils), and installed British political officers in their stead (Tripp 2000, 37).[28] In August 1915, the Ottoman Penal and Criminal Procedure Code was removed; its replacement, modeled on the Indian Civil and Criminal Codes, was called the Iraq Occupied Territories Code.

Direct rule displaced former Iraqi officers and government officials with British counterparts. By August 1, 1920 the Civil Administration consisted of 534 high-ranking officers and personnel, but only 20 of these were Iraqi (Atiyyah 1973, 214). The British military presence was also pervasive. One American observer of the British occupation noted in March 1917 that "the British meant to show the native population that there would be no trouble in the city while they were running it. Every man on the street had his rifle and bayonet" (Mathewson 2003, 54).

The British increased the scope of their rule by providing Iraqis with the bulk of their collective goods. Funding for education and medical services, although meager, increased almost threefold from 1915 to 1918. The British army and civil administrations employed Iraqi laborers to build roads as well as railway and irrigation systems (Atiyyah 1973, 219, 224).

In some respects – particularly regarding tribes – British rule remained indirect, largely because their initial efforts at direct rule spurred resistance. Initially, the British miscalculated the tractability of tribal shaykhs, only to discover that they could pose serious threats to social order. For example, when the British took Qurna in 1914, they relied on the support of Shaykh Khaz'al, known to command obedience from a number of different tribes in the area. But most tribesmen soon deserted Khaz'al, causing him to demand aid from the British lest the tribes rise up against him. The British faced similar experiences with other tribes. When force was used to subdue the tribes, tribesmen readily declared their support for the occupiers, but as soon as the British forces retreated, the tribesmen turned against them (Atiyyah 1973, 109–112). The British eventually gave generous amounts of money to shaykhs to secure order indirectly (Atiyyah 1973, 219). They also enacted the Tribal Civil and Criminal Disputes Regulation, which gave shaykhs the authority to adjudicate disputes within their tribe as well as to collect taxes for the government (Tripp 2000, 37).

The initial reaction to British occupation varied by region. Leading figures in Basra, for example, first accommodated British authorities, as

---

[28] This was not done in the Kurdish territories, which were least amenable to direct rule due to the mountainous terrain (Kocher 2004).

reflected in the words of an Expeditionary Force commander, who telegraphed, "We were cordially welcomed by the inhabitants, who appeared eager to transfer their allegiance to the British Government" (Atiyyah 1973, 87). This acceptance arose because leading figures in Basra had preexisting economic relationships with British merchants desiring access to the Persian Gulf. Since the British were at war with the Turks, this appeased Arab nationalists (Atiyyah 1973, 86–87; Tripp 2000, 32).

Kurdish tribal authorities initially welcomed the British as well. Leaders in Sulaimaniyya handed control of the region over to Britain, which shortly thereafter granted Shaykh Mahmud Barzinji, believed to be influential among the Kurds, the governorship of Lower Kurdistan. By passing its control capacity to a local notable, the British hoped to rule the region indirectly. But they miscalculated the scope of Shaykh Mahmud's influence. Conflicts between Kurdish shaykhs, as well as Shaykh Mahmud's ambitions, resulted in a series of revolts. When Shaykh Mahmud declared Kurdistan an independent state in May 1919, the British dispatched a military unit to reclaim Sulaimaniyya. Although it successfully suppressed Shaykh Mahmud, this increase in state penetration nonetheless stirred new opposition against British intrusion into Kurdistan (Tripp 2000, 34).[29]

In other areas, however, resistance to the occupiers appeared almost immediately. In early 1918, a group of clerics, shaykhs, and other influential persons in Najaf and Karbala formed the Society of Islamic Revival to defend Islam against the British (Tripp 2000, 33). When a British officer in Najaf was killed in 1919, the British blockaded the city and responded with sweeping arrests and executions. Shi'i clerics and civilians also opposed the British, some even forming alliances with Sunni groups who shared their sense of frustration over losing jobs and status under direct rule (Yaphe 2003). By April 1920, resistance to the British became increasingly organized. Shi'i Ayatollah al-Shirazi issued a *fatwa* against employment in the British administration. Shi'is and Sunnis met to formulate strategies for obtaining Iraqi independence, as did Shi'i *'ulama* and tribal shaykhs of the mid-Euphrates region (Tripp 2000, 41). A number of secret organizations and parties also emerged, including Haras, the leading nationalist party of the time, whose success can largely be attributed to Sunni–Shi'i cooperation.

---

[29] "Often local in nature, these could be aimed against neighbours as much as against the British authorities, but they stemmed from a similar desire, even compulsion, on the part of the Kurdish tribal chieftains to exploit any perceived weakness of central power and to assert their own autonomy. They resented any attempt by outside powers to curb their own freedom of action" (Tripp 2000, 34).

Much of the response to British direct rule was framed in terms of Arab self-determination. A goal of Iraq's major political parties, for example, was to obtain Iraqi independence for Basra, Baghdad, and Mosul. The British reacted to these developments by strengthening direct rule: they increased the number of security forces and intelligence officers in the cities, making public protest virtually impossible. Iraqi resisters were forced to meet in mosques, which quickly became forums for stimulating Arab nationalism. With 130 mosques in Baghdad, 35 in Basra, and 51 in Mosul, anti-British propaganda was easily spread throughout the Iraqi population (Marr 2003, 23; Atiyyah 1973, 275–280). By 1920, therefore, most of Iraq was resistant to British rule.

Despite this, in April of 1920, the League of Nations awarded Britain the mandate to rule Iraq (Dodge 2003, 5). This fueled even more anti-British sentiment and two months later culminated in outright revolt. An estimated 130,000 Iraqis rebelled, but the movement was not effectively organized; it lacked the support of some Sunni groups who feared the movement would undermine their traditional dominance in the region (Tripp 2000, 44; Marr 2003). Even so, the British only managed to quell the rebellion by the end of October. Thus direct rule fared no better under the British than it had under the Ottomans.

After the revolt the British abruptly changed course, abandoning direct rule. The subsequent government included Iraqis and adopted a variety of once-spurned Ottoman institutions. Iraqi officials replaced British political officers in the provinces. To further economize on control costs, the Royal Air Force (RAF) was enlisted to pacify rebellious tribes in the countryside by bombing them (Dodge 2003, 154; Sluglett 2003, 7).[30] In 1921, the annual military budget for Iraqi operations was reduced from £25 million to £4 million (Mathewson 2003, 57).

In 1921, the British installed the Hashemite Amir Faisal as King, marking the beginning of a period of indirect rule in Iraq that lasted thirty-seven years under three different Hashemite monarchs. Despite Faisal's exalted title, the British maintained much control over Iraqi politics. British "advisors" functioned behind the scenes, while Britain maintained control of the country's foreign relations as well as veto power over military and financial matters (Sluglett and Sluglett 1990, 11). Faisal – a non-Iraqi Arab widely perceived as a British puppet – had little legitimacy among the Iraqi people (Bengio 2003, 16). Because he

---

[30] Winston Churchill, the responsible minister, chose the air force because planes could "police the mandated territory of Mesopotamia for less cost than the traditional method of military occupation" (Omissi 1990, 16). Arthur Harris, the strategist who devised the bombing strategy to control the tribal areas of Iraq, later employed the same tactics in the bombing of Dresden.

was too weak militarily to withstand tribal opposition, Faisal was largely dependent on the British, and specifically the RAF, to enforce order. But Faisal was also less tractable than the British had hoped. From the start, he insisted on playing the key leadership role in Iraq, a demand that the British conceded to only to avoid any resistance that might have emerged were the government seen as illegitimate (Dodge 2003, 20). This tension between Faisal and the British reflects a fundamental problem with indirect rule: local autonomy can spur noncompliance with state authority.

Given the abysmal failure of the experiment with direct rule, however, the British were willing to take this risk. Faisal's strategy for ruling the tribes was shaped after the Ottomans' – namely, the parceling out of land rights; and, like them, he used it to bind the shaykhs to his regime. In 1933, the monarchy passed the Law Governing Rights and Duties of Cultivators. This law protected and increased the landowning rights handed to shaykhs during the Ottoman empire, but afforded the cultivators fewer rights. Peasant tribesmen were required to pay money rents and shares of their crops to their shaykhs. If they did not have enough money or crops, they were required to remain on the land and work until their debts were paid off (Tripp 2000, 47–52).[31] This strategy bound tribesmen to their local rulers; as a result, they were more dependent on their shaykhs than on the state for goods and control.

Faisal also attempted to build an Iraqi army, at first consisting of Sharifian officers and Sunni tribesmen. The Sharifian officers held strong pan-Arab ideologies that left Shi'i and Kurdish elements in Iraq feeling marginalized; for them, the military was an arm of the Sunni-dominated government and not a mechanism for national integration (Kelidar 2003, 31). Later, the army consisted largely of Kurdish and Shi'i conscripts, antagonizing members of these communities who were not inclined to fight for a country that did not afford them much political representation (Kelidar 2003, 31; Tripp 2000, 87).

Faisal's rule was a balancing act: while reining in potential challengers he also tried to keep British interference at bay. Although the monarchy was a retreat from direct rule and a response to the liabilities of direct rule, indirect rule proved no panacea for the British either. The Sunni-dominated state was anything but evenhanded in its distribution of collective goods. Government jobs were provided primarily to Sunnis,

---

[31] By the late 1950s, 55% of cultivable land was held by only 2,500 people, mostly Sunni. Further, 70% of Iraq's arable land consisted of 3,400 large haciendas. By 1957, a large proportion of the rural population was landless. In short, augmented indirect rule immiserated the peasantry. The Law also reduced urban migration, effectively tying many peasants to their shaykhs' lands (Cole 2004).

and though the Iraqi educational system preached Arab nationalism, this message rang hollow to many non-Sunnis (Tripp 2000, 95). The Kurds were incensed when, despite British promises to grant Kurdish autonomy, the 1930 Anglo-Iraqi treaty failed to even mention minority rights, much less Kurdish self-determination (Natali 2001, 263). Dissatisfaction with these policies led to the formation of new political and potentially threatening organizations among underrepresented cultural groups.

Despite a series of military coups in the mid-1930s, British hegemony remained unchallenged.[32] In 1941, however, a coalition of nationalists and constitutionalists raised the stakes when they tried to topple the monarchy, end British control, and open the territory to Axis influence. The British responded by increasing its military assets in Iraq, thereby ramping up direct rule. Anti-government protests were violently repressed.

By creating a highly personalized and generous central governing body – now enriched by the growth of oil revenues – the monarch was for the most part successful in pitting groups in civil society against one another. Consider the state's response to Shi'i demands for greater representation in government. In the 1920s, the state hired only twenty-one Shi'i ministers, but by the 1950s, this number had risen to seventy-six. This increase in Shi'i representation is misleading, however, because it does not take into account the growth of the state apparatus. Despite the doubling of Shi'i representation in government from 18 to 36 percent between the 1920s and 1950s, Sunnis continued to hold key positions and the Shi'i remained underrepresented (Nakash 1994, 127).

Demonstrations and uprisings continued to pose challenges for the British-backed government. Many demonstrators were killed in *al-Intifada* of 1948. Courts martial led to the imprisonment of hundreds of agitators. Oppositional groups gained more ground; the Iraqi Kurdish Democratic Party (KDP), for example, held its founding congress in Baghdad in 1946 (Tripp 2000, 117; Natali 2001, 263). The Shi'i disseminated literature attacking pan-Arabism and the state and submitted petitions to the government demanding freedom of expression and a greater share of various public goods (Marr 2003, 42; Nakash 1994, 119). Moreover, class-based oppositional groups emerged for the first time; various artisan associations began to coalesce and form the Iraqi Communist Party (ICP) (Sluglett and Sluglett 1990, 22). The class divisions fostered by indirect rule – and an

---

[32] Although both Kurds and Shi'is rebelled, these actions were largely confined to specific tribal groups rather than a grand coalition of Kurds or Shi'is. While some Shi'i tribes revolted, others either sided with the state or remained neutral, unwilling to risk their own arms and tribesmen without first witnessing the outcome of other uprisings.

upsurge in Arab nationalism in the Middle East – set the stage for a violent
military coup in 1958 led by 'Abd al-Karim Qasim (Tripp 2000). So ended
British domination in Iraq.

To some extent, the era of British rule recapitulates the fate of direct
and indirect rule under the Ottomans. Although the British imposed
direct rule to strengthen their control of Iraq, the strategy backfired.
Direct rule fostered Iraqi nationalism and increased the solidarity of
different religious and ethnic groups. When the British reverted to a
more indirect form of rule, order was restored, but only temporarily.
Indirect rule under the Hashemites was unsuccessful primarily because
the British failed to recognize that its effectiveness rests on the basis of
equitable treatment of solidary groups. Because Iraqi society was so
culturally diverse, and because the Hashemite monarchs favored one
status group over all others, social order was continually at risk.

Why was indirect rule under the Ottomans more successful? Although
the Ottomans also played favorites, they did not allocate collective goods
on a cultural basis. Nor was any particular tribe persistently favored over
its rivals. The Ottomans provided goods such as land rights to different
tribal leaders, but they did not hesitate to rescind them, as well. Pref-
erential treatment was so short-lived and indeterminate that no local
group felt permanently disfavored. Moreover, under British rule, the
military was afforded more freedom to mobilize against the occupation;
this helped bring about the coup that ended British rule in Iraq
altogether.

Iraq under Qasim and Saddam

Qasim's regime marked the beginning of an era of an unprecedented
growth in direct rule. Qasim transformed himself into the personification
of Iraq, a tactic later adopted by Saddam Hussein. He dramatically
increased state penetration, repressing rebellious groups more vigorously
than his predecessors.

This repression is exemplified by Qasim's relationship with the Kurds.
Qasim initially provided the Kurdish population with its own cultural
space: Kurds were awarded positions in government, opportunities in
education, and even some cultural rights. For a brief time Kurds and
Arabs experienced a sense of unity, and the KDP even publicly recognized Qasim for acknowledging Kurdish cultural rights. By 1959,
however, the Kurds began to use their autonomy to distinguish themselves from Arabs. Despite regarding themselves as Iraqis, they insisted
on being recognized as members of a distinct culture with a non-Arab
language and heritage. For a short while, a Kurdo-Arab state seemed

possible, and Kurdish relations with Qasim were positive (Natali 2001, 267–268).

External influences (not least those emanating from the United States) convinced Qasim to change his policies toward the leftist Kurds. Ultimately, he arrested Kurdish nationalists and bombed Kurdish rural areas, fueling greater Kurdish resistance to the regime (Natali 2001, 269). Qasim's policies toward the Iraqi Communist Party (ICP) – like those toward the Kurds – ran hot and cold. Initially, Qasim lent some support to the ICP, which reached the height of its power between 1958 and 1959. The ICP grew rapidly, building a people's army of up to 11,000 volunteers, as well as organizing a number of protests, student movements, and trade unions (Sluglett and Sluglett 1990, 53–54, 63). But Qasim later withdrew his support from the communists, and toward the end of his rule the state banned ICP newspapers, broke up communist unions, and even shut down other leftist groups such as the Youth Federation, the Partisans for Peace, and the Women's League (Sluglett and Sluglett 1990, 75–76; Batatu 1978, 948; Yousif 1991, 187).

While Qasim's increasing penetration of the north spurred the Kurds' demands for cultural autonomy, heightened state scope undercut the ICP by replacing it as a source of collective goods. Qasim increased state scope dramatically. Like other Third World nationalists of that era, Qasim extended direct rule by nationalizing Iraq's oil, increasing state welfare, and distributing land to the impoverished peasantry (Al-Eyd 1979, 41). His efforts were only partially successful, however. The oil industry, the major source of foreign exchange, remained in private hands.[33] Nonetheless, Qasim was able to divert funding from infrastructural projects to public housing schemes and housing loans in the cities. Educational investment trebled and many new schools and hospitals were built (Tripp 2000, 167). Qasim imposed ceilings on individual holdings (618 acres in irrigated areas, 1,236 acres in rainfall areas), and promised that the sequestered land would be redistributed to landless peasants in plots of about 20–40 acres each (Dann 1969, 57;

---

[33] Although Qasim tried to nationalize the oil companies, he first had to settle a number of old disputes and work toward self-sufficiency in production and the market. The government attempted to negotiate with the Iraq Petroleum Company (IPC) for control of unexploited areas of oil resources. When negotiations failed, the state passed a law that withdrew the IPC's concession rights to the area. The state also imposed cargo dues and port charges on IPC shipments through Basra (Al-Eyd 1979, 19). The IPC did not accept the law, and in an act of defiance cut production in order to penalize the country and put pressure on Qasim. This move ultimately cost Iraq 550 million dollars between 1950 and 1970. The state responded by establishing the Iraqi National Oil Company (INOC), but this venture failed to remove the state's dependence on the IPC. In ensuing years, the IPC and the INOC collaborated on joint ventures.

Sluglett and Sluglett 1990, 138). Due to inadequate enforcement, however, little redistribution actually occurred (Khadduri 1970, 117; Sluglett and Sluglett 1990, 38). Even so, Qasim's concerns for the poor won him much popular support.

Since direct rule is so costly to implement, how did Qasim fund this increased state largesse? Half of the new funds came from appropriation of revenue from oil wealth, and half from loans offered by the Soviet Union and Czechoslovakia. The increased scope provided by these resources was successful in muting much class-based opposition to the regime (e.g. by the ICP), suggesting that extreme levels of direct rule are effective at maintaining order. However, the increased level of penetration stimulated opposition among disadvantaged status groups. The Kurds were particularly eager to see Qasim overthrown, so much so that they looked to pan-Arab groups – like the Ba'ath – for support (Tripp 2000, 168). In fact, it was the Ba'ath who staged a coup against Qasim. The Ba'ath Party ruled for only a few months before being overthrown by members of the armed forces. Five years later it reemerged to overthrow the existing regime.

The Ba'athists – and Saddam Hussein in particular – vastly increased direct rule. Saddam completed Qasim's mission against class-based opposition by emasculating the country's trade unions (Dodge 2003, 160). Following a huge increase in the price of oil in 1973, he used oil revenues (which increased eightfold from 1973 to 1975 [Tripp 2000, 314]) to substantially increase state employment, the size of the military, and the quantity of state-provided welfare benefits. State employment rose from 20,000 to more than 580,000 from 1958 to 1977 (Dodge 2003, 160). The army and security services grew rapidly, as well. In 1967, the ratio of military manpower relative to population was 10 per 1,000; by 1984, this ratio was 42 per 1,000 people (Makiya 1998, 34).[34] All told, the civilian arm of the state is estimated to have employed 21% of the working population, with 30% of Iraqi households dependent on government payments in 1990–1991. These revenues also enabled

---

[34] "The army that carried out party policy in the second half of the 1970s was different from the one that waltzed in and out of governments in the 1960s. It had metamorphosed into a creature of the Ba'ath party. Three things account for this. The first change was the comprehensive series of purges of all influential high-ranking officers ... The second change ... was the establishment of a new system of accountability in which party men could thwart the orders of their senior non-Ba'athist officers if they suspected them ... The third change was to separate ideology from the military. Comprehensive party organization robbed officers of the opportunity to see themselves as surrogates and guardians of a national identity otherwise in jeopardy" (Makiya 1998, 25–26).

Saddam to establish a patronage system that divided potential rivals.[35] He invested heavily in schools, hospitals, food subsidies, and housing projects. In 1968, Saddam also implemented land reform: "Tribal Shaykhs were no longer paid off for their expropriated land. The government helped form a large number of agricultural cooperatives and became the primary distributor for agricultural surplus, and there were genuine improvements in rural standards of living" (Khadduri 1970, 119). These measures laid the foundation for a high degree of social order by increasing dependence on the state and by aligning personal and state interests.

Saddam's state immensely increased its penetration. On assuming power, Saddam expanded the party militia and restructured the secret police to forestall political opposition. Saddam established three separate secret police agencies, each independently responsible to the Revolutionary Command Council. The *Amn*, designed with the help of the Soviet KGB, was responsible for internal security. The *Estikhbarat* was set up to root out dissidents operating outside of Iraq. And the *Mukhabarat* – or Party Intelligence – was the most powerful and feared agency among the three (Makiya 1998, 14). The *Mukhabarat* penetrated every aspect of Iraqi life, to the extent that Iraqis never knew when or by whom they were being spied on. Members of Saddam's regime were themselves spied on (Roberts 2000). Spying created a heightened sense of fear and paranoia that kept dissent and political unrest at a minimum. Saddam also resorted to torture and execution to keep people in line (Makiya 1998).[36]

Although Saddam's access to oil revenue and foreign aid funded the growth of direct rule, his resources were hardly sufficient to counter the opposition of disfavored groups. Resistance principally emanated from two directions. Tensions between the state and the Kurds had been

---

[35] Thus, "The capacity of certain Shi'i figures to command respect and to exercise authority within the community clearly unnerved a regime based on narrow circles emanating from the Sunni lands of the north-west ... It was the hidden potential of these forms of social solidarity which worried ... Saddam Husain. Consequently, like previous rulers of Iraq, they tried to undermine that solidarity, channeling resources towards the Shi'i community at large, whilst ensuring that certain groups, families and individuals were more favored than others. In this way, a patronage network was established, drawing many Shia into the widening circle of those who were in some sense complicit in the order being established in Iraq" (Tripp 2000, 204).

[36] "As the terror struck deeper into the population – and no longer solely at its margins – withdrawal, cynicism, suspicion, and eventually pervasive fear replaced participation as the predominant psychological profile of the masses ... The post-1968 stratification of Iraqi society, unlike that of other Third World countries, evolved by compromising people in the violence of the Ba'ath, by sucking them into the agencies of the secret police, the army, and militia. The inordinate role of fear in Iraq can only be understood from this standpoint" (Makiya 1998, 58).

escalating, as Ba'ath promises for Kurdish autonomy were only honored in the breach. When oil production in Kirkuk was nationalized in 1974, the Kurds demanded a proportionate share in oil revenues. Saddam refused, and a Kurdish revolt broke out with Iranian support. When this support dried up, the Kurds were defeated. But far from securing stable order, increased penetration encouraged the creation of a new Kurdish party – the Patriotic Union of Kurdistan (PUK). Whereas the PUK opposed the regime, its competition with the KDP gave Saddam political leverage to divide the Kurds (McDowall 1992, 27–29).

The secularism of the (now much more efficacious) central government encouraged greater Shi'i solidarity, however. Saddam's secular clientelism harassed the Shi'i population. For example, in the course of a 1969 territorial dispute with Iran, the Ba'ath regime demanded that the Shi'i Ayatollah Muhsin al-Hakim condemn the Iranian government. Al-Hakim refused and Saddam responded by shutting down a university in Najaf. Demonstrations by the Shi'i followed, as sermons turned into political protests. The state arrested high-ranking religious leaders and shut down Islamic schools, spurring riots and demonstrations the violent oppression of which only furthered the cycle of protest and violence. The Safar *intifada* of 1977 was soon followed by the expulsion of the Shi'i leader Ayatollah Khomaini (Tripp 2000, 202–203) and the Iranian Revolution fostered more Iraqi Shi'i Islamist resistance. To counter this threat, Saddam initiated the Iran–Iraq war with the tacit support of the United States and the Soviet Union (both alarmed by the Shi'i takeover of Iran). Finally, the failure of Iraq's Kuwaiti occupation opened the door for a series of spontaneous revolts in the Shi'i south (Cockburn and Cockburn 2002, 188). The increase of state penetration was only effective in the short term. The imposition of direct rule stimulated opposition among culturally disadvantaged groups, especially those, like the Shi'i, which already had an organized base. Thus, as had occurred under Qasim, Ba'ath Party direct rule favored some groups and severely repressed others.

The Iran–Iraq war (1980–1988) lasted far longer than anyone had anticipated, not least Saddam. At the war's end, Iraq faced a severe recession. Since direct rule is costly to maintain, the downturn in the country's economic fortunes posed a grave challenge to the regime. To forestall the possibility of a military coup, Saddam purged and divided the officer corps, and replaced and killed high-ranking political officials with members of his clan, transforming the regime in a sultanistic direction. Last, he attempted to overhaul the economy through economic liberalization; the failure of this policiy motivated his invasion of Kuwait.

Following the Gulf war, many anticipated that the no-fly zones and United Nations sanctions would significantly weaken Saddam's regime. But this did not occur. By allowing for indirect rule in the northern part of the country, the no-fly zones compromised Iraq's territorial integrity.[37] Ironically, the no-fly zone shored up the regime by relieving the resource-poor center of much of the cost of controlling Kurdish territory. Although the United Nations sanctions severely affected the Iraqi economy and the standard of living, Saddam also found a way to use these to his advantage. He created a government food-rationing system to dissuade dissent in the general public, and rewarded his supporters in the party and military by giving them privileged access to food. Moreover, Saddam and his immediate circle profited handsomely from kickbacks in the United Nations Oil for Food Programme (Alnasrawi 2002, 100). For these reasons, invasion was arguably the only means of toppling the regime.

Whereas Saddam's use of direct rule did not fully succeed in quashing the opposition – both Kurds and the Shi'i Marsh Arabs caused him trouble – it provided the greatest level of social order in Iraqi history. High scope – in the form of welfare benefits and government employment – left much of the population dependent on the state and unwilling to challenge it. At the same time, high penetration instilled such fear in the country that merely to express disapproval of the regime was to court the prospect of the harshest of punishments.

But this level of direct rule could only be sustained in Iraq by exogenous windfalls derived from oil revenues and foreign aid. After 1973 the price of oil soared, and after 1979 both the Soviets and Americans turned a blind eye on Saddam's efforts against the Iranian revolutionaries. Once the center lost these sources of revenue and political support, however, direct rule should have been imperiled. Paradoxically, foreign intervention – in the form of United Nations sanctions and the no-fly zones – helped Saddam economize on control costs and maintain a higher-than-expected level of direct rule.

Implications for present-day Iraq

Full-scale direct rule is a surer means of attaining social order in culturally diverse societies than indirect rule. But since direct rule results in a shift in dependence – for jobs, security, insurance, education, and other collective goods – from traditional authorities and intermediate

[37] In contrast, Iraqi helicopter gunships were permitted in the southern no-fly zone, substantially reducing Shi'i autonomy.

social groups to the central state, it is extremely costly to implement.[38]
The center has but three means of providing the requisite largesse. First,
it can do so by its capacity to generate revenue and public goods
endogenously on the basis of robust economic development. This is
difficult to accomplish in less developed countries (and no option in the
near term for Iraq), but the examples of the four Asian tigers and
Market-Leninist China reveal that it is not impossible.[39] A second
endogenous means of doing so is through central control over the revenues provided by the export of key resources, like oil. Were it not for
Iraqi oil wealth, it is highly unlikely that Saddam would have been
effective in implementing direct rule. Absent these means, direct rulers
must rely on exogenous sources of aid.

In addition to its manifest costs, direct rule can stir opposition.
Competition over collective goods and resistance to encroachments on
autonomy can result in challenges to state hegemony by ethnic, religious, or tribal groups. In response to British direct rule, for example,
new political parties emerged in Iraq, Sunni and Shi'i groups collaborated, and traditional tribal affiliations were strengthened. Extreme direct
rule, as occurred under Saddam, was more effective because it combined
extensive welfare benefits with the harshest of sanctions for noncompliance.

Although indirect rule imposes considerably fewer costs on central
authorities, it too is costly.[40] In addition to agency costs, which substantially cut into potential central government revenues (Kiser 1999),
indirect rule is only effective when it devolves decision-making to groups
that are willing to comply with central authorities. What determines
whether a given group will be compliant? This question is akin to the
classic problem of federalism (Riker 1964), and the solution resides in

---

[38] The socialist USSR and its Warsaw Pact allies probably represent the apex of direct rule
in modern history. Given their level of economic development, these states did attain
high levels of social order – especially when compared to the more liberal successor
regimes. But maintaining socialism in a global economy proved to be infeasible in the
medium run (see Przeworski 1991, 51–99).

[39] Likewise, Ireland's entrance into the European Union spurred rapid investment-led
economic growth.

[40] In the physical world, the second law of thermodynamics states that systems
spontaneously change toward greater entropy. The cell, for example, does not exist
in isolation: "it takes in energy from its environment in the form of food, or as photons
from the sun ... and it then uses this energy to generate order within itself. In the
course of the chemical reactions that generate order, part of the energy that the cell uses
is converted into heat. The heat is discharged into the cell's environment and disorders
it, so that the total entropy – that of the cell plus its surroundings – increases, as
demanded by the laws of physics" (Alberts et al. 2002, 71). To the extent that these
laws also apply in the social world, this would explain why all forms of social order are
costly to attain.

the center's ability to render the groups (and sub-units) dependent on it for access to vital resources. To the degree that groups are dependent on the center, their leaders' interests will be aligned with those of the state, and they will therefore be motivated to curb their members' oppositional proclivities. This dependence derives from, but is not limited to, financial, kinship, military, and welfare relations with the center.[41] Indirect rule of Iraq by the Ottoman empire, for example, was largely enforced by the looming threat of an Ottoman invasion. Indirect rule by the British during the first Hashemite monarchy also hinged on the RAF's ability to subdue subversive elements in Iraq.

What implications does this analysis have for the current Iraqi state? How can it bring order to this turbulent land? Direct rule of Iraq is simply not an option; it has resulted in social disorder throughout Iraqi history, save during the Ba'ath regime when Saddam's rule was absolute. Just as the British did in the aftermath of World War I, the Americans banked heavily on direct rule in post-invasion Iraq. But like the British before them, this attempt was hampered by inadequate military and economic commitment by the Bush administration (Ricks 2006; Bremer 2006; Diamond 2005).[42] American failure at securing order has left Iraqis with a mess to contend with. A hardly functioning Iraqi economy and insufficient financial support from other countries doom any effort at direct rule. Iraq's cultural and ethnic diversity also poses grave challenges to centralized rule. Attacks on American troops and Iraqi police have emanated from tribal, ethnic, and religious organizations. Members of the Iraqi state are themselves so divided along ethnic and religious lines that it is hard to imagine them reaching a consensus on how to directly govern their culturally fractured society.

Indirect rule has been effective in Iraq only when the center has refrained from systematic differential treatment of cultural groups. The British, Qasim, and Saddam all played favorites, and when they did revolts ensued. Indirect rule of the tribes under the Ottomans, however, was most successful because it did not *perpetually* favor one tribe over another. The likelihood of obtaining state-provided goods was just as

---

[41] Group dependence is maximized in hierarchical societies like Japan (as reflected in Japan's *keiretsu*, headed by large financial institutions [Gerlach 1992]), and minimized in loosely integrated warlord societies like contemporary Afghanistan (Fairbanks 2002).

[42] Paul Bremer states that he requested more troops from Rumsfeld on several occasions, only to be rejected. Bremer also claims to have told Bush, Rumsfeld, and Rice that free and fair democratic elections required a voting infrastructure that Iraq lacked, and installing it would take months. But faced with pressures at home, particularly by an upcoming election and the need to represent the occupation as successful and brief, the Bush administration repeatedly urged Bremer to administer Iraq as though speed was of the utmost importance (Bremer 2006).

great for one tribe as the next; ditto for the likelihood that such goods would be withheld. Since local leaders in such regimes were always on edge, challenging the regime was seldom in their long-term interests. Indirect rule in Iraq today may only be effective if the state treats its constituent cultural groups equitably. Although a divide-and-rule strategy might seem attractive, it is unlikely that the competing sectarian elements within the Iraqi state would be willing deny their own constituents resources at any time.

Had the US occupiers rejected centralization in favor of some kind of federation, some disorder might have been averted (Galbraith 2006). The Coalition Provisional Authority (CPA) could have relied on solidary intermediate groups to control their own members, thereby reducing the cost of state scope and penetration.[43] This strategy would have also provided Iraqis with more legitimate rulers than the US occupiers (Diamond 2004). The CPA did not take this course because they deemed it unwise; Bremer and others worried about placing power in the hands of leaders who could very well use their enhanced position to disrupt the nascent state (Bremer 2006). Given that the strongest local rulers, like Muqtada al-Sadr, have now proven to be the most significant threats to order, these concerns appear to have been well founded. But indirect rule need not have been untenable. So long as local groups – qua groups – were made dependent on the center for their welfare and security, and so long as none was perpetually disfavored by the state, indirect rulers could have been dissuaded from sabotaging state-building efforts.[44]

What should the Iraqi state do now, given that the CPA failed to rely on indirect rulers? The effectiveness of indirect rule hinges on the solidarity of local groups. Therefore, the Iraqi state should rely on groups that would be most solidary in each of the territory's many regions. Unfortunately, over the past few years, some of the most solidary local Iraqi groups, such as al-Qaeda's "Organization in Mesopotamia" and al-Sadr's Mahdi Army, have proven the most threatening to state stability. It would be difficult for the Iraqi state to see eye to eye with these insurgent groups, much less to make them dependent on its largesse. But not all local solidary groups threaten the state. For example, the Grand Ayatollah Ali al-Sistani has denounced involvement in sectarian

---

[43] These remarks about American policy in Iraq were written in the spring of 2007, and have not been amended in the wake of subsequent developments.

[44] Further, the more that membership in these groups cross-cuts the major axes of conflict, the greater the resulting order (Varshney 2002). However, at the present time, prospects for the establishment of socially integrated intermediate groups in Iraq are exceedingly slim.

violence (International Crisis Group 2006). The Iraqi regime can capitalize on Sistani's ability to manage a large Shi'i local population as well as his loyalty to the state, which is based on a mutual antipathy to the insurgents. The Iraqi government must move fast, however: as the violence persists, Sistani's influence wanes (International Crisis Group 2006). Where other solidary groups (such as tribes) exist, the state can nurture them and rely on them to establish order. These groups' bases of affiliation are not significant; what matters is the state's ability to create interdependent and evenhanded relationships with them. The state could also invest in reinvigorating civil society such that new groups can emerge, groups bound by a common interest in quashing violent insurgent organizations.

To accomplish these goals on the cheap is dubious at best; moreover, it cannot occur overnight. In the meantime, an increasingly vigorous resistance consumes resources that could otherwise be used for vitally important civil investment. Indeed, the headlines continue to trumpet the news that sectarian violence is reaching unprecedented levels. Also remarkable is the extent to which American forces are targets. The sentiments behind this violence are strengthened by the Iraqis' perception that sooner, if not later, the Americans will go home. Insurgent groups are attempting to shore up their political position when this day comes by targeting one another today.

These events hark back to the 1920 revolt against British rule. As the baseball player Yogi Berra would have it, this is *déjà vu* all over again.

REFERENCES

Ahmadi, Nader. 2003. "Migration Challenges Views on Sexuality." *Ethnic and Racial Studies* 26 (July): 684–706.
Al-Eyd, Kadhim A. 1979. *Oil Revenues and Accelerated Growth: Absorptive Capacity in Iraq*. New York: Praeger.
Alberts, Bruce, Alexander Johnson, Julian Lewis, Martin Raff, Keith Roberts, and Peter Walter. 2002. *Molecular Biology of the Cell*. New York: Garland Science.
Alnasrawi, Abbas. 2002. *Iraq's Burdens: Oil, Sanctions, and Underdevelopment*. London: Greenwood Press.
Althusius, Johannes. [1614] 1964. *Politics*. Boston: Beacon Press.
Atiyyah, Ghassan R. 1973. *Iraq, 1908–1921: A Socio-Political Study*. Beirut: Arab Institute for Research and Publication.
Batatu, Hanna. 1978. *The Old Social Classes and the Revolutionary Movements of Iraq*. Princeton University Press.
Beissinger, Mark R. 2002. *Nationalist Mobilization and the Collapse of the Soviet State*. Cambridge University Press.

Beissinger, Mark R., and Crawford Young. 2002. *Beyond State Crisis?: Postcolonial Africa and Post-Soviet Eurasia in Comparative Perspective*. Washington DC: Woodrow Wilson Center Press.

Bengio, Ofra. 2003. "Pitfalls of Instant Democracy." In *U.S. Policy in Post-Saddam Iraq*, ed. Michael Eisenstadt and Eric Mathewson. Washington DC: Washington Institute for Near East Policy, 15–26.

Blau, Peter Michael, and Joseph E. Schwartz. 1984. *Crosscutting Social Circles: Testing a Macrostructural Theory of Intergroup Relations*. Orlando: Academic Press.

Bremer, Paul. 2006. *My Year in Iraq*. New York: Simon & Schuster.

Brubaker, Rogers. 2002. "Ethnicity Without Groups." *European Journal of Sociology* 43 (August): 163–189.

Bunce, Valerie. 1999. *Subversive Institutions: The Design and the Destruction of Socialism and the State*. Cambridge University Press.

Chehabi, H.E., and Juan J. Linz. 1998. *Sultanistic Regimes*. Baltimore: Johns Hopkins University Press.

Chwe, Michael Suk-Young. 2001. *Rational Ritual: Culture, Coordination, and Common Knowledge*. Princeton University Press.

Cockburn, Andrew, and Patrick Cockburn. 2002. "Saddam at the Abyss." In *Inside Iraq*, ed. John Miller and Aaron Kenedi. New York: Marlowe & Company, 167–207.

Cole, Juan. 2004. "The Three-State Solution?" *The Nation* 278 (March): 27–30.

Cooper, Frederick, and Ann Laura Stoler. 1997. *Tensions of Empire: Colonial Cultures in a Bourgeois World*. Berkeley: University of California Press.

Dann, Uriel. 1969. *Iraq under Qassem*. Jerusalem: Israel University Press.

Diamond, Larry. 2004. "Testimony to the Senate Foreign Relations Committee." www.stanford.edu/~ldiamond/iraq/Senate_testimony_051904.htm (October 7, 2006).

2005. *Squandered Victory*. New York: Henry Holt and Company.

Dodge, Toby. 2003. *Inventing Iraq*. New York: Columbia University Press.

Elias, Norbert. 1983. *The Court Society*. Oxford: Blackwell.

1993. *The Civilizing Process*. Cambridge, MA: Blackwell.

Ertman, Thomas. 1997. *Birth of the Leviathan: Building States and Regimes in Medieval and Early Modern Europe*. Cambridge University Press.

Fairbanks Jr., Charles H. 2002. "Weak States and Private Armies." In *Beyond State Crisis?: Postcolonial Africa and Post-Soviet Eurasia in Comparative Perspective*, ed. Mark R. Beissinger and Crawford Young. Washington DC: Woodrow Wilson Center Press, 129–160.

Fearon, James D., and David D. Laitin. 1996. "Explaining Interethnic Cooperation." *American Political Science Review* 90 (December): 715–735.

Galbraith, Peter W. 2006. *The End of Iraq: How American Incompetence Created a War Without End*. New York: Simon & Schuster.

Gellner, Ernest. 2003. "Trust, Cohesion and the Social Order." In *Theories of Social Order: A Reader*, ed. Michael Hechter and Christine Horne. Stanford University Press, 310–316.

Gerlach, Michael L. 1992. *Alliance Capitalism: The Social Organization of Japanese Business*. Berkeley: University of California Press.

Gorski, Phillip. 2003. *The Disciplinary Revolution.* University of Chicago Press.
Granovetter, Mark. 1973. "The Strength of Weak Ties." *American Journal of Sociology* 78 (May): 1360–1380.
Hayek, Friedrich A. von. 1973. *Rules and Order.* University of Chicago Press.
Hechter, Michael. 1987. *Principles of Group Solidarity.* Berkeley: University of California Press.
    2000. *Containing Nationalism.* Oxford University Press.
    2004. "From Class to Culture." *American Journal of Sociology* 110 (September): 400–445.
Hechter, Michael, Debra Friedman, and Satoshi Kanazawa. 1992. "The Attainment of Global Order in Heterogeneous Societies." In *Rational Choice Theory: Advocacy and Critique,* ed. James S. Coleman and Thomas J. Fararo. Newbury Park, CA: Sage Publications, 329–344.
Hechter, Michael, and Christine Horne. 2003. *Theories of Social Order: A Reader.* Stanford University Press.
Hobbes, Thomas. [1651] 1996. *Leviathan.* Oxford University Press.
Hourani, Albert Habib. 1991. *A History of the Arab Peoples.* Cambridge, MA: Belknap Press of Harvard University Press.
Hudson, Michael C. 1977. *Arab Politics: The Search for Legitimacy.* New Haven: Yale University Press.
Human Rights Watch/Middle East. 1995. *Iraq's Crime of Genocide: The Anfal Campaign Against the Kurds.* New Haven: Yale University Press.
Huntington, Samuel P. 1968. *Political Order in Changing Societies.* New Haven: Yale University Press.
International Crisis Group. 2006. "The Next Iraqi War? Sectarianism and Civil Conflict." *Middle East Report* 52 (February).
Jabar, Faleh A. 2003. "Sheikhs and Ideologues: Deconstruction and Reconstruction of Tribes Under Patrimonial Totalitarianism in Iraq, 1968–1998." In *Tribes and Power: Nationalism and Ethnicity in the Middle East,* ed. Faleh Abdul-Jabar and Hosham Dawod. London: Saqi, 69–109.
Kelidar, Abbas. 2003. "Iraqi National Integration Under the British." In *U.S. Policy in Post-Saddam Iraq,* ed. Michael Eisenstadt and Eric Mathewson. Washington DC: Washington Institute for Near East Policy, 27–37.
Khadduri, Majid. 1970. *Socialist Iraq: A Study in Iraqi Politics Since 1968.* Washington DC: The Middle East Institute.
Khoury, Dina Rizk. 1997. *State and Provincial Society in the Ottoman Empire.* Cambridge University Press.
Kiser, Edgar. 1999. "Comparing Varieties of Agency Theory in Economics, Political Science, and Sociology: An Illustration from State Policy Implementation." *Sociological Theory* 17 (July): 146–170.
Kocher, Matthew. 2004. "Human Ecology and Civil War." Ph.D. dissertation, University of Chicago.
Kohli, Atul. 2002. "State, Society and Development." In *Political Science: State of the Discipline,* ed. Ira Katznelson and Helen V. Milner. New York: W.W. Norton; Washington DC: American Political Science Association, 84–117.

Lapidus, Ira M. 1990. "Tribes and State Formation in Islamic History." In *Tribes and State Formation in the Middle East*, ed. P.S. Khoury and J. Kostiner. Berkeley: University of California Press, 25–47.

Lyall, Sarah. 2002. "Lost in Sweden: A Kurdish Daughter is Sacrificed." *New York Times*, July 23: A3.

McDowall, David. 1992. "The Kurdish Question: A Historical Review." In *The Kurds: A Contemporary Overview*, ed. Philip G. Kreyenbroek and Stefan Sperl. New York: Routledge, 10–32.

Makiya, Kanan. 1998. *Republic of Fear*. Berkeley: University of California Press.

Marr, Phebe. 2003. *A History of Modern Iraq*. Boulder, CO: Westview Press.

Mathewson, Eric. 2003. "Rebuilding Iraq: Assessing the British Military Occupation." In *U.S. Policy in Post-Saddam Iraq*, ed. Michael Eisenstadt and Eric Mathewson. Washington DC: Washington Institute for Near East Policy, 52–66.

Nakash, Yitzhak. 1994. *The Shi'is of Iraq*. Princeton University Press.

Natali, Denise. 2001. "Manufacturing Identity and Managing Kurds in Iraq." In *Right-Sizing the State*, ed. Brendan O'Leary, Ian S. Lustick, and Thomas Callaghy. Oxford University Press, 253–288.

Nettl, J.P. 1968. "The State as a Conceptual Variable." *World Politics* 20 (July): 559–592.

Nieuwenhuis, Tom. 1981. *Politics and Society in Early Modern Iraq*. Boston: Martinus Nijhoff.

Oates, Wallace E. 1972. *Fiscal Federalism*. New York: Harcourt Brace Jovanovich.

Omissi, David. 1990. *Air Power and Colonial Control: The Royal Air Force 1919–1939*. Manchester University Press.

Packer, George. 2005. *The Assassin's Gate: America in Iraq*. New York: Farrar, Straus, and Giroux.

Przeworski, Adam. 1991. *Democracy and the Market: Political and Economic Reforms in Eastern Europe and Latin America*. Cambridge University Press.

Putnam, Robert D. 2000. *Bowling Alone: The Collapse and Revival of American Community*. New York: Simon & Schuster.

Ricks, Thomas E. 2006. *Fiasco: The American Military Adventure in Iraq*. New York: Penguin Press.

Riker, William H. 1964. *Federalism: Origin, Operation, Significance*. Boston: Little, Brown.

Roberts, Paul William. 2000. "Saddam's Inferno." In *Inside Iraq*, ed. John Miller and Aaron Kenedi. New York: Marlowe & Company, 101–124.

Roeder, Philip G. 1991. "Soviet Federalism and Ethnic Mobilization." *World Politics* 43 (January): 196–232.

Simmel, Georg. [1922] 1955. "The Web of Group Affiliations." In *Conflict and the Web of Group Affiliations*, ed. Georg Simmel. New York: Free Press, 125–196.

Sluglett, Marion Farouk, and Peter Sluglett. 1990. *Iraq Since 1958: From Revolution to Dictatorship*. New York: I.B. Tauris.

Sluglett, Peter. 2003. "The British Legacy." In *U.S. Policy in Post-Saddam Iraq*, ed. Michael Eisenstadt and Eric Mathewson. Washington DC: Washington Institute for Near East Policy, 3–14.

Tocqueville, Alexis de. [1848] 1969. *Democracy in America*. New York: Anchor Books.

Traub, James. 2004. "Making Sense of the Mission." *New York Times Magazine*, April 11.

Tripp, Charles. 2000. *A History of Iraq*. Cambridge University Press.

Varshney, Ashutosh. 2002. *Ethnic Conflict and Civic Life: Hindus and Muslims in India*. New Haven: Yale University Press.

Weber, Max. [1919–1920] 1958. "The Protestant Sects and the Spirit of Capitalism." In *From Max Weber: Essays in Sociology*, ed. Hans Gerth and C. Wright Mills. Oxford University Press, 302–322.

Wilson, A.T. 1931. *Loyalties, Mesopotamia*, vol. II: *1917–1920: A Personal and Historical Record*. Oxford University Press.

Woodward, Susan L. 1995. *Balkan Tragedy: Chaos and Dissolution after the Cold War*. Washington DC: Brookings Institution.

Yaphe, Judith. 2003. "The Challenge of Nation Building in Iraq." In *U.S. Policy in Post-Saddam Iraq*, ed. Michael Eisenstadt and Eric Mathewson. Washington DC: Washington Institute for Near East Policy, 38–51.

Yousif, A.S. 1991. "The Struggle for Cultural Hegemony During the Iraqi Revolution." In *The Iraqi Revolution of 1958*, ed. Robert Fernea and Roger Louis. New York: I.B. Tauris, 172–196.

4 Factors impeding the effectiveness of partition in South Asia and the Palestine Mandate

Lucy Chester

Introduction

Contemporary international affairs are imbued with the legacy of partition. Conflict has continued for decades in partitioned areas as diverse as the Korean peninsula, South Asia, and Ireland, demonstrating that partition is not the straightforward solution to ethnic or religious conflict that it may seem. To divide warring parties may appear simple in conception, but implementing an effective partition – one that contributes to conflict resolution and minimizes violence – is dauntingly complex. Members of the international community, and the United States in particular, expend enormous resources on these problems. They maintain a military presence, as the United States does in South Korea, and Britain in Northern Ireland; they invest in repeated attempts at peacemaking, as in the Middle East; or they suffer the consequences, often global in impact, of failing to keep the peace. The utility of partition, as well as its long-term repercussions, are therefore issues of great significance to international security.

This essay seeks to aid decision-makers considering partition as a solution to violent conflict by exploring two contrasting cases from British imperial history: the Palestine Mandate, where the British discussed various partition plans at great length, but ultimately refused to implement a division, and South Asia, where the British resisted any discussion of partition, then implemented a division hastily.[1] My comparative analysis of these two cases, which in many ways are very different, reveals four crucial common factors:

(a) a population made up of intermingled religious, ethnic, or other groups;

---

[1] I define partition as the division by a third party of an area previously under a single administration (see also Klieman 1980, 281).

(b) militarization of competing factions within the civilian population;

(c) waning or undeveloped state power;

(d) political influences that are masked rather than openly acknowledged.

Not only are these conditions likely to prevail in any situation where decision-makers are considering partition, but they are difficult to ameliorate. As a result, they will likely undermine attempts to use partition as a means of imposing order.

So too will they undermine attempts to avoid partition. The fact that the Arab–Israeli conflict continues, even though the British withdrew without an organized partition in Palestine, suggests that walking away will not necessarily produce a more orderly result.[2] Whether the factors identified above play as important a role in all partitions as they do in these two cases remains to be seen. For the moment, my analysis suggests that scholars can fruitfully employ these factors as variables to be considered in future studies.

The need for such studies is pressing, because diplomats and political leaders still turn to partition as a solution to conflicts involving ethnic and religious strife. The most notable recent case is the 1995 Dayton Peace Accords, which divided Bosnia and Herzegovina. Some observers have even proposed partition for Afghanistan and for Iraq (Kinzer 2001).[3] But while partition may bring significant gains to the political leaders who take power in newly independent areas, it can also exact a toll, which is paid mostly by the poor and weak.

This essay offers a brief overview of the historical background to the South Asian and Palestinian conflicts. It then examines the operation of four factors common to these cases and demonstrates that each of these factors played havoc with the decision on whether to impose partition in Palestine and limited the effectiveness of the South Asian division. The next section draws conclusions about the role that these factors may play in partition in general, followed by a discussion of the price paid by those who have least power in the decision-making process. Finally, I explore the possibility that partition-based attempts to impose order may be inherently contradictory.

Previous scholarly discussion of partition falls into three categories. First, there are a large number of single case studies, which by definition do not involve a comparative element (for example Klieman 1980).

---

[2] The first Arab–Israeli war produced a *de facto* division, in contrast with a third-party partition.

[3] See also *The McLaughlin Group*, host John McLaughlin. PBS television program, September 10, 2004.

Such studies often provide provocative insights that can be usefully applied to broader examinations of partition in general. Building on these studies and on my own earlier research on the South Asian partition, this essay pays close attention to the particularities of each case. Because violence and other repercussions of partition were particularly severe in the Punjab province of northwest India, the South Asian portion of this comparison focuses on Punjab.[4]

The second category of scholarly discussion examines multiple partitions but does so individually, mentioning comparative aspects only in a brief introduction or conclusion (Hachey 1972; Fraser 1984). It includes, too, studies of partition that focus on regional or other groupings (Asiwaju 1985; Schaeffer 1999). This approach limits scholars' ability to measure the relative importance of the many factors that play a role in each case and to identify common elements. This essay, by contrast, identifies key commonalities between cases and analyzes the impact of those commonalities.

The final category often takes the form of debate over whether partition is effective or ineffective as a means of resolving conflict (Kaufmann 1996; Mearsheimer and Van Evera 1995; Kumar 1997; Sambanis 2000). Because the outcome of partition depends heavily on the context in which it is used and on the details of its implementation, this framework must be supplemented by comparative discussion of the conditions involved in specific cases. In conducting a comparative historical analysis, I seek to identify practical challenges involved in implementing partition, not to determine whether partition is good or bad.[5]

Historical context

During the first half of the twentieth century, British imperial leaders made repeated attempts to use partition in order to resolve particularly difficult conflicts. Although imperial decision-makers have been accused of carelessness in their implementation of partition in South Asia, it cannot be said that they approached the use of partition blithely. Earlier in the century, Britain had suffered a humiliating setback: its 1905 partition of Bengal, undertaken in order to strengthen imperial control, failed when nationalist resistance forced the government to reunite the

---

[4] Casualty statistics for partition are unreliable at best, but it is clear that the majority of deaths occurred in Punjab.

[5] This essay is part of a larger book project comparing both imperial and nationalist experiences of the postwar period in South Asia and the Palestine Mandate.

province in 1911. In the early 1920s, their experience with the bloody Irish partition left British leaders – and the British public – keenly aware of the difficulties inherent in partition. And yet British policymakers would turn to partition again as they sought to reconcile Britain's stated support for a Jewish homeland with its obligations to Palestinian Arabs.

Moreover, despite this discouraging history, the British government turned to partition yet again in a desperate attempt to resolve Hindu–Muslim conflict in India. Their decision was surprising given the fact that, during the same period, a British-sponsored conference of Arab and Jewish leaders had broken down so badly that the British had abandoned the notion of brokering a Palestinian partition and referred the matter to the United Nations. The aftermath of partition brought not only independence for India and Pakistan, but also mass violence, one of the largest forced migrations in history, and lasting unresolved tensions. Meanwhile, Britain's decision to refer the Palestine question to the United Nations rather than impose partition did not bring a markedly improved result: Israeli independence also brought with it immediate war and lasting regional conflict.

For the purposes of this essay, the story in Palestine began during the First World War, when British troops occupied the region and brought an end to Ottoman control. After the war, the League of Nations granted Britain a "Mandate" making it responsible

for placing the country under such political, administrative and economic conditions as will secure the establishment of the Jewish national home, as laid down in the preamble, and the development of self-governing institutions, and also for safeguarding the civil and religious rights of all the inhabitants of Palestine, irrespective of race and religion. (Hurewitz 1979c, 306)

This mandate obligated the British to rule Palestine for the benefit of its people.

Britain's obligation to Palestine's inhabitants was complicated, however, by earlier commitments. In 1915 and 1916, Sir Henry McMahon, the British High Commissioner for Egypt, had engaged in correspondence with Hussein ibn Ali, the *sharif* of Mecca, an influential Arab leader. British leaders saw Arab support as crucial to Britain's war effort, and in hopes of stimulating an anti-Turkish uprising, McMahon's correspondence had promised British support for an independent Arab state (Hurewitz 1979b). The British never defined the exact parameters of this state, but Hussein and many other Arabs were left with the impression that this new state would include Palestine.

In 1917, Britain had also issued a public pledge to Zionists seeking to establish a Jewish homeland in Palestine. Fearing that "international

Jewry" might support Germany if Britain did not offer concessions, the British foreign minister, Arthur Balfour, declared that

His Majesty's Government view with favour the establishment in Palestine of a national home for the Jewish people, and will use their best endeavours to facilitate the achievement of this subject, it being clearly understood that nothing shall be done which may prejudice the civil and religious rights of existing non-Jewish communities in Palestine. (Hurewitz 1979a, 106)

This statement came to be known as the Balfour Declaration. Like McMahon's intentionally vague statements, it never defined the area included in the Jewish homeland, let alone what exactly a "national home" was and how much sovereignty it could expect. The Balfour Declaration and the Hussein–McMahon correspondence meant that the British had incurred conflicting obligations even before the Mandate began.

Jewish–Arab tensions increased significantly during the Mandate period. After bloody riots in August 1929, conflict peaked in 1936, when a sustained Palestinian Arab uprising began. During this period, the British gave serious consideration to the possibility of dividing Palestine into two states, one Arab and one Jewish. As Britain's relations with Germany worsened and European conflict loomed, however, British officials saw Arab alliances as increasingly important. These allies, who had displayed keen interest in the outcome of the Arab–Jewish conflict in Palestine, made it clear that they disapproved of any plan to partition Palestine. As a result, by 1938 many British officials opposed partition. Wartime exigencies soon meant that resolution of the problem was delayed indefinitely.

British officials eventually concluded that Britain should remove itself from Palestine altogether. In late December 1946, British Prime Minister Clement Attlee and Foreign Secretary Ernest Bevin decided that the best way to extricate Britain from Palestine was to turn the Mandate over to the United Nations (Louis 1986, 15). On February 25, 1947, this decision became official when Colonial Secretary Arthur Creech Jones stated, "I have been instructed by His Majesty's Government to announce, with all solemnity, that they have ... decided that in the absence of a settlement they must plan for an early withdrawal of British forces and of the British administration from Palestine" (Louis 1984, 473). One prominent scholar argues that this plan was a British attempt to maintain a façade of impartiality while maneuvering the majority pro-Arab UN into imposing a solution that Britain could not afford to impose for fear of alienating the United States (Louis 1986, 18). In August 1947, the UN Special Commission on Palestine (UNSCOP) recommended that Britain withdraw and that its mandate be terminated. British leaders were unhappy with the anti-imperial tone of UNSCOP's report but, more importantly, were relieved at the opportunity to abandon what had become an increasingly heavy burden (Louis 1986, 21). Although the UN approved a partition plan in November 1947, by March 1948 it concluded that the plan could not be carried out (Cohen 1987). By this time, an Arab–Jewish civil war was already well underway. British troops, despite their rapidly diminishing practical power, remained in Palestine until the official expiration of the Mandate, at midnight on May 14, 1948.

In South Asia, Britain faced similar problems, albeit in a very different context. Perhaps most importantly, Britain's colonial presence in the subcontinent was longstanding, in contrast to Palestine. Palestine was not only a more recent acquisition, but it was a mere mandate, not an actual colony. British India, the pride of the empire, provided a *raison d'être* for many other British holdings, including, to a certain extent, Palestine. Protecting the routes to India was one of the highest British imperial priorities, and the Suez Canal through Egypt was the most important route. British leaders considered Palestine a vital element of the Middle Eastern strategic picture, key to the protection of the Suez (Louis 1986, 16).

The British understood conflict in South Asia to be primarily between Hindus and Muslims (not recognizing that their own policies had contributed to the increasing division of South Asian society along religious lines) (Cohn 1987). Matters came to a head in the years after World War II. As it became clear that Britain intended to withdraw from South Asia, nationalist leaders debated the appropriate form that independence should take. The Muslim League, previously a minor player but now revitalized by its victories in the 1946 elections, demanded partition and an independent Muslim state, while the Indian National Congress pressed for a united India. British leaders, including the weary Indian Viceroy Lord Archibald Wavell, a wartime appointee who had stayed on, cast about for a solution that would satisfy all parties and, most importantly, allow Britain to save face. British leaders preferred to keep India whole for two reasons: in practical terms, their military advisors counseled that a divided India would be much less useful militarily; on the ideological level, Britain's success in uniting India had long been a justification for the Raj, and partition would undermine the contention that Indians had benefited greatly from British rule (French 1997).

In March 1947, Attlee replaced Wavell with Lord Louis Mountbatten, the last viceroy, giving Mountbatten a mandate to get Britain out of

South Asia. Shortly after his arrival, concluding that Muslim League–Congress reconciliation was impossible, Mountbatten determined that it would be necessary to partition the subcontinent in mid-1948. In early June 1947, however, he advanced the partition deadline to August 15 of the same year. The South Asian partition was thus hastily arranged; there was little time allowed for any of the parties involved to consider the major practical problems that they faced.

In both South Asia and Palestine, the aftermath of Britain's withdrawal was bloody and chaotic. In India and Pakistan, riots over the summer of 1947 spiraled into ethnic cleansing. Casualty figures are unreliable, but most scholars agree that roughly 500,000 people died. Another ten million refugees crossed the new boundaries in both directions. The two new states of India and Pakistan thus came into existence at a time of great bloodshed and trauma, trauma that contributed to three wars between the two states and continues to poison Indo-Pakistani relations. In the Middle East, Zionist leaders declared the creation of Israel on May 15, 1948. Conflict escalated with the British departure, which allowed both sides freedom to resupply their fighting forces, and Israeli forces ultimately proved victorious. Although several thousand people were killed, the scale of violence in Palestine was nowhere near that seen in Punjab. Hundreds of thousands of Palestinian Arabs fled their homes, however, and their situation remains a source of great tension between Israel and its neighbor states.

A comparative study of the Palestine Mandate and South Asia

There are a number of intriguing similarities between conditions in the two territories in question. Many of the same concerns and priorities shaped British responses to problems of religious conflict in Palestine and South Asia. The basic condition of intermixed populations set the stage for partition demands, while the increasing militarization of those populations made the situation more dangerous. The colonial state's weakness hindered its attempts to disarm civilians, and political forces played an important role in the endgame of empire, despite British efforts to present an apolitical façade.

Mixed populations

In both Palestine and South Asia, the decades leading up to Britain's withdrawal were characterized by increasing division within a mixed population. In Palestine, the question of population distribution was controversial from the beginning of the Mandate. The terms of the Mandate, in fact, required a delicate demographic balancing act:

The Administration of Palestine, while ensuring that the rights and position of other sections of the population are not prejudiced, shall facilitate Jewish immigration under suitable conditions and shall encourage, in co-operation with the Jewish agency referred to in Article 4, close settlement by Jews on the land, including State lands and waste lands not required for public purposes. (Hurewitz 1979c, 306)

These requirements resulted in a situation where Zionists sought to enable the immigration of as many Jews as possible, while the British sought to restrain immigration.

Britain's aggrieved Foreign Secretary, Ernest Bevin, complained to the House of Commons in 1945:

The problem of Palestine is itself a very difficult one. The Mandate for Palestine requires the Mandatory to facilitate Jewish immigration, and to encourage close settlement by Jews on the land, while ensuring that the rights and position of other sections of the population are not prejudiced thereby. His Majesty's Government have thus a dual obligation, to the Jews on the one side and to the Arabs on the other. The lack of any clear definition of this dual obligation has been the main cause of the trouble which has been experienced in Palestine during the past 26 years. (PRO CAB 104/264)

The result was a gradually shifting demographic balance. British census figures are problematic, but they provide a rough idea of demographic change during the Mandate period. According to British figures, Palestine's population at the beginning of the Mandate, in 1922, was roughly 11% Jewish (PRO CAB 104/264). By 1945 it was about 32% Jewish, despite higher fertility rates among Palestinian Arabs (McCarthy 1990). Many Jewish settlers, however, lived in enclaves surrounded by Arab-populated areas. Any partition boundary would have left large numbers of people on the wrong side of the line.

In addition, Palestinian Arabs were far from a monolithic group. They included both Muslims and Christians, as well as minorities like the Druze. Although Arab consciousness had risen significantly, particularly since the 1930s (Antonius 1938), clan divisions and the difficulties of everyday life meant that many Palestinian Arabs had little interest in questions of nationhood in the years leading up to Britain's withdrawal (Morris 1999, 192). Mandate society was not easily divisible into the two neat categories of "Arab" and "Jew." There were divisions within the Jewish community as well, but overall Jews were far more united than were Palestinian Arabs.

The Punjabi population distribution presented a similar problem. In 1947, India's Punjab province was home to Hindus, Muslims, Sikhs, and a number of smaller minority groups, including Christians and Parsis. Muslims numbered roughly 57% of the province's total population, Hindus about 28%, and Sikhs some 13%. Although there were more Muslims than Hindus and Sikhs in western Punjab, and more Hindus and Sikhs than Muslims in eastern Punjab, overall settlement patterns made any easy division impossible. In fact, the Sikhs were concentrated in central Punjab, meaning that any division would cut their ancestral homelands in two. The solution some Sikh leaders hoped for – a line that would keep central Punjab united and allot it to one side or the other – would have left either a very large minority of Hindus in Pakistani Punjab or a very large minority of Muslims in Indian Punjab.

Decision-makers took a curious approach to this problem, imposing a binary solution on a region inhabited by three major groups. The boundary commission responsible for drawing the partition boundary was directed to "demarcate the boundaries of the two parts of Punjab on the basis of ascertaining the contiguous majority areas of Muslims and non-Muslims" (Mansergh and Moon 1983, 744). In other words, Hindus and Sikhs were combined into the single and rather peculiar category of "non-Muslims." (Other, less politically powerful groups like Christians, Parsis, and untouchables were also shoehorned into this category.) Hindus and Sikhs did not necessarily share the same political goals, however, as demonstrated by the very different boundary proposals their representatives submitted to the Punjab boundary commission. For a time, in fact, some Sikh leaders considered aligning with Pakistan, while other Sikh leaders called for Khalistan, an independent state of their own.

Even the three major groups, however, were not monolithic entities with well-defined political goals. There were cleavages within each group.[6] Neither were separations between groups well defined. Demographic statistics were based on the British designed and administered census, which categorized individuals into neat religious classifications, with no overlap. In reality, however, elder sons in some Hindu families traditionally became Sikhs, and there is additional evidence of a high number of conversions to Sikhism as leaders sought to cement and arm their following in the years before partition (Jalal 2001, 525–526). In

---

[6] The Ahmadiyya sect of Muslims, for example, was declared heretical by the Government of Pakistan in 1974, even though its prominent members included Zafrullah Khan, who argued the Muslim League case before the Punjab boundary commission and later represented Pakistan at the United Nations.

short, dividing population groups based on religious identity was a trickier business than imperial census statistics made it seem.

Once the probable path of the new boundary became publicly known, Sikh militants responded violently.[7] They were a far more powerful minority than the Palestinian Christians, and they had a disproportionate impact on the outcome of partition. Although the question of which side – Hindus, Muslims, or Sikhs – bore the most responsibility for partition violence is a vexed and difficult question, there is no doubt that militant Sikh groups played a prominent role in the killing (Aiyar 1998). Government efforts to resolve the Punjabi conundrum by lumping Sikhs in with Hindus had failed, and the Government of India would later be forced to reckon with Sikh demands. In 1966, Punjab was further partitioned, in order to create a new Sikh-majority Punjab, as well as the states of Haryana and Himachal Pradesh. Conflict between Sikh groups and the central government continued, however, culminating in Prime Minister Indira Gandhi's 1984 assassination by her Sikh bodyguards and a bloody decade-long separatist conflict in Punjab. The attempt to take a shortcut to partition by conflating Sikh interests with those of Punjabi Hindus was not a success.

Militarized populations

In Punjab as in Palestine, the years immediately preceding Britain's withdrawal were marked by increasing violence. In both cases, the fact that many civilians had access to weapons made the situation ever more dangerous. In Palestine, British officials had tried to prevent the free distribution of firearms. However, both Jewish and Arab armed groups were active during this period. The British themselves had given military training both to the Haganah, the Jewish defense force, and to Arab forces, including the Arab Legion of Transjordan. During World War II, some 50,000 Jews had served in Allied armies, gaining vital military training and experience (Freedman 1972, 198). By 1945, British Members of Parliament were already complaining about the danger posed by well-armed paramilitary groups. One noted that "considerable quantities of arms now exist on both sides – Jews and Arabs – and a threatening situation persists" (PRO CAB 104/264). Efforts to disarm civilians were problematic, however, particularly as the law and order

---

[7] Leaks about a week before independence indicated that Pakistan would receive a salient projecting into Indian Punjab, south of the sacred Sikh city of Amritsar. Although the final boundary line eliminated this salient, an August 9 attack on a train carrying government servants to Pakistan has been interpreted as the opening sally in a Sikh militant campaign to meet such a line with violence.

situation worsened. In early 1948, a Colonial Office official noted that "there were serious complaints from both Jews and Arabs that, while we would not let them arm themselves, we could not protect them. The present position was hardly tenable" (PRO CAB 134/527). Preventing civilians from protecting themselves without providing them effective security left the British on shaky ground, both ethically and in terms of their international reputation.

In addition, a top-secret report showed that thousands of foreign militants, including Muslim fighters from Yugoslavia, were present in Palestine (PRO CAB 134/527). There were also foreign fighters supporting the Jewish forces (Morris 1999, 193). But some British officials maintained a steadfastly optimistic viewpoint; a senior member of the Palestine government reported that the High Commissioner "thought that fears of large-scale fighting during out [sic] withdrawal might prove somewhat exaggerated, for while Jews and Arabs might want to fight each other, neither would want to fight the other and the British as well" (PRO CAB 134/526). This prediction proved sadly mistaken.

By 1947, the population of Punjab was even more highly militarized than the population of Palestine. Punjab was a traditional recruiting ground for the (British) Indian army, and Punjabi Muslims and Sikhs were among the "martial races" the British deemed most effective as soldiers. As a result, Punjab was home to a disproportionate number of soldiers. During World War II, there were many Punjabis not only in the Indian army but also in the Indian National Army, the Subhas Chandra Bose-led force that fought with the Japanese against the British (Fay 1993). After the war, demobilized soldiers from both armies returned home, bringing with them their training, their uniforms, often their weapons, and, crucially, their combat-tested group bonds. Many soldiers put these tools to brutally effective use in 1947.

In the months before partition, Muslim, Sikh, and Hindu groups all built up private armies (Aiyar 1998, 35, fn. 60). There are conflicting reports about the level of preparations carried out by each group, and it remains difficult to find objective appraisals of their role in the violence (Zafar 1995; Talib 1950). As early as 1946, however, Punjabi militarization was on the rise. The author of the best available study points to the role of Sikh jathas (gangs) as decisive, although she notes that Muslim and Hindu armies were also being expanded and drilled (Aiyar 1998, 35, fn. 60). In the partition violence, well-armed fighters used both sophisticated military arms and locally produced weapons. They sometimes applied military tactics to train attacks, with covering fire from light machine guns and rifles protecting raiders who rushed the trains using spears and knives (Tuker 1950, 485–488). In short, extensive military experience and easy access to weapons contributed to the devastatingly effective ethnic cleansing that characterized the Punjabi partition.

State weakness

In the months before Britain ended its administration, it gradually but very publicly lost much of its real authority in both Palestine and Punjab, as it became increasingly clear that the British intended to withdraw their forces. One symptom of this problem was a rapidly worsening law and order situation, which, as noted above, complicated British disarmament efforts in both Palestine and Punjab. In early 1948, the Palestine government reported that "British officers and officials were having to show their passes at Arab road blocks," prompting the Colonial Office to comment that "when British policemen had to produce passes to Arabs it might be said that the administration had already broken down" (PRO CAB 134/527). The primary concern of the Official Committee on Palestine, a British government body formed somewhat hastily as the imminence of Britain's withdrawal became clear, was the effect that the weakness of the Palestine government would have on British military security. There was much debate over the timing of the British withdrawal and about means of ensuring the withdrawal or destruction of military stores in such a way that they could not be used by either Arabs or Jews in a subsequent civil war (PRO CAB 134/526 and 527).

In addition, the British were particularly concerned about the damage to their authority that would result from the arrival of the UN Commission to partition Palestine. The Colonial Office argued that

The partition plan now before the United Nations Assembly visualised the early dispatch to Palestine of a United Nations Committee to take over the administration of the country and the Official Committee had felt that the premature arrival of this Commission in Palestine would be extremely embarrassing, since, whatever its precise status might be, the Jewish organisations in Palestine would at once transfer their allegiance to it, and the Arabs would be provoked by its presence and activities. (PRO CAB 134/526)

As a result, British officials concluded that they could maintain control for only fifteen days after the UN Commission's arrival. Britain therefore pressured the UN not to send its Commission to Palestine until early May at the soonest. This requirement severely limited the effectiveness of the Commission, which found itself expected to take over the running of the entire Mandate in a two-week period. The Commission chairman belatedly asked Britain to stay on for longer than two weeks after the Commission's arrival, pleading that otherwise the Commission's task would be "beyond human possibility," but Britain stood firm (PRO CAB 134/527). Waning state control posed too great a risk to British military plans and to British prestige.

In South Asia in 1947, as in Palestine during the same period, it was public knowledge that the British Raj was ending. The fact that it would soon cease to exercise power damaged its prestige; their evident loss of local control affected government officials' decisions. Both the central and provincial governments found themselves decreasingly effective; traditionally highly disciplined military and police units began to succumb to communal resentment. The British felt themselves to be in a race against time, struggling to transfer power before it disappeared entirely. However, the new states of India and, especially, Pakistan also lacked effective means of exerting power. It took them months after partition to build up their authority, all the while grappling with a huge influx of refugees.

Decision-makers were keenly aware of their loosening grip on authority, and this awareness had practical results. Despite specific intelligence reports that Sikh militants were planning attacks, including an assassination attempt on Muhammad Ali Jinnah (soon to be Pakistan's first Governor General), the British decided not to arrest them. One reason for this decision was that, as the Governor of the Punjab wrote to the Viceroy, "I could hardly send them to what will in a few days be a Pakistan jail; on the other hand if I left them in East [Indian] Punjab, they would be a centre of agitation" (Mansergh 1983, 637). The British hold on Punjab had weakened to such an extent that they preferred to leave such extremists free rather than risk the consequences of arresting them; neither did they have much faith in the ability of their successor governments to enforce law and order.

The role of politics: sensitivity to international opinion

As they contemplated the final procedures by which they hoped to extricate themselves from both Palestine and in South Asia, British officials were keenly aware of international opinion. However, international pressure played a more powerful and more consistent role in Palestine than in South Asia, for there were more external groups interested in Palestine than with an eye on British India. In Palestine, both neighboring Arab states and worldwide (but especially American) Zionist pressure were of grave concern to British policymakers. After attempts to mollify both sides, impending war prompted the British to calculate that Arab favor would be more important in wartime than Jewish allies. In 1939, Prime Minister Neville Chamberlain went so far as to admit that "we are now compelled to consider the Palestine problem mainly from the point of view of its effect on the international situation ... if we must offend one side, let us offend the Jews rather than the Arabs" (PRO FO 371/23234). External considerations had come to the fore. In South Asia, American pressure to decolonize played an important role in the endgame of empire, but was not a central factor before World War II. British India itself was, conversely, a vital factor on the international scene, particularly because of the power projection capabilities Britain derived from its Indian troops.

Another significant similarity between British policy in Palestine and in South Asia was the use of ostensibly independent and apolitical commissions to accomplish political ends. In South Asia, I have argued, the commission responsible for drawing the Indo-Pakistani boundary legitimated the fundamentally political partition process by providing a vital façade of objectivity and judicial fairness (Chester 2002). In Palestine, various elements of the British government used a parade of theoretically independent bodies to achieve their goals. The common thread that linked these goals was a desire to appear evenhanded and objective, whether before a colonial audience or in the eyes of international observers.

In 1947, South Asian nationalist leaders, along with the British, attempted to portray the process of defining the partition boundary as purely objective. They did so by establishing a pseudo-judicial boundary commission. But political pressures from all sides meant that the commission members were all political nominees from the leading nationalist parties. Its chairman was a British lawyer, Cyril Radcliffe, who had never been to India and had no experience in boundary-making, but was familiar with British imperial interests.[8] Radcliffe has been subject to allegations, from Indian observers but particularly from the Pakistani side, that he bowed to pressure from the Viceroy to change the line in India's favor at the last moment. These criticisms of the boundary commission as biased toward one side or the other, however, buy into the myth that partition was an objective, apolitical process, when in fact it was anything but. The commission members were nominated by political parties and their advice to Radcliffe was driven by their political loyalties. Radcliffe himself does not seem to have been partial to either Congress or the Muslim League; his loyalty was to the British state, and

---

[8] Radcliffe's boundary lines were, however, surprisingly sound, given the impossible requirements dictated by the larger partition process (Chester 2002, 211–222).

to its interests, particularly its interest in speedily extricating itself from its South Asian responsibilities (Chester 2002, 73–114).

Commissions served a similar purpose in Palestine. After the 1929 riots between Arabs and Jews, for example, British officials pressured their Palestinian judiciary to hold Jews and Arabs relatively equally culpable (Segev 2000, 329). The Peel Commission, however, provides perhaps the most notable example. In the eyes of Israeli historian Tom Segev,

> The royal commission had not, of course, come to "study" anything; it had come to help the government divest itself of Palestine. Lord Peel seems to have brought with him a foregone conclusion: "The social, moral and political gaps betweens the Arab and Jewish communities are already unbridgeable." (Segev 2000, 401)

The commission was intended as cover to help the British find a relatively graceful exit from an increasingly uncomfortable situation. Segev (2000, 413) refers to this kind of commission of inquiry as a "ritual procedure." Such rituals were intended less to formulate new policy or to seek Arab–Jewish rapprochement than to prove, rather cynically, that the British were "playing fair" (Segev 2000, 437).

As Michael J. Cohen writes, the so-called "independent" commission was actually an "invaluable political instrument" (Cohen 1978, 189). Such commissions served their (British-designed) purposes in 1938, when Whitehall used the Woodhead Commission to ease the British move away from partition, and in 1946, when the Anglo-American Commission of Inquiry provided cover for British delay after the strain of World War II and allowed the British to work, at least temporarily, hand in hand with the United States (Cohen 1978, 184). Such bodies allowed the British to maintain the appearance of judicial objectivity and rationality, when in fact political considerations played a determining role in policy decisions.

Factors likely to impede partition

What insights can the Palestinian and Punjabi cases offer for the general use of partition? They provide little comfort for those considering partition as a tool to resolve conflict and achieve lasting order. They suggest that attempts at partition are likely to meet with mixed success at best. Division offers valuable political power to some but at a high cost, particularly to those who lose their homes, their families, or even their lives. Both the South Asian and the Palestinian cases suggest that the very conditions that seem to call for partition may impede the implementation of an effective division. We turn now to an examination of those conditions' broader policy relevance.[9]

Population mix

A population mix of some kind is a necessary condition for partition. If there were no population mix, there would be no one to divide. However, the territorial distribution of this mix is often such that there is no clear line that can separate the groups in question without leaving significant minorities on the "wrong" side of the new line. Drawing a line through an area with mixed settlement patterns can have a number of potentially dangerous results. Boundary-makers may be tempted to use salients, strips of land that jut into neighboring territory, as a means of including members of a group on the "right" side of the line. Salients are strategically useful (as well as strategically dangerous) features that can be destabilizing. Another possibility is that large minorities may be left on one or both sides of the line, where they may be vulnerable to persecution at the hands of the majority community. If they are fearful enough, these minorities may attempt to migrate across the new line, causing a refugee crisis. It takes time, patience, and a high level of cooperation to draw a line through a mixed population area – exactly the qualities that are in short supply when conflict is so severe that decision-makers are contemplating partition.

Although any division of two groups will be difficult, the presence of a third significant minority complicates matters further. If decision-makers decide that a three-way partition is impossible, they must consider with which side the third party is more closely aligned and ensure that the third party will find its interests adequately represented on that side. In order for a settlement to be widely accepted, the interests of all major parties must be considered. Ignoring the interests of a third group in an effort to simplify the problem will merely exacerbate minority dissatisfaction. Similarly, effective policies must recognize the varied interests and goals of a diverse community, rather than assuming that it is a monolithic whole.

Militarized populations

In a situation where groups are so fearful that they prefer partition to any other solution, the population to be divided will likely be armed. If the

---

[9] Additional problems that complicated these two cases are likely to be present in other cases of partition; the discussion below is not intended to be exhaustive.

partition is to take place in an area with a military tradition, where a significant percentage of the population has military experience, that violence may be organized and efficient. Such conditions can provide ready tinder for a conflagration of ethnic violence. One solution is to disarm the local population. However, this approach is itself difficult to implement for a variety of reasons. Disarmament can be nearly impossible where large rural areas are involved or where weapons can be easily hidden. There is little point in confiscating weapons that can be replaced quickly from local resources. Some weapons have other legitimate uses, as agricultural implements (e.g. machetes) or as religious objects (e.g. kirpans, an edged weapon carried by observant Sikhs), making their confiscation problematic. In short, militarized populations may be an inescapable feature of the background for some attempted partitions.

The use of locally made weapons, as in Punjab in 1947, demonstrates the difficulty of offering any simple policy prescription for disarmament. One contemporary observer described seeing spearheads or daggers being made in a local shop a few weeks before independence (Spate, diary entry for August 3, 1947). Although seizing grenades and automatic weapons would likely have reduced the effectiveness of mass violence, it would not have eliminated it completely. Furthermore, such an undertaking would have required a tremendous investment of time and manpower at a time when the reliability of the Raj's police and military forces was increasingly unsure.

State weakness

Another factor that complicates partition in general – and disarmament in particular – is weak state and local authority. This problem is especially prevalent in the actual locality to be partitioned, where the power of the old state is waning and the power of the new state is yet to be established. The state loses prestige because the public recognizes that it will soon cease to exist. Its practical ability to enforce law and order is compromised, particularly if administrators and police officials must move to new posts as part of the partition plan. Multiethnic police or administrative units may find that ethnic tensions impede their work, while forces composed of members of only one party will be considered illegitimate by members of the other party. This slow process of the waning of state authority will accelerate rapidly in the final months and weeks before partition unless steps are taken to counter it or compensate for it.

With waning state power, those who bear grievances may seize the opportunity to take revenge on members of other groups. In addition, common criminals may take advantage of a general atmosphere of lawlessness to commit crimes for their own gain. It is crucial to prevent such crimes not only because in the short term they spark escalating violence, but also because in the long term they contribute to lasting resentments that make post-partition reconciliation and cooperation even more difficult.

The role of politics

Decision-makers may be unwilling to acknowledge the role of politics in the partition process. They may attempt to portray aspects of the partition process as purely objective and fair, in an effort to give them greater legitimacy and to ensure their public acceptance. However, it is difficult, if not impossible, to remove politics completely from any partition process. Simply ignoring the influence of politics can leave leaders unprepared to deal with the repercussions of politically influenced decisions. Furthermore, revelations that an apparently apolitical element of partition was in fact influenced by politics can have a devastating effect on public perceptions of its legitimacy.

If political differences could be overcome easily, it would not be necessary to resort to partition in the first place. Rather, policymakers (and those affected by their decisions) would do better to recognize the role of politics in partition and attempt to compensate for it in such a way that all sides feel that their interests are fairly represented. Unfortunately, the fraught circumstances that accompany partition planning make this prescription a tall order.

The most to lose, the least influence

A further factor must be considered here – the fact that those who have the most to lose from any partition often have the least real influence on the decision-making process. Key decisions about partition will be made at the administrative center. However, those in the peripheral areas to be divided have superior knowledge of local reality. For example, they possess information about social or agricultural links that may not be displayed on official maps or in other government records, but will have a direct impact on the success of any partition attempt. Local knowledge is crucial to drawing a boundary line, because lack of this low-level detail can lead to problems such as lines that divide farmers from their fields or cut through essential infrastructure facilities. But inhabitants of the areas that are to be partitioned often have little influence over decisions at the center. They will bear the brunt of decisions that, especially in rural areas with poor communications, they may have known little about. Although inhabitants of borderland areas may feel that events at the center have little to do with them, in reality they are likely to be at the center of partition's disruption of daily life. Local inhabitants may suffer communal attacks or even ethnic cleansing; even if they are not forced to leave their homes, they will have to adjust to new and often more precarious patterns of life in areas that have been transformed into borderlands.

Conclusions

The British adopted very different approaches to their withdrawal from South Asia and from Palestine. In Palestine, there were lengthy discussions of key issues, including boundary location, infrastructure problems, and demographic factors. Ultimately, however, British leaders dropped the notion of partition for fear of alienating the Arab leaders whose support they saw as crucial. In South Asia, there was nearly no contemplation of these issues until very late in the game, as the British avoided any discussion of partition for fear of giving the idea legitimacy. In both cases, I argue, the British were willing to consider partition, however temporarily, because they thought that it might help preserve British prestige. The goal of imposing lasting order was secondary to the goal of burnishing Britain's international image.

These two cases, despite their different outcomes, help us understand the contradictions inherent in partition. First, the primary requirement for resolving the problems outlined above may be cooperation between political leaders of rival groups. Unfortunately, cooperation is often lacking precisely where it is needed most; if the parties involved had been able to cooperate, partition might not have seemed necessary in the first place. Second, the leaders involved in such cases are human beings, operating in a situation of great uncertainty and complexity. If partition requires near-perfect knowledge, courage, stamina, and wisdom to implement effectively, it must remain a tool of last resort. Here, however, we encounter the final paradox of partition: its successful implementation requires extensive planning, preferably well in advance. Decision-makers with responsibility for conflicted regions have the unenviable task of balancing, on the one hand, the need to consider all options short of partition before resorting to division with, on the other, the need to make extensive preparations for partition in order to provide any chance of success.

Why would decision-makers undertake such a difficult task? The answer lies in the fact that partition does offer significant benefits. For one, political leaders on both sides may be able to consolidate their power within the post-partition state. In addition, a withdrawing power can point to the partition as an attempt to impose order. If local leaders can be brought into the process, the withdrawing power can go further and claim that those leaders are responsible for any resulting violence. In other words, partition offers a tempting means of saving face in situations that seem insoluble. But this gain for the withdrawing power, as valuable as it may be, will do little to address the complex problems on the ground. This is so partly because of the inherent structure of partition, which is based on the assumption that there are neat and meaningful divisions within the society in question, which can be divided along those lines with some precision. Partition is an attempt to impose a simple division on a complex society – in most cases, treating as dualistic a problem that is multifaceted.

In the cases discussed here, the debate over whether or not to use partition had less to do with attempts to impose order and resolve conflict than it did with Britain's need to protect its own security. I do not mean to argue that the British actively worked to foment disorder. Rather, I argue that Britain's postwar policy reflected the fact that its top priority was protecting its own long-term interests – not establishing lasting order in various troublesome holdings. The ideologies that Britain used to justify colonial rule, like the terms of the Palestine Mandate, focused on the welfare of people under British control. Under pressure, however, local interests came a distant second to imperial security needs. British leaders divided South Asia because it provided the quickest exit from a situation on the verge of collapse, but decided not to implement a partition in Palestine because it would alienate vital Arab allies. These case studies suggest that partition will continue to tempt decision-makers with the promise of political gains, including a relatively dignified exit. Unfortunately, it is also likely to result in continuing conflict and violence.

REFERENCES

Manuscript sources
Cambridge University South Asian Archive:
    O.H.K. Spate, 1947 Diary, Spate Papers
Public Record Office (UK National Archives):
    CAB 104/264
    CAB 134/526
    CAB 134/527
    FO 371/23234

Other sources

Aiyar, Swarna. 1998. "'August Anarchy': The Partition Massacres in Punjab, 1947." In *Freedom, Trauma, Continuities: Northern India and Independence*, ed. D.A. Low and Howard Brasted. Walnut Creek, CA: AltaMira Press, 15–38.

Antonius, George. 1938. *The Arab Awakening*. London: Hamish Hamilton.

Asiwaju, A. I. 1985. *Partitioned Africans: Ethnic Relations Across Africa's International Boundaries*. London: C. Hurst.

Chester, Lucy. 2002. "Drawing the Indo-Pakistani Boundary During the 1947 Partition of South Asia." Doctoral dissertation, Yale University.

Cohen, Michael. 1978. *Palestine, Retreat from the Mandate: A Study of British Policy, 1936–45*. New York: Holmes & Meier.

ed. 1987. "Resolution Adopted on the Report of the Ad Hoc Committee on the Palestinian Question." November 29, 1947. Official Records of the General Assembly, 181 (II). Cited in *The Rise of Israel: United Nations Discussions on Palestine 1947*. New York: Garland Publishing, 163–184.

Cohn, Bernard. 1987. "The Census, Social Structure and Objectification in South Asia." In *An Anthropologist among the Historians and Other Essays*, Bernard Cohn. Oxford University Press, 224–254.

Fay, Peter Ward. 1993. *The Forgotten Army: India's Armed Struggle for Independence 1942–1945*. Ann Arbor: University of Michigan Press.

Fraser, T. G. 1984. *Partition in Ireland, India, and Palestine: Theory and Practice*. New York: St. Martin's Press.

Freedman, Robert. 1972. "The Partition of Palestine: Conflicting Nationalism and Great Power Rivalry." In *The Problem of Partition: Peril to World Peace*, ed. Thomas Hachey. University of Chicago Press, 175–212.

French, Patrick. 1997. *Liberty or Death*. London: HarperCollins.

Hachey, Thomas E., ed. 1972. *The Problem of Partition: Peril to World Peace*. University of Chicago Press.

Hurewitz, J. C., ed. 1979a. "The Balfour Declaration." *The Times (London)*, November 2, 1917. Cited in *The Middle East and North Africa in World Politics: A Documentary Record*, 2nd edn, vol. II. New Haven: Yale University Press, 106.

1979b. "The Husayn–McMahon Correspondence." July 14, 1915–March 10, 1916. Great Britain. Parliamentary Papers, 1939. Misc. no. 3. Command Paper 5957. Cited in *The Middle East and North Africa in World Politics: A Documentary Record*, 2nd edn, vol. II. New Haven: Yale University Press, 46–56.

1979c. "The Mandate for Palestine." July 24, 1922. Great Britain. Parliamentary Papers, 1922. Command Paper 1785. Cited in *The Middle East and North Africa in World Politics: A Documentary Record*, 2nd edn, vol. II. New Haven: Yale University Press, 305–309.

Jalal, Ayesha. 2001. *Self and Sovereignty: Individual and Community in South Asian Islam since 1850*. Oxford University Press.

Kaufmann, Chaim. 1996. "Possible and Impossible Solutions to Ethnic Civil Wars." *International Security* 20 (4) (Spring): 136–175.

Kinzer, Stephen. 2001. "Break Up Afghanistan? Why Not?" *New York Times*, December 1: A15.

Klieman, Aaron S. 1980. "The Resolution of Conflicts Through Territorial Partition: The Palestine Experience." *Comparative Studies in Society and History* 22 (2) (April): 281–300.

Kumar, Radha. 1997. *Divide and Fall?* London: Verso.

Louis, Wm. 1984. *The British Empire in the Middle East*. Oxford: Clarendon Press.

1986. "British Imperialism and the End of the Palestine Mandate." In *The End of the Palestine Mandate*, ed. Wm. Roger Louis and Robert W. Stookey. Austin: University of Texas Press, 1–31.

McCarthy, Justin. 1990. *The Population of Palestine: Populations Statistics of the Late Ottoman Period and the Mandate*. New York: Columbia University Press.

Mansergh, Nicholas, and Penderel Moon, eds. 1983. *The Transfer of Power 1942–7*, vol. XII. London: Her Majesty's Stationery Office.

Mearsheimer, John J., and Stephen Van Evera. 1995. "When Peace Means War." *New Republic*, December 5: 16–21.

Morris, Benny. 1999. *Righteous Victims: A History of the Zionist–Arab Conflict, 1881–1999*. London: J. Murray.

Sambanis, Nicholas. 2000. "Partition as a Solution to Ethnic War: An Empirical Critique of the Theoretical Literature." *World Politics* 52 (4) (July): 437–483.

Schaeffer, Robert K. 1999. *Severed States: Dilemmas of Democracy in a Divided World*. Lanham: Rowman & Littlefield Publishers, Inc.

Segev, Tom. 2000. *One Palestine, Complete: Jews and Arabs under the British Mandate*, trans. Haim Watzman. New York: Henry Holt and Company.

Talib, S. Gurbachan Singh, comp. 1950. *Muslim League Attack on Sikhs and Hindus in the Punjab, 1947*. Amritsar: [n.p.].

Tuker, Francis. 1950. *While Memory Serves*. London: Cassell and Co. Ltd.

Zafar, Rukhsana, comp. 1995. *Disturbances in the Punjab 1947*. Islamabad: National Documentation Centre.

5 The social order of violence in Chicago and Stockholm neighborhoods: a comparative inquiry

Robert J. Sampson and Per-Olof H. Wikström

We know surprisingly little about interpersonal violence in cross-national, comparative context. Owing partly to the difficulties in collecting data that can reasonably be compared, research has tended to focus on stylized facts generated in separate fashion. For example, we know that violence is ecologically concentrated based on numerous, separate studies of American and European cities. But we do not know why. We also know that violence tends to correlate with structural factors such as neighborhood poverty, again in many different cities. Yet we do not know whether concentrated poverty, defined similarly, can explain cross-national differences in violence, nor even how the distributions of inequality directly compare at the neighborhood level. Perhaps more important, when it comes to the social mechanisms that generate or inhibit violence, the limits of our knowledge become apparent. By focusing primarily on correlates of violence at the level of social composition (namely poverty), prior research has tended toward a risk factor rather than an explanatory approach that posits social mechanisms.

Our goal for this essay is to move beyond the dominance of exclusively American studies of interpersonal violence and the canonical correlate of poverty. We do so by addressing the neighborhood social order of interpersonal violence in the contemporary urban settings of Chicago and Stockholm. The move we make is to link comparative measures of structural inequality with community-level mechanisms that are hypothesized to predict violence in similar ways despite vastly different national contexts. We thus consider the problem of moving from community-level correlations, or markers, to the underlying social mechanisms theoretically at work. We conceptualize a social mechanism as a

This essay was originally presented at the conference on "Order, Conflict, and Violence" at Yale University, April 30–May 1, 2004. We thank the conference participants and Cambridge University Press reviewers for helpful comments.

plausible (unobservable) contextual process that accounts for a given phenomenon, in the ideal case linking putative causes and effects (see Wikström and Sampson 2003; Hedström and Swedberg 1998). We do not claim to demonstrate causation, but the goal is nevertheless to aim at a preliminary understanding of collective processes that predict violence in a strategic comparative setting.

The comparison of interest is at first blush counterintuitive – why Chicago and Stockholm? After all, Sweden and the US are worlds apart along a number of dimensions, including the concentration of poverty, welfare support, the planned nature of housing, and, not least, violence. Chicago is violent, segregated, and rank with economic inequality compared to Stockholm. Yet from a comparative perspective, this is analytically strategic if our goal is to uncover general, structural characteristics that transcend cultural and national boundaries. Following the "most different" research design for comparative studies (Przeworski and Teune 1970, 34–46), our motivation is therefore to discover whether there are common relationships in highly disparate cities, and if so along what dimensions. Chicago and Stockholm not only fit the bill but represent the third-largest and largest city in the US and Sweden, respectively.

There are also practical reasons for our choice. Capitalizing on serendipity and a last-minute opportunity, we were able to leverage and unite two separate studies. One of us is the director of a large-scale ongoing study of Chicago neighborhoods, a major component of which was an original survey of 8,872 residents of that city that was fielded in 1995. The basic idea was to conduct a cluster-based survey to measure key dimensions of neighborhood social process and advance a methodology we have termed "ecometrics" (Raudenbush and Sampson 1999). The other was the principal investigator of a longstanding study of violence and social ecology in Stockholm who was about to launch a survey in early 1996. Learning of each other's work, we met and designed a replication to measure survey-reported violence, social control, social trust, and disorder in Stockholm in a way that was identical to Chicago. Over the past several years we also collected geo-coded police records of similarly defined violent events and census data on structural differentiation in economic structure and housing. This essay reports our first attempt to unite these data sources to study comparative variations in the neighborhood-level context of violence. In fact, in our search of the literature we were unable to find a single study that integrated comparable measures of social processes, structural inequality, and interpersonal violence in the US and any European country, much less Sweden.

Our specific focus is the explanation of variation in interpersonal violent events across neighborhoods. We believe our approach presents an interesting case for thinking about the problem of conflict and social order. Although not necessarily group-oriented in the sense of war, civil strife, or revolution, interpersonal violence is a quintessentially social act, requiring the intersection in time and space of three elements – motivated offenders, suitable targets, and the absence of capable guardians (Cohen and Felson 1979). Common wisdom tends to attribute most of the action in violence to offenders rather than the social structure of the community settings that generate violent acts. The insight of thinking about events rather than persons is that even if motivated offenders are present, violence cannot occur absent a social interaction among, or intersection of, actors. It follows that violence can be ecologically concentrated in certain areas because of the presence of targets or the absence of third-party guardianship (e.g. low social control or public surveillance), even if the pool of latent or motivated offenders is more evenly distributed across the city.

In addition, the violent events we study tend to be serious in nature (e.g. homicide, aggravated assault) and reasonably well measured across space, a crucial ingredient for comparative work. Through a multi-method combination of survey-reported and official records, we were thus able to tap the more general concept of the violence potential of areas.

Theoretical backdrop

Our approach draws its motivation from an intellectual tradition in sociology that seeks to explain variation in rates of crime by neighborhood. Products of the early Chicago School, Shaw and McKay (1942) argued that low economic status, ethnic heterogeneity, and residential instability led to community disorganization, which in turn accounted for delinquent subcultures and ultimately high rates of delinquency. It was not until the 1970s and 1980s, however, that social disorganization was defined more explicitly as the inability of a community structure to realize effective social controls (Kornhauser 1978; Bursik 1988; Sampson and Groves 1989). As Janowitz (1975) argued, social control should not be equated with repression or forced conformity. Rather, social control refers to the capacity of a social unit to regulate itself according to desired principles – to realize collective (as opposed to forced) goals. The data seem clear that residents desire to live in safe environments free of predatory violence.

In practice, the theoretical definition of social disorganization has been operationalized largely in systemic terms – that is, the local community is viewed as a complex system of friendship, kinship, and acquaintanceship networks, and associational ties rooted in family life and ongoing socialization processes (Kasarda and Janowitz 1974; Bursik 1988). The unfortunate side effect is that scholars of the city have tended to equate socially organized communities with strong social ties, such as friends and kinship bonds. Neighborhoods bereft of dense social ties came to be seen as less able to realize common values and maintain the informal social controls that foster safety. A common approach, for example, has been to examine the association of the density of acquaintanceship or friendship ties with rates of crime and violence.

This move is problematic and glosses over an original thrust of social disorganization theory that connected structural forms of community disadvantage with diminished capacity for social control. Strong ties among neighbors are no longer the norm in most urban communities – friends and social support networks are decreasingly organized in a parochial, local fashion (Fischer 1982). Moreover, as Granovetter (1973) argued in his seminal essay, "weak ties" – including less intimate connections between people based on more infrequent social interaction – may be critical for establishing social resources, such as job referrals, because they integrate the community by bringing together otherwise disconnected subgroups. Bellair (1997) extended this logic to the study of community crime by demonstrating that weak but still existing ties among neighbors, as manifested by less frequent patterns of social interaction, are predictive of lower crime rates. Research on dense social ties thus reveals something of a paradox. Not only do many urbanites interact with their neighbors on a limited basis, poor city dwellers whose strong ties are tightly restricted geographically may actually produce an environment that discourages collective responses to local problems (Wilson 1987).

Addressing these urban realities, Sampson et al. (1997) proposed a tighter focus on mechanisms of social control that may be facilitated by, but do not necessarily require, strong ties or associations. Rejecting the outmoded assumption that neighborhoods are primary groups characterized by dense, intimate, and affective relations, Sampson et al. (1997) defined neighborhoods in ecological terms and highlighted the combination of working trust and shared willingness of residents to intervene in social control. For example, are there shared expectations that residents will take action if there is a fight or children are skipping school and hanging out on a street corner? Extending Bandura's foundational thinking (1997) to the neighborhood level, shared expectations for control that emerge in a context of trust and cohesion were conceptualized theoretically in terms of the higher-order construct of "collective efficacy." Just as self-efficacy is situated rather than global (one has self-efficacy relative to a particular task), a neighborhood's efficacy exists relative to specific tasks such as maintaining public order.

Moving from a focus on private ties to social efficacy signifies an emphasis on neighbors' conjoint capability for action to achieve an intended effect, and hence an active sense of engagement on the part of community residents. As Bandura (1997) argues, the meaning of efficacy is captured in expectations about the exercise of control, elevating the agential aspect of social life over a perspective centered on the accumulation of stocks of resources. This conception is consistent with the redefinition of social capital by Portes and Sensenbrenner as "expectations for action within a collectivity" (1993, 1323). Some density of social networks is essential, to be sure, especially networks rooted in social trust. But the key theoretical point is that networks have to be *activated* to be ultimately meaningful. The theoretical framework proposed here thus recognizes the transformed landscape of modern urban life, holding that while community efficacy may depend on a working trust and social interaction, it does not require that my neighbor or the local police officer be my friend (see Sampson 2006).

Structural inequality in resources matters greatly for explaining the production of collective efficacy. Concentrated disadvantage and homeownership, in particular, predict levels of later collective efficacy, and the associations of disadvantage and housing stability with violence are significantly reduced when collective efficacy is controlled (Sampson *et al.* 1997). These patterns are consistent with the inference that neighborhood constraints influence violence in part through the mediating role of neighborhood efficacy. Prior work thus suggests that social resources and social networks create the capacity for collective efficacy, but it is the act of exercising control under conditions of trust that is the most proximate to explaining violence.

Research design

In this essay, we present an attempt to comparatively assess neighborhood-level variations in structural differentiation (e.g. economic disadvantage, residential stability), social control, public "disorder," and violence. Taking Chicago and Stockholm as our comparative sites, a set of measures was designed to bear on the theoretical framework of interest. We specifically collected three sets of data that were matched to allow comparison.

Community surveys

In Chicago the data on neighborhood social processes stem from the Community Survey of the Project on Human Development in Chicago Neighborhoods (PHDCN). The extensive social-class, racial, and ethnic diversity of the population was a major reason Chicago was selected for the study. Chicago's 865 census tracts were combined to create 343 "Neighborhood Clusters" (NCs) composed of geographically contiguous and socially similar census tracts. NCs are smaller than Chicago's 77 community areas (average size = 40,000) but large enough to approximate local neighborhoods, averaging around 8,000 people. Major geographic boundaries (e.g. railroad tracks, parks, freeways), knowledge of Chicago's local neighborhoods, and cluster analyses of census data were used to guide the construction of relatively homogenous NCs with respect to distributions of racial–ethnic mix, socio-economic status, housing density, and family structure. The Community Survey (CS) of the PHDCN was conducted in 1995, when 8,782 Chicago residents representing all 343 NCs were personally interviewed in their homes. The basic design for the CS had three stages: at stage 1, city blocks were sampled within each NC; at stage 2, dwelling units were sampled within blocks; and at stage 3, one adult resident (eighteen or older) was sampled within each selected dwelling unit. Abt Associates carried out the screening and data collection in cooperation with PHDCN, achieving an overall response rate of 75 percent.

The Stockholm study was modeled in part to replicate key portions of the Chicago Community Survey. The main survey was carried out in the early part of 1996. Questionnaires were administered to a random sample of 5,000 residents of the county of Stockholm, which includes both the inner city and Greater Stockholm suburbs. Based on a response rate of 80 percent, the final sample is comprised of 3,992. These respondents are spread across geographic neighborhoods (average size = 5,000) where boundaries were constructed by city planning authorities based on family status, housing tenure (e.g. nonprofit, single family), transportation access, and other land-use patterns (see Wikström 1991, chapter 6). For the present study, Stockholm neighborhoods with at least five survey respondents (representing over 90 percent of the original sample) were selected for the comparative analysis, yielding 200 areas. Combined with the Chicago sample of 343 NCs, the total number of neighborhoods analyzed below is thus 543.

In both the Chicago and Stockholm surveys the design was explicitly multilevel, whereby respondents were asked about personal and household characteristics along with a set of questions designed to assess neighborhood context. At the individual level we constructed the following measures in both sites in a way that is directly comparable: *age, sex, college education* (1 = yes, 0 = no), *length of residence* in the household, *homeownership, married* (1 = yes, 0 = no), residence in *public or government housing* (1 = yes, 0 = no), and *unemployment* (1 = yes, 0 = no). Each respondent was also asked whether he/she had been victimized by a violent crime in the neighborhood in the six months prior to the survey. We are therefore able to examine individual-level risk of violent crime in addition to the effect of neighborhood social context.

Racial or ethnic status is of course a different matter when it comes to cross-national comparison, the subject of another paper altogether. Nevertheless, in the analysis below we do make some attempt to examine the ecological distribution of what we think of as the "disadvantaged" group with respect to discrimination or "outgroup" status in each country. In Chicago, as in the US at large, African-Americans have long been segregated and a long line of research suggests they occupy a disadvantaged minority-group position. In Sweden, race/ethnicity makes little sense as a concept, but immigration is a salient topic (Martens 1997). Immigration from Turkey and the former Yugoslavia in particular is increasing and there is some evidence of spatial clustering and segregation of non Swedish-born immigrants. We thus created an indicator in Stockholm of foreign-born status, which we selectively compare to African-American status in Chicago. They are not tapping the same manifest characteristic, of course, but may tap a larger and more interesting factor, namely the ecological segregation of "minority" groups that are seen as disadvantaged or undesirable by the societal mainstream.

To facilitate cross-comparative analysis, a common set of items was designed to be asked in an equivalent fashion in each city about key social processes. For conceptual clarity, and in keeping with the focused nature of the ideas traced earlier, we highlight the fusion of two major constructs: informal social control and social trust/cohesion. The wording of the items comprising the main scales is as follows.

Informal social control

1. "If some children were spray-painting graffiti on a local building, how likely is it that your neighborhoods would do something about it? Would you say it is very likely, likely, unlikely, or very unlikely?"
2. "If there was a fight in front of your house and someone was being beaten or threatened, how likely is it that your neighbors would break it up?" (Would you say it is very likely, likely, unlikely, or very unlikely?)

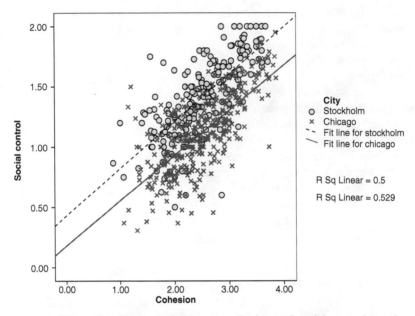

Figure 5.1 Similar link between cohesion and social control, by city

Note that these items are designed to tap the likelihood of neighbors' willingness to intervene and not the respondent's. Each respondent is thus utilized as an informant and asked to rate the collective properties of neighborhood social control (Raudenbush and Sampson 1999).

Trust/cohesion

Respondents in each city were also asked the following:

1. "People around here are willing to help their neighbors." Would you say you strongly agree, agree, disagree, or strongly disagree?
2. "People in this neighborhood can be trusted" (with same response set).

As seen in Figure 5.1, at the neighborhood level these constructs are strongly and similarly related in both cities, with a correlation in excess of .7. Consistent with Sampson *et al.* (1997), we thus created a modified collective efficacy scale that combined the constituent items.

In criminological theory much is often made of the concept of "public disorder," or the existence of signs of physical decay and so-called incivilities (Wilson and Kelling 1982). Visual cues such as graffiti on buildings, public intoxication, and abandoned cars are thought to attract offenders who assume from such disorder that residents are indifferent to what goes on inside the neighborhood. The idea is that violence is more likely to occur in ecological niches signifying a lack of public order. One of us has written critically about this concept in the past (Sampson and Raudenbush 1999), but we sidestep here the main debate. Our intent is merely to examine the cross-national variations in disorder, and specifically to assess whether the main relationships of interest are robust to controlling for disorder. A scale was developed from the following items:

1. "How much of a problem is litter, broken glass or trash in the sidewalks and streets?"
2. "How much of a problem is graffiti on buildings and walls?"
3. "How much of a problem is drinking in public?"
4. "How much of a problem is groups of teenagers or adults hanging out in the neighborhood and causing trouble?"

Each item was followed with: "Would you say it is a big problem, somewhat of a problem, or not a problem in your neighborhood?"

Scales for each of the three social-process measures resulted in neighborhood-level reliabilities (see Raudenbush and Sampson 1999) in the range of .7 and above.

Census structural characteristics

Although our community surveys measure key aspects of social stratification, we chose to collect independently measured census characteristics. In each site we specifically measure percent female-headed families, percent on public assistance, and percent in poverty. We spent an inordinate time trying to measure poverty in a similar fashion, settling on the percent of families below the poverty line in Chicago, which we determined was roughly below the 20th percentile distribution of income for the city. For Stockholm, we therefore defined a similar measure of the percentage of families with incomes below the 20th percentile distribution of Stockholm. These are relative to each city, by definition, but they are parallel and correlate very strongly and similarly with other measures that are defined the same, such as female-headed families. Finally, we constructed percent home ownership and percent living in the same house as previous census. By matching the census measures nearly identically to the individual-level survey, we can assess the contextual characteristics of disadvantage and residential stability.

Police records

To assess method-induced associations between outcomes and predictors, we collected independent event data from the Chicago and
Stockholm police on violent offenses. Locating the occurrence of the
crime, we tallied the counts of all interpersonal violence (homicide,
aggravated assault, and robbery) matched to the years of the survey. A
long line of research has suggested these serious violent offenses are well
measured, especially homicide. In a supplemental analysis we therefore
separately examine a count model of homicide as an indicator of neighborhood violence both because of its indisputable centrality to debates
about violence and because it is widely considered to be the most
accurately recorded of all crimes. For total violence we examine the log
of the event rate per 100,000 persons at risk.

Neighborhood inequality in cross-national perspective

We begin by examining the means and distributions of neighborhood characteristics in Chicago and Stockholm. The first message from
Table 5.1 is unambiguous: Chicago fares poorly in comparison with
Stockholm no matter what the dimension we consider. Whether survey-
reported violence, officially recorded violence, poverty, segregation, or
stability, Chicago is significantly worse off. The violence differentials are
very pronounced – the official violence rate is some eight times higher in
Chicago than in Stockholm, and prevalence of survey-reported violent
victimization is over five times higher.

Based on a theoretical desire to assess the differential effects of the
core concepts of disadvantage and stability, we constructed two "a
priori" scales from the census measures in Table 5.1. *Concentrated disadvantage* is defined by the percentage of families with low income,
percentage of families receiving public assistance, and percentage of
families with children that are female-headed. *Residential stability* is
defined as the percentage of residents five years old and older who lived
in the same house five years earlier, and the percentage of homes that are
owner-occupied. We also conducted a principal components analysis to
assess the dimensionality of items by city. As shown in Table 5.2, the
economic indicators load in a similar pattern in both cities – areas that
are high in public assistance are also low income and characterized by
the concentration of female-headed families. This finding corresponds
with a long line of research on the concentration of urban poverty (see
reviews in Sampson and Lauritsen 1994; Land *et al.* 1990). In the
pooled sample the second factor of what we label stability is dominated

Table 5.1. *Means and standard deviations for comparative city data, neighborhood level (n = 343 Chicago, n = 200 Stockholm)*

	Chicago		Stockholm		t-ratio for difference
	Mean	SD	Mean	SD	
Survey data:					
% Minority[a]	39.90	40.80	17.58	16.70	−8.92**
Collective efficacy	−0.46	1.60	0.47	1.70	6.34**
% Violent victimization	12.83	8.80	2.46	4.60	−17.93**
Census data:					
% Public assistance	17.47	15.06	6.33	4.98	−12.57**
% Female-headed families	32.95	18.55	21.58	10.03	−9.26**
% Home owners	42.44	23.50	54.27	27.10	5.14**
% Same house 5 years	56.02	12.67	64.15	6.69	9.77**
Police recorded					
Violence rate per 100,000	6551.88	4266.90	807.31	605.47	−24.51**

Independent samples t-test, equal variances not assumed; **$p < .01$
[a] Black in Chicago; immigrant in Stockholm

Table 5.2. *Principal components analysis of neighborhood characteristics: varimax dimensions, by city (loadings over .60 underscored)*

	Dimensionality components:				
	Pooled sample		Chicago		Stockholm
	1	2	1	2	1
Neighborhood characteristic					
% Residential stability	0.05	0.96	0.17	0.96	−0.79
% Owner-occupied housing	−0.55	0.75	−0.54	0.79	−0.91
% Public assistance	0.95	−0.04	0.98	0.09	0.74
% Female-headed families	0.95	−0.11	0.96	0.01	0.88
% Low income	0.91	−0.20	0.95	−0.21	0.92
Eigenvalues	3.21	1.26	3.21	1.47	3.64
Variance explained	64.20	25.30	64.30	29.50	72.87

by percent living in the same house as five years earlier (stability), and percent owner-occupied homes. The emergence of a residential stability factor is likewise consistent with much past research.

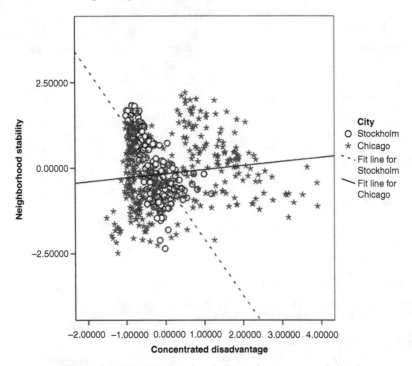

Figure 5.2 Neighborhood stability and concentrated disadvantage, by city

The main comparative difference is that residential stability is more closely linked to economic status in Stockholm. That is, in Stockholm there are few neighborhoods that are residentially unstable and yet well-to-do, which is by contrast a fairly common scenario in the upscale rental areas on the north side of Chicago. In addition, Chicago has stable areas that are poor (Wilson 1987). As a result, the stability factor is more independent from disadvantage in Chicago. This differential ecological pattern is seen clearly when graphically portrayed as in Figure 5.2. Stability is tightly clustered in Stockholm and strongly negatively related to poverty.

In Table 5.1, moreover, there are two clear factors in Chicago, whereas in Stockholm the stability indicators load negatively on one factor dominated by poverty. Yet disadvantage and stability can still be independently defined in Stockholm, and if we modify the eigenvalue criterion, two dimensions emerge. Based on these results in conjunction with our theoretical framework, our main analysis focuses on the two

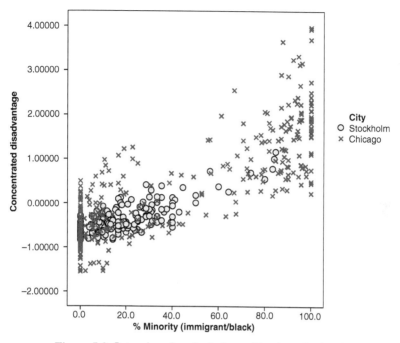

Figure 5.3 Intensity of ecological stratification of minority groups by concentrated disadvantage, by city

scales of disadvantage and stability. In preliminary analysis we constructed a number of different definitions of disadvantage (e.g. using aggregated survey measures of unemployment and low income), but the main pattern remained. Furthermore, we conducted all analyses with and without the low-income measure as a defining feature of the disadvantage dimension, again obtaining similar results.

In a separate analysis we also introduced the "minority" group variable, which loaded on the disadvantage factor using either principal components or alpha-scoring factor analysis with an oblique rotation. The loading was, however, much higher in Chicago than Stockholm, reflecting the neighborhood segregation mechanisms that concentrate the poor, African-Americans, and single-parent families with children in American cities (Wilson 1987; Massey and Denton 1993; Land *et al.* 1990).

The intensity of ecological stratification of disadvantage by race/ immigrant group is reflected graphically in Figure 5.3. There are considerably more segregated areas in Chicago than in Stockholm, and they

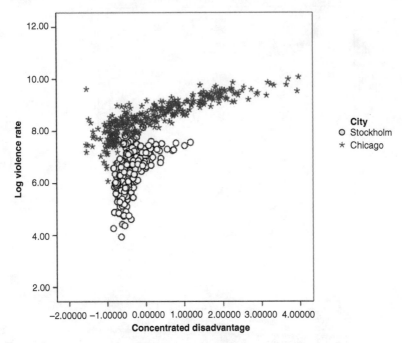

Figure 5.4 Violence by concentrated disadvantage in comparative context

are more sharply related to concentrated disadvantage. In the analysis below we therefore replicated all models with a disadvantage factor that included percent minority group as a defining feature. The results were similar. Because minority-group status is so different across context, we prefer the more parsimonious definition of disadvantage. As a precaution we replicated all analyses by separately controlling for minority-group status in models assessing the effects of concentrated disadvantage (reported below).

Violence and collective efficacy

The data introduced thus far show both similarity and difference in the ecological structure of Stockholm neighborhoods. Major questions remain. Despite these differences in neighborhood inequality, what is the nature of the relationship with violence? What is the relationship with collective efficacy? We first examine the bivariate association of concentrated inequality with log violence rate, disaggregated by city. Figure 5.4 is intriguing, as it demonstrates visually the macro-level

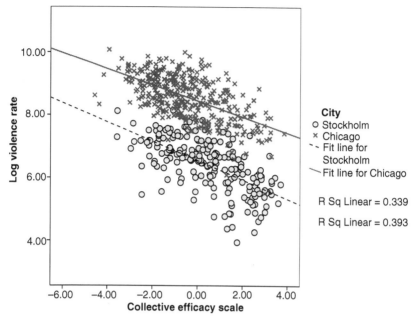

Figure 5.5 Similar collective efficacy–violence link by city

consequences of housing policies and social inequality. Namely, there is a positive association of violence with disadvantage in both cities but there are many more disadvantaged neighborhoods in Chicago, where the association with violence begins to tail off. There are more affluent neighborhoods in Chicago as well – note the areas to the left of graph. Overall Figure 5.4 appears to reflect an "equality compression" of ecological distributions in Stockholm, characterized by restricted variation in disadvantage and lower violence. Indeed, Chicago "sits atop" Stockholm at virtually every level of disadvantage, and its extended range of concentrated disadvantage is pronounced. As such the city effects appear strong even though the association of violence with disadvantage is similarly positive. In further analysis this pattern held for each constituent measure of disadvantage.

We also found that structural disadvantage and residential stability significantly predict variations in collective efficacy in both cities at the bivariate level (data not shown). The relationships were consistently stronger in Stockholm than Chicago, but the bottom line is that disadvantage is associated with lower levels of collective efficacy, and residential stability is associated with higher levels of collective efficacy.

Perhaps most interesting is the relationship of collective efficacy with violence. Figure 5.5 shows a clear negative association, linear in pattern, and similar in slope. In fact, a t-test for the difference of coefficients was not significant at $p < .05$. The variance-explained statistics are virtually identical as well and the shape of the relationship is invariant. Therefore, although Chicago again sits atop Stockholm in a disadvantaged position of structural risk, as collective efficacy increases the log violence rate decreases in an invariant way in both cities.

Multivariate patterns

Tables 5.3–5.5 present a multivariate assessment of the independent nature of the predictive patterns observed above. Table 5.3 shows the independent association of disadvantage and stability with the official log violence rate. The pattern of relationships is similar in both cities, although the sample-specific statistics reveal a higher explained variance in Chicago than Stockholm. Table 5.4 shows that disadvantage and stability independently predict variations in collective efficacy as well, this time with Stockholm showing greater explanatory power of the overall model. In both tables, however, each structural factor shows predictive strength.

In Table 5.5 we turn to a simultaneous consideration of structural differentiation and neighborhood social organization as predictors of violence. Collective efficacy emerges as a significant predictor of lower violence rates independent of structural differentiation. In both cities, collective efficacy appears to mediate part of the relationship of stability and disadvantage with violence. Still, the direct effect of disadvantage looms large, especially in Chicago.

We conducted a series of tests to assess the basic robustness of findings. First, we replicated the main analysis with an over-dispersed Poisson model of homicide counts, allowing for spatial clustering by neighborhood. We know that homicide is measured extremely well, and moreover the negative binomial distribution allows for unobserved heterogeneity of the variance parameter. Despite the very rare nature of homicide – especially in Stockholm – the results were largely consistent with the above set, with collective efficacy emerging as a significant predictor of lower homicide in each city.

Second, we introduced public disorder to see if the relationship between collective efficacy and violence was altered (Skogan 1990). It may well be that the results thus far stem from endogeneity or what some might think of as the "reflection" problem, with collective efficacy tapping aspects closely associated with the outcome of violence itself. To

Table 5.3. *Structural differentiation and prediction of violence rate, by city*

	Chicago		Stockholm	
	Coeff.	t-ratio	Coeff.	t-ratio
Neighborhood predictors				
Intercept	8.45	394.32**	6.72	129.99**
Concentrated disadvantage	0.51	28.30**	0.86	5.65**
Residential stability	−0.11	−5.84**	−0.24	−2.39*
Variance explained	0.70		0.44	

*p < .05; **p < .01

Table 5.4. *Structural differentiation and prediction of collective efficacy, by city*

	Chicago		Stockholm	
	Coeff.	t-ratio	Coeff.	t-ratio
Neighborhood predictors				
Intercept	−0.19	−2.88**	−0.30	−3.68**
Concentrated disadvantage	−0.80	−14.49**	−1.41	−5.90**
Residential stability	0.71	11.91**	1.10	7.10**
Variance explained	0.47		0.67	

*p < .05; **p < .01

Table 5.5. *Structural differentiation and collective efficacy predict violence rate, by city*

	Chicago		Stockholm	
	Coeff.	t-ratio	Coeff.	t-ratio
Neighborhood predictors				
Intercept	8.44	400.28**	6.68	127.76**
Concentrated disadvantage	0.45	20.05**	0.66	4.10**
Residential stability	−0.01	−2.55*	−0.01	−0.76
Collective efficacy	−0.01	−4.60**	−0.14	−3.15**
Variance explained	0.72		0.46	

*p < .05; **p < .01

Table 5.6. *Structural differentiation, disorder, and collective efficacy predict violence, by city*

	Chicago		Stockholm	
	Coeff.	t-ratio	Coeff.	t-ratio
Neighborhood predictors				
Intercept	8.44	203.15**	6.47	82.31**
Concentrated disadvantage	0.45	17.43**	0.46	2.72**
Residential stability	−0.01	−2.54*	−0.11	−0.10
Collective efficacy	−0.01	−4.30**	−0.13	−2.88**
Disorder	0.00	−0.13	0.63	3.40**
Variance explained	0.72		0.50	

*p < .05; **p < .01

assess this possibility we can control for the reports of disorder in the neighborhood by the same people that report as informants in collective efficacy. The results in Table 5.6 show that public disorder does predict violence but only in Stockholm, an interesting result considering the much higher levels of disorder in Chicago than Stockholm (Table 5.1) and the fascination in the US for "broken-windows" style policing. Nevertheless, the processes by which collective efficacy predicts violence and disadvantage predicts violence remain remarkably similar and unaffected by disorder.

Furthermore, we introduce a control for the burglary rate in the neighborhood as a way to control for common third causes of a crime that are conceptually distinct from violence. Although this is not a foolproof method and serves as a conservative test (collective efficacy has been shown to predict burglary rates in past research), it sheds some light on the robustness of the main results. Surprisingly, the pattern was virtually unchanged. Burglary was indeed a marker for increased violence rates in both Chicago and Stockholm, yet the strong predictive power of collective efficacy remained (t-ratios of −2.61 and −3.02, respectively). Whether we control for concurrent patterns of burglary or disorder in public spaces, then, the double combination of structural disadvantage and lower collective efficacy remains a potent predictor of variations in the log rate of violence in these two distinct settings.

Despite the similarity of patterns, however, it is not the case that we can explain away the violence differential between Chicago and Stockholm with measured neighborhood factors. When we add a city-level indicator variable for Chicago it is highly significant (t-ratio = 16.7), and the models in Tables 5.3–5.5 explain only a small fraction of the original city difference.

A multilevel analysis of violent victimization

Our results to this point have been restricted to a common outcome source – police incident records. We turn now to a very different strategy for assessing violence – reports of violent victimization by survey respondents. It is highly unlikely that the error sources are similar in these distinct methods of measuring violence. Therefore if we obtain similar or near-similar results we are on a stronger footing with respect to making inferences about the distribution of violence in relation to structural characteristics and social processes.

Capitalizing on the survey yields another, independent benefit. Namely, we now have recourse to a rich set of individual-level covariates of violence, including sex, marital status, homeownership, age, and length of residence. By conducting a multilevel analysis that simultaneously models individual- and neighborhood-level associations, we provide a different handle on possible selection bias. We therefore estimate a multilevel logistic regression where 1 indexes a violent victimization in the neighborhood in the past six months and 0 indicates no victimization. At the within-neighborhood level, we model $\eta_{ij} = \log \left[\varphi_{ij} / \left(1 - \varphi_{ij} \right) \right]$, the natural logarithm of the odds ratio. Specifically,

$$\left(\eta_{ij} \text{Violence} \right) = \beta_{0j} + \Sigma_{(q=1-9)} \beta_q X_{qij} + e_{ij},$$

where β_{0j} is the intercept; X_{qij} is the value of covariate q associated with respondent i in neighborhood j; and β_q is the partial effect of that covariate on the log odds of violence. The error term, e_{ij}, is the unique contribution of each individual, which is assumed to be independently and normally distributed with constant variance σ^2.

The basic between-neighborhood model is:

$$\beta_{0j} = \theta_{00} + \theta_{01} \text{ (concentrated disadvantage)} + \theta_{02} \text{ (stability)} + \theta_{03} \text{ (collective efficacy)} + U_{0j},$$

where θ_{00} is average neighborhood violence, and θ_{01} through θ_{03} are the regression coefficients of the effects of concentrated disadvantage, residential stability, and collective efficacy, respectively, on neighborhood violence. Because the person-level covariates at level 1 are centered about the sample means, β_{0j} serves as an indicator of the mean violence in a neighborhood *after* the effects of the nine covariates have been

Table 5.7. *Multilevel analysis of survey-reported violent victimization, Chicago and Stockholm*

Predictors	Victimization	
	Coeff.	t-ratio
Intercept	−2.42	−51.90**
Neighborhood level		
Collective efficacy	−0.19	−4.83**
Concentrated disadvantage	0.15	2.77**
Residential stability	−0.15	−2.65**
Person level		
Female	0.07	1.03
Married	−0.29	−3.82**
Minority	0.07	0.76
Homeowner	0.22	2.57*
Length residence	0.58	7.23**
Age	−0.01	−4.12**
Unemployed	0.24	3.13**
Education	0.01	0.12
Public housing	−0.55	−2.87**
Level 1 variance	0.88	
Level 2 variance	0.24	

Note: Pooled n = 9,121 persons and 541 neighborhoods.
*P < .05; **P < .01

controlled. U_{0j} is the neighborhood-level error term, assumed to be normally distributed with a variance of τ. Based on preliminary analysis, we constrain the person-level slopes to be constant across neighborhoods and do not estimate multilevel interactions. Our primary interest is the main effects on parameter variance across neighborhoods in violent victimization, controlling for individual-level differences.

The findings from the pooled city samples in Table 5.7 reveal that survey-reported violence is higher in neighborhoods characterized by neighborhood instability, disadvantage, and lower collective efficacy, controlling for nine observed characteristics of the person. The estimated association of collective efficacy with violence maintains when we control for public disorder. It also holds when we enter a dummy variable for Chicago, consistent with the official violence results reported above. Specifically, the "Chicago effect" is large (odds ratio = 5.3) but the coefficient for collective efficacy is literally unchanged (−.19) and remains highly significant. Disadvantage and stability, however, are rendered insignificant when city is controlled.

Conclusion

Although we recognize that our data are marked by important limitations, this is the first study of which we are aware that has systematically compared the neighborhood social order of violence in a cross-national, city-comparison framework. Our tentative conclusion is that neighborhood-level variations in ecological structure, informal social control, social disorder, and violence accord with theoretical predictions in a consistent fashion in two cities with a vastly different makeup and history. Indeed, Chicago and Stockholm could not be more different in fundamental respects, and our results in fact uncovered important differences in how social resources are ecologically distributed, as demonstrated most starkly in Figure 5.3. Stockholm, by stereotype and in fact, appears much more equal at the neighborhood level.

Yet the nature of the relationship between community social structure and violence is remarkably similar at the broader level. Because the same features account for violence in both cities, while the very same features are differentially allocated by neighborhood according to larger principles of societal social organization, we have in essence tapped into a partial explanation of the city differences in violence. It remains to be seen how well our framework stands up to future tests, and the data confirm that the "Chicago" effect remains large, possibly owing to cultural differences. Still, it appears that there is something fundamental and generic about community social order and violence that cuts across international boundaries.

REFERENCES

Bandura, Albert. 1997. *Self Efficacy: The Exercise of Control.* New York: W. H. Freeman.

Bellair, Paul. 1997. "Social Interaction and Community Crime: Examining the Importance of Neighbor Networks." *Criminology* 35: 677–703.

Bursik, Robert J. 1988. "Social Disorganization and Theories of Crime and Delinquency: Problems and Prospects." *Criminology* 26: 519–552.

Cohen, Lawrence, and Marcus Felson. 1979. "Social-Change and Crime Rate Trends: A Routine Activity Approach." *American Sociological Review* 44: 588–608.

Fischer, Claude. 1982. *To Dwell among Friends: Personal Networks in Town and City.* University of Chicago Press.

Granovetter, Mark. 1973. "The Strength of Weak Ties." *American Journal of Sociology* 78: 360–380.

Hedström, P., and R. Swedberg. 1998. *Social Mechanisms: An Analytical Approach to Social Theory.* Cambridge University Press.

Janowitz, Morris. 1975. "Sociological Theory and Social Control." *American Journal of Sociology* 81: 82–108.

Kasarda, John, and Morris Janowitz. 1974. "Community Attachment in Mass Society." *American Sociological Review* 39: 328–339.

Kornhauser, Ruth. 1978. *Social Sources of Delinquency.* University of Chicago Press.

Land, Kenneth, Patricia McCall, and Lawrence Cohen. 1990. "Structural Covariates of Homicide Rates: Are There Any Invariances Across Time and Space?" *American Journal of Sociology* 95: 922–963.

Martens, Peter. 1997. "Immigrants, Crime, and Criminal Justice in Sweden." In *Ethnicity, Crime, and Immigration: Comparative and Cross National Perspectives,* ed. M. Tonry. University of Chicago Press, 183–256.

Massey, Douglas, and Nancy Denton. 1993. *American Apartheid: Segregation and the Making of the Underclass.* Cambridge, MA: Harvard University Press.

Portes, Alejandro, and Julia Sensenbrenner. 1993. "Embeddedness and Immigration: Notes on the Social Determinants of Economic Action." *American Journal of Sociology* 98: 1320–1350.

Przeworski, Adam, and Henry Teune. 1970. *The Logic of Comparative Inquiry.* New York: Wiley.

Raudenbush, Stephen, and Robert J. Sampson. 1999. "'Ecometrics': Toward Science of Assessing Ecological Settings, with Application to the Systematic Social Observation of Neighborhoods." *Sociological Methodology* 29: 1–41.

Sampson, Robert J. 2006. "Collective Efficacy Theory: Lessons Learned and Directions for Future Inquiry." In *Taking Stock: The Status of Criminological Theory,* ed. Francis T. Cullen, John Paul Wright, and Kristie Blevins. New Brunswick: Transaction Publishers, 149–167.

Sampson, Robert J., and W. Byron Groves. 1989. "Community Structure and Crime: Testing Social-Disorganization Theory." *American Journal of Sociology* 94: 774–802.

Sampson, Robert J., and Janet L. Lauritsen. 1994. "Violent Victimization and Offending: Individual-, Situational-, and Community-Level Risk Factors." In *Understanding and Preventing Violence: Social Influences,* vol. III, ed. Albert J. Reiss Jr. and Jeffrey Roth. Washington DC: National Academy Press, 1–114.

Sampson, Robert J., and Steve Raudenbush. 1999. "Systematic Social Observation of Public Spaces: A New Look at Disorder in Urban Neighborhoods." *American Journal of Sociology* 105: 603–651.

Sampson, Robert J., Stephen Raudenbush, and Felton Earls. 1997. "Neighborhoods and Violent Crime: A Multilevel Study of Collective Efficacy." *Science* 277: 918–924.

Shaw, Clifford, and Henry McKay. 1942. *Juvenile Delinquency and Urban Areas.* University of Chicago Press.

Skogan, Wesley. 1990. *Disorder and Decline: Crime and the Spiral of Decay in American Neighborhoods.* Berkeley: University of California Press.

Wikström, Per-Olof. 1991. *Urban Crime, Criminals, and Victims.* New York: Springer-Verlag.

Wikström, Per-Olof, and Robert J. Sampson. 2003. "Social Mechanisms of Community Influences on Crime and Pathways in Criminality." In *Causes of Conduct Disorder and Serious Juvenile Delinquency*, ed. Ben Lahey, Terrie Moffitt, and Avshalom Caspi. New York: Guilford Press, 118–148.

Wilson, James Q., and George Kelling. 1982. "Broken Windows: The Police and Neighborhood Safety." *Atlantic Monthly* (March).

Wilson, William Julius. 1987. *The Truly Disadvantaged: The Inner City, the Underclass, and Public Policy*. University of Chicago Press.

6 Traditions of justice in war: the modern debate in historical perspective

Karma Nabulsi

This chapter will focus on the conflicting traditions of justice in war, traced through the seventeenth to the twentieth century, and is an introduction to the modern debate on justice in war in an historical context. When exploring recent frameworks and conceptualizations of particular types of modern war, such as "unequal war" and "asymmetrical war," scholars claim to be exploring new phenomena, and draw their evidence from very recent practices of the late twentieth and early twenty-first centuries (MacKenzie 2000, 3). They analyze suicide bombing, acts of terrorism by subnational and religious groups, and other acts that are seen as outside the bounds of traditional warfare. They also look at the responses to these tactics of modern war, such as the aerial bombardment that was practiced during the two Gulf wars, or in Afghanistan, or Falluja, or Gaza (Rodin 2004). But are these practices of war truly modern phenomena? I will demonstrate in this chapter that they are not. By setting out the historical context of the debates concerning the nature of war and concepts of justice in war in the nineteenth century and before, this essay will demonstrate the debate has always been about cases of asymmetrical and unequal wars. War, more often than not, is between an army and a people, not between two professional armies.

Just war is not only about the just causes for going to war in the first place; it is also about the just means of fighting it. Accordingly, the main rule to establish in being able to set standards of justice in war is those who may fight (Harries 2006, 225). In these wars, the issue is always: who is just? Or more importantly, who is the just warrior? Equally, who is the criminal? The different answers to this fundamental question actually come from differing philosophical conceptions of political justice. Indeed, the laws of war were created to get around this very problem. It removes itself from the highly political concept of *just war*, where one side is just and one not, and relies instead upon a modern concept of justice *in* war, which is designed to be ideologically neutral. This latter concept introduced a foundational principle on the modern laws of war: the distinction between combatant and noncombatant

(McMahan 2005, 1–6). Only by separating classes of those who could and those who could not fight (it was argued), could moderation be introduced into the act of war itself, and important restrictions and restraints introduced. Yet the whole dilemma of the laws of war is here – this issue about who these laws applied to was actually never solved, and remains a contested practice as well as concept.

But first we will explore the modern origins of this just war debate, especially the question as to how one can distinguish between just war and justice in war, given the conditions of unequal war and asymmetrical war, and from there we will set out the ideology of justice in war in such conditions. So we begin with Hugo Grotius, who is answered by Jean-Jacques Rousseau – who associates Thomas Hobbes' vision of war with that of Grotius. We begin in the seventeenth century and go into the eighteenth with Rousseau's response, before coming to the modern debate in the late nineteenth century between just war and justice in war, and the formation of the modern laws of war, the great attempt to regulate war with the Hague treaties 1899 and 1907 and Geneva Conventions of 1949.

Grotius and the nature of war

Much like Hobbes' *Leviathan*, the ambition of Grotius' *De Jure Belli ac Pacis* can be found in its title. Grotius' goal was not to establish whether there could be rules that governed war and peace, but what those rules were. He proceeded by first defining war as broadly as possible, in order to include a comprehensive range of permissible activity within the scope of its laws:

In treating of the rights of war, the first point, that which we have to consider, is, what is war, which is the subject of our enquiry, and what is the right, which we seek to establish … war is the state of contending parties, considered as such. This definition, by its general extent, comprises those wars of every description, that will form the subject of the present treatise. (Grotius [1625] 1990, 41)

He also created a system of law which could offer bilateral rights to both belligerents in war, an additional principle to traditional *jus ad bellum*. Writers on the laws of war before Grotius had argued that either there could be bilateral rights in war (that is, each belligerent could have an equal right to make war on the other), or there was only one just party. Grotius, unsurprisingly, took a position in between these two, and suggested an entirely new legal approach. He argued that although sovereigns could *not* have bilateral rights, their subordinates *could*, so that belligerents in the field of battle could both be lawful and just. This was put forward as a custom of war, sourced in a type of contractual *jus gentium*. It allowed Grotius to put forward a theory that claimed states had tacitly agreed that, irrespective of the objective justice of their claims, their representatives in battle (commanders and soldiers) could be recognized as having mutual and legitimate rights against each other in war.

Grotius' method of analysis was driven by both principal and subsidiary purposes. The principal goal was to counter what he believed were the two established theories of war and peace, thus advancing his own system in their place. He claimed the alternate philosophies of war and peace were both too excessive and too absolute in the extent and limits they sought to place upon war. In his famous statement in the introduction to his book on the laws of war and peace, the *Prolegomena*, Grotius defined his philosophy as a response to the problems encountered in each extreme view:

Confronted with such utter ruthlessness, many men who are the very furthest from being bad men, have come to a point of forbidding all use of arms to the Christian, whose rule of conduct above everything else comprises the duty of loving all men. To this opinion sometimes John Ferus and my fellow countryman Erasmus seem to incline, men who have the utmost devotion to peace in both Church and State; both their purpose, as I take it, is, when things have gone in one direction, to force them in the opposite direction, as we are accustomed to do, that they may come back to a true middle ground. But the very effort at pressing too hard in the opposite direction is often so far from being helpful that it does harm, because in such arguments the detection of what is extreme is easy, and results in weakening the other statements which are well within the bounds of truth. *For both extremes therefore a remedy must be found, that men may not believe either that nothing is allowable, or that everything is.* (Grotius [1625] 1990, 21; emphasis added).

His secondary purpose was to introduce a concept of "moderation" into the practice of warfare. His appeal for the application of this virtue formed several chapter headings of Book III of *De Jure Belli et Pacis*, which was concerned chiefly with the customs and practices of war. The manner in which Grotius introduced the notion of *temperamenta* was typical. After listing a particularly brutal range of customs which he described as acceptable under various types of law, he began, "I must retrace my steps, and must deprive those who wage war of nearly all the privileges which I seem to grant them" (Grotius [1625] 1990, 76). Indeed, his system of introducing improvement was to illustrate the possibility and limits of change. His method of seeking moderation, *temperamenta*, was crucial, and laid a foundational stone for the nineteenth-century Grotian tradition of the laws of war. Although it is the last phrase in his quotation about finding the middle way that is most remembered, it was his method of introducing change stated earlier that was much more consequential: the search for a *media res* between "both extremes" that he believed so disastrous.

Here Grotius develops a concept, which was aptly captured in Hirschman's notions of perversity and jeopardy, which posits the idea that any substantive change is dangerous, because it either has the reverse effect to that intended or endangers the positive values already achieved, some "previous, precious accomplishment." (This concept in practice will also be illustrated in more depth later by an example of its development in the late nineteenth century). Further, Grotius maintained this method of seeking change by "pressing too hard in the opposite direction," actually undermining various customs which ought to be maintained; this amounted to a belief on his part that the more utilitarian and harsh practices of war had a recognized place *within* the law.

Accordingly, Grotius' system defined all customs and practices as legitimate in wartime, but advanced a more normative claim to moderate these customs. Both the normative claim and the customary practices could, according to Grotius, be sourced from divine law, natural law, the law of nations, or volitional law. His method in establishing a theory using this eclectic procedure represented his unique contribution to the foundations of a new school of thought on war. There are five features of the Grotian system that are particularly worthy of mention. The first of these concerns his way of defining customary practices of war, searching for illustrations of these customs in ancient history and examples from his own century. He explained the reasons for choosing this procedure:

History in relation to our subject is useful in two ways; it supplies both illustrations and judgements. The illustrations have greater weight in proportion as they are taken from better times and better peoples. Thus we have preferred ancient examples, Greek and Roman, to the rest. And judgements are not to be slighted, especially when they are in agreement with one another; for by such statements the existence of the laws of nature, as we have said, is in a measure proved, *and by no other means, in fact, is it possible to establish the law of nations.* (Grotius [1625] 1990, 30; emphasis added)

His selection at first may appear simply arbitrary; on a complete reading of his work, however, it is apparent that the examples used are purposely and selectively chosen. Among the Romans he had a particular devotion to Livy, Machiavelli's favored promoter of savage war.

The second theoretical feature concerned the artificial contrivance Grotius deemed necessary to achieve his desired *media res*. As he selected an enormous collection of brutal practices of war, a structural imbalance developed within his system. As the architectural pillar supporting barbaric practices at one end of his scale was so heavily loaded, its weight destabilized the more normative pillar which he had constructed to embody the other end, thus abandoning a true middle ground. The hypothetical *media res* was not merely conjectural, it was not even in the middle. Accordingly, Grotius' work drew more heavily from the conservative view of history than the progressive in constructing this ersatz "middle."

A third feature was the moral relativism in Grotius' vision of war which, along with the ideological relativism set out earlier, remained unresolved both in his work and in tradition. This was a conflict between procedural and substantive conceptions of pluralism. The normative pillar, which held up one end of Grotius' theoretical edifice, claimed to need the more "realist" positivist pillar in order to constitute a balanced structure. This was perceived as the only means of finding the just route: the gate at the center of Grotius' edifice through which one had to pass in order to navigate a true middle path between the absolutist claims of any single ideology. Yet the normative pillar, by its nature, consisted of moral claims that established the absolute virtue of specific values and principles, such as the justness of choosing such a middle path. Likewise the positivist pillar claimed that the theoretical structure must encompass both extremes of the discourse on war. Yet the pluralistic procedures took precedence over the pluralistic substance. These discourses embodied a mechanism which allowed different moral visions to coexist, making adherence to any one ethical claim near impossible.

The fourth feature lay in his declared attempt to make a moral claim for moderation in warfare, using the techniques of inclusivity. The contradiction between making a moral claim, based on Christian law, the law of nature, or any other law, while simultaneously maintaining the ability to detach from any ethical scheme whatsoever, created irreconcilable tensions. Yet the uniqueness of this approach had to do with Grotius' ability to cite ethical claims within the same system (and alongside others) that denied other moral claims; these precepts could equally be claimed by the humanitarian, "normative" Grotian tradition of the more "realist" Grotian lawyers.

Finally, a notable feature in Grotius' theory of moderation in war was his audience. The appeal for moderation was made specifically to rulers and princes in authority. His entire argument rested on the fact that only by writing for, and about, power and powerful leaders, could incremental change be brought about. By sustaining, and indeed constructing, legitimizing arguments which endorsed rulers' actions, the entire body of the work assumed an asymmetrical character, seeming to offer an endless range of rights for rulers, and mere obligations for subjects and slaves.

Indeed this was the essence of the Grotian legacy to the founding of the laws of war. At the heart of the Grotian system was an essential dichotomy between the rights of states and armies on the one hand, and the position of ordinary members of society on the other. Although he devoted some effort to justifying private wars, the thrust of Grotius' writings was to concentrate the legitimate recourse to war in public hands. Within these limits, however, states and armies were given an open field to visit destruction and mayhem upon each other; these actions were justified by the hallowed principles of practice and custom. On the other side of the equation lay the hapless subjects of their respective states, condemned to wallow in the private sphere, enjoying no political or civic rights either in war or in peace, and with the peculiar formulation of Grotian charity as their only hope for salvation. Between the public sphere of the state and the private realm of the subject, there was no question in Grotius' mind as to which enjoyed the primary position. Sown by Grotius, the seeds of the distinction between the rights of states and armies and the subordinate position of civilians – expressed in the legal dichotomy between lawful and unlawful combatant – germinated in the later nineteenth century and remains with us today.

Rousseau and the nature of asymmetrical war

In his opening paragraphs of *Principes du Droit de la Guerre*, Rousseau descends upon Grotius' and Hobbes' philosophies of war with a remarkable literary force. After attacking their methods, he goes on to address their motives in equally scathing terms:

What human soul would not be sickened by such sad scenes? But one is no longer considered a man if one pleads the cause of humanity. Justice and truth must be bent in the interests of the strongest. That is now the rule. Since the poor cannot provide pensions or employment, since they do not grant tenure or endow university chairs, why should we protect them? (Rousseau 1964, vol. II, 602)

Finally he assaults the principles upon which their version of the nature of war is based. His aim is not only to destroy their logic, demonstrate the poverty of their principles, or illustrate the viciousness of the ethics of the old world, but also to reveal his own system with as much lucidity as possible. Only by dramatically crushing the opposition could he clear the way for an entirely new formulation. Within his system was a way to guide relations between states with radically different political structures. Accordingly, he needed to juxtapose the new world of his virtuous republic with the old world of power politics, brute force, and conquest, and in so doing demonstrate that there was no fatality about the latter phenomena. Unequal wars of occupation did not have to be endured with stoic resignation, but could (and in fact needed to) be met with a firm collective response by the citizenry.

Rousseau illustrates the nature of war by defining it in a wholly original way. As he repeatedly professed in *Principes*, and went on to argue in *Du Contrat Social* as well, there is a political nature to both just and unjust war. In his *Principes*, he argues that in fact war arises directly from Hobbes' unjust "peaceful" institutions:

> For a moment let us put these ideas in opposition to the horrible system of Hobbes. We will find, contrary to his absurd doctrine, that far from the state of war being natural to man, war is born out of peace, or at least out of the precautions men have taken to assure themselves of peace. (Rousseau 1960, vol. II, 610)

He next focuses his attack on Grotius' claims in *De Jure Belli et Pacis*. Grotius' world of unjust war endorses three principles that Rousseau rejects: private war, conquest, and the rights that naturally accrue to conquest – in short, slavery and the principle of might is right. Chapter 3 of *Du Contrat Social* is actually entitled "The Right of the Strongest." He explains, "'the right of the strongest,' a right that apparently seems to be ironic, is in reality an established principle," and asks, rhetorically, "But will no one ever explain to us this phrase?" Rousseau argues that force is only a "physical power, and I cannot see what morality can result by its effects. To yield to force is a necessity and not an act of will; at most it is prudence." He concludes, "In what sense can it become a duty? ... This so-called right can only produce a bewildering nonsense" (Rousseau 1960, vol. II, 354). In his next chapter on slavery he points the finger more directly:

> Grotius and the others claim to find another justification in war for the alleged right of slavery. According to them, the victor's having the right to kill the vanquished implies that the vanquished has the right to purchase his life at the expense of his liberty; a convention thought to be the more legitimate because it proves profitable to both parties. But it is clear that the so-called right to kill the vanquished cannot be derived from the state of war ... The right of conquest has no other foundation than the law of the stronger. And if war gives the conqueror no right to massacre a conquered people, no such right can be invoked to justify their enslavement ... Hence far from the victor having acquired some further authority besides that of force over the vanquished, the state of war between them continues; their mutual relations is the effect of war, and the

continuation of the rights of war implies the absence of a treaty of peace. A convention has been made, but that convention, far from ending the state of war presupposed its continuation. (Rousseau 1960, vol. II, 356–357)

Hence unjust war, in his definition, emanated from the "first world" of empire and inequality – the worlds inhabited by Hobbes and Grotius and all those who subscribed to their "desolate philosophies." Just war, as derived from the true principles of the nature of man, was a war fought not by the professional soldiers in the pay of kings, but by citizens of the republic, who rallied to its aid in times of crisis. Rousseau explained the difference between the two in no uncertain terms in his advice to Poland: "Regular troops, the plague and depopulators of Europe, are good for only two purposes, to attack and conquer neighbours, or to shackle and enslave Citizens." He then added, "I know that the state should not remain without defenders; but its true defenders are its members. Each citizen ought to be a soldier by duty, none by profession" (Rousseau 1960, vol. II, 1014).

An essential feature of his paradigm, however, is the fact that this republic was not utopian. Unlike the Abbé St. Pierre's *Projet*, Rousseau did not believe that total peace was always possible, because within his system these two worlds could coexist simultaneously. A natural consequence of this multidimensional vision was that once these two worlds were juxtaposed, wars coming from the old world were unjust wars of conquest, while wars from the new world were just wars of self-defense. Here, in a recommendation to the Polish people on how to preserve their sovereignty, he juxtaposed the old world with their potential new one to illustrate this point:

To look for a means of guaranteeing yourselves against the will of a neighbour stronger than you is to seek a chimera. It would be of an even greater one to try and make conquests and to acquire offensive force; it is incompatible with the form of your government. Whoever wants to be free ought not to want to be a conqueror. (Rousseau 1960, vol. II, 1013)

In summary, Rousseau's perception of the nature of war was underpinned by his belief in its political nature. War, he believed, was the result of a particular type of government. He expressly rejected any justification for wars of conquest, but did not imagine they might be banned from existence; rather they would cease only when corrupt empires transformed themselves into virtuous republics (and he had no illusions about the time this might take). Even so, his belief that republics were less aggressive toward their neighbors was heavily qualified as he noted the ability of unprincipled leaders to pervert or confuse the general will.

Even more ingeniously, as his system allowed for the past and the future to coexist, he could suggest policies for the republic, and rules which could guide relations between states during different stages of their development, thus allowing for prescriptions to proto-republics such as Poland. Central to this view was that citizens could not be detached from the defense of the state. A just war of self-defense was by its nature a war in which the state was defended by the sovereign citizens, who acted in the very name of public authority under such circumstances. Hence unequal war only occurs if there is an absence of common rules in the international arena of justice and fairness. Commonly used to describe a strategic reality, unequal war for Rousseau meant inadequate laws to deal with the problems that were created by an unjust balance of power.

The modern laws of war from 1874 to 1949

By 1874 the European powers had agreed upon two international conventions, the Geneva Convention on Prisoners of War of 1864, inspired by Henri Dunant's book, *Un Souvenir de Solférino*, an eyewitness account of extreme suffering endured by wounded soldiers on the field during the Austro-Italian war, and the St. Petersburg Declaration of 1868, which contained the famous statement of the principle that the "only legitimate object which States should endeavour to accomplish during war is to weaken the forces of the enemy state" (Roberts and Guelff 1989, 30–31). Still unresolved were the lawful practices of armies on land, and the difficulties these caused, notably the distinction between combatant and noncombatant and the rights and duties of occupying powers and occupied inhabitants (Graber 1949, 13–36). The one existing national codification, the Lieber Code, introduced a set of legal guidelines at the time of the Civil War in the United States, and provided the basis for a draft text presented to the various delegations which gathered at Brussels in the summer of 1874 ("Actes" 1879–1880, 15).

The Brussels conference took place against the express wishes of Bismarck, and in origin was a scheme devised by the heads of two royal families. From European capitals' archives it is clear that very few diplomats wanted it to take place at all. The reason for their reluctance was the following. Lesser powers, with Britain and France on their side, had no ambition to see the Prussian army's occupation practices of 1870–1871 codified into international law, while even Bismarck could see little advantage in such a development. German war ambitions were, in fact, more suited to an uncodified customary "might is right" philosophy, which the Chancellor had no desire to see challenged in a public arena. The smaller powers' fears were confirmed by the Russian draft of the convention circulated to delegates in the summer of 1874. The legal norms proposed so obviously favored occupying forces that this text became known in European ministries as "The Code of Conquest" (PRO, Foreign Office Archives 1874, FO83/481).

It was the Franco-Prussian war of 1870 that fundamentally confirmed the tenet that force equalled law, and so disturbed the French diplomats cited above, and which illustrated that the right of conquest was still a legitimate feature of the international system. International law was seen as an exclusive tool of states, and indeed states were regarded as the only recognized actors in the international system. But the relationship among these states was clearly ordered: empires remained the dominant political norm, and the hierarchical role they enjoyed within the Concert of Europe meant that their interests were always given priority. This strictly hierarchical conception of international society was also in evidence during negotiations, where there was no equality in the decision-making process among the European states invited – lesser powers had little real negotiating ability. Lambermont, the Belgian host, noted how all the diplomats invited were terrified about "compromising" themselves with the great powers, but nonetheless could not be absent from the conference:

Saturday, Sunday and Monday I successively received all the delegations. Except for the Russians and the Germans ... all are vague, all perplexed, all desperate not to compromise themselves. (Ministry of Foreign Affairs Archives, Brussels, Dossier B.7484)

In the end, the Brussels conference broke up after a month of debates without any clear agreement, except for a pretty useless draft "Brussels Declaration." The next set of negotiations on the laws of war took place at the Hague in the summer of 1899. The international atmosphere was radically different (although the underlying fissures remained). The Hague was one of a series of grand international "peace" treaties envisioned by diplomats and politicians from various corners of the world to resolve such vexing issues as world disarmament and international arbitration. There were also several strands of broadly divergent political ideologies which gave support to the general notions of disarmament and peace; the peace internationalists, organizations promoting the economic values of free trade, institutes such as the Nobel Institute, which established a peace prize in 1897, and the more rarefied Institute of International Law of 1873.

As at Brussels, it was the Russian emperor who gave the impetus for the conferences. However, this time it was the growing realization of the dangers of Europe's rapid over-militarization that pushed statesmen to the table, rather than the desire to regulate the manner in which wars were fought. A convention entitled "The Laws and Customs of War on Land" (known as the Hague Regulations) emerged from the first round. It omitted the majority of troublesome issues which wrecked the Brussels conference of 1874 (Breucker 1974, 1–15).

The period between the Hague conferences and the Geneva Conventions in 1949 saw an acceleration of the pace in international legal codification. The 1929 Geneva Convention on Prisoners of War constituted a great advance from the previous regulations, but still failed to raise the question of civilians who resisted occupation and whether they should be granted the privileges of belligerency (POW status). Equally, the efforts in the 1930s of the International Committee of the Red Cross (ICRC) to persuade the major powers to sign a convention protecting civilians proved fruitless (McCoubray 1990, 144). However, two other international treaties of the era also bore indirectly on the laws of war: the Covenant of the League of Nations and the Kellogg-Briand Pact (1928). Both were informed by the liberal internationalist view that war could be eradicated through enlightened diplomacy and collective action (Draper 1972). Also directly influencing the Geneva negotiations in 1949 were the various national and international positions on war crimes during and after World War II, in particular the Nuremberg Trials of 1946, and the Universal Declaration of Human Rights of 1948 (see Paulson 1975). Indeed, one of the most important legal precedents was the 1942 "London Declaration of War Crimes," issued at the height of the war by the Allies, which proclaimed hostage-taking and other customary occupying army practices a war crime. This gave an enormous impetus to states to create a legal convention that would actually reflect this politically inspired stance ("Declaration of War Crimes, adopted by the Inter-Allied Conference at St. James's Palace on January 13, 1942," in Schwarzenberger 1943, 140).

A final set of negotiations resulted in the four Geneva Conventions of 1949, which covered different aspects of the limitations on war. Two of these contained issues which addressed the distinction between lawful and unlawful combatant: the Prisoners of War Convention, and the Civilians Convention, the latter being related to individuals who came under military occupation. However, although comprehensive, these conventions still did not provide a clear solution to the central problem of the distinguishing between lawful and unlawful combatant.

The legal controversy

The challenge of formulating a distinction between lawful and unlawful combatant drove most aspects of the legal controversy at conferences between 1874 and 1949.

The first problem was the definition of occupation: the precise conditions necessary for its legal commencement. For invading armies, the sooner an overrun territory was declared occupied, the more rapidly they were recognized as occupying powers, so for them, simply tacking a poster to a tree was sufficient to declare that a military occupation had begun in that area. It was thus the only condition needed by an invading army to require the complete passivity of the population (Birkhimer 1892, 3). Others, however, believed a large number of conditions had to be met; not only did the local population first have to be completely subdued, but also for an occupation to continue, it needed to be maintained by force. The object of stipulating such exacting conditions was tactical: the further a state of occupation could be delayed, the longer citizens had a right to bear arms in defense of the country.

The second problem was the question of legitimate combatants. In the traditional customs of war, only professional soldiers were granted belligerent status. Accordingly, all civilians who participated in hostilities were considered outlaws, and were to be "delivered to justice" ("Actes" 1879–1880, 223–224, 302). Those contesting this legal norm argued that all citizens who bore arms for the nation were legitimate combatants (Clarke et al. 1989, 11). In the debates for the Convention on Prisoners of War, small countries sought to protect armed defenders – citizen militia and others – from reprisals if captured (as professional soldiers already were). A further debate centered on the concept of levée en masse. The larger powers sought to have the conditions for a legitimate uprising restricted in several ways, above all by requiring its necessary organization under military command. It was also to be limited both temporally and spatially, in that it was to be launched only at the moment of an invasion, and occur only in territories not yet subjected to occupation (Meyrowitz 1966, 144).

Finally there was the question of permitted army methods in occupied territories, such as reprisals, levies, and requisitions. The first of these, reprisals, was a customary method used by armies to punish illegal acts by the inhabitants of occupied territories. There were three views. The first argued for the rights of armies and wanted to maintain and consolidate the practice; second were those who campaigned for the rights of resistance and advocated its complete abolition; and finally, those who saw themselves as introducing a degree of "humanity in warfare" desired to mitigate the practice of reprisals (Kalshoven 1971).

Conceptions of justice, emerging from distinct traditions of war

All of the legal controversies were driven by the problem of distinguishing between who was a lawful fighter in wartime, and who was not granted this privileged status. The challenge of maintaining this distinction between classes of those who could fight arose in a particular historical and political context in the nineteenth and twentieth centuries. It also emerged under the specific circumstances of this period of time in Europe, which was replete with wars of foreign rule, invasion, and occupation. It was from this crucible that the three distinct articulations of war emerged; hence, the recurrence of such themes as conquest, resistance, obedience, patriotism, sovereignty, and independence in their ideological discourse. These three philosophical traditions of war also held a particular and exclusive view of what political justice ought to consist of. The final part of this essay will outline the three traditions of conceptions of justice, and demonstrate how the debate set out between the positions of Rousseau, Hobbes, and Grotius continued up through the nineteenth and twentieth centuries (Nabulsi 1999).

The martial conception of justice

The term "martialism" defines an ideology which glorified war and military conquest, and quite simply can be defined as the view that war is both the supreme instrument and the ultimate realization of all human endeavor. It was a doctrine which manifested itself most emphatically in the practices of conquest and foreign rule. Indeed, it could be said that martialism constituted the political philosophy of occupying armies. In this sense, its precepts were entirely favorable to the practices of occupation, and strongly hostile to all manifestations of resistance to its moral and political authority. For those who advanced this position, war was seen as natural, and could not (and should not) be codified. At the conferences on the laws of war, various proponents of this ideology set forth this position, and in doing so illustrated the martialist conception of justice, as well as their paradigm and understanding of unequal war.

The official Prussian position on war during the mid- and late nineteenth century represented martial ideology in full. Their response to their own legal expert Bluntschli was paradigmatic. Bluntschli had attempted to write a manual on the laws of war, involving many other international lawyers, but his draft reflected the more conservative view on war in Europe. Major von Hartmann wrote the official reply of the Prussian Ministry of War to Bluntschli's proposal for a "Codification of the Laws of War" of 1880, entitled *Military Necessities and Humanity*. "The expression 'civilised warfare,' used by Bluntschli, seems hardly intelligible; for war destroys this very equilibrium ... If military authority recognises duties it is because it imposes them upon itself in full sovereignty. It will never consider itself subject to outside compulsion. Absolute military action in time of war is an indispensable condition of military success" (Hartmann 1877–1878, 123). But there was worse in store for Bluntschli. Von Moltke, the military hero of Prussia, used the opportunity to compose his now infamous exposition on war and peace: "Perpetual peace," he wrote to Bluntschli, "is a dream, and it is not even a beautiful dream: war forms part of the universal order constituted by God. In war are displayed the most noble virtues, courage and abnegation, fidelity to duty, and the spirit of sacrifice which will hazard life itself; without war humanity would sink into materialism" (Andler 1913, 23).

Some British jurists agreed with this conservative view held by Prussia, and advanced a notion of political justice that claimed almost total rights for the occupying power over the civilian population. Halleck's manual of war, in 1871, took this position. Occupied civilians were "virtually in the condition of prisoners of war on parole. No word of honour has been given, but it was implied; for only on that condition would the conqueror have relinquished the *extreme right of war which he held over their lives*" (Halleck 1871, 386; emphasis added).

In 1949, at the negotiations at Geneva that would create the four Geneva Conventions, the British War Office Delegate William Gardner continued in this tradition. He attempted to have the practice of hostage-taking preserved behind the back of his own delegation who were seeking to ban it absolutely, and in spite of the fact that his own government had loudly and publicly proclaimed this practice a war crime a few years earlier. In 1941, at the Allies conference in London, President Roosevelt had declared that the "practice of executing scores of hostages in reprisals for isolated attacks ... revolts a world already inured to sufferings and brutality" (Schwarzenberger 1943, 140). Churchill had added, "the cold blooded executions of innocent people will only recoil upon the savages who order and execute them ... the atrocities in Poland, Yugoslavia, in Norway, in Holland, in Belgium, and above all behind the German Fronts in Russia surpass anything ... Retribution for these crimes must henceforward take its place among the major purposes of the war" (Schwarzenberger 1943, 142). Four days after his secret meeting with the ICRC official, which was unsuccessful, Gardner publicly set out this position with the rest of the delegation: "The foundation on which to rest in argument was that the Occupying Power must have certain powers which went beyond the normal peacetime powers of the Government, for example, the right to take hostages and the right to destroy property as a reprisal" (PRO FCO 369/4150). For the martialist, all activity by civilian population was seen as a crime, even passive resistance. In 1949, the War Office directed the position at the international conference to be, "[The] Occupying Power must have powers to take stern measures against passive resistance" (PRO FCO 369/4156).

The Grotian conception of justice

The Grotian tradition of justice developed in a particular manner from 1874 to 1949 in the context of the framing of the laws of war. It was the most dominant tradition, in that its core principles lay at the heart of the very project of the laws of war. Although Hugo Grotius devoted some effort to justifying private wars, the thrust of his writings was to concentrate the legitimate recourse to war in public hands. This was the essence of the Grotius' legacy to the founding of the laws of war. At the heart of the Grotian legal system on war was an essential dichotomy between the rights of states and armies on the one hand, and the position of ordinary members of society on the other. Important values were law, order, power, and sovereignty of the state. The Grotian tradition was thus "index-linked" to legitimate power. Accordingly, absolutely central to the Grotian position was the ambition to limit the rights of belligerency to a particular class of participant (the soldier), and to exclude all others from the right to become actively involved in it, no matter if they were being invaded.

Keeping the concept of *jus ad bellum* theoretically separate from that of *jus in bello* made it easier to establish and maintain a legal parity between belligerent parties. An important principle in the Grotian ideology was a pragmatic rule upholding the equality of belligerents: "International law has no alternative but to accept war, independently of the justice of its origin, as a relation which the parties to it may set up if they choose, and to busy itself only in regulating the effects of the relation. Hence both parties to every war are regarded as being in an identical legal position, and consequently possessed of equal rights" (Holland 1876, 5–7).

The military rulebook at the time of the Hague conference in 1899 reflected this position: "The right of the non-combatant population to protection for their persons and property, the limits and extent of which right we have hitherto been discussing, necessarily involves on the part of those who have obtained this protection on the faith of their being non-combatant a corresponding duty of abstaining from all further hostilities against the invaders" (Wheaton 1889, 469).

The Russian delegate at Brussels in 1874 explained, when advancing his draft treaty: "It has been said that the Russian project paralyses the rights of defense. This reproach is not founded ... But war has changed its nature. It was once a sort of drama where strength and personal courage played a great role. Today, individuality has been replaced by a formidable machine which genius and science has put into motion. Therefore it is our imperative duty to regulate inspirations such as patriotism ... The great explosions of patriotism that occurred at the start of our century in several countries cannot be reproduced today" ("Actes" 1879–1880, 132).

In order to underscore this normative conception of civilian passivity, Grotian jurists attempted to assert that certain historic forms of resistance by civilians were imaginary. At the Geneva 1949 conference, for example, the existence of the *levée en masse* was dismissed out of hand by the representative of the ICRC, even though the facts on the ground proved otherwise, and were well documented in archives and by eyewitnesses and participants throughout the nineteenth century in Europe. The method was to introduce state practice only, and to deny the existence of resistance. This was, of course, much harder in 1949, after the Second World War, and the various uprisings throughout it, such as in Warsaw.

The republican conception of political justice

Wars of empire and of foreign occupation occurred in Europe throughout the nineteenth and twentieth centuries, and it was the republican response to this predicament that directed the trajectory and development of the tradition's ideology. The tradition emerged as a direct result of the quest for independence, and developed subsequently into a distinct republican doctrine of patriotism. Its main features were liberty and equality, individual and national self-reliance, patriotism and public-spiritedness (and the importance of education to arouse these virtues), and a notion of just war combined with justice in war.

"There can be no patriotism without liberty, no liberty without virtue, no virtue without citizens. You will have all these if you train citizens; without doing so, you will have only wicked slaves, from the rulers of the State downwards. To form citizens is not the work of a day; and in order to have men it is necessary to educate them when they are children" (Rousseau 1960, vol. II, 1054).

For republicans, defense by civilians and citizens to an invasion and occupation was always legitimate. Indeed, in republican ideology, there was the duty to disobey the occupying power, and the duty to resist the invasion and occupation. For the republican conception of political justice in war, the cardinal precept was the legitimacy of civilian defense. Unlike the Grotian and martial traditions, which clearly saw military occupation as the end of formal war and the collapse of legitimate authority of the occupied state, republicans saw military occupation as a continuation of the state of war. Equally important for republicans was that although the formal institutions of their state may have collapsed through the actions of the invading army, the source of their government's legitimacy came from the people. Therefore, the locus of authority and sovereignty reverted to the individual and collective inhabitants of that state, the sovereign citizens, who became its representatives and agents during its suspension.

From the nineteenth century onward, smaller countries consistently asserted that there was no legal obligation of obedience to the occupying power, arguing that citizens' resistance to occupation was a "sacred duty." By 1949 some countries reinterpreted their domestic law to reflect this view. At two important postwar trials in the Netherlands in 1946, a judge ruled that the Hague Conventions did not create legal obligations in conscience binding on the inhabitants. The Dutch Court of Cassation ruled that resistance was a "permissible weapon to use against the occupant." And Yugoslavia's postwar constitution specifically prohibited the acceptance of foreign occupation by the officials or the population.

Thus, for republicans, there were two types of crime in war. The first was that invasion and aggression itself was criminal. This view was reflected in the development of early twentieth-century international law, such as the Kellogg-Briand Pact. For republicans, unlike the Grotian legal position, law came before war, not after it. At the negotiations at Geneva in 1949, the Danish delegation argued that "all States agreed that wars of aggression constituted an international crime, and it was therefore obvious that resistance by the civilian population should in such a case be considered as an act of legitimate defence" (*Final Record* 1949, vol. II, A, 252).

The second conception for republicans emerged from their broader notion of political justice: war crimes are acts by an invading or occupying army against its defenders. At Brussels in 1874, the Greek delegate stated the obvious: "one can punish the population if it is not considered as a belligerent, but if we accept this status then they are in a condition of legal resistance" ("Actes" 1879–1880, 101). There was the attempt, equally, by republicans to resist the codification of reprisals into treaty law. The Belgian representative Lambermont argued this at the first conference on the laws of war in Brussels in 1874: "There are some things done in wartime that will always be done, and this one must accept. But it is proposed here to convert them in law, into positive prescriptions, and international ones at that. If the citizens are to be taken to the execution posts for having attempted to defend their country at the peril of their lives, they should not have to find, inscribed on the post at the foot of which they are to be shot, a treaty signed by their own government that has condemned them to death in advance" (Archives Belgium, Dossier B.7484).

Conclusion

Throughout the modern era, of which this essay traces just a fraction of a rich debate, there has always been a sharply contested concept about the nature of war, and the just causes for engaging in it. Equally, the notions of asymmetrical and unequal wars were predominant concerns of many of the key philosophers, legal jurists, and advocates in the past, just as they are today (Rodin 2006, 154). Wars have rarely been the chessboard rule-bound games set on a playing field as described by military theorists and strategists that the rules were intended to codify. The rules introducing humanity into warfare in the late nineteenth century through the early treaties on the laws of war had consistently served the already stronger party of an invading state in unequal wars. Through the gradual increase of introducing humanity into warfare by means of international humanitarian law over the last half of the twentieth century, this imbalance has been, at least partially, addressed (Chesterman 2001, 14). Sadly, it may go some way toward illustrating why the stronger parties in various current conflicts refuse to apply these legal constraints to themselves.

REFERENCES

"Actes de la Conférence Réunie à Bruxelles, du 27 juillet au 27 août 1874, pour régler les lois et les coutumes de la guerre." *Nouveau Recueil Général de Traités*, 2nd series, vol. IV (1879–1880).
Andler, Charles. 1913. *Frightfulness in Theory and Practice*. London: Fisher Unwin.
Birkhimer, W. 1892. *Military Government and Martial Law*. Boston: J.J. Chapman.
Breucker, J. de. 1974. "La déclaration de Bruxelles de 1874." *Chroniques de Politique Étrangère* 27 (1).

Chesterman, Simon. 2001. *Just War or Just Peace?* Oxford University Press.

Clarke, M., T. Glynn, and A. Rogers. 1989. "Combatants and Prisoner of War Status." In *Armed Conflict and the New Law*, ed. Michael Meyer. London: British Institute of International and Comparative Law, 1–35.

Draper, Gerald. 1972. "The Ethical and Juridical Status of Constraints in War." *Military Law and Law of War Review* 55 (January): 169–185.

Final Record of the Diplomatic Conference of Geneva of 1949. Berne: Federal Political Department (1949).

Graber, Doris. 1949. *The Development of the Law of Belligerent Occupation*. New York: Columbia University Press.

Grotius, Hugo. [1625] 1990. *De Jure Belli ac Pacis*, trans. A. Campbell. London: Hyperion Press.

Halleck, H. W. 1871. *International Law or Rules Regulating the Intercourse of States in Peace and War*. New York: D. Van Nostrand.

Harries, Richard. 2006. "Application of Just War Criteria in the Period 1959–89." In *The Ethics of War: Shared Problems in Different Traditions*, ed. R. Sorabji and D. Rodin. London: Ashgate, 222–234.

Hartmann, J. von. 1877–1878. "Militärische Notwendigkeit und Humanität" [Military Necessities and Humanity]. *Deutsche Rundschau* 13.

Holland, T. E. 1876. "A Lecture on the Brussels Conference of 1874, and Other Diplomatic Attempts to Mitigate the Rigours of Warfare." In *Lectures 1874–84*. Oxford University Press.

Kalshoven, Frits. 1971. *Belligerent Reprisals*. Leyden: Sijthoff.

McCoubray, M. 1990. *International Humanitarian Law: The Regulation of Armed Conflicts*. Aldershot: Dartmouth Publishing.

MacKenzie, K. 2000. "The Revenge of the Melians: Asymmetrical Threats." MacNair Paper 62. Washington DC: National Defense University Press.

McMahan, Jeff. 2005. "Just Cause for War." *Ethics and International Affairs* 19 (3): 1–21.

Meyrowitz, H. 1966. "Le statut des saboteurs dans le droit de guerre." *Revue de Droit Pénal et de Droit de Guerre* 5: 144.

Nabulsi, K. 1999. *Traditions of War: Occupation, Resistance, and the Law*. Oxford University Press.

Paulson, S. L. 1975. "Classical Legal Positivism at Nuremberg." *Philosophy and Public Affairs* 4 (2): 132–158.

Roberts, Adam, and Richard Guelff. 1989. *Documents on the Laws of War*. Oxford: Clarendon Press.

Rodin, D. 2004. "Terrorism Without Intention." *Ethics* 114: 752–771.

——— 2006. "The Ethics of Asymmetric War." In *The Ethics of War: Shared Problems in Different Traditions*, ed. R. Sorabji and D. Rodin. London: Ashgate, 153–168.

Rousseau, Jean-Jacques. 1964–1969. *Œuvres complètes*, ed. B. Gagnebin and M. Raymond. Paris: Pléiades.

Schwarzenberger, Georg. 1943. *International Law and Totalitarian Lawlessness*. London: Stevens.

Wheaton, H. 1889. *International Law*. London: G. G. Wilson.

7   Problems and prospects for democratic
      settlements: South Africa as a model for
      the Middle East and Northern Ireland?

Courtney Jung, Ellen Lust-Okar, and Ian Shapiro

In the 1970s, the political conflicts in South Africa, Northern Ireland, and the Middle East were often grouped together as among the world's most intractable. They exhibited profound racial and ethnic animosities, reinforced by linguistic, cultural, economic, and religious differences, and solidified by decades of more-or-less violent confrontation. They were often held out as paradigms of "divided" societies, and there seemed little chance of a transition to peaceful, let alone fully democratic, arrangements in any of them. Whether one focused on the players contending for power, the histories of the conflicts, or the capacities of outsiders to influence events, the prospects for negotiated settlements seemed dim.

The conflicts have diverged remarkably in subsequent decades. South Africa, often depicted in the grim 1970s as the most intractable of intractables, moved through a comparatively peaceful four-year transition to majority rule in a unitary state. Democratic elections in 1994, 1999, and 2004 put the African National Congress (ANC) securely in power without civil war, economic collapse, or catastrophic white exodus. To be sure, the continuing economic and social challenges are enormous, with a third of the population unemployed and one in nine infected with HIV, but by most measures South Africa has weathered the transition well. Democracy may not yet be entrenched in South African politics, but it seems at least to have a fighting chance.

Northern Ireland has also made important advances since negotiations began in earnest in 1996. Both Republicans and Loyalists committed to ceasefires that have held, and most serious violence has abated sufficiently that people have started to think peace a realistic possibility. The two sides signed an agreement in 1998 that majorities of both Catholics and Protestants supported. Yet the future of that 1998 Good Friday agreement remained precarious, at best, through 2004. The failure of the power-sharing government to work had led to its repeated suspension by Westminster, and eventually the reimposition of direct rule in October 2002. Whether the paramilitary groups would disband and the Executive and Assembly would be revived remained to be seen.

Establishing peace between the Palestinians and Israelis has been even more elusive. There have been some major turning points in the Arab–Israeli conflict and periods of great optimism, most notably following the negotiation of the Camp David Accords and subsequent signing of the Israeli–Egyptian peace treaty in 1979 and the Palestinian–Israeli negotiation of the Oslo Accords in 1993. There have also been numerous less dramatic "openings" from one side or another. The Palestine Liberation Organization (PLO) acceptance of a two-state solution in 1988, Syria's decision to support the multilateral Madrid conference in 1991, and Israel's decision to negotiate directly with the PLO all provided windows of opportunity for their negotiating partners. However, the principals have often been either unable or unwilling to seize the opportunities that emerge when one side makes concessions. For instance, in 1998 Benjamin Netanyahu rendered Yasser Arafat's concessions in the Wye Accords useless when he unilaterally suspended implementation, and Arafat refused Ehud Barak's concessions at Camp David II in 2000.

Backtracking and disappointing failure have been so frequent that the peace process often seems ritualistic and pointless. Different leaders participate more or less grudgingly at different times, almost always under intense American pressure. This was manifest in President George W. Bush's "road map" for peace in the summer of 2003. Israeli Prime Minister Ariel Sharon was induced to use the word "occupation" for the first time in relation to the conflict, but his insistence that this referred to people and population centers, not the West Bank as such, made the seeming concession nearly meaningless. The concessionary speech delivered by Palestinian Prime Minister Mahmoud Abbas at the Aqaba summit, widely reported to have been drafted by the White House, led Hamas to break off talks with the Palestinian Authority on ending the violence, and further depletion in his already negligible approval ratings among Palestinians.[1] It was unsurprising that the unilaterally declared "truce" by Hamas and other militant groups quickly collapsed in light of the vast differences that remained over territory, settlements, "the right of return," disarmament, prisoners, and the dearth of popular support on both sides for politicians showing any inclination to bridge these gulfs. The Middle East peace process continues to vindicate

---

[1] See "Sharon Backtracks on Israeli 'Occupation,'" Newsmax.com Wires (May 28, 2003) at www.newsmax.com/archives/articles/2003/5/28/100340.shtml (6/13/2003) and Bennett (2003).

the 1970s' diagnosis by going nowhere – if often by Byzantine routes at enormous human and economic cost.

Whence these divergent outcomes? We argue that there are lessons to be drawn from South Africa's comparative success that can illuminate the ongoing dynamics in Northern Ireland and the Middle East – both why they have not yet succeeded and whether they can succeed in the future. We label these conflicts with the compound acronym SAMENI, to signal that ours is an inductive effort based on the South African experience and a close examination of how similar dynamics have played out in the Middle East and Northern Ireland. In making this case, we agree with others that the three conflicts exhibit important similarities, but we believe that they have been misconstrued (Knox and Quirk 2000; Lustick 1994a; 1994b; Akenson 1992; Adam 1990; Giliomee and Gagiano 1990; Gidron *et al.* 2002). Scholars have focused on the putatively "divided" character of the societies – suggesting that conflicts engendered by ethnic, racial, and religious divisions preclude reconciliation. Hence the dire predictions about South Africa in the 1960s, 1970s, and 1980s.

In our account, negotiations in these settings are best seen as a distinctive class of transplacements or negotiated settlements.[2] Their distinctiveness resides not in their "divided" character, but rather in their being imperfect democracies – subject to electoral constraints and dependent on democratic norms, that they violate, for legitimation. The *ancien régime* is a flawed democracy, not a conventional authoritarian system. No doubt all democracies are flawed to some degree, but in these situations the unusually large gulf between the democratic ideal the government claims to embrace and the reality on the ground produces dissonance both for those advantaged by the system and for those excluded from the government. The government's lack of legitimacy provides the impetus for regime change in these circumstances. It shapes the negotiations in distinctive ways and structures the available settlements. Success depends not on the key players finding the Holy Grail, but rather on their converging on a solution that their constituents will accept as legitimate.

It will be clear from this claim that ours is not a deterministic argument. Individual players make decisions that could be made differently, often with consequential results. Moreover, many contingencies affect the outcomes of negotiations. Had F. W. de Klerk been shot by a

---

[2] So for example we rely on Huntington (1991), O'Donnell and Schmitter (1986), and Przeworski (1991) to think through the logic of SAMENI conflict resolution. These three negotiations have rarely been analyzed in the transplacement literature. One notable exception is Sisk (1995). In Jung and Shapiro (1995) we also used the model of transplacements to think through the dynamics of negotiation in South Africa.

disgruntled right-winger before the 1992 referendum, the South African transition might have fallen apart. Had Yitzhak Rabin not been shot in 1995, a successful agreement between Israelis and Palestinians might by now have been concluded and implemented. We might then be trying to explain Middle East success in contrast to South African failure.[3] This is not to say that resolution is exclusively dependent on luck and contingencies of leadership – defying the possibility of useful theory. Such contingencies make it impossible to predict success in any given instance, but this does not exhaust the theoretical agenda. For one thing, on our account it is possible in many situations to predict failure, and, perhaps more important, to say something about how those situations would have to change for success to become a possibility. For another, when success is possible, we can and do develop accounts of the conditions under which it becomes more or less likely.

Our procedure is as follows. We begin, in part 1, by explaining why the conditions that gave rise to these negotiations can usefully be classed together. In part 2 we then elaborate on the ways in which SAMENI negotiations constitute a distinctive class of negotiated settlements. In parts 3 and 4 we explore the conditions that facilitate the initiation, negotiation, and consummation of SAMENI agreements, explaining how circumstances coincided to allow South Africa to overcome the barriers to democratic legitimation, moving through all three stages with comparative ease, while negotiations in the Middle East and Northern Ireland have continually snagged. This leads to a discussion, in part 5, of how negotiations could have succeeded in the Middle East and Northern

---

[3] Counterfactual speculation is inherently difficult, though we adduce considerable evidence in support of these claims below. With respect to South Africa it merits reporting that F.W de Klerk believes that had he been assassinated after the March 1992 referendum the negotiations would likely have been concluded successfully, but that this is much more doubtful had it occurred before the referendum when the government was losing by-elections to conservatives. De Klerk reports that the decision to call the referendum was the only unilateral decision of his presidency. He consulted no one in the cabinet or the National Party (NP) leadership because he knew they would oppose it. Even if a new leader wanted to call a referendum, he doubts that either of the likely contenders (Pik Botha and Roelf Meyer) would have been able to do so, given the need to establish themselves in the party leadership. At the very least the process would have been significantly delayed (interview with author, December 9, 2003). Given our discussion of the importance of timing below, this might well have been sufficient to derail it permanently.

If de Klerk had been killed, the only conceivable replacement who might have been able to carry the NP and the military through negotiations was Roelf Meyer. But Meyer was a very junior minister, without much standing in the party. It seems more likely that Pik Botha would have assumed leadership and resorted to reforming apartheid. Support by the South African Defence Force (SADF) for the transition was at best tenuous at the time of the referendum.

Ireland, the conditions under which they might do so in the future, and the ways in which we may better address the study of such conflicts.

1.   Comparability of SAMENI negotiations

The South African, Israeli, and Northern Irish regimes have all depended heavily on appeals to democratic legitimacy to which they conspicuously failed to live up. The National Party government in South Africa was first elected in 1948 on a platform of "separate development" that would guarantee democratic representation for every race in its "own" territory. The maldistribution of land and other resources at the core of this plan, not to mention the forced removals of tens of thousands from their homes, meant that it was always hopelessly illegitimate in the eyes of nonwhite South Africans and much of the rest of the world. Israel, too, was conceived of as a democratic state from the beginning. If the presence of Israeli Arabs as second-class citizens made this problematic from the start, it was nothing compared with the legitimacy problems that would pile up in the decades after the occupation of the West Bank and Gaza in 1967. In both cases, the introduction of partial democratic reforms failed to remove the stain of exclusion.

The democratic legitimacy of Northern Ireland was also undermined by the gerrymandered origins of the state. From the beginning, Catholics rejected British rule as imperialism. The great majority of them saw the partition in 1921 as a cynical ploy to create an artificial Protestant majority, resisting it – often violently. As a result, the partition could only be sustained through repression. The British resorted repeatedly to special powers legislation and "proscription," with results similar to the emergency regulations that would become semi-permanent features of Apartheid South Africa and Israel's Occupied Territories.[4] In all three cases the government faced inescapable tension between its need for democratic legitimacy and its undemocratic practices. This supplied impetus for reform.

---

[4] Under the Special Powers Act (1922) the Minister for Home Affairs could, among other things, "arrest without charge or warrant, intern without trial, prohibit the holding of coroners' inquests, flog, execute, use depositions of witnesses as 'evidence' without requiring them to be present for cross-examination or rebuttal, destroy buildings, requisition land or property, ban any organization, be it political, social, or trade; prohibit meetings, publications, and even gramophone records" (McGuffin 1973, 22). Proscription is the power to outlaw organizations, enshrined in the 1887 Criminal Law and Procedure (Ireland) Act. "Proscription in its contemporary guise is located in Section 21 of the Northern Ireland (Emergency Provisions) Act 1978." "A person is guilty of an offense if he belongs or professes to belong to a proscribed organization" (Walker 1988, 612).

Even imperfect democracy constrains the players, however. Unlike authoritarian leaders negotiating transplacements, as in Spain, governments in flawed democracies can be voted out of office. This is critical, for it means that both sides must keep an eye on their constituents as well as their opponents. Not only must they protect their positions vis-à-vis the opposition until negotiations have been concluded, but they must also outflank opponents on their own side and build constituencies in support of the new dispensation. This means that elites' abilities to maneuver through public opinion are vital for success. Flawed democracy plays an important role in pushing negotiators to the table, but it also affects whether they can stay there and what they can achieve.

Some might still object to our classification on other grounds that the three conflicts are not relevantly alike. The issues, stakes, and constraints may seem so different that each situation follows an independent logic. After all, South Africa achieved a transition to majority rule within a unitary state whereas in both the Middle East and Northern Ireland negotiations have focused on creating or maintaining partitions with power-sharing. But this gets the cart before the horse. In fact, stakeholders in all three conflicts have entertained variations on each of these solutions at different times and, if our argument is correct, different solutions might have been negotiated in any of them. Indeed, and ironically, partition might reasonably have been judged more likely in South Africa, ex ante, than in the other two conflicts – if only for demographic reasons. The question is not: What is the right outcome? Rather it is: Is there an outcome on which elites can converge while maintaining their popular support and, if so, will they in fact converge on it and remain there for long enough to implement it?

One might concede this yet still wonder about Northern Ireland's fitting the transplacement logic, given the roles of multiple players in several countries. It is true that political leaders in Great Britain and the Republic of Ireland have influenced the conflict and attempts to resolve it. But what matters is not the geographic location of the participants. Rather, it is the ways in which the existence of a flawed democracy both exacerbates the crisis and permits grass-roots constituencies to constrain negotiators' attempts to arrive at solutions. By the time the last round of negotiations began in the mid-1990s, Northern Ireland had been under direct rule from Westminster for twenty-five years. Continuing sectarian violence against British rule undermined the government's claim to democratic legitimacy and, in particular as the EU began to develop European standards for the treatment of minorities, Prime Ministers John Major, and then Tony Blair, grew impatient to resolve the conflict. In fact, as we will see, many of the negotiating dynamics that shaped the South African transition evolved similarly in Northern Ireland – notwithstanding their transnational character. As a result, it meets the test for all fruitful comparative research: that the cases be sufficiently similar to make comparison possible and sufficiently different to make it illuminating.

Perhaps more powerful challenges to our comparison are related to the Middle East. Some will contend that the conflict there is fundamentally different from that in Northern Ireland or South Africa on the grounds that the stakes for the actors – both Israelis seeking to defend a Jewish state and Palestinians invested in regaining their homeland – are inherently zero-sum. The great lesson of the wars of religion of the seventeenth century is often taken to be that when national sovereignty becomes bound up with collective religious identities, the result is perpetual war. The standard solution has long been thought to lie in the de-emphasis of such exclusionary grounds for citizenship via mechanisms such as religious disestablishment. Most players in, and commentators about, the Middle East operate on the assumption that this is not possible there. It is said to be too threatening to the Zionist self-understanding, and to its mirror image: that the Palestinian people have an inalienable right to national self-determination.

But consider a South African perspective on this objection. Apartheid was self-consciously exclusionary, built on an ascriptive basis that left no room for assimilation. Moreover, the racial ideology of apartheid was underpinned with a religious mission; its architects were doctrinaire Calvinists who saw themselves as one of the last outposts of Christian civilization – defending it from communism in the east and a corrupt and degenerate west. As recently as 1985, had anyone seriously suggested that white South Africans would endorse a multiracial state – let alone under a majority-rule, black government – they would have been laughed out of town or locked up. Nor should we forget that, whereas five million Jews face a similar number of Palestinians in Israel, Gaza, and the West Bank, in South Africa five million whites faced twenty-five million blacks. Demography alone might lead one to believe that the zero-sum character of the South African conflict in the mid-1980s looked less tractable than is the case in the Middle East. The magnitude of the unexpected South African transformation suggests that analogous changes in beliefs about religion and ethnicity might indeed be possible in the Middle East.[5]

---

[5] In this connection it is perhaps heartening that at a conference on democratic transitions and consolidation consisting of some 100 academic experts from 36 countries plus 33 heads and former heads of state held in Madrid in October/November 2001, a final

A different lack-of-comparability objection focuses less on the stakes involved in the conflict and more on the proposed solution. One reason for this claim is that the two-state solution will never be perceived as legitimate. Manifest disparities of wealth, status, and power, combined with the partial character of most proposed variants of the Palestinian state, call its sustainability into question. It is doubtless true that any two-state solution would confront legitimation problems reminiscent of "separate but equal" in the American south. But this does not mean that it could not endure for a long time; indeed, the American example suggests that it could. It simply suggests that in the longer term it may be a weigh station en route to a different destination. Living with a settlement can change what people can live with. *Brown* v. *Board of Education* would not have been possible in 1896.

A similar objection is that the two-state solution that became the underpinnings of the Oslo process would have been unenforceable. Any future Israeli government would remain free to roll tanks into the West Bank or Gaza if it became unhappy with the settlement. In contrast, this reasoning goes, in South Africa the enforcement problem was dealt with by a fundamental shift in power to the ANC. However, as we argue in part 3, the enforcement difficulties associated with SAMENI negotiations should not be judged by standards that are not met in most political circumstances. Switzerland and Costa Rica are substantially demilitarized states that could be invaded by neighbors but are not. Moreover, it is not obvious that the enforcement problem was solved by the ANC's triumph in South Africa. The army might have defected at various points – as indeed it still could. In short, the similarities underlying these conflicts should not be missed because they have evolved differently since the 1970s, because of the location of the parties as insiders and outsiders, or because of other alleged sui generis features of one situation or another.

2.   The character of SAMENI negotiations

SAMENI negotiations resemble other transplacements in three ways. First, like other transplacements SAMENI negotiations occur in a power stalemate in which no one can impose change. Neither the regime nor its opponents can dictate a solution, yet there is a potential coalition of

report was adopted in which it was agreed that "rights of citizenship should apply equally to all citizens" and that the majority "must avoid all temptation to define the nation in ethnic terms in the constitutional text or its political practice." See Hidalgo (2002, 34) and Shavit (2003).

government reformers and opposition moderates who may be able to negotiate an agreement both prefer to the status quo.[6] For transplacements to succeed, the innovative coalition must remain sufficiently strong that, should an agreement be reached, its members can carry their constituencies along and impose the settlement on government hardliners and opposition radicals who resist it. Because multiple factors must come together in the right sequences, there are many more ways for all negotiated settlements to fall apart than for them to succeed.

Second, SAMENI negotiations resemble other transplacements in that because they concern political fundamentals, the stakes are inevitably high. Questions of sovereignty, involving regime type, territorial boundaries, or both, are at issue. If an agreement is reached and implemented, it will lead to irreversible changes in a major part of political reality. The negotiations involve intertwined issues of personal security, economic survival, and collective destiny that have been politicized by decades of conflict. Even if negotiations fail, or the agreement is not implemented, the power balance is likely to change, making return to the status quo ante difficult or impossible. Political futures are on the line for the principals, giving them large and increasing stakes in the outcomes. In short, like other transplacements, SAMENI negotiations exhibit the life-or-death quality of politics that is about the basic rules of the game.

This is why transplacement negotiations are so fragile. Government reformers and opposition moderates are still, in most ways, adversaries who must constantly judge one another's agendas and abilities, as well as reassess their own. They can signal to each other their intention to continue in the process, but to do so they must take decisive steps in facing down opposition within their own ranks even before it is clear that an enforceable agreement will be reached. As a result, although the principals know that success may write them into the history books, the risks are huge. At critical junctures they must be willing to confront historical allies on their own flanks to gain a prize that will be theirs only if their negotiating adversaries can do the same thing. Moreover, they have little reason to trust those with whom they are dealing. It is, in short, one thing for there to be a potential coalition in favor of a negotiated settlement; quite another for it to form and sustain itself long enough to get the job done. Because this requires splintering existing

---

[6] The language of hard-liners and reformers, moderates and radicals, is used in the literature on democratic transitions. See Przeworski (1991, 67–70) and Huntington (1991, 151–164). The terms reformers and moderates do not refer to the content of political ideologies. Rather, they denote players who are willing to entertain outcomes that differ from their political ideals in search of a mutually acceptable solution.

coalitions and fending off attacks from historical allies who feel threatened or even betrayed, it takes creative ingenuity, courage, and luck.

A third way in which SAMENI negotiations resemble other transplacements often goes unnoticed due to the widespread proclivity to hive them off as "divided societies." Viewed in that way the conflicts seem to involve particularly intractable forms of political violence. It is true that there have been periods of considerable violence in South Africa, the Middle East, and Northern Ireland, but this scarcely differentiates them from other transplacements – as in Chile in the 1970s or El Salvador in the 1980s for example. Yet it is not so much the amount of violence that commentators focus on as the type, and in particular the fact that it occurs among groups that define themselves by reference to such categories as race, religion, or ethnicity. The common assumption that these categories are ascriptive, if not primordial, leads people to misidentify the conflicts as inherently zero-sum, and to miss the possibilities for unanticipated alliances and the redefinition of political identities as negotiations evolve. That there was a non-Solomonic settlement in South Africa surprised many people. If our analysis is correct they should not have been surprised, and those who continue to insist on the sui generis character of the violence in the Middle East and Northern Ireland should not make the same error.

Yet on our account SAMENI transplacements are nonetheless distinctive because they are both complicated and motivated by conditions of imperfect democracy. Unlike standard transplacements in countries like Spain, Poland, and Chile, the government is democratically elected. Yet, as we have noted, they are imperfectly democratic because large populations under the government's control are disenfranchised or partly enfranchised in ways that are widely seen as unjust. This reality gives the regimes inherent legitimacy problems because they must claim to be democratic when they obviously are not. By entering negotiations, reformers acknowledge, however implicitly, this deficiency in their system. This means that they are usually on the defensive – arguing about the terms and pace of change rather than its necessity. This in turn means that no settlement can succeed unless there is broad agreement that the democratic deficit that gave impetus to negotiations has been substantially attenuated, if not abolished. Once parties to a conflict appeal to democracy as their source of legitimation, widely accepted democratic norms rule out racial oligarchies, and in today's world they even make religious and ethnic oligarchies suspect. Moshe Halbertal explained this imperative well following the collapse of the July 2000 Palestinian–Israeli Washington summit: "Between the Mediterranean and the Jordan there are roughly five million Jews and five million

Palestinian Arabs. You cannot have a Jewish and democratic state without dividing this land, and those who oppose that are dooming Israel to an apartheid state, which might have secure borders, but might not be worth securing. Barak is on a purely Zionist mission to bring Israel back into borders where it can be Jewish, just, democratic – and secure."[7]

The opposition in SAMENI conflicts often emanates from a liberation movement (the ANC, the PLO, and the IRA, in these cases) and is not, as such, democratically elected, but it gains significant leverage from the fact that the government lacks democratic legitimacy. By entering negotiations, the opposition inevitably becomes democratically constrained as well. Its leaders must be able to claim plausibly that they represent a major constituency, if not the majority, and to move toward a settlement that will be popularly validated. In short, although the regime and its opponents may both be imperfectly democratic, they claim to be democrats and depend on popular support in a more robust sense than the players in other transplacements. The need for democratic legitimation greatly complicates negotiations, defying attempts to reduce them to stylized elite games. We are thus sympathetic to Elisabeth Wood's (2000) contention that the transitions literature has been overly focused on elite interactions, with insufficient attention to the larger political contexts within which they occur. But where Wood contends that such negotiations are driven from below, we take a more interactive view. Negotiators are constrained by popular opinion, but to succeed elites must make the right choices at critical junctures – including choices about how to respond to popular opinion and when to try to shape it. One of the trickiest problems arises from the reality that negotiating a settlement usually involves concessions that force the principals to move away from their mandates. The challenge then becomes finding ways to avoid alienating constituencies whose endorsement is essential to the settlement's legitimacy.

The central question in all transplacements is: can the reformers and moderates agree on a settlement and successfully face down the hardliners and radicals on their flanks? However, SAMENI transplacements are distinctive in that the parties must also maintain enough grass-roots support that backers of the *ancien régime* continue to see the settlement as legitimate while partisans of the new dispensation regard it as repairing the democratic deficit. Quite simply, negotiators must be able to hold onto power until a settlement has been concluded, and this, in the presence of uneven progress and the subsequent vicissitudes of

---

[7] Moshe Halbertal, as quoted in Friedman (2000, A21).

public opinion, is extraordinarily difficult. The potential to disrupt negotiations by using democratic institutions to pressure the opponent, ironically, provides new opportunities and sources of power to those who seek to scuttle agreements, as spikes in suicide bombings in Israel have often demonstrated.

Moreover, the dynamics of negotiations will be affected by democratic turnovers in power. If the negotiating government falls at the polls, as has often been the case in Israel, new players must then establish their credentials as bona fide reformers intent on concluding an agreement. As well as constantly reassessing their own interests in proceeding, both sides must thus worry about whether the other can maintain enough support among their core constituencies to carry through their own side of the bargain. They must also worry about how concessions they might make threaten to alienate their own supporters. Barak's willingness to put sovereignty over parts of Jerusalem on the table for the first time in the failed 2000 Washington negotiations is a case in point. His subsequent loss of popularity at home was partly linked to the realization that it would be difficult, if not impossible, for any Israeli leader to declare Jerusalem off-limits in future negotiations.[8]

3.   Onset of SAMENI negotiations

Catalysts for SAMENI negotiations can take the form of sticks, carrots, or – more likely – both. For government reformers the main stick will likely be an increasingly costly, deteriorating status quo, depleting their political capital and increasing their will to negotiate. This may be because of internal developments such as terrorist bombings or an ungovernability campaign or because of external factors such as sanctions, pressure from international human rights groups or a powerful ally. Changing structural, global, or popular constraints may render the status quo less viable, and alternatives more readily imaginable. Evolving ideological paradigms can also shift perceptions of the viability or meaning of persisting in conflict. For instance, the fall of communism, or the increasing bankruptcy of race as an organizing principle of political and social life, or the development of international norms regarding

---

[8] A poll conducted by the Palestinian Center for Policy and Survey Research (PCPSR) in Ramallah and the Harry S. Truman Research Institute for the Advancement of Peace at the Hebrew University, Jerusalem found that 55.7% of Israelis surveyed believed that "Israel made too much of a compromise" at the Camp David summit. PCPSR, "Results of Israeli Public Opinion Poll: July 27–31, 2000." www.pcpsr.org/survey/polls/2002/p1israelipoll.html (6/17/03).

minority rights, might highlight the democratic deficit and undercut the grounds that have justified violence hitherto. Carrots could include the prospect of peace and an end to pariah status in world opinion, a variety of economic incentives, or a desire to do the right thing and go down in history as a statesman.[9]

Comparable considerations apply to the opposition. Sticks might include the inability to sustain grass-roots support for a costly and unwinnable guerrilla war, international pressure, depleted weapons, or dissension within the liberation movement. Among the carrots may be the legitimation afforded by recognition and talks with the government, the allure of power, access to international players, promises of economic support from third parties, or the advantages of peace and prosperity. In all three cases under discussion, the combination of sticks and carrots ushered in unprecedented negotiations that held out the hope of ending decades of intractable conflict.

How the unthinkable became thinkable in South Africa

Throughout the 1980s the South African government faced a deteriorating status quo. The ungovernability campaign mounted by the United Democratic Front (UDF) massively raised the costs of keeping order in the townships by organizing a generation of young black activists with a more militant opposition style than their parents'.[10] The currency collapse that followed South Africa's inability to meet international debt obligations in 1985 sent the economy into a tailspin, and the relentless chorus of outside political and economic pressure began to be matched by attacks on apartheid from growing numbers of Afrikaner intellectuals.[11] By the second half of the 1980s, polls revealed that most whites believed that apartheid threatened the country's future, decreasing dramatically the costs facing elected officials entering negotiations (Booysen 1989). NP confidence in the medium-term viability of the apartheid state was particularly shaken by the escalation of violence

---

[9] Some incentives are longstanding. For example, most observers argue that business elites in South Africa, Northern Ireland, and Israel have long favored a peace settlement, and we have found striking evidence of this in Israel, where eighteen out of twenty-five top business executives we surveyed in 2003 favored an Oslo-style solution and only two opposed it (see Appendix). However, there is no evidence in any of these cases that the pressure from the business community was responsible for either beginning or continuing negotiations.

[10] The UDF was the backbone of internal opposition to apartheid in the 1980s, and widely considered the internal wing of the then-banned ANC. See Seekings (2000).

[11] An anti-Apartheid Afrikaner intellectual movement had its foundation in the late 1960s. See Adam and Giliomee (1979).

following the collapse of the second phase of CODESA roundtable negotiations in May 1992.[12]

The two most important carrots had to do with the collapsing Soviet empire after the mid-1980s. Because the leaderships of the ANC and the South African Communist Party (SACP) overlapped substantially, white fear of majority rule was conflated with fear of communism. After 1989 a communist government in South Africa was no longer a serious threat, and white elites began to realize that majority rule need not mean the destruction of capitalism or the expropriation of private property.[13] The political corollary of this was a more flexible and pragmatic ANC leadership with whom serious negotiations, if not yet partnership, could be considered. That this would also mean an end to pariah status, the possibility of economic revival, unfettered overseas travel, and countless other benefits of normalization no doubt also helped. Once white South Africans began thinking the unthinkable, it could start looking attractive.

NP carrots were ANC sticks. In the early 1980s a strapped USSR had stopped ANC and SACP financial backing and military training on the grounds that South Africa was not in a revolutionary situation.[14] This was a closely held secret within the ANC leadership, but it was only a matter of time until the government would know it as well. Overtures to China led nowhere, forcing the ANC-in-exile to rethink its military strategy and start building up internal opposition. The UDF was formed in 1983 in opposition to Tricameral Parliament elections which had offered some representation to "coloured" and other disenfranchised racial minorities. This ushered in a new era of populist opposition with a massive ungovernability campaign in the townships.[15] Widespread internal unrest raised the stakes for the NP government at the same time as it marginalized the Pan Africanist Congress (PAC) and Inkatha forces within the liberation movement. But the government's ferocious repression of the opposition, particularly after 1986, as well as its huge

---

[12] The acronym stands for Conference on a Democratic South Africa. These were part of the "prenegotiations" in that the government insisted in involving over twenty interests, including those who had no interest in a democratic transition such as the extreme white right and the Inkatha Freedom Party. Predictably they went nowhere. See Jung and Shapiro (1995, 285–286).

[13] In fact white economic elites realized this before the politicians, and began secret talks with the ANC as early as 1986, in Lusaka and Dakar. See Sisk (1995, 78).

[14] "Statement of the National Executive Committee of the African National Congress on the Question of Negotiations," Lusaka, October 9, 1987, cited in Friedman (1993, 10–11).

[15] The Tricameral Parliament was a last-ditch attempt by the NP to refashion the tatters of apartheid's divide-and-rule strategy by creating separate houses of parliament for Coloureds and Indians (though none for Blacks).

reserves of military and paramilitary power (South Africa had – and has – by far the most powerful and best equipped army in Africa), made it plain that the Soviets were right about the low odds of successful revolution.

The most important carrot in getting the ANC leadership to the bargaining table was the prospect of power. The low odds of military success meant that de Klerk government's willingness to negotiate had to be taken seriously. Even if the ANC had to accept the prospect of power-sharing in an interim government at least, this was surely better than nothing. Moreover, it opened up the possibility of a new status quo that could subsequently develop into full majority rule – as turned out to be the case.

Shifting constraints and possibilities in the Middle East

The Israeli decision to enter negotiations mirrored the South African one in several ways. Maintaining the status quo had become more expensive with the eruption of the first *intifada*. The anger of Palestinian youth, and organizational efforts by the Unified National Leadership of the Uprising (UNLU), took a toll on Israeli public support for the occupation. Israelis returned increasingly to their pre-1967 beliefs that occupation of the West Bank and Gaza was neither feasible nor desirable.[16] No doubt a drop-off in world support for Israel, caused by vivid nightly depictions of the confrontation between stone-throwing youth and well-armed Israeli soldiers on CNN, reinforced this. By the early 1990s, the Israeli economy was also suffering from the influx of Soviet Jews, adding an economic dimension to the political malaise and prodding the leadership in the direction of negotiations.[17] Shifting public opinion meant conditions were ripe for a solution that could not only create peace and order, but also restore the democratic legitimacy of the Israeli state.

---

[16] Israeli support for talks with the PLO consequently increased. A *New York Times* poll in April 1987 found that only 42% of respondents favored such talks. In contrast, a *New York Times* poll conducted in March 1989 found 58% of Israelis supported negotiations with the PLO if it recognized Israel and ceased terrorist activity. A poll by Yediot Aharonot found similar results the following month, with 59% of respondents supporting talks with the PLO. See Tessler (1994, 724–725). An independent poll conducted for PM Rabin on the eve of the Oslo agreement also confirmed that the public would support an agreement, even if Arafat was involved. See Makovsky (1996, 62).

[17] During the 1990s, 900,000 former Soviet immigrants arrived, the largest immigration to Israel since the mid-1950s. Over 330,000 of these arrived in 1990 and 1991. Yaffee and Tal (2000, 4).

By 1991, there were increasing pressures within Israel for an agreement with the Palestinians. After the Gulf war, which neutralized Syria and moved moderate Arab states into closer alliance with the US, the Bush administration decided that the time for negotiations was ripe – adding both to the pressure and to the sense of opportunity for Israel (Baker 1995, 422). There was also a growing domestic constituency supporting an agreement with the Palestinians. Frustrated by the *intifada* and alarmed by the noticeable decrease in US government support, army generals, the business community, and a large segment of the Israeli political left called for a peace process.[18] Rabin capitalized on this frustration when he ran successfully against Shamir, promising an "autonomy agreement" with the Palestinians and restoration of US–Israeli relations (Makovsky 1996, 12). In 1993, Rabin decided for the first time to talk to the PLO and Arafat, then the most powerful Palestinian leader, who would be essential to any deal.[19]

At the same time, the costs of entering negotiations were falling for Arafat. He had weathered the internal criticism for acknowledging the state of Israel in 1988 and, with the help of political platforms set forth during the *intifada*, gained general Palestinian acceptance for a two-state solution.[20] He also faced less opposition from Arab leaders to entering negotiations, with Egypt's move toward peace in 1979, King Hussein's relinquishing of the West Bank in 1988, and Syria's willingness to participate in the multilateral Madrid conference in 1991. His perception of Israel's strength might not have changed, but his expectations about the domestic and regional costs of negotiating were notably lower after 1991 than at any previous time.

The *intifada* had strengthened the Palestinians by putting pressure on Israel to negotiate, but the PLO also faced mounting pressure to enter negotiations. It had become increasingly isolated since the early 1980s – abandoned by Egypt in the 1979 Camp David agreement and thrown out of Lebanon in 1982. Yet these challenges paled by comparison with

---

[18] On the development of business community support for agreement/continuing peace process, see "In the Middle East: 'Peace is now irreversible,'" *Business Week*, November 20, 1995, 62–64. A survey we conducted showed that twenty-two of twenty-five business executives believed the peace agreement would have a positive impact on their businesses, and twenty of twenty-four believed that it was of major importance. See Appendix.

[19] Rabin continued to oppose direct deals with the PLO until mid-1993, and only after August approved the draft Oslo Accord. See Shlaim (1994, 32).

[20] Pamphlets distributed during the *intifada*, as well as a coordinated demonstration of Palestinian, Israeli, and international actors in 1990, called for "Two States for Two Peoples," a marked contrast from earlier calls for the elimination of Israel (Ashrawi 1995; Tessler 1994).

the events of 1990–1991. The fall of the Soviet Union and Eastern Bloc diminished military and financial support. Then, Arafat took the wild, and ultimately disastrous, gamble of supporting Iraq during the Gulf war – leading the PLO to the edge of financial and political bankruptcy.[21] Dismayed Gulf states withdrew financial support and Kuwait threw Palestinian workers out of the country. Defeated Iraq was in no position to help. The PLO could not pay monthly salaries, let alone support its functions.[22] Finally, Syria had seized the opportunity of the Gulf war to move closer to the US, first agreeing to join in the US-led coalition and then accepting an invitation to the Madrid conference. So it is not surprising that, following the failed USSR coup attempt in August and the Syrian acceptance of the Madrid conference, the PLO authorized a Palestinian delegation, led by Haider Abdul Shafi, to start negotiations. As Farouq Qaddumi explained, it was time for the PLO to join the peace process or exit history (Sayigh 1997, 660).

Both the *intifada* and the presence of a non-PLO negotiating team at Madrid were creating an alternative Palestinian leadership. Much as Arafat welcomed the new legitimacy for the idea of a Palestinian state, it was becoming alarmingly possible for Palestinians and others to imagine this state without a role for him and the PLO. Negotiating at Oslo was a way to preserve their role, though it came at a price because negotiations involve concessions, and, until an agreement is actually consummated, making concessions increases the leadership's vulnerability to a flank attack. Fear of losing his grip on the Palestinian leadership propelled Arafat to accept concessions, and it also forced him to confront the possibility of an endgame rather than an endless peace process. Time and momentum were on his side, but if things dragged on for long enough without an agreement, they would turn against him.

Opportunities to end stalemate in Northern Ireland

Negotiations in Northern Ireland resulted from a different mix of sticks and carrots. Neither Britain nor the Irish Republic suffered unsustainable damage from the conflict in Northern Ireland, and the conflicting parties within Northern Ireland had ample popular legitimacy and access

---

[21] PLO coziness with Iraq was not new. In the late 1980s, Iraq had promised it that it would commit fifty-four army divisions against Israel after the end of the Iran–Iraq war, and Arafat had described Iraq as the defender of the "eastern gate" of the Arab nation. Similarly, in December 1989, Arafat praised the unveiling of a new Iraqi ballistic missile as a "gift to the intifadah" (Sayigh 1997, 640–641).

[22] Approximately 400,000 Palestinians were thrown out of the Gulf countries, and the PLO lost an estimated $10 billion between 1991 and 1993 (Usher 1995, 1–2).

to the limited type of military equipment needed to continue the conflict. The Northern Ireland economy was depressed, but economic problems were not generally blamed on the Troubles, and budget transfers from Britain ensured that Northern Ireland was able to spend beyond its means.[23] Nonetheless, most relevant parties were engaged in talks to end the conflict for much of the 1990s. Why?

Solving this puzzle requires attention to the unusual combinations of participants to the Northern Ireland conflict. The transplacement model of hard-liners, reformers, moderates, and radicals, which captures the principal dynamics of negotiations in South Africa and the Middle East, is complicated there by the fact that there are four sets of players, each with its own moderate and hard-line factions powerful enough to scuttle an agreement: Great Britain, the Irish Republic, the Ulster Unionist Party (UUP), and the Social Democratic and Labour Party (SDLP) and Sinn Fein together on the Nationalist side. Once the "external" players (Britain and Ireland) decided to work toward settlement, the participation of the "internal" players was gradually achieved through a combination of political sticks and carrots, guarantees, and pressure.

The 1985 Anglo-Irish agreement marked the start of a new peace process. When Irish Taoiseach Garret FitzGerald came to power in 1982, he immediately began to shift relations with both Britain and the North. The agreement between the British and Irish governments "formalized cooperation on conflict resolution" between the two governments and would eventually set the terms of the accord (O'Leary and McGarry 1996, 226; Darby 1997; Mallie and McCittrick 1996). It required that the constitutional status of Northern Ireland would not be changed without majority consent. This guaranteed the status of Northern Ireland as part of the United Kingdom in the short run, but it opened the door to the possibility that its status could be changed in future. And it did more than that. The very fact that the British government agreed to this possibility underscored that they acknowledged Northern Ireland's questionable democratic legitimacy. Imagine them signing on to something similar about Surrey.

Albert Reynolds was elected Irish Taoiseach in 1992. He pushed "talks about talks" forward by starting parallel dialogues with John Major's government in Britain and with the SDLP and Sinn Fein in Northern Ireland. In 1993 Major and Reynolds announced the

---

[23] The difference between what Northern Ireland collects in revenue and what it receives in transfers from London is the subvention. Northern Ireland's is higher than Scotland or Wales'. Interview with Dr. Esmond Birnie, former Member of the Legislative Assembly (MLA), UUP, July 29, 2003.

Downing Street Declaration as the starting point of a peace process. The British government reiterated that it had "no selfish strategic or economic interest in Northern Ireland," and went on to acknowledge that the possibility of a united Ireland was in the hands of the Irish people alone (Darby 2003). By signaling that it would not guarantee the Unionist position indefinitely, Britain raised the cost of recalcitrance to Unionists and ceded the contestability – if not illegitimacy – of the status quo. The Irish Republic in turn promised that a settlement would include amending the Irish Constitution to remove the claim that the Irish Parliament had in principle the right to incorporate and govern Northern Ireland. The Declaration thus moved further toward establishing the framework within which both sides would pursue their aspirations.[24] It also made clear that any future settlement would have to come to grips with Northern Ireland as a distinct entity, at least for the foreseeable future.

The Downing Street Declaration stated that negotiations would be limited to those parties not engaged in paramilitary violence. In response, the IRA announced a complete cessation of all military activity in August 1994, forcing Loyalists to parry with a ceasefire. Within six months, the British and Irish governments issued a Frameworks for the Future policy document, aimed at translating the Joint Declaration into concrete terms. The guidelines for a final settlement included the structure of relations between Ireland, Britain, and Northern Ireland, and the composition of a devolved government within Northern Ireland. As in South Africa and the Middle East, then, negotiations over a settlement in Northern Ireland were seriously underway by the early 1990s. Understanding why the outcomes diverged as they did concerns us next.

4.   Theory and practice of commitment

If negotiations are to lead to viable agreements, the adversaries must rely on one another. A potential obstacle is the classic commitment problem described by Schelling: if each side knows that the other might subsequently defect, why should either agree (Schelling 1960)? In theory, commitment problems are ubiquitous in democratic politics, given the lack of third-party enforcement. Despite numerous attempts to show that compliance with democratic outcomes can be in the interests of all, no theoretical account has been developed that shows why electoral

---

[24] We are grateful to Brendan O'Leary for suggesting this interpretation of the effect of the Declaration on aspirations. See O'Leary (1995, 862–872).

losers with the power to defect so often do not do so (Przeworski 1991; 1999). It would be unthinkable for an American president who lost an election to order tanks down Pennsylvania Avenue, even if he has no realistic hope of ever regaining power through the ballot box. The same could be said of politicians in many other democracies who routinely accept results that consign them to political oblivion. We must therefore take care not to judge potential settlements in the transition context by a standard that predicts perpetual civil war throughout the democratic world (Shapiro 2003, 88–93).

That said, there are reasons to expect commitment problems surrounding transplacements to be particularly acute. Following decades of sometimes violent conflict, they are marriages of convenience among parties with little reason for mutual trust. As Rabin put it in 1993: "Peace is not made with friends. Peace is made with enemies, some of whom – and I won't name names – I loathe very much."[25] Even if reformers and moderates are willing to move toward agreement, they will be skeptical of one another's good faith.

This is further complicated in the quasi-democratic settings characteristic of SAMENI transplacements because the negotiating partners must be responsive to public opinion. Indeed, it might be possible for opponents of negotiations to use public opinion to undermine reformers or even to remove them from power. Unless the reformers and moderates build support for the idea of an agreement among the grass-roots constituencies they depend on, the rug will be pulled out from under them. Yet by the same token negotiators can also employ the constraints of democratic legitimation to signal their commitment to a settlement. By making concessions public, political elites tie themselves to positions they will not easily be able to abandon without damaging their political careers. In so doing they burn bridges to existing sources of legitimation, forcing them to look for new ones. In this sense the quasi-democratic character of SAMENI negotiations may offer possibilities for dealing with commitment problems that are not available in other transplacements.

Reformers and moderates have incentives to do what they can to help strengthen one another to deal with hostile flanks, but these incentives are mixed. On the one hand they need to strengthen their adversaries. Because negotiated transitions occur only when government reformers and opposition moderates are too weak to achieve unilateral change but strong enough to achieve it if they cooperate, they must have adversaries who can stay in power long enough to deliver. Yet, on the other hand,

---

[25] "From Setbacks to Living Together." *New York Times*, September 5, 1993: 10.

they must not strengthen their adversaries too much. Both sides will want to extract the best possible terms for their supporters so far as the content of an agreement is concerned, and they have no reason to make this task more difficult than necessary. Moreover, in many cases the protagonists will expect to compete for political support in the new order, if it arrives, and a stronger adversary is more difficult to compete with than a weaker one. Even if the eventual settlement is expected to be a partition, other considerations create similar pressures. Strengthening your adversary will turn out to have been costly if there is no agreement and the situation reverts to one of open conflict. While each side has incentives to optimize its own political strength vis-à-vis conservative and revolutionary flanks, it is thus optimal for them if their adversary merely satisfices: becomes just strong enough to deliver an agreement from which potential spoilers can be marginalized if they cannot be co-opted (Jung and Shapiro 1995, 280–282).

The capacity to demonstrate commitment is shaped by how bad things are likely to get should the negotiations fail. If the principals believe that withdrawing from negotiations is either unlikely or exceedingly costly for them, this will stiffen their backs to stay the course when the going gets rough. More important, passing a costly or unacceptable reversion point helps them signal to their negotiating adversaries that they are serious about achieving a successful agreement. This is why things sometimes have to get worse before they can get better. An unpalatable reversion point for either or both parties by no means guarantees agreement – there are other possibilities such as civil war or military coup. But if your adversary knows that the status quo ante is decreasingly tenable for you, it becomes easier for him to believe that you are serious about looking for an accommodation.

Both sides must be concerned not only with an adversary's political will to reach an agreement, but also with their capacity to deliver. As a result, the credibility of negotiating commitments is unavoidably dependent on how successful reformers and moderates are at co-opting or marginalizing flank attacks. You have little reason to trust even an adversary you believe to be sincere if you think that the ground may be cut from under him. This belief can be forestalled in various ways. One is to actually be the flanking force. This Nixon-to-China logic suggests that the closer negotiators are to the ideological extremes in their parties, the more credible their commitments will be. The alternative is to face down the flanking opposition at critical junctures, or visibly to burn bridges with it while retaining the support of the military. One way or another, the negotiating principals must ensure that their adversaries have good reasons to believe that they can deliver down the stretch.

South African success

These commitment problems were managed in three ways in South Africa. First, the situation on the ground became decreasingly attractive to the NP and eventually even to the ANC. The combination of economic malaise, a sustained national uprising, and international opprobrium took an increasing toll on white South Africans. The September 1992 Bisho massacre made graphic the possibility that escalating violence could spiral out of control, forcing both sides to look into the abyss and resume (secret) negotiations that had been abandoned with the breakdown of CODESA II (Jung and Shapiro 1995, 288). Second, potential flank attacks were effectively neutralized. De Klerk's history as an orthodox Afrikaner and conservative member of the NP initially strengthened his hand within his own party. Similarly, Mandela had substantial political capital on entering the negotiations that stemmed from his personal legitimacy. In contrast to Inkatha leader Mangosuthu Buthelezi, who was compromised by his dealings with the apartheid regime in the 1980s, Mandela's refusal to renounce violence as a condition for release from twenty-seven years in prison made him unassailable within the ANC. A radical flank did emerge during negotiations, but Mandela's legendary status and position as founder of the ANC's military wing made his authority impossible to challenge.

Third, and perhaps decisively, decisions made by Mandela and de Klerk early in the negotiations helped diminish their commitment problems. De Klerk's bold steps in 1992 showed how bridge burning enhances credibility and how even flawed democracy can be used to move negotiations forward. In 1990 and 1991 he lost a series of by-elections while he was negotiating with the ANC, emboldening right-wing attacks on him. He called their bluff, however, by holding a snap referendum in March 1992 that he won by a two-thirds majority among the white electorate in every region of the country. He insisted throughout the referendum campaign that the critical issue of power-sharing (the political equivalent of sovereignty over Jerusalem for Israelis or policing and IRA decommissioning in Northern Ireland) was non-negotiable. In fact he was forced to moderate this demand later in the negotiations, but even then this was obscured by the fact that the ANC, which had steadfastly rejected all compromise on majority rule, gave de Klerk the wiggle room he needed by agreeing to a constitutionally mandated interim government of national unity. The ANC nonetheless refused to commit to a permanent government of national unity. They kept constitutionally mandated power-sharing out of the statement of entrenched principles the Constitutional Court would eventually use to judge the acceptability of the final constitution. By the time the final constitution, which dropped power-sharing, was negotiated in 1995, the NP was no longer in a position to insist on anything.

This was one of several respects in which the ANC played its cards perfectly during the negotiations. At the time of the referendum, no one knew how long an interim settlement would last or what the final agreement was going to look like. In many places interim settlements have been known to drag on for decades, and some may reasonably have expected this in South Africa. Once de Klerk had made his move, the ANC helped him satisfice by compromising on the power-sharing issue in the interim constitution. This was essential for him to retain his grass-roots support. By then he had burned his bridges with the far right and legitimated the negotiated transition among the white electorate, even though – fortuitously, as we argue later – it was not entirely clear where it would lead.

Governments have an initial advantage in transition negotiations because they control the military and hence the possibility of a return to authoritarianism should negotiations fail. However, that advantage diminishes for a leader who alienates the conservative flank (which often has its own links to the military hierarchy), and moves toward the position of his adversary during negotiations. Facing down the hard right magnified de Klerk's personal political investment in achieving the successful negotiated settlement. Failure would have been immensely costly for him, possibly not survivable. It would likely have been followed by a massive escalation of violence for which he would have been held responsible by the whites who had trusted him, opening the way for an authoritarian leader, or the army, to seize the initiative. We cannot be sure de Klerk had passed a point of no return by the time of the referendum, but clearly he was well into his Rubicon treading in deep water. He would have been in dire straits had he found himself there alone.

The ANC pooh-poohed the referendum at the time as one more illegitimate "whites only" vote, but once it was over they had de Klerk exactly where they wanted him. He could no longer point to constraints coming from the right as a way of limiting the concessions he could make. By the time of the final agreement in 1993 it was the government that had made the decisive power-sharing concession, and by then there was no going back for de Klerk.

The compromise over power-sharing also illustrates how the opposition can deal successfully with potentially hostile flanks within its own ranks. During negotiations, the initiative was not most seriously in danger of shifting to more radical organizations outside the ANC (which by this point were hopelessly weak), but rather to a radical flank of youth within the ANC mobilized by Winnie Mandela, Peter Mokaba, and Chris Hani. Conceding power-sharing for an interim settlement only enabled the ANC leadership to keep critics on board at the critical meeting of February 1993 (Jung and Shapiro 1995, 290–291). The ANC leadership could plausibly (and correctly, as it turned out) make the case that time was on their side, and that once the reality had changed on the ground, they would be negotiating over the final settlement from a position of much greater strength.

To be sure, they were helped by a variety of factors: the ANC's good organization compared with that of potential opposition interlopers, Mandela's legendary status, and the assassination of Chris Hani in April 1993, which removed the most popular radical leader from the scene and reinforced the commitment of both sides to a settlement. Hani's murder might have unraveled the peace process altogether as millions of African youth emptied into the streets to mourn and seek revenge. As it happened, however, de Klerk and Mandela moved quickly, and with a united front, to forestall such an outcome. But the main reason the ANC coalition stayed together was that the negotiations took place within the context of a flawed democracy whose legitimacy was deteriorating. Thus, the moderate leadership, which included tough-minded and pragmatic negotiators like Cyril Ramaphosa with unassailable anti-apartheid credentials, could make a plausible case that by conceding power-sharing in the interim arrangement they had not conceded anything of importance. It meant that within four years the ANC would have achieved an outcome through negotiations – majority-rule democracy with themselves in decisive control – that they lacked the military capacity to impose on the government at any time before the transition.

If the ANC played its cards perfectly in the 1992 settlement, does this mean that they got the better of de Klerk in the negotiations? Making that case would require establishing that the ANC leadership could have both remained intact and continued as the principal protagonist on the opposition side while agreeing to a permanent power-sharing arrangement. This is doubtful, not only because of the internal conflict it would have provoked in the ANC, but also because any such deal would have empowered Buthelezi's Inkatha as an important opposition player with a share in power. Inkatha was the third largest party in South Africa and the best bet for the NP to dilute ANC power and support. The NP, which had long courted Inkatha as a moderate alternative to the ANC, would have insisted on maximizing the strength of all minority parties with an eye to weakening the

ANC.[26] Having successfully marginalized Buthelezi, the ANC had no reason to travel down that path. "Ordinary democracy" rather than power-sharing was thus their reservation price for the permanent constitution, making their optimizing and satisficing strategies identical. Agreeing to interim power-sharing was needed to move de Klerk toward, if not past, his point of no return; resisting anything more was essential to maintaining their own position. For this reason it seems clear that although de Klerk could have scuttled the negotiations, paying whatever political price that entailed, he could not have negotiated better terms for the NP.

Notice, however, that massive though the concession was to give away constitutionally mandated power-sharing in the final constitution, the outcome could have been worse for the NP. This is not a negligible list of what they achieved: entrenched democratic principles with a constitutional court to interpret them; a two-thirds majority requirement to alter the constitution; entrenched protections of property rights and civil freedoms; absence of high representation thresholds that would disenfranchise minor parties; the guarantee of an amnesty process and protection of civil service jobs for at least five years; and a powerful party whip system that the NP believed would strengthen its leverage in Parliament. Three general elections later, ANC hegemony still means that there is little meaningful national political competition.[27] If and when the ANC begins to fracture, leading to a more fluid political environment, then the entrenched democratic guarantees will be important devices in giving minority parties the chance to become more consequential political players.[28] Accordingly, it would be a mistake to say that de Klerk was giving away the store in accepting constitutionally mandated power-sharing. Arguably the NP made some unnecessary minor concessions, and to that extent did not get the ANC to satisfice in areas where it might have done (Jung and Shapiro 1995, 300–301). But on the major constitutional questions of democratic politics,

---

[26] Inkatha played an important role in the government of national unity in the decade after the transition, but on sufferance from the ANC which found it expedient to co-opt Buthelezi by keeping him in the cabinet.

[27] However, there is meaningful local and regional political competition. In the Eastern Cape, the United Democratic Movement (UDM) formed by Bantu Holomisa, who was expelled from the ANC in 1997, and Roelf Meyer, who had led the NP negotiating team in the transition, took away a substantial portion of the ANC vote to become the official opposition party in 1999. The Christian Democratic Party did the same thing in the Northern Transvaal. In both 1994 and 1999 Inkatha won elections in Natal, and the NP (in coalition with the Democratic Party after 1999) governs the Western Cape.

[28] After the first election much of the NP defected to other opposition parties, and in 2004 the party effectively ceased to exist when its leaders decided to join the ANC.

commitments were extracted from the ANC that might not have been, and indeed have not been in other transitional contexts.

This is not to say other outcomes are unimaginable. A more strategically astute NP leadership in the 1980s might have made a deal with Buthelezi to partition the country before the UDF had consolidated itself as the principal opposition player. Had that happened, the South African conflict today might look more like the Middle East does, with disputes over sovereignty, borders, refugees and other displaced persons and an endlessly debated "peace process" amid the ebb and flow of a war of attrition. Alternatively, the NP could have staggered on during the 1990s (and perhaps even beyond) as it had in the 1980s, repressing the opposition and thumbing its nose at outside pressure. Given the erosion of its support among Afrikaner intellectuals, this would have meant an increasingly authoritarian militarized society with scant hope for improvements in the economy. Yet it might have been survivable for a long time. True, the deteriorating political and economic climate supplied the NP with the impetus to begin the negotiations and to stay the course, but it did not compel them to do so. Structural factors predispose things in one direction or another, but agency is required as well. Had P. W. Botha remained at the NP helm it is unlikely negotiations would have started in 1990 or, if somehow they had begun, ended successfully in 1993.

Missed opportunity in the Middle East

Though in some ways more challenging, the commitment problems facing the principals in the Middle East in the early 1990s were not insuperable. Like Mandela and de Klerk in South Africa, Rabin and Arafat were both well placed to manage hostile flanks. Israelis viewed Rabin as a war hero dedicated to Israeli security, better positioning him to move the process forward than Shimon Peres would be. Arafat also had the clout of being a long-time Fateh leader-in-exile. Indeed, Rabin's decision to deal with Arafat directly through the "back channels" at Oslo was a clear recognition that the Palestinian delegation depended on and deferred to Arafat (Savir 1999, 5; Makovsky 1996, 39). He risked a breakaway by his radical flank, but he quickly demonstrated his ability to gain the acquiescence of the majority and to marginalize the remaining opponents.

Yet the Middle East negotiations differed from those in South Africa from the perspectives of both sides to the negotiations. The Oslo formulation was widely seen as Arafat's attempt to shore up his personal power, and it was far from clear that when push came to shove many

Palestinians would accept the agreement that could be extracted as superior to the status quo (Sayigh 1997, 658–660). Nor was the Israeli side propelled by an imperative to consummate an agreement. Israel's decision to enter negotiations was based, in part, on the perception that a weakened Arafat would be easy to bargain with. The *intifada* and then significant US pressure had moved the Israeli government into concessions in 1993, with an eye to getting an agreement rather than merely going through the interminable motions of the peace process. Like Arafat, Rabin seems to have been personally committed to reaching a settlement, but few can have doubted that Israel could cut and run if the going got rough.

This reality generated commitment problems that Arafat and Rabin both dealt with by burning bridges on their flanks. Convinced that Rabin was serious about a settlement that would involve a sovereign Palestinian state and focused, perhaps, on his own political survival, Arafat accepted a partial agreement that postponed deciding the most important issues such as control over Jerusalem, full establishment of a state, the return of refugees, and water rights.[29] He also stepped decisively into the Rubicon by recognizing Israel's right to exist and committing himself to policing the West Bank to provide Israel security from Palestinian attacks. Opposition heightened, and the situation threatened to turn into a civil war in November 1994 when Palestinian police faced down several thousand Hamas supporters demonstrating outside the largest mosque in Gaza. In addition to the Islamist resistance, Arafat also faced increasing opposition from leftist and nationalist critics who decried the "Bantustan solution" (Said 1995; Usher 1995, 14–20, 25–34).

Rabin also tried to face down hard-line opponents. Labour dominance in the Knesset allowed him to move forward in negotiations with little real attention or recognition of opposition. But as he converged on the peace settlement, signing Oslo II in September 1995, an increasingly vitriolic opposition attacked his cooperation with Arafat, shouting "Death to Arafat" and portraying Rabin wearing Arafat's trademark kaffiyeh.[30] As Netanyahu remarked in that same month, "I don't want to say isolated, but we were in the minority. [Now] I think the government is in the minority" (Gellman 1995).

---

[29] According to Edward Said, as early as 1992 Arafat seemed to be "staking his entire future on Rabin's electoral win" (Said 1995, 179).

[30] On opposition in the settlements, see Friedman (1994, 54–56); Sprinzak (1999); "Rabin Decides to Close Gazan Roads near Settlements, Arafat Condemns Attacks." *New York Times*, October 4, 1995; and "Five Killed in Suicide Bombing of Bus 26 in Jerusalem." *New York Times*, August 21, 1995.

Rabin and Arafat demonstrated their commitment to the process, continuing to cooperate even as they became targets of increasing attack. Rabin and Peres minimized Palestinian violations in an attempt to shore up the process. After a spate of bombings in 1995, for example, Arafat offered his condolences while Rabin vowed to continue the peace process, telling Arafat, "We must work together to prevent terrorism, and you must remember that terrorists are not just our enemies, but yours as well."[31] Arafat showed similar patience when on February 25, 1994, Dr. Baruch Goldstein from Kiryat Arba walked into the Ibrahimi Mosque in Hebron's Tomb of the Patriarchs and fired on worshiping Muslims, killing 29 and wounding nearly 100. Rather than call off the process, Arafat recalled that he told Rabin in a call following the massacre: "There are clearly fanatics in the settlements, and the government of Israel needs to take steps against them. They want to destroy the peace process" (Wallach and Wallach 1997, 460). That reaction, too, was met with harsh Palestinian criticism.

Had they been able to keep going, Arafat and Rabin might well have consummated an agreement whose benefits would have replenished their political capital on the South African model, but Rabin's murder in November 1995 put this possibility on ice.[32] Importantly, however, it was not the removal of Rabin from office through undemocratic methods that thwarted the peace process, but ultimately Peres' inability to take advantage of the opportunities that negotiating in a flawed democracy can afford that froze negotiations. His failure to call a snap election as soon as he replaced the fallen Rabin was surely one of the most consequential missed opportunities in the history of Middle East politics.[33] The evidence suggests that it might well have served the same function as de Klerk's March 1992 referendum, at a time when public opinion on both sides favored a two-state solution and the outrage at Rabin's assassination had all but the most fanatical Israeli right on the defensive.[34] Perhaps US pressure could have moved Peres at this point

[31] "Rabin Decides to Close Gazan roads near Settlements, Arafat Condemns Attacks." *New York Times*, October 4, 1995. See also Bruck (1995).

[32] In our survey of business executives in 2003 twenty of twenty-five respondents believed that Rabin's assassination increased the likelihood that Oslo would fail. However, only twelve of them said that they recognized this in 1995.

[33] Fifteen out of the top business executives we surveyed in 2003 thought this had been a strategic mistake by Peres. Nine of them thought his hard-line strategy in the run-up to the 1996 election harmed the prospects for peace.

[34] According to polls conducted by the Tami Steinmetz Center for Peace Research (TSC) at the University of Tel Aviv, the Oslo peace index of Israeli public opinion rose from 46.9 in October 1995 to 57.9 on November 8, immediately following Rabin's assassination. The index remained at 58 at the end of November, dropping to 55.8 in December. TSC, "Peace Index, 1995." http://spirit.tau.ac.il/socant/peace/ (June 18,

but the timing for this was not propitious in the run-up to the November 1996 US presidential election.

True, many critical issues remained unresolved, but as the ambiguity around permanent power-sharing during the South African referendum underscores, this does not mean that a workable settlement was unavailable. Indeed, in South Africa this ambiguity was essential to moving things forward. Had the South African negotiations fallen apart, many analysts would subsequently have said that the negotiations could not have succeeded because the whites would never have given up power-sharing. Plausible as such arguments might have sounded, they would have been wrong. Negotiations themselves shift conceptions of what is possible, which in turn changes what is possible.

In the event, Peres missed his opportunity, tacking instead to the right. He permitted the assassination of Yahya Ayyash in January 1996, which further contributed to the cycle of violence and closures on the West Bank and Gaza Strip. In addition, Peres responded to attacks from southern Lebanon by bombing Lebanese refugee camps in Operation Grapes of Wrath. At the same time, the wave of suicide bombings in the spring of 1996[35] led Israelis to seek a "firmer stance" in negotiations.[36] Likud was able to regroup while Peres alienated himself from Israeli supporters of the negotiations, particularly Israeli Palestinians. Palestinian radicals thus helped secure the victory of the Israeli right, and when elections were held in May 1996, Peres lost the race to be Israel's first directly elected prime minister by only 29,000 votes. In marked contrast to Peres, the incoming Prime Minister Benjamin Netanyahu had made no secret of his hostility to the Oslo Accords on which the negotiations had been predicated, leaving them on life support at best.

Facing defeated partners in peace left Arafat massively weakened. Initially, he responded by attempting to push the peace process forward at all costs. He courted Netanyahu, waiting for the call and meeting that would eventually confer recognition on him as a legitimate negotiating partner. Netanyahu, facing US pressure and an Israeli constituency pressing for a "secure peace," finally agreed not only to a meeting

---

2003). 72.5% of Palestinians polled in October 1995 supported the peace process. JMCC Public Opinion Poll no. 10 www.jmcc.org/publicpoll/results/1995/no10.htm. For additional discussion of the missed opportunities for settlements under Rabin and Peres, see Lust-Okar and Organski (2002).

[35] By March 1996, Israelis had experienced twelve suicide bombings during the Oslo process. Four of these came in February and March 1996 alone, killing fifty-nine Israelis (HaTorah 2003).

[36] A June 1996 poll by the TSC found that 70.7% of Israeli Jews supported a firmer stance toward the Palestinians. TSC, "Peace Index June 1996." http://spirit.tau.ac.il/socant/peace/peaceindex/1996/files/JUNE96e.pdf (June 25, 2003).

but also to signing the Hebron Accord and Wye agreement. Arafat responded with increased concessions, but it was clear that Netanyahu was neither a willing nor a committed partner in the peace process. Facing competing constituencies at home, he refused to implement the agreement and continued expanding settlements in the Occupied Territories. Democracy was no longer pushing toward an agreement.

Palestinians became increasingly disillusioned with the peace process, and with the Palestinian Authority's (PA) ability to deliver a positive solution. The Palestinian standard of living had fallen sharply since the signing of the 1993 Accords. Palestinians faced economic and social difficulties, and an unresponsive, authoritarian PA. International support from donors dropped as they lost confidence in the PA. Israel closed territories, continued expanding the settlements,[37] and dragged its feet in withdrawing from the Occupied Territories.[38] This compounded Palestinian alienation (Brynen 2000, 140–144). Support for the PA declined, with the majority of Palestinians coming to see it as corrupt.[39] The costs of selling any agreement with compromises thus rose dramatically for Arafat after the collapse of the Hebron Accord and Wye agreement. Seventy percent of Palestinians polled in June 1999 continued to support the peace process, but their trust in Israel had declined.[40] Arafat faced opposition not only from Hamas and Islamic Jihad, but also from former Fateh supporters, academics, and the Palestinian middle classes who had been willing at least to "wait and see" through 1996.

---

[37] The number of settlers rose from 99,065 in 1991 to 186,135 in 1999 (Foundation for Middle East Peace 2001).

[38] Had the aborted Wye Memorandum of October 1998 been implemented, Palestinians would have had control over 18.2% (Area A) of the West Bank and shared control (Area B) over 21.8%. Israelis would maintain full control (Area C) over 60% of the territory. Of the scheduled transfers, only 1% was territory moved from Area C to Area A, and 3% of territory designated Area B would have remained in "nature reserves" in which Palestinians would be prohibited from building. This agreement was signed after the initially declared deadline for the establishment of a Palestinian state. Ministry of Foreign Affairs, "Wye Memorandum Agreement, October 23, 1998." www.mfa.gov.il/mfa/go.asp?MFAH07o10 (June 25, 2003).

[39] A poll conducted by the Center for Palestine Research and Studies (CPRS) from June 3–5, 1999 found that 71% of Palestinians believed the PA was corrupt, and 66% believed that the level of corruption would remain the same or increase in the future. CPRS, "Public Opinion Poll no 41." www.pcpsr.org/survey/cprspolls/99/poll41a.html (June 17, 2003).

[40] The CPRS poll conducted from June 3–5, 1999 found that 70% of Palestinians surveyed supported the peace process, while 27% opposed it. At the same time, however, 66% of the respondents did not trust the peaceful intentions of the Barak government, in contrast to 23% expressing trust in the newly elected Israeli government. Similarly, 55% did not believe that final status negotiations would lead successfully to a permanent settlement, and 45% supported the continuation of armed attacks against Israel. CPRS, "Public Opinion Poll no. 41."

Thus, by the time Barak went to Camp David in 2000, intending to make major concessions, Arafat could no longer meet him halfway.[41] Elected in May 1999, Barak was riding a wave of anti-Netanyahu sentiment and knew his landslide victory was largely in response to the Israeli demands to "end this process" and make an agreement.[42] As a directly elected prime minister, he enjoyed a degree of independent legitimacy, and the possibility of holding a referendum on an agreement even in the face of a hostile Knesset. That he was willing to make bold moves was readily apparent as, in an attempt to force a peace agreement with the Syrians, he announced the unilateral withdrawal from southern Lebanon. The attempt to conclude an agreement with Hafez al-Asad was bold and creative. It was made in the apparent belief that the Syrian treaty was easier to conclude than the Palestinian agreement, and that peace with the Syrians would ease the way for the latter treaty.[43] After the strategy failed, Barak turned fully to the Palestinian track in the spring of 2000, signaling his commitment to make more concessions than any previous Israeli leader.[44] The resulting anger in the Knesset, marked by a failed no-confidence vote and threats to bolt the coalition, bolstered his credibility.[45]

The difficulty was that Arafat was now too weak to make concessions on such key issues as Jerusalem and the Palestinian "right of return." Palestinians' skepticism toward Barak's intentions had only heightened since the previous summer, as they saw themselves sidelined in favor of Syrian–Israeli negotiations. By the time he came to Camp David in the summer of 2000, against his will and under strong pressure from Bill Clinton, his hands were tied. Survey data showed the majority of Palestinians opposed to the meetings, with little confidence in Arafat's

---

[41] The extent to which concessions offered at Camp David were "major" and intended to meet Arafat halfway remains controversial. However, it appears clear that these concessions went beyond previous Israeli offers (much to many Israelis' dismay), and indeed exceeded offers which Arafat had previously found more acceptable.

[42] Barak won the 1999 elections for prime minister with 56.08% of the popular vote, vs. 43.92% for Netanyahu. See "Election Results 1999." *Jerusalem Post.* http://info.jpost. com/1999/Supplements/Elections99/final.html (June 22, 2003).

[43] "Barak Survives No-confidence Vote as Raids on Lebanon Resume." CNN.com World, February 14, 2000. www.cnn.com/2000/WORLD/meast/02/14/mideast.02/ (June 22, 2003).

[44] Thus William Safire would attack Barak for making concessions in violation of his own election pledges by offering Arafat virtually all of the West Bank (including the Jordan Valley which would have meant relocating 40,000 Israeli settlers), a virtual guarantee of a right of return to all Palestinians around the world, and shared sovereignty with a new Palestinian state over portions of Jerusalem, "unthinkable only a year ago" (Safire 2000, A25).

[45] "Barak Survives No-confidence Vote in Parliament." CNN.com World, July 10, 2000. www.cnn.com/2000/WORLD/meast/07/10/mideast.summit.02/ (June 22, 2003).

negotiating team.[46] By then Arafat was likely unable to restore the levels of support he had obtained in the early 1990s; his only hope of maintaining Fateh dominance and his leadership position was by responding to Palestinian popular opinion.[47] Unless Barak was willing to concede to Palestinian demands, which seemed vanishingly unlikely, Arafat would thus be unable to respond. This was clear to the lead writers for *The Economist* a week before the negotiations collapsed. Citing opinion polls giving only 32% support among Palestinians (with over 50% believing that he would be pressured into concessions at Camp David), they noted with great perspicacity that "the more he withstands the heat, the higher his stock will rise."[48] Former Secretary of State James Baker reached the same conclusion in his post-mortem following the collapse. Quoting Palestinian sources to the effect that "Arafat's ability to maneuver is nil,"[49] he concluded: "what was not enough for Mr. Arafat was too much for many Israelis, to whom any agreement will be submitted by referendum" (Baker 2000, A25). In short, the window of opportunity was no longer open because Arafat was not in a position to commit to anything that Barak could accept.

The Israeli–Palestinian negotiations demonstrate how easily potentially viable solutions to the commitment problem can be destroyed. Rabin had put himself and his leadership on the line, first in making and then defending his decision to negotiate with the PLO. His solid, if slim, Labor majority in the Knesset enabled him to act with little regard for his opponents. The bridges he burned along the way suggested that he would do what was needed to deliver an agreement once made. Arafat, who had his own reasons to negotiate, could thus anticipate that if he took the risk and signed the Oslo agreement the Israeli government would fulfill its part of the bargain and move forward on the final status issues. Rabin took similar risks, even if somewhat less was at stake for

---

[46] A Jerusalem Media and Communications Centre (JMCC) poll conducted July 16–17, 2000 found that 52.8% of respondents did not expect the delegations to reach an acceptable final agreement, while only 37.3% expected an agreement. More importantly, when asked "Are you confident or not confident in the Palestinian negotiating delegation in Camp David?" 34.7% lacked confidence and 7.8% "did not know." JMCC, "JMCC public opinion poll no. 38 on Palestinian attitudes towards the Camp David Summit, July 2000." www.jmcc.org/publicpoll/results/2000/no38.html (June 17, 2003).

[47] According to a PCPSR poll, 68% of Palestinians believed Arafat's overall position at Camp David was "just right," while 15% believed he had compromised too much. PCPSR, "Public opinion poll no. 1," July 27–29, 2000. www.pcpsr.org/survey/polls/2000/pla.html (June 17, 2003).

[48] "The Ballad of Camp David." *The Economist*, July 2: 43.

[49] For data supporting this conclusion, see PCPSR, "Public opinion poll no. 1."

him initially. He had reason to believe that Arafat would deliver on his commitments, given the political costs he had paid for entering negotiations. Certainly it was clear that if anyone could deliver the Palestinian side in 1995, it was he.[50] But the derailing of the process eroded his political power, and with it his ability to deliver the Palestinian side in any agreement. Opponents of Oslo grew from small Islamic and leftist fringe groups into the mainstream of Palestinians, who came to believe that years of interim agreements weakened them while providing no benefits. They continued to support "peace," but by 2000 the vast majority did not expect the then current process to succeed.[51]

Northern Irish vulnerability to multiple vetoes

Negotiations in Northern Ireland have faced two limitations. Moderate leaders have not had the success of Mandela and de Klerk in facing down their radical flanks, particularly on the Unionist side, and neither side has been sufficiently motivated by a deteriorating status quo to take the irreversible steps to consolidate agreement. The absence of an *intifada* or other serious threat to governability makes it remarkable that there has been an agreement at all, but unsurprising that the agreement has been in perpetual danger of falling apart.

Frustrated by the failure of the British government and the Unionists to negotiate seriously, the IRA suspended its ceasefire in February 1996 with a bomb explosion that injured 100 people in London (Stevenson 1996). As in South Africa, violence was effective in galvanizing a recalcitrant negotiating partner, and three weeks later the Irish and British governments announced that inclusive all-party negotiations on Northern Ireland would follow elections to a negotiating Forum. Chaired by former US Senator George Mitchell, talks began in June 1996 under rules of "sufficient consensus," so that no proposal could

---

[50] Even those who question whether Arafat turned Hamas and the Islamic Jihad "loose" on the Israelis argue that he did so in order to increase his bargaining position and ultimately gain a better settlement. Few seriously question whether he really sought to end the conflict and see a Palestinian state develop before his imminent death. As he made clear in his March 2002 interview with Christiane Amanpour, he sees the establishment of the Palestinian state (including East Jerusalem) not only as his personal mission, but as the very definition of who he is. See www.cnn.com/2002/WORLD/meast/03/29/arafat.cnna/ (March 29, 2002).

[51] In July 2000, 75% of Palestinians polled supported the Palestinian–Israeli peace process, but 60% believed that lasting peace was impossible. Moreover, 66% of Palestinians polled also believed that Israelis do not believe lasting peace is possible with Palestinians. PCPSR, "Public opinion poll no. 1."

pass if vetoed by Britain, Ireland, the Unionist UUP, or the Nationalist SDLP.[52]

These talks remained bogged down in party brinksmanship and infighting until a Labour landslide put Tony Blair into office in May 1997. Blair was free of the ties and debts to Unionist parliamentary partners that had hampered John Major's room to move the peace process. Blair immediately expressed his commitment to "solving" the Northern Ireland crisis. His first trip was to Northern Ireland, where he warned Sinn Fein that "the settlement train is leaving. I want you on that train. But it is leaving anyway and I will not allow it to wait for you. You cannot hold the process to ransom any longer. So end the violence now" (Mitchell 1999, 101). In June and July the British government worked hard behind the scenes to bring Sinn Fein into talks, to the growing ire of Unionists who feared Britain would sell them out to achieve peace. But the British and Irish governments recognized that no settlement would be enforceable without Sinn Fein's participation. Here the negotiators made a key decision that Israel and the US had not made in 2003 when they sought to marginalize Hamas from the road map: to include all potential spoilers to the agreement.

But bringing Sinn Fein into talks jeopardized the political strength and negotiating position of Trimble's UUP. If Unionist support for negotiations crumbled, forcing Trimble to leave the table, the peace process would disintegrate. Moderators and guarantors were therefore careful to shore up the Unionist side, to protect it from its own right wing (Mitchell 1999, 104). Moderators catered to the Unionist demand for IRA arms decommissioning, for example, by giving the issue prominence at the start of the talks.[53]

The IRA responded by announcing a second ceasefire on July 20, 1997, while continuing to refuse to decommission. Since the Unionists had made decommissioning a precondition of negotiations, Trimble took the risky decision to enter talks that could have gutted his support base. He had evidently reached a personal point of no return, as demonstrated by his private admission to Blair that "we are not in the mode of walking out" (Mitchell 1999, 108). On July 22, the debate over whether Sinn Fein should be admitted to talks without prior decommissioning came to a head in a vote. The UUP, Democratic Unionist Party (DUP), and UK Unionist Party (UKUP) all voted against it, with

---

[52] The idea of sufficient consensus was drawn directly from the South African CODESA negotiations, and predictably facilitated Unionist stonewalling. See Mnookin (2003).

[53] No agreement was in fact reached over decommissioning, however, which of course continued to act as a stumbling block to implementation as late as 2003.

the result that when talks reconvened in September Sinn Fein was at the table but the Unionist parties were gone (Mitchell 1999, 109). The DUP and UKUP had left for good, and tried to force the UUP to walk out through accusations that the party was betraying its people. Opinion polls showed that the UUP had popular support for remaining in the talks, but the party leadership was also under extreme pressure, even from within its own ranks (Mitchell 1999, 111, 117). This was the situation when the UUP finally entered negotiations under Trimble's leadership. Talks between the governments and the parties began seriously in October 1997.

Negotiations were organized in three strands. The first dealt with political arrangements within Northern Ireland, the second with North–South relations, and the third with relations between London and Dublin. Strand Two, concerning the relations between Ireland and Northern Ireland, was the most contested. In February, all parties agreed to an Easter deadline, and after a delay caused by ceasefire violations on both sides, the parties began serious negotiations in mid-March. As they came down to the wire, London and Dublin negotiated an agreement on Strand Two that was blatantly unacceptable to the Unionist side. At the insistence of the moderators, who argued that Trimble was not bluffing when he said he could not agree to this document, both sides returned to the table to renegotiate (Mitchell 1999, 166). Strand Two was reworked in the final week before the deadline to include the controversial provisions demanded by each side: a North–South council and an elected Assembly expected to operate in mutual interdependence. The Good Friday agreement, also known as the Belfast agreement, was concluded in April 1998.

The accord included five main constitutional principles: Northern Ireland's future constitutional status, as part of Ireland or the UK, would be in the hands of its citizens; the people of Ireland, north and south, could vote to unite; Northern Ireland would remain, for the time being, within the United Kingdom; Northern Irish citizens could choose to identify as Irish, British, or both; and the Irish state would drop its territorial claim on Northern Ireland (Darby 2003). A copy of the agreement was delivered to every household in Northern Ireland in anticipation of the referendum, and a clear majority in both Ireland (56% turnout; 94% approval) and Northern Ireland (81% turnout; 71% approval) approved it. This included majorities of both Unionists and Nationalists, although the Unionist majority was slim (Bew 1998, 1).

As with the Oslo Accord, but unlike the ANC–NP agreement, the Belfast agreement did not mark the end of negotiations and the beginning of implementation. For almost two years, London continued to govern Northern Ireland as implementation snagged on the controversial issues that had been left outstanding in the Good Friday agreement. It seems clear that part of the obstacle to implementing the Belfast agreement was that a substantial portion of Unionists never believed that the status quo was unsustainable. Unlike in South Africa, where polls indicated that most whites had concluded apartheid was no longer feasible by the end of the 1980s, most Protestants in Northern Ireland continued to believe direct rule from London, or majority rule in which they would be the majority, were sustainable alternatives. They believed that a compromise with Nationalists could only weaken their position.[54] In this they were analogous to the Jewish settlers in the Occupied Territories who refuse to see flawed democracy as unsustainable. Achieving a settlement might require that their government force them to accept it.

But this is easier said than done in SAMENI settings. Given democratic constraints in the Unionist movement, Trimble and the moderates have been unable to face down the right wing that opposes agreement. From the outset, moderate Unionists had only a narrow margin of support for the accord. Exit polls from the May 1998 referendum on the agreement showed Protestants almost evenly divided between support and opposition. The Protestant middle class appeared ready to defect from the settlement over the early release of prisoners (Hayes and Dowds 2001, 2; Millar 2000a, 1). Whereas the March 1992 South African referendum returned a solid endorsement for continued negotiations, the results of the Northern Ireland referendum were sufficiently ambiguous that they could still be used to political advantage by those who opposed a settlement, highlighting again the fickle role of democracy in negotiations (Breen 1998). Although 96% of Catholics supported the agreement, only 55% of Protestants did (Elliot and Flackes 1999, 125). Moreover, the Protestant vote was exceedingly fragile. According to the *Northern Ireland Referendum and Election Study*, one-quarter of all Protestants had considered changing their vote during the campaign, mostly from a Yes to a No vote. Among Catholics, only 7% had considered changing theirs (Hayes and McAllister 2001, 81).

Elections for the Northern Ireland Assembly were held in June 1998. The UUP won 28 seats, the SDLP 24, DUP 20, Sinn Fein 18, Alliance 6, Women's Coalition 2, UKUP 5, Progessive Unionist Party (PUP) 2, and Anti-Agreement Unionists (AAU) 3. Although the UUP won a plurality

[54] In late 2000 The Northern Ireland Life and Times survey found that 14% of Protestants who voted "yes" in 1998 would now vote against the agreement because of declining support for devolution and lack of progress on decommissioning (Hayes and McAllister 2001; Hayes and Dowds 2001).

of seats (not of votes), its slim margin of victory actually represented a loss for the party, whose 1997 returns at Westminster presaged a win of as many as 39 seats, and only 16 for Ian Paisley's DUP. The 1998 election results suggested that the moderate center of Unionism was eroding. Moreover, the UUP was comparatively vulnerable as the anti-agreement camp (DUP, UKUP, and AAU) also won, between them, 28 seats. Analysts predicted before the election that the UUP would need to win at least 30 seats to avoid deadlock in the Assembly and to make the North–South council work (Moriarty 2000b, 2). Therefore, although the UUP won the election and emerged as the largest party in the Assembly, anti-agreement parties were also able to interpret the election result as a victory, in particular because the transfer system of voting favored the UUP (Moriarty 2000a).

The election campaign also laid bare differences within the UUP over the agreement. Jeffrey Donaldson, a UUP Member of Parliament at Westminster, emerged as the most important opposition figure within the party but almost half of the leadership of the UUP openly opposed the accord. Some of these took seats in the Assembly, but they could not be counted on to vote the party line, further diluting the pro-agreement bloc (Bew 1998). Trimble barely squeaked by in elections for party leadership after 1998, as he faced powerful challenges over the issue of implementation of the accord. When Trimble agreed in 2000 that it might be possible to reenter government with Sinn Fein without prior decommissioning, Martin Smyth mounted an internal challenge for party leadership which, though unsuccessful, exposed deep and continuing fault lines within the Ulster Unionist Party and the weakness of Trimble's support base (Tonge and Evans 2001, 113–114). Under pressure from Britain, Trimble nevertheless twice entered a power-sharing government without IRA decommissioning.

On August 15, 1998 a bomb exploded in Omagh, killing 28 people (mostly women and children) and injuring 220 – the largest loss of life of any single act of violence during the Troubles. The Real IRA, a breakaway faction of the IRA opposed to the settlement, claimed responsibility and immediately apologized for the deaths, announcing the suspension of all military operations. But the act was so widely condemned, including by the IRA, that it backfired against hard-line Republicans, reminding everyone of the gruesome alternative to peace. Omagh played an important role in solidifying a commitment to peace across Northern Ireland and in marginalizing those from the Nationalist right who would scuttle the process. Since then, Sinn Fein and the IRA have faced less of the hard-line censure that has limited Trimble's room to maneuver in the implementation phase of the process.

The UUP blocked Sinn Fein's entry to the Executive for sixteen months, insisting again on prior IRA decommissioning, while Britain, Ireland, and mediators continued to try to broker a compromise.[55] In November 1999, a slim majority of 58% of UUP delegates approved entry into a joint government, and the British and Irish governments transferred power from London to Belfast within days. Under a power-sharing formula, Trimble became First Minister, and Seamus Mallon, leader of the Nationalist SDLP, the coequal Deputy First Minister. Ten other cabinet seats were divided proportionally among Ulster Unionists, the SDLP, Sinn Fein, and the DUP. The UUP was left deeply divided by the split vote, and the terms of entry included a clause committing the party council to reconvene in February to review the decision. If the IRA had not by then begun to disarm, the party would use its majority position to dismantle the government (Hoge 1999).

As in South Africa, moderates in the opposition helped government reformers face down their recalcitrant flanks. When the IRA initially refused to move on decommissioning, London responded by suspending the Assembly in February 2000 to protect Trimble from another divisive UUP vote that threatened to sink his leadership. This made the IRA realize that it had to help Trimble survive, just as the ANC had helped de Klerk do the same thing by agreeing to power-sharing in the interim constitution and Arafat had helped Rabin by dampening Palestinian response to the massacre in the Ibrahimi Mosque. Hours after the suspension, the IRA made its first commitment to dismantle its arsenal (Hoge 2000a). The result was that in March Trimble won an internal challenge to his party leadership, if with only 57% support (Hoge 2000b).

But it was enough for him to move forward. In a bid to face down his opponents, Trimble announced his intention to sever ties with the Loyalist Orange Order. Although the move was part of a longstanding agenda to reduce the party's sectarian connections, the timing was clearly calculated to hive off naysayers within the party (Millar 2000b). The IRA cooperated, agreeing to put their guns and bombs beyond use and to weapons-dump inspections by international assessors Cyril Ramaphosa and Martti Ahtisaari. The Unionists responded by supporting Trimble's return to a power-sharing government with Sinn Fein by a two-thirds majority (Breen 2000). The UUC finally voted at the end of May to resume implementation, and Britain transferred power

---

[55] At the time, Trimble insisted that his hands were tied, and Ken Maginnis, a leading moderate within the party, agreed that the plan would split the party and was impossible to sell to rank-and-file supporters (Pogatchnik 1999).

back to the Northern Ireland Assembly and its twelve-person joint cabinet.[56]

Devolution was suspended three more times over the next three years, so that the power-sharing government in Northern Ireland was operational for only twenty of the possible fifty-four months that it might have functioned.[57] In September 2002 the Ulster Unionist Council issued a statement affirming that the UUP would "not sit in government with unreconstructed terrorists," again demanding the total disbandment of all terrorist groups including the IRA.[58] In October 2002 devolution was suspended again because Trimble threatened to withdraw his ministers from the Executive in protest against the continued participation of Sinn Fein in government.[59] Blair has repeatedly backed the Unionist position, noting that the Irish Republic has refused to let Sinn Fein take seats in government without IRA dissolution, whereas Unionists in the North had been forced into a power-sharing arrangement with Sinn Fein.[60] Gerry Adams complained that London should not have the latitude to suspend the institutions of the Good Friday agreement every time the UUP threatened to walk out, pointing out that Blair would be unlikely to do the same if Sinn Fein threatened to leave the government.[61] Trimble made the contrary case that Britain should not have suspended devolved government; that it ought instead to have suspended Sinn Fein.

Post-agreement negotiations have nevertheless settled a number of other issues that were left outstanding in April 1998. In November 2001 the Royal Ulster Constabulary was renamed the Police Service of Northern Ireland, and the new Policing Board replaced the Police Authority. Although the UUP contested the arrangement, the PSNI committed to recruiting on the basis of 50:50 representation.[62] This is potentially important. In South Africa the integration of the police force

[56] Reuters, "Northern Ireland Rivals Try for Home Rule Again." *New York Times*, May 30, 2000. www.nytimes.com/reuters/international/international-irish-1.html (May 31, 2000).

[57] Text of a speech made by Gerry Adams, Monaghan, October 26, 2002. CAIN Web Service http://cain.ulst.ac.uk/events/peace/docs/ga261002.htm (November 11, 2002): 6.

[58] Text of document agreed at the Ulster Unionist Council meeting on Saturday September 21, 2002. CAIN Web Service http://cain.ulst.ac.uk/issues/politics/docs/uup/uup210902.htm (November 11, 2002).

[59] This occurred after a scandal in which Sinn Fein was accused of spying on other parties and government at Stormont.

[60] Speech by Tony Blair, Harbour Commissioners' Office, Belfast, October 17, 2002. CAIN Web Service http://cain.ulst.ac.uk/events/peace/docs/tb171002.htm (November 11, 2002).

[61] Speech made by Gerry Adams, Monaghan, October 26, 2002. CAIN Web Service http://cain.ulst.ac.uk/events/peace/docs/ga261002.htm (November 11, 2002).

[62] CAIN Web Service, Chronology of the Conflict, http://cain.ulst.ac.uk/othelem/chron/ch00.htm (June 5, 2003).

before the transition greatly eased enforcement problems. The IRA also made an important symbolic statement in July 2002, apologizing for killing and injuring noncombatants during the Troubles.[63] IRA decommissioning persisted as the main obstacle to implementation, however, leading analysts to assume that the relevant question was "what would have induced (or might in future induce) the IRA to disband as a paramilitary organization?"

But the South African experience suggests otherwise. South Africa's NP also insisted initially on disarmament as a precondition for talks with the ANC, but when the ANC refused, talks proceeded almost without a pause. Considering that an international monitoring team repeatedly verified that IRA weapons were beyond use[64] and that Loyalists perpetrated most of the post-accord violence (Hayes and McAllister 2001, 88), it is far from obvious that the IRA's refusal to change its rhetoric was a literal threat to security in Northern Ireland or Britain in the late 1990s.[65] Yet Tony Blair repeatedly suspended power-sharing governments out of sensitivity to Unionist demands. For instance, in May 2003 he again halted implementation by postponing legislative elections. He deemed insufficient Gerry Adams' statement that the IRA would "disarm fully as part of the Northern Ireland peace settlement if other parties to the accord fulfill their obligations" (Hoge 2003, A2), despite declarations by the Irish government and most pro-agreement parties that the insistence on disarmament caused more problems than it solved. American envoy Richard Haass also called for elections to take place "as soon as possible" (Lavery 2003, A2). By July 2003, many politicians in Northern Ireland, including pro-agreement Unionists, agreed that postponing elections placed tremendous pressure on the settlement and seriously undermined the credibility of the agreement among voters.[66] Pro-agreement members of the Ulster Unionist Party were particularly concerned that party infighting would mean that postponed elections could favor those who opposed the agreement.[67]

---

[63] Full text of IRA statement of apology, July 16, 2002. CAIN Web Service http://cain. ulst.ac.uk/events/peace/docs/ira160702.htm (June 5, 2003).

[64] The IRA suspended contact with the Independent International Commission on Decommissioning (IICD) on October 30, 2002, full text of IRA statement, CAIN Web Service http://cain.ulst.ac.uk/events/peace/docs/ira301002.htm (November 11, 2002).

[65] DUP party member David Ervine argues for example that it was destructive of the UUP to insist on a condition that they should have known the IRA would be unable to comply with. (Interview, June 20, 2003.)

[66] Interviews with David McNarry and Dr. Esmond Birnie (UUP), Rachel Steert (Women's Coalition), David Ervine (DUP), and James Cooper (UUP).

[67] Interviews with Dr. Esmond Birnie and James Cooper (UUP).

SAMENI negotiations are prone to forms of myopia that lead pressure to be applied in the wrong places. Blair's repeated suspension of power-sharing was a failure of vision and nerve that ranks with Peres' missed opportunity in 1995, playing into the hands of those Unionist leaders for whom stonewalling against change has always been the name of the game. This is not to say that great and continuing pressure on the IRA would not have been needed to move the process forward. It is to say that Blair was uniquely placed, among recent British prime ministers, to bring no less essential pressure to bear on the Unionists. They too had to be told that the "settlement train is leaving the station." The relevant South African precedent here is not the failed CODESA idea of "sufficient consensus" which empowers and emboldens spoilers, and which, notably, fell apart twice without moving the process forward. Rather it is that powerful players committed to a settlement must garner enough popular support that spoilers realize that they will be marginalized if they do not join the process. Recall that the NP and ANC negotiated the core elements of the South African settlement in secret in 1992, and then announced them as nonnegotiable. Inkatha added its name to the ballot only days before the 1994 election, once Buthelezi finally realized that it could not be derailed.

This merits particular note in light of the fact that in other areas there have been moves toward the type of normal politics in Northern Ireland that are the ultimate goal of SAMENI negotiations. When government has been in session, much (though not all) of what goes on is politics as usual. Statements and proposed legislation about road safety, health-care, unemployment, and pork barrel-type projects dominate the websites of all the major parties. The Women's Coalition and the Alliance Party explicitly eschew sectarian designation and are self-consciously attempting to generate a new political dialogue that will expand the possibilities of political identity in Northern Ireland. Polls indicate that a majority of Protestants and Catholics alike had also moved beyond the conflict in the new century, agreeing that issues like health service and unemployment were most pressing.[68]

To sum up, the obstacles to peace in Northern Ireland were as formidable in the 1990s as they were in the Middle East. Yet our analysis suggests that had different choices been made at critical junctures, things could have turned out differently, and there might have been settlements comparable to what was achieved in South Africa. Indeed,

---

[68] In the 1999–2000 the Northern Ireland Life and Times survey, respondents were asked to identify the most important priorities for the new assembly: 40% chose improving health services and 37% cited employment. www.qub.ac.uk/ss/csr/nilt (June 5, 2003).

underscoring the fluidity of SAMENI negotiations and their critical dependence on contingencies of choice, we saw that the South African transition might well have derailed at various points, just as the others have done.

5.   Implications

There is nothing intrinsic to the conflicts in the Middle East and Northern Ireland that renders them less tractable than South Africa's. People miss this because they focus on the alleged divided character of societies involved in these conflicts. They would do well to remember that similar claims about South Africa were conventional wisdom in the 1980s. The divided society lens directs attention either to the wrong features of the conflicts or to the wrong features of negotiations. Recognizing SAMENI conflicts as negotiated settlements in the context of flawed democracies redirects our attention to the importance of achieving agreements that can sustain popular support as a condition for making them stick. In what follows, we elaborate on the conditions that facilitate and undermine settlements, discuss the future prospects for the Middle East and Northern Ireland, and spell out some larger implications for conflict studies.

Lessons learned

In contrast to conventional analyses of SAMENI conflicts, we find that successful negotiations do not depend on the nature of the solution. Rather, what is vital is that the solution – whatever its form – gains enough legitimacy that potential spoilers decide that challenging it is too costly. This means building popular support for the new dispensation while it is being negotiated. It is far from clear that this could not have occurred had the negotiations between Rabin and Arafat been able to conclude in 1995, or had Peres adopted a different policy than he did immediately following Rabin's death. We saw in part 3 ("Shifting constraints") that at that time the two-state solution enjoyed considerable legitimacy. Blair was in an even stronger position to solve the enforcement problem by appealing to popular support in Northern Ireland after 1998, given his historic mandate in 1997 and the enthusiasm for the agreement in both communities. In the end, it is only the legitimacy of the agreement itself that can get potential spoilers to adhere to the conditions of a peace settlement.

Because a viable agreement must enjoy popular support, radicals and hard-liners cannot be marginalized until their supporters desert them and back the negotiations. This happened dramatically with de Klerk's referendum, and it could have happened, we argued, in the Middle East in 1995–1996. Unfortunately, because analysts frequently underestimate the importance of democratic legitimacy to a negotiated settlement, they often focus on, and pin their hopes upon, moderate leaders who are willing to push a peace agreement forward – "sensible chaps" who are appealing to deal with – regardless of whether they have the requisite popular support. For instance, Gerry Adams' emergence on the scene in 1988 as a new kind of pragmatic IRA leader "with a human face" led to endless speculation about whether a settlement could now be anticipated. But Adams and his behavior were irrelevant until the Blair government came to power in the UK in 1997 – given the dependence of the Tory governments on Unionist support under Thatcher and Major.

By the same token, both US and Israeli negotiators often focused on Palestinian players who could not reasonably be expected to deliver. The 2003 Middle East road map was a case in point. Arafat's corrupt government had lacked grass-roots legitimacy since the mid-1990s, and the appointment of Mahmoud Abbas as Prime Minister was scarcely a solution to this problem. With its political legitimacy, not to mention its security apparatus, in tatters, the PA was in no position to rein in the violence that followed the Aqaba summit.[69] The more Abbas was praised

---

[69] The Oslo process weakened Fateh and the PA vis-à-vis Hamas, which both provided critical social services to an increasingly impoverished Palestinian people. See Fisher (2003). Support for Hamas grew at Fateh's expense. In December 1996, support for Fateh was 35.2% and for Hamas 10.3%. Similarly, 41.2% of Palestinians most trusted Yasser Arafat, and 4.8% trusted Sheikh Yassin. Only 19.5% of Palestinians did not trust anyone. By December 2001, support for Fateh dropped to 26.1%, while that for Hamas rose to 21.3%. Similarly, trust in Arafat declined to 24.5% and that in Yassin rose to 12.8%. This trend has continued. By April 2003, Fateh remained the single most-trusted faction in Palestinian politics, with 22.6%, although overall support for Fateh trailed the combined support for Hamas and leftist factions (22.0%), Islamic Jihad (6.3%), PFLP (2.0%), and other factions (3.1%). However, more, 34.3%, responded they "don't trust anyone." (Fisher 2003; JMCC, "Public Opinion Poll no. 43." www.jmcc.org/publicpoll/results/2001/no43.htm [June 25, 2003]; JMCC, "Public Opinion Poll no. 18." www.jmcc.org/publicpoll/results/1996/no18.htm [June 25, 2003].) A poll conducted by JMCC in April 2003 found that the majority of Palestinians believed that Abbas' appointment as Prime Minister would have little effect on the PA reform process: of respondents, 28.7% felt the appointment would further PA reforms, 17.4% felt it would hinder reforms, and 43.2% felt it would have no effect. It is telling that 67.8% of respondents believed that the creation of a prime ministry was due to external influences alone, 19.2% felt that it was due to external influences and a conviction that the reforms were in the interests of the Palestinian people, and only 6.2% believed the reform was undertaken purely in order to benefit the Palestinian people. Furthermore, only 1.8% of respondents named Abu Mazen as the Palestinian personality that they most trust, vs. 21.1% for Yasser Arafat, and 9.7%

as "reasonable" in Jerusalem and Washington, the weaker he was bound to become in Ramallah. Caught between a rock and a hard place, any popularity he could hope to sustain would depend on delivering what Arafat could not: better living conditions, an end to curfews, and open borders – all of which depend on Israeli goodwill and US pressure.

The presence of a strong radical flank need not itself bode poorly for peace, provided efforts are made to incorporate them if they cannot be marginalized. That Hamas was not at the table in the early negotiations over the road map is the functional equivalent of the South African government's trying to strike a deal with Buthelezi in 1992, or of talks in Northern Ireland excluding Sinn Fein. Notwithstanding IRA failure to decommission as late as 2003, Sinn Fein support for the agreement was unwavering, as its electoral base grew in the years following the accord. Hamas and other violent Palestinian nationalist groups are doubtless aware that their strategy will never lead to outright victory over Israel, but their immediate target is not Israel. They are engaged in a struggle for control over the representation of the Palestinians, and failure of the peace process has solidified their support base. Effective marginalization of Hamas was likely impossible by 2003, so that any lasting peace must involve dealing with them, perhaps in secret – at least initially.[70] Contrary to press reports at the time, Sharon's overture to the Palestinian Authority was not a case of Nixon going to China (Diamond 2003, 1). It was more like Nixon being dragged to Hong Kong.

Even when the right actors are on board, they may have to sell mutually incompatible solutions to their constituencies – at least until people realize that they can live with outcomes they had previously dismissed as unthinkable. Constructive ambiguity can help. There seems to be little question that in the Middle East obscurity about the final outcome, and even the interim steps, was essential for moving the process forward in 1995. Lack of clarity about such issues as the final status of Jerusalem, borders, settlements, and the right of return has been harshly criticized, but ambiguity about these issues was essential to creating a new reality in which Palestinians and Israelis accepted a two-state solution as legitimate. The South African success depended on the final agreement to abandon constitutionally mandated power-sharing not being fully apparent earlier in negotiations. As this process illustrates, the very fact of participating in negotiations can loosen up fixed perceptions.

---

for Ahmed Yassin. (JMCC, "JMCC Public Opinion Poll no. 48," April 2003. www. jmcc.org/publicpoll/results/2003/no48.htm#results [June 22, 2003].)

[70] Hamas moderates have signaled their willingness to enter negotiations (Hass 2003).

This is not to deny that constructive ambiguity can create implementation problems later. Northern Ireland and the Middle East have revealed all too clearly that it can. But without it they will not move forward, and the creative ingenuity of the players will never become focused on dealing with the implementation problems.

If the SAMENI cases suggest that negotiations proceed best if the final details are left for later, they also suggest that there is urgency in getting to an agreement. That the South African negotiations moved quickly and concluded decisively contributed greatly to the result. Conversely, the slowing down of Middle East negotiations has repeatedly strengthened the hands of stonewallers and led windows of opportunity to close. The Bush administration seemed to appreciate this in the summer of 2003, when Secretary of State Colin Powell argued forcefully for the need to "move urgently," not giving time for the "terrorists to win."[71] Even the most committed moderates must outrun the radicals and reactionaries who will be determined to prevent an agreement. The sooner a negotiated arrangement is seen as the new status quo, the less likely it is that recalcitrant forces will be able to destroy it.

Future prospects

Taken together, these observations inform our expectations over the prospects for settlements in the Middle East and Northern Ireland. Despite continuing setbacks to the implementation of the Good Friday agreement, the Northern Ireland conflict appears considerably closer to resolution than the Middle East. Once decommissioning is seen in perspective, it becomes clear that the window of opportunity has been open for a good part of the time after 1998. Members of the Legislative Assembly speculate that support for the agreement has eroded in part precisely because it has been suspended so often that it seems unworkable.[72] The fact that it is suspended by Westminster makes it seem additionally undemocratic in the sense of being more vulnerable to external

---

[71] "Powell Condemns Hamas Role." June 21, 2003, 00:53 GMT 01:53 UK, BBC News. http://news.bbc.co.uk/2/hi/middle_east/3008420.stm (June 24, 2003). Note that the 2003 Geneva Accord recognizes the importance of moving quickly toward a final settlement which is specified with a degree of detail that would not have been possible but for the Oslo Accord.

[72] Author interview with Esmond Birnie. A poll conducted in January 2003 showed that only 36% of Protestants would still vote for the Good Friday agreement. But 60% of Protestants would be willing to support the peace process if it could be made to work (Irwin 2004).

than electoral pressure. Blair was unwilling through 2004 to pay the political cost of putting real pressure on the Unionists, but he had both the mandate and the leeway so to do. Moreover, it seems reasonable to think that he might have done so, and that there may well be future opportunities for him or others to implement the Good Friday agreement – particularly for a Labour government with a large majority.

In 2004 there seemed to be three possibilities for Northern Ireland. Implementation could continue to move forward in fits and starts, but with everyday politics revolving less around the agreement and more around tangible improvements in areas like healthcare and employment. Polls show that popular support for the agreement has been diminishing ever since it was signed, but also that most people in Northern Ireland believe that social welfare and the economy are more pressing issues than the relative political status of Unionists and Republicans.[73] It remains to be seen whether the voting public will be able to move the parties toward a similar consensus. Alternatively, if the stalemate on decommissioning persists, there might be another big international push (possibly again led by the US) to reach agreement on the outstanding issues. Publicity, attention, and deadlines would be used again, as they were in 1998, to generate a groundswell of support and excitement for implementation. Another possibility is a reversion to violence – even if the trend toward normal politics against the background of the Good Friday agreement makes this outcome less likely. But completely ruling it out assumes more backbone from the British government than Blair exhibited in facing down Unionist recalcitrance in his first five years in office, and it takes too static a view of the IRA leadership which could always revert to a military strategy.

Successfully maneuvering through the Middle East road map would require a great deal from Palestinian, Israeli, and international actors. The toll of the *intifada*, as well as the changing regional situation after the US–Iraq war, led several key players to return to negotiations. At the same time, however, these same conditions limited the trust each side holds in the other, and hence the likelihood that moderates can deliver an agreement. Prime Minister Sharon held his position largely due to the weakness of the traditional Israeli peace camp. Given this reality, not to mention his history and ideology, he was unlikely to become a reformer.[74] Indeed, his 2002 decision to construct a massive fence in the West Bank was less likely meant to ensure the end of terrorism – at

---

[73] See www.qub.ac.uk/ss/csr/nilt (June 5, 2003).
[74] We should not be surprised, therefore, by his equivocal statements on Israel's "occupation" of the West Bank in May and June 2003 (Kifner 2003; Shipler 2003).

which it failed – than to make conditions unbearable, thus stimulating Palestinian emigration from the Occupied Territories (Shaheen 2003).[75] Yet, if he appeared less than eager to negotiate, he was capable of delivering. Deteriorating conditions had led many settlers to announce that they would accept evacuation from the settlements in return for economic compensation, thus weakening the right flank.[76] If Sharon chose to enter into the negotiations full-steam ahead, he could sideline his right-wing supporters and offer Labor participation in his government (Lust-Okar 2003, 3–7). As the historical champions of the peace process, they would have little choice but to join. Sharon would have burned his bridges behind him, enhancing, from the standpoint of our analyses, the prospects for peace.

Success would require significant US pressure on the Israeli administration to make concessions in the face of continuing, right-wing, domestic opposition and Palestinian violence. The Israeli government would eventually need to convince its own supporters that they are better off with an agreement with the Palestinians and withdrawal from the Occupied Territories than they are with either continued occupation of the West Bank and Gaza Strip (WBGS) or the ethnic cleansing of Eretz Israel. This had become a tall order by 2002, when Israeli support for the "transfer" of Palestinians living in the WBGS reached 46%, and the support for transfer of Palestinians living inside the Green Line stood at 31% (Jaffee Center 2002).[77] Perhaps even more difficult, however, was that Israelis also needed to convince Palestinians that they would no longer solve immediate crises by rolling tanks into Palestinian towns or assassinating leaders with military aircraft. Without that conviction, it is difficult to see how support for any settlement would be forthcoming.

---

[75] The fence is expected to affect the lives of 600,000 West Bank Palestinians. See "U.N. Estimates Israeli Barrier Will Disrupt Lives of 600,000." *New York Times*, November 12, 2003.

[76] According to a 2003 poll, 54% of settlers stated that they would resist forced dismantlement, but 74% would entertain moving inside the Green Line in return for compensation. Moreover, 71% of settlers thought a peace agreement should be reached (up from about 55% in 2002) and 44% accepted a Palestinian state (up from 19% the previous year). Israelis also increasingly see settlers as isolated in their struggle to secure settlement. The same survey found that about 64% of settlers expect themselves to be alone, and 75% of Israelis inside the Green Line see settlers as isolated in their struggle with the government. "Poll: 71% of Settlers Say There Will Be Deal with the Palestinians." *Haaretz*, July 23, 2003.

[77] See also "Growing Popularity of a Transfer in Israel, Removing Palestinians from the West Bank and Gaza and Distributing Them Throughout the Arab World." National Public Radio Morning Edition, October 21, 2002. www.npr.org/programs/morning/transcripts/2002/oct/021021.gradstein.html (June 24, 2003).

The tasks facing the Palestinians were equally difficult. Those intent on a settlement would need to restrain or incorporate the radical flank, demonstrating to Israelis not only that they could, but that they consistently would, ensure Israeli security. This was particularly difficult at a time when the security infrastructure of the Palestinian Authority had largely been demolished, and when support for the Fateh leadership and confidence in the Israelis were both at record lows. With a strong radical flank, the PA could not afford to sideline Hamas completely. Rather, it would need to gain at least tacit Hamas support, most likely by granting Hamas moderates what they have most fervently wanted: a place at the table. Because even this would be unlikely to satisfy the hard-liners who wanted only to see Israel pushed into the sea, the need for security remained. A successful solution would thus require a significant change in the attitudes of both Palestinian and Israeli hard-liners in the long run.[78]

Western prognosticators rushed to hail Arafat's death in November 2004 as creating a window of opportunity for peace. Our account of the conditions needed for a settlement suggest that such optimism was misplaced. Mahmoud Abbas confronted many of the same legitimacy problems that plagued Arafat by 2000. Yet the US State Department and the Western press immediately zeroed in on him as a sensible chap with whom business could perhaps be done. Their inattention to figures like the imprisoned Marwan Barghouti (the most popular secular leader among Palestinians) underscores how little they grasped that it is the legitimacy of leaders, not their pliability to others' agendas, that is essential to a tractable settlement. For Arafat's death to create an opportunity on the Palestinian side, not only Barghouti but also Hamas would have to participate, becoming invested in solving the problem rather than in derailing potential solutions. Even in that eventuality, no settlement would be feasible without significant changes in Israeli politics. In the years since the 2000 Camp David debacle, the Sharon government had made it plain to all who were willing to look that it was more interested in a military victory than a political settlement. Without a change in that attitude, there would be no more chance of a settlement in the Middle East than there had been in Northern Ireland before 1997.

The difficulty of achieving settlements in SAMENI settings should not surprise us. We have seen that the windows of opportunity that make

---

[78] People-to-people programs and efforts to revise history textbooks on both sides are part of the efforts to change fundamental attitudes toward "the other" on both sides. See Moughrabi (2001) and Israel/Palestine Center for Research and Information program on Peace Education (www.ipcri.org/index1.html) and *Jerusalem Post* (Internet edition), "Teachers Greet the Enemy." April 3, 2003 at www.ipcri.org/index1.html.

such settlements possible open rarely, and they seldom stay open for long. Few politicians are willing to take the considerable risks involved in moving through them. Indeed, they often fail to see either the possibilities or how fleeting they might be. A better and more widespread understanding of the dynamics of SAMENI negotiations, and of their consistency with the logic of transplacements, might diminish that possibility.

Rethinking conflict studies

Conflict studies have long been driven in part by a debate, often implicit, over whether conflict is driven from above – by political elites manipulating followers to gross acts of violence – or from below – by ancient and primordial hatreds nurtured in families, communities, and places of worship. The study of conflict resolution is similarly riveted, and focuses either on elite dispositions to negotiate or on grass-roots initiatives to foster tolerance. One of the functions of the imperfect democratic settings we study in these cases is to draw the link, both empirically and analytically, between the two levels of focus.

In the middle of a peace process, a society lacks the security both of hard-line retaliation (which represents the status quo ante), and of a democratically legitimate settlement (which is the final goal). Suspended thus between an unsustainable past and an unreachable future, elite politics becomes polarized. In the politics of peace, as each side breaks into two or more factions, the most important contests are those that take place among the factions. And in these fights, the primary weapon is popular support.

In both the Middle East and Northern Ireland the way forward seems primarily constrained not by elites or masses alone, but by the link between them. In both places those factions that reject a settlement, or that reject the particular settlement that is on the table, have gained ascendance since the heady days (1994 in the Middle East, 1998 in Northern Ireland) when a majority on all sides favored reconciliation. As negotiations have dragged on, a reforming center has lost ground partly because its members have failed to lock in their advantage by making peace work.

Facing failure, or at most limited success, people grow impatient, or unnerved. Skittish, they swing among factions. In the last four Israeli elections voters returned Rabin, Netanyahu, Barak, and Sharon – in that order. David Trimble has been operating on an exceedingly thin margin of support almost continuously since 1998, the Nationalist SDLP has lost support to Sinn Fein, and Arafat and the PLO have grown steadily more vulnerable to Hamas and Islamic Jihad. Electoral volatility and slim margins of support stop any side from declaring a mandate in such circumstances, undermining the chances of any significant move in one direction or another. Then democracy, the link between elites and a support base, can paralyze transformation rather than facilitate it.

But paralysis is no more sustainable than the status quo ante was once considered to be, and the specter of failure will continue to hang over these societies so long as some democratic peace is not reached. The factionalized character of the politics of peace draws the link between leaders and constituents even more starkly than normal politics, and their mutual dependence offers the possibility of both vicious and virtuous cycles. A decisive swing in favor of a settlement will require some success – some sense that moving forward is better than moving backward. Achieving success lies in the hands of elites. But support for an agreement, or for implementation, which is what is needed before elites can move decisively toward peace without risk of losing power altogether, lies with their constituencies.

APPENDIX: SURVEYS OF ISRAELI BUSINESS ELITES

In December 2003–February 2004, we conducted a survey of twenty-five Israeli business elites. A Jewish Israeli citizen administered the survey through face-to-face interviews with top executives. They were chosen in a stratified sample to include large enterprises in a range of economic sectors: Investment Banking and Holdings, Venture Capital, Insurance, Advertising, Media and Communications, Energy, Airlines, Industrial Manufacturing, and Technology. The businesses varied in labor-intensiveness: twelve had fewer than 50 employees; five had 50–100 employees; three had 100–500 employees; and five had more than 500 employees, with the largest business employing 15,000 workers. Few of the companies (only two of seventeen respondents answering this question) had employed Palestinian workers in the past decade, with only one of these enterprises continuing to do so today. The enterprises varied as well in the nature of production, with fourteen respondents targeting the domestic market and seven engaged in export production.

A range of executives was interviewed. All had deep knowledge of and vested interests in their company, with respondents including business owners, CEOs, Vice-Presidents, and Directors of Sales and Marketing. They came from a range of political backgrounds: three defined their political affiliations as right-wing; four were from the middle/center; nine from the left; one from the mid-left; and one self-described "Democrat neutral," and six who failed to identify themselves.

The data from questions reported here:

3. (When you first learned of the Oslo negotiations), would you say that your attitude toward the proposed settlement was

a. Very favorable	b. Somewhat favorable	c. Neutral	d. Somewhat unfavorable	e. Very unfavorable
10	8	4	1	1

4. At that time, how optimistic were you that the settlement would be achieved?

a. Very optimistic	b. Somewhat optimistic	c. Neutral	d. Somewhat pessimistic	e. Very pessimistic
5	9	4	3	3

5. Do you think the Rabin assassination made the peace process

a. More likely to succeed	b. More likely to fail	c. Did not have an affect on the process
1	20	4

6. Was this immediately apparent to you when he was assassinated?
a. Yes: **13** b. No: **11**

9. In particular, do you think that Peres made a strategic error in not calling for immediate elections after Rabin's assassination?

a. Yes	b. No	c. Don't know
15	3	7

10. Was it clear to you that Peres' strategy before the May 1996 elections made peace

a. More likely	b. Less likely	c. Did not have an affect on the process
2	9	12

16. At what point over the past two decades do you think a settlement could most easily have been reached and implemented?

a. Before the Oslo agreement	b. When Rabin was Prime Minister	c. When Peres was Acting Prime Minister	d. When Netanyahu was Prime Minister	e. When Barak was Prime Minister	f. When Sharon was Prime Minister	g. Other (please specify)
	12	1		2	2	3

19. How important do you think that concluding the peace process is to your own business prospects?

a. Of major importance	b. Somewhat important	c. Not important at all
20	4	

20. Specifically, how would concluding the process affect your business?

a. Have a positive effect	b. Have a negative effect	c. No effect
22	1	1

26. Do you think that the peace process is a major concern for other business elites as well?

a. No	b. Yes
2	20

REFERENCES

Adam, Heribert, ed. 1990. *Comparing Israel and South Africa: Prospects for Conflict Resolution in Ethnic States*. University Press of Colorado.
Adam, Heribert, and Hermann Giliomee. 1979. *Ethnic Power Mobilized: Can South Africa Change?* New Haven: Yale University Press.
Akenson, Donald. 1992. *God's Peoples: Covenant and Land in South Africa, Israel, and Ulster*. Ithaca: Cornell University Press.
Ashrawi, Hanan. 1995. *This Side of Peace*. New York: Touchstone.
Baker, James A., III (with Thomas DeFrank). 1995. *The Politics of Diplomacy: Revolution, War and Peace, 1989–1992*. New York: Putnam's Sons.
2000. "Peace, One Step at a Time." *New York Times*, July 27: A25.
Bennett, James. 2003. "Hamas Breaks off Talks on Stopping Attacks on Israel." *New York Times*, June 11: A1, A7.
Bew, Paul. 1998. "Initiative to Trimble but his Edge over Opponents is Thin." *Irish Times*, April. www.ireland.com/special/peace/results/analysis/analysis10.htm.
Booysen, Suzanne. 1989. "The Legacy of Ideological Control: The Afrikaner Youth's Manipulated Political Consciousness." *Politikon* 16 (1): 7–25.
Breen, Suzanne. 1998. "United No Parties Set their Sights on Assembly." *Irish Times*, May 25. www.ireland.com/special/peace/results/road/ahead3.htm (May 25, 2000).
2000. "Most Ulster Unionists Want Trimble in Executive." *Irish Times*, May 12. www.ireland.com/newspaper/ireland/2000/0512/north4.htm (May 25, 2000).

Bruck, Conni. 1995. "A Reporter at Large: The Wounds of Peace." *New Yorker*, October 8: 64–91.

Brynen, Rex. 2000. *A Very Political Economy: Peacebuilding and Foreign Aid in the West Bank and Gaza*. Washington DC: USIP.

Darby, John. 1997. *Scorpions in a Bottle*. London: Minority Rights Group.

——. 2003. "Northern Ireland: The Background to the Peace Process." http://cain. ulst.ac.uk/events/peace/darby03.htm (June 17).

Diamond, John. 2003. "Sharon's Support for Road Map Historic." *USA Today*, May 26: 1. www.usatoday.com/news/world/2003-05-26-mideast_x.htm (June 24, 2003).

Elliot, Sydney, and W.D. Flackes. 1999. *Conflict in Northern Ireland: An Encyclopedia*. Belfast: Blackstaff Press.

Fisher, Ian. 2003. "Defining Hamas: Roots in Charity and Branches of Violence." *New York Times*, 16 June.

Foundation for Middle East Peace. 2001. *Special Report* 11 (6) (November–December). www.fmep.org/reports/2001/v11n6.html (June 25, 2003).

Friedman, Robert. 1994. "Report from the West Bank: An Unholy Rage." *New Yorker*, March 7: 54–56.

Friedman, Steven. 1993. *The Long Journey: South Africa's Quest for a Negotiated Settlement*. Johannesburg: Raven Press.

Friedman, Thomas. 2000. "Yasir Arafat's Moment." *New York Times*, July 28: A21.

Gellman, Barton. 1995. "Likud Leader Hammers Rabin, PLO Premier; Hopeful Netanyahu Claims Ascendancy of Israeli Opposition." *Washington Post*, September 9: A22.

Gidron, Benjamin, Stanley Nider Katz, Yeheskel Hasenfeld, eds. 2002. *Mobilizing for Peace: Conflict Resolution in Northern Ireland, Israel/Palestine, and South Africa*. Oxford University Press.

Giliomee, Herman, and J. Gagiano. 1990. *The Elusive Search for Peace: South Africa, Israel, Northern Ireland*. Oxford University Press.

Hass, Amira. 2003. "What the Doctor Orders." *Haaretz*, June 20. www.haaretz. com/hasen/pages/ShArt.jhtml?itemNo= 307203&. (June 22, 2003).

HaTorah, Aish. 2003. "Myths and Facts." www.aish.com/Israel/articles/Suicide_ Bombings.asp (June 25).

Hayes, Bernadette, and Lizanne Dowds. 2001. "Underpinning Opinions: Declining Levels of Support among Protestants for the Good Friday Agreement." Paper presented at roundtable discussion by Democratic Dialogue April 10, 2001, Europa Hotel, Belfast.

Hayes, Bernadette C., and Ian McAllister. 2001. "Who Voted for Peace? Public Support for the 1998 Northern Ireland Agreement." *Irish Political Studies* 16: 73–93.

Hidalgo, Diego, ed. 2002. *Conference on Democratic Transitions and Consolidation*. Madrid, Spain: Siddharth Mehta Ediciones.

Hoge, Warren. 1999. "Ulster Unionists Open Way for Ruling with Sinn Fein." *New York Times*, November 28. www.nytimes.com/library/world/europe/ 112899nireland-unionists.html (May 25, 2000).

2000a. "Britain Suspends System of Power Sharing in Ulster." *New York Times*, February 12. www.nytimes.com/library/world/europe/021200nireland-talks.html (May 25, 2000).

2000b. "Ulster Leader Holds on, but Power Lessens in Unionist Vote." *New York Times*, March 26. www.nytimes.com/library/world/europe/032600nireland-trimble.html (May 25, 2000).

2003. "Sinn Fein Leader Pledges Full Disarmament of the I.R.A." *New York Times*, April 28: A2.

Huntington, Samuel. 1991. *The Third Wave.* University of Oklahoma Press.

Irwin, Colin. 2004. "Devolution and the State of the Northern Ireland Peace Process." www.peacepolls.org. January 12.

Jaffee Center for Strategic Studies. 2002. "Memorandum No. 61: Israeli Public Opinion on National Security." Tel Aviv University, July.

Jung, Courtney, and Ian Shapiro. 1995. "South Africa's Negotiated Transition: Democracy, Opposition, and the New Constitutional Order." *Politics and Society* 23 (3): 269–308.

Kifner, John. 2003. "The Bush Plan: Put the Toughest Hurdles First." *New York Times*, June 8.

Knox, Colin, and Pádraic Quirk, eds. 2000. *Peace Building in Northern Ireland, Israel and South Africa: Transition, Transformation and Reconciliation.* Basingstoke: Palgrave.

Lavery, Brian. 2003. "US Envoy Wants Elections." *New York Times*, May 8: A2.

Lustick, Ian. 1994a. "Necessary Risks: Lessons for the Israeli–Palestinian Peace Process from Ireland and Algeria." *Middle East Policy* 3 (3): 41–59.

1994b. Unsettled States, Disputed Lands: Britain and Ireland, France and Algeria, Israel, and the West Bank–Gaza. Ithaca, NY: Cornell University Press.

Lust-Okar, Ellen. 2003. "Israeli Elections 2003: What Likud's Victory Doesn't Tell You." *Yale Israel Journal* (Spring): 3–7.

Lust-Okar, Ellen, and A. F. K. Organski. 2002. "Coalitions and Conflict: The Case of Palestinian–Israeli Negotiations over the West Bank." *Journal of Conflict Management and Peace Science* (Spring): 23–58.

McGuffin, John. 1973. *Internment!* Tralee, Ireland: Anvil Books.

Makovsky, David. 1996. *Making Peace with the PLO: The Rabin Government's Road to the Oslo Accord.* Washington DC: Washington Institute for Near East Policy.

Mallie, Eamonn, and David McCittrick. 1996. *The Fight for Peace: The Secret Story Behind the Irish Peace Process.* London: Heinemann.

Millar, Frank. 2000a. "London is Relieved but Difficulties Lie Ahead." *Irish Times.* www.ireland.com/special/peace/results/road/ahead3.htm (May 25, 2000).

2000b. "Trimble Stakes his Future on the Drive to Modernise," *Irish Times*, April 21. http://scripts.ireland.com/search/ . . . wspaper/opinion/2000/0421/opt2.htm (May 25, 2000).

Mitchell, George J. 1999. *Making Peace.* New York: Alfred Knopf.

Mnookin, Robert H. 2003. "Strategic Barriers to Dispute Resolution: A Comparison of Bilateral and Multilateral Negotiations." *Journal of the Institute of Theoretical Economics* 159 (1): 199–220.

Moriarty, Gerry. 2000a. "Even Split for Anti, Pro-Agreement Parties." *Irish Times*. www.ireland.com/special/peace/results/news/news3.htm (May 25, 2000).

2000b. "How the Parties Could Share Out Seats." *Irish Times*. www.ireland. com/special/peace/results/road/ahead4.htm (May 25, 2000).

Moughrabi, Fouad. 2001. "The Politics of Palestinian Textbooks." *Journal of Palestine Studies* 31(1): 5–19.

O'Donnell, Guillermo, and Philippe Schmitter. 1986. *Transitions from Authoritarian Rule: Comparative Perspectives*. Baltimore: Johns Hopkins University Press.

O'Leary, Brendan. 1995. "Afterword: What is Framed in the Framework Documents?" *Ethnic and Racial Studies* 18: 862–872.

O'Leary, Brendan, and John McGarry. 1996. *The Politics of Antagonism: Understanding Northern Ireland*, 2nd edn. London and Atlantic Heights, NJ: Athlone.

Pogatchnik, Shawn. 1999. "Ultimatum Irks Northern Ireland." *Detroit News*, July 4. www.detnews.com/1999/nation/9907/04/07049902.htm (May 18, 2000).

Przeworski, Adam. 1991. *Democracy and the Market*. Cambridge University Press.

1999. "Minimalist Conception of Democracy: A Defense." In *Democracy's Value*, ed. Ian Shapiro and Casiano Hacker-Cordón. Cambridge University Press.

Safire, William. 2000. "Why is Arafat Smiling?" *New York Times*, July 27: A25.

Said, Edward. 1995. *Peace and its Discontents*. London: Random House.

Savir, Uri. 1999. *The Process: 1,100 Days that Changed the Middle East*. New York: Vintage.

Sayigh, Yazid. 1997. *Armed Struggle and the Search for State: The Palestinian National Movement*. Oxford: Clarendon Press.

Schelling, Thomas C. 1960. *The Strategy of Conflict*. Cambridge, MA: Harvard University Press.

Seekings, Jeremy. 2000. *The UDF: The United Democratic Front in South Africa, 1983–1991*. Athens, OH: Ohio University Press.

Shaheen, Edward R.F. 2003. "The Map and the Fence." *New York Review of Books* 50 (11), (July 3): 8–13.

Shapiro, Ian. 2003. *The State of Democratic Theory*. Princeton University Press.

Shavit, Ari. 2003. "Cry, the Beloved Two State Solution." *Haaretz*, August 7. www.jfjfp.org/BackgroundQ/two-states_aug03.htm.

Shipler, David K. 2003. "Sharon Has a Map: Can He Redraw It?" *New York Times*, June 1.

Shlaim, Avi. 1994. "The Oslo Accord." *Journal of Palestine Studies* 91: 32.

Sisk, Timothy D. 1995. *Democratization in South Africa: The Elusive Social Contract*. Princeton University Press.

Sprinzak, Ehud. 1999. *Brother Against Brother: Violence and Extremism in Israeli Politics from Altalena to the Rabin Assassination*. New York: Free Press.

Stevenson, Richard W. 1996. "Bomb Wounds 100 in London as IRA Truce is Said to End." *New York Times*, February 10.

Tessler, Mark. 1994. *A History of the Israeli–Palestinian Conflict.* Bloomington, IN: Indiana University Press.

Tonge, Jonathan, and Jocelyn A.J. Evans. 2001. "Faultlines in Unionism: Division and Dissent Within the Ulster Unionist Council." *Irish Political Studies* 16: 113–114.

Usher, Graham. 1995. *Palestine in Crisis: The Struggle for Peace and Political Independence after Oslo.* London: Pluto Press.

Walker, Clive. 1988. "Political Violence and Democracy in Northern Ireland." *Modern Law Review* 51(5): 605–622.

Wallach, Janet, and John Wallach. 1997. *Arafat: In the Eyes of the Beholder.* New York: Birch Lane.

Wood, Elisabeth. 2000. *Forging Democracy from Below: Negotiated Transitions in El Salvador and South Africa.* Cambridge University Press.

Yaffee, Nurit, and Dorith Tal. 2000. "Immigration to Israel from the Former Soviet Union." www.cbs.gov.il/engprfl.htm (accessed June 18, 2003).

Part 2

Challenging, transforming, and destroying order

8 Civil wars and guerrilla warfare in the contemporary world: toward a joint theory of motivations and opportunities

Carles Boix

The use of systematic and organized violence to effect political change is a generalized phenomenon around the world. Singer and Small (1994) put at 137 the number of civil wars that killed at least 1,000 during the period from 1820 to 1990. The death toll from civil wars fought after World War II has been estimated at a minimum of 16.2 million (Fearon and Laitin 2003). According to the data gathered by Banks (1997), between 1919 and 1997 there were over 500 spells of guerrilla warfare around the world. In the same period of time, close to 1,500 politically motivated assassinations or attempted assassinations of high government officials or politicians were committed – at a rate of one every three weeks. Banks codes a similar number of revolutionary or rebellious acts against the central government and about 4,000 political riots – or almost one per week.

A first generation of researchers working on the causes of political violence emphasized the presence of "structural" causes to explain civil wars and guerrilla warfare. Modernization scholars traced rebellion to economic inequality (Muller 1985; Paige 1975; Russett 1964) and the impact of economic modernization and the position or claims of particular social groups (Huntington 1968; Wolf 1969; Gurr 1973). A later line of research related violent conflict to ethnic nationalism (Horowitz 1985; Connor 1994).

More recently, scholars working on civil wars have offered a strong critique of the central assumption made by the former generation of scholars that rebellious activities occur when "grievances are sufficiently acute that people want to engage in violent protest" (Collier and Hoeffler 2001, 2). According to this position, the presence of economic resentments, ethnic antagonisms, and personal or clique grudges are too

A first version of this essay was prepared for the Yale conference on "Order, Conflict, and Violence," April 30–May 1, 2004. I thank the comments of the participants and particularly of Robert Bates, Stathis Kalyvas, David Laitin, and Nicholas Sambanis.

widespread to specify the cases in which political violence will erupt. Similarly, they claim that maintaining that all cases of violence point to the existence of *exaggerated* grievances is useless since the concept (and presence) of "acute grievances" is particularly difficult to pin down. Hence, in a world full of "grievances," researchers must abandon any examination of the political and economic motivation of actors to focus on the "opportunity" structures that facilitate the actual outbreak of violence. Accordingly, Collier and Hoeffler (1999; 2001) have explained the occurrence of civil wars as a function of greed (at least in their initial work). In their account greed is fueled by the abundance of "natural resources" (measured through the percentage of primary products) and by the relatively low life chances of potential rebels (proxied by rates of secondary-school enrollment for males). In turn, Fearon and Laitin (2003, 75–76) hypothesize that "financially, organizationally, and politically weak central governments render insurgency more feasible and attractive due to weak local policing or inept and corrupt counterinsurgency practices" and then conclude that civil wars happen in "fragile states with limited administrative control of their peripheries" (88).

There is no doubt that, as forcefully stated by the political opportunities' scholars, the first generation of work on civil wars and guerrilla warfare was too broad and even ambiguous about the causes and agents that motivated the generation of systematic and organized political violence. Yet the alternative theory, based on the idea of stressing the opportunities that may be open to potential insurgents, remains equally unconvincing, at least when interpreted in a strict manner. Civil war and guerrilla onsets may be more likely in mountainous terrain and in mining areas. Weak police and military forces are an invitation to chaos and violence. Still, Switzerland and Norway have extremely mountainous terrain (and their per-capita income was not very high in the nineteenth century, at least by post-World War II standards), but they have not undergone any civil war in the past 150 years – Switzerland's civil war of 1848 resulted in a handful of deaths and would clearly not qualify as such in any of the current datasets we have. Many nineteenth-century and twentieth-century nations have sustained long spells of peace without particularly well-developed bureaucracies and road systems.

A more sensible theoretical approach to explain systematic political violence is to acknowledge that different opportunity structures constrain or facilitate the eruption of violence, in the same way they prevent or ease the commission of a crime. But, to paraphrase Collier and Hoeffler (2001), the commission of the crime itself requires some motives, which we still need to identify if we wish to make serious progress in the determination of the causes of political violence. In other words, a convincing model of civil war and guerrilla warfare requires, as with almost all crimes, both motivation and opportunity.

Accordingly, this chapter departs from the assumption that civil wars and guerrilla warfare occur whenever the expected net gains from employing violence exceed the net gains derived from accepting the status quo among some political actors (such as unions, peasant organizations, a clique of army officers and so on). The status quo is here defined as a situation in which either a section of society holds the (public) monopoly of violence and policymaking uncontested by those that are excluded from the decision-making process or political differences are settled peacefully (through either voting procedures or bargaining) among all parties in contention.

More precisely, the decision to engage in violent activities is a function of two factors. On the one hand, violence becomes more likely as the difference between the benefits accrued under a new regime obtained through the use of violence and the gains obtained under the status quo increases. The use of violence to alter the political and economic status quo increases as the distribution of relatively immobile assets becomes more unequal in any given economy. As income inequality rises, the resistance of the well-off to the introduction of democratic, peaceful means to set government policy hardens – the losses they would incur from majority rule would be simply too substantial. Correspondingly, resorting to violence becomes more attractive to those that are excluded from the state apparatus – the prize of victory raises with inequality. Political violence becomes particularly acute in unequal economies in which assets are fixed and are not complementary to the skills of their current owners. In those cases the potential rebels can apply violence to overturn the existing regime with the relative certainty that assets will not be moved out of the country and that the elimination of their owners will not reduce their economic value.[1]

On the other hand, the occurrence of political violence declines as its costs go up, thus accommodating the current literature on civil wars that insists on the key role played by the structure of "political opportunities" within which rebels launch violent actions against the state. As detailed

---

[1] The literature on greed and civil wars becomes easily embedded in the theory of this chapter as follows. The presence of abundant *natural* resources (rather than all sorts of resources, which, prima facie, could also finance any type of illegal activity) fits squarely with the idea that only fixed assets can be easily expropriated and controlled by the rebels. Educational attainment similarly points to the type of assets in society and, in a way to be discussed later, to the underlying pattern of income distribution in society.

later, the costs of violence to the parties in contention vary with their organizational and mobilizational capabilities, the military technology they employ, and other factors such as the type of terrain, the distribution of the population, and the infrastructures of the state.

After developing the theory in the first section, this chapter turns to examine its empirical validity. The second section describes the distribution of violence over time and provides a first cut into the underlying causes of violence. The third section tests in a systematic way the theory presented in the first section. The empirical analysis is original in two directions. First, I move beyond current studies of civil wars, which have focused on post-1945 data, by looking at civil wars since the middle of the nineteenth century and guerrilla and revolutionary outbreaks since World War I. Second, I consider more fine-grained measures of the nature and distribution of wealth and I show that several factors, such as per-capita income and ethnic composition, which have been claimed to be strongly correlated to violence, are of little or no interest in more broadly specified models.

Theory

To explore the circumstances that may lead to civil wars and guerrillas, let me proceed in the following manner. I will first characterize the structure of any economy along two dimensions – the level of capital endowment of each individual, and the extent to which capital is mobile and can be actually taxed. I will then consider and discuss the distributional consequences that different political regimes have on different types of individuals (given their position in the economy) and the political strategies they will be likely to adopt. This will allow me to describe the conditions under which they may choose to engage in violent strategies and civil confrontation.[2]

Economic structure

To approximate the economic structure of any country, assume in the first place that assets are distributed unequally. That is, there are different individuals with different skills and assets, and thus income, who choose to work variably. By assumption, in that economy the distribution of skills and incomes is skewed so that the median individual, who is the individual with 50 percent of the others above and below her on the

---

[2] This discussion follows, in an abbreviated manner, the model developed in Boix (2003).

income ladder, is poorer than the average income individual, that is, the person with the mean income.[3]

In addition to having a particular distribution of assets and income, economies are also defined by their types of assets. Assets vary in an economy according to the extent to which they can be more or less easy to tax. The extent to which assets may be "taxable" will be determined by two factors. In the first place, their specificity, which grows when the difference of the income or returns it generates at home and abroad increase. For example, some assets, such as land or oil wells, are completely specific to the country they are located: they cannot be moved anywhere else. Other assets, such as high skills or money, can be moved abroad to generate rents very similar to the returns they yield at their country of origin. The more specific assets are to the country in which they are being used, the more taxable they are since the cost of moving them abroad (in response to higher taxes) is higher. In the second place, the "taxability" of assets varies with the degree to which the tax authority can monitor any given asset and its return. A fully "taxable" asset is one that cannot be hidden for tax purposes and therefore yields the expected tax return. A nontaxable asset is one whose income flow is hard to monitor and whose owner can easily escape from the tax enforcement authority – this is the case, for example, of certain professional skills, the provision of consulting services, or the transactions of small shopkeepers.

Taxation

Assume further that in this economy the state sets a linear tax income.[4] All tax revenues are redistributed lump sum (i.e. an equal amount) to everyone. That transfer, which is the total tax revenue divided by the number of individuals in the economy, equals the taxes paid by the voter with average income. As a result, all the individuals poorer than the average income will favor a positive tax since the transfer they will receive will be larger than the amount they pay. Conversely, all the individuals richer than the average income voter will oppose a tax.

In a democratic setting, with a one-person one-vote rule, and following the median voter theorem, the policy that is adopted is the one most preferred by the median voter. Since the income of the median individual is lower than the average income, the result will be a positive

[3] As a matter of fact, all real world income distributions match this assumption.
[4] The description of the taxation model departs from (and then extends) the optimal taxation mechanism introduced by Meltzer and Richards (1981).

tax and positive transfers. Moreover, the poorer the median voter is relative to the average income individual, the larger the tax rate he will favor, because the difference between the tax he pays and the transfer received becomes larger. In other words, as the income distribution becomes more skewed and unequal, the tax pressure should increase.

The level of taxation will only be constrained by two parameters. First, the median voter is bound by the distortions that come from tax rates: the median voter will never impose taxes that lead to an overall decline in total revenue.[5] Second, he will be constrained by the mobility and taxability of assets. As capital becomes more mobile, that is, as it can be moved abroad to obtain a return equal to the domestic return, the tax rate will decline since otherwise the capital holder would have an incentive to transfer his assets abroad. Similarly, whenever capital can be easily hidden from the state or it becomes of a kind that can only be used by its owner, the temptation to confiscate it also declines.

Political institutions

Economists have always treated the voting rule of this taxation model (where all individuals vote and the median voter determines the tax policy) as a fixed or exogenous parameter. Yet this theoretical decision is wrong.[6] The choice of the voting rule precedes the actual process of voting about the tax rate and the distribution of assets. As a matter of fact, all political actors determine who will vote (and how the vote will take place) informed by the tax outcomes they anticipate will take place under each alternative voting rule. Rich voters will be interested in excluding the poorest voters (and thus moving the median voter toward them) to minimize the tax to be paid. Conversely, the voters with the low incomes will press for their full political participation.

More precisely, as inequality in a given country goes up, the demand and political pressure for redistribution will intensify. As a result, to avoid paying high, quasi-confiscatory taxes, the wealthy will be even more inclined to establish an authoritarian regime that excludes the majority of the population. Naturally, since the introduction of an authoritarian regime requires bearing some costs of repression, the well-off will only act to exclude the poorest if those repression costs are larger

---

[5] Without this restriction, the median voter would always set the tax rate equal to 1 and hence expropriate from individuals with an income equal to or larger than the average income.

[6] In fact, this mistake explains why the Meltzer-Richards model performs very weakly to explain the level of taxes in the empirical arena.

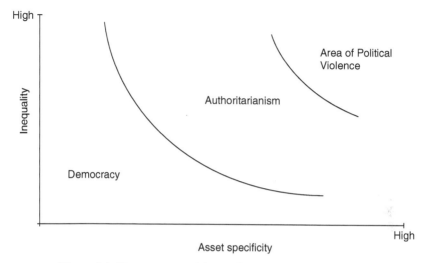

Figure 8.1 Democracy and inequality

than the taxes they would have paid under a democratic regime. Similarly, as the distribution of income becomes more equal among individuals, redistributive pressures from the poorest social sectors on the well-off voters diminish. The relative costs of tolerating a mass democracy, that is, the taxes they would pay, decline for the holders of the most productive assets to the point that they become smaller than the costs of repression they would have to bear to exclude the majority of citizens. And democracy becomes acceptable to all parties.

The type of political solution that will prevail will also depend on the types of assets in the economy. As assets become less specific (more mobile), the redistributive pressures from noncapital holders on capitalists diminish and, as a result, the likelihood of democracy rises. By contrast, economies with a large proportion of fixed assets, such as the oil countries, will generally remain authoritarian (conditional on having a skewed distribution of income).

To sum up, the combination of the distribution of assets and income and the nature of wealth leads to the set of predictions displayed in Figure 8.1. A stable democracy prevails at low levels of either inequality or specificity of wealth. As the cost of taxation increases (due to increases in wealth inequality and asset specificity), authoritarianism starts to pay off. Finally, for high levels of inequality and asset specificity, authoritarianism becomes the dominant strategy of high-income individuals.

Political violence

For sufficiently high levels of inequality and asset specificity or immobility, political violence will erupt as a systematic means to effect political change. As already pointed above, with growing income inequality and asset specificity, the resistance of the well-off (such as landowners or government officials in control of mining resources in rentier states) to democracy grows – the losses they would incur from majority rule become too large. In turn, those that are excluded from governing and setting taxes have a strong incentive to revolt. At high levels of inequality, the prize of victory is substantial. Political violence will become particularly acute in unequal economies in which assets are fixed and not complementary to the skills of their current owners. In those cases the potential rebels can apply violence to overturn the existing regime with the relative certainty that assets will not be moved out of the country and that the elimination of their owners will not reduce their economic value. In short, political violence will tend to appear in countries located in the upper right-hand corner of Figure 8.1.

Still, the prediction that violence will happen in that region should be simply taken as a probabilistic statement. The potential rebels of highly unequal, highly asset-specific economies will only resort to armed action if they believe they have a reasonable chance of winning. Those beliefs are generally formed under conditions of incomplete information. Hence, their guesses or estimations about their probability of success will be shaped by their assessment of the strength of their own organizational capacities and the perceived military capabilities of the state.

It is in this context that the "political opportunities" literature can be fully integrated with a theory of political motivations to explain a strategy of violent engagement. Certain objective or structural traits, such as the existence of mountainous terrain, inaccessible forests, poor roads, geographically fragmented states (e.g. archipelagos), and so on, will likely play an important role in bolstering the decision to engage in violent activities. Likewise, the availability of finance (in the form of natural resources such as oil wells, diamond mines, or coca plantations) should encourage rebellious activities as well.

Finally, the organizational and mobilizational capacity of insurgents is central in explaining when violent rebellions will flare up and progressively transform into guerrilla warfare or even civil wars. We can put this point in a slightly broader historical context. It is reasonable to assume that in many countries the underlying conditions of high inequality and wealth specificity did not change substantially from the eighteenth to the twentieth century or that, at least, did not worsen dramatically. Yet the number, length, and harshness of civil wars, guerrillas, and rebellious outbreaks increased over time – eventually culminating in all the large civil wars of the mid-twentieth century such as those fought in Russia, China, or Vietnam. Such a secular, long-durée trend toward more violence was triggered by the growing agitation and organization of certain social sectors such as the peasantry, which had remained isolated and poorly communicated until that time. With the advent of "political modernization" (functional states, city networks, and literate minorities), a set of "enlightened" elites provided those that were discontent with the means to challenge the status quo (or, in a different interpretation, pushed them to engage in violence). Still, those "revolutionary vanguards" were only successful when certain conditions obtained on the ground. In the absence of broad inequalities, violence hardly evolved into civil war. To put it in other words, a theory that dismisses motivation and that only emphasizes the supply of the means to be violent (either because the state has imploded or because some Polpotian characters have appeared to force, by pure intimidation, a segment of the population) would be unconvincing. It could not explain the empirical patterns I unveil in the third section.

The distribution of political violence

To explore the validity of the explanatory model, I examine data on the occurrence of civil wars and guerrilla warfare. The data for civil wars come from two datasets: the dataset of the "Correlates of War" (COW) project developed by Singer and Small (1994), which includes data from 1816 through 1992, and the dataset built by Fearon and Laitin (2003), spanning from 1945 to 1999. Generally speaking, a civil war is defined as a conflict in which military action took place between agents of (or claimants to) a state and organized, nonstate groups who sought to take control of the state (in the entire country or in part of the country) or to change governmental policies, and where at least 1,000 battle deaths resulted from the war.[7] The Fearon-Laitin dataset is more expansive than the COW: for the period 1945 to 1990, whereas the former reports 80 war onsets and over 600 years of civil war, the latter includes 60 war onsets and roughly 400 years of war. The data on guerrillas are taken from Banks (1997) and cover the period from 1919 to 1997. Episodes of

---

[7] Fearon and Laitin (2003) further qualify a civil war as a conflict where at least 100 were killed on both sides. For a full specification of conditions see Fearon and Laitin (2003, 76, footnote 4).

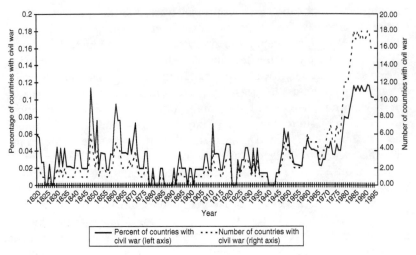

Figure 8.2 Civil wars, 1820–1994

guerrilla warfare are any armed activity, sabotage, or bombings carried on by independent bands of citizens or irregular forces and aimed at the overthrow of the present regime.

Figure 8.2 shows the number and proportion of sovereign countries with an ongoing civil war (as defined in COW) from 1820 to 1994. The proportion of countries under civil war has been relatively stable – around 2 to 4% for the whole universe of sovereign countries. Within a pattern of general stability, two periods stand out as more conflict-ridden: the middle decades of the nineteenth century and the last quarter of the twentieth century. Spurred by considerable political turmoil over the introduction of liberal institutions in Europe and the construction of new states in America, the proportion of countries at war rose to 5% between 1848 and 1871, with two peaks in 1848 and 1861. Except for a spike around World War I, civil wars became very infrequent from 1880 to 1945. In the postwar period, the COW dataset shows an upward trend, particularly after 1975. The last three decades have been the most turbulent with about 10% of all sovereign countries at war (or an average of 15% in the Fearon-Laitin database).

Figure 8.3 depicts the number and proportion of countries experiencing guerrilla warfare every year. About 10% of all countries suffered a guerrilla movement in the interwar period. The proportion increased to about 15% after 1945, peaked in the late 1960s, and then gradually

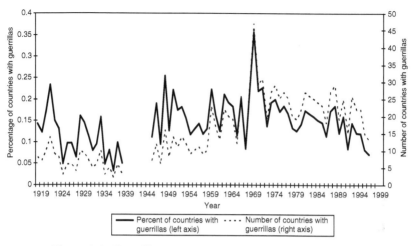

Figure 8.3 Guerrillas, 1919–1997

declined. By 1997 there were guerrillas in thirteen countries or 7% of all sovereign states.

Empirical analysis

The central hypothesis of this essay is that political violence should erupt as income inequality and asset-specificity increase. Additionally, the model also predicts that the costs of choosing violence will shape the level and type of violence. More expensive forms of violence should be rarer. This is indeed true observing the empirical evidence presented in Figures 8.2 and 8.3. Civil wars are less frequent than guerrilla movements. Similarly, better organized states with easy access to all their territory and population should have less violence.

Inequality and asset specificity

Figures 8.4 and 8.5 show the distribution of civil war onsets and guerrilla warfare onsets across the world by the average level of industrialization and urbanization (on the x axis) and the percentage of family farms (on the y axis). The percentage of family farms captures the degree of concentration and therefore inequality in the ownership of land. That measure, gathered and reported by Vanhanen (1997, 48), is based on defining as family farms those "farms that provide employment for not more than four people, including family members, ... that are

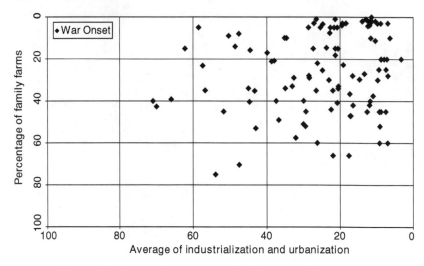

Figure 8.4 Economic structure and civil wars, 1850–1994

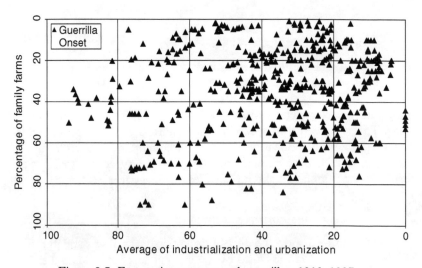

Figure 8.5 Economic structure and guerrillas, 1919–1997

cultivated by the holder family itself and ... that are owned by the
cultivator family or held in ownerlike possession." The definition, which
aims at distinguishing "family farms" from large farms cultivated mainly
by hired workers, is not dependent on the actual size of the farm – the
size of the farm varies with the type of product and the agricultural

technology being used.[8] The dataset, reported in averages for each decade, ranges from 1850 to 1999.[9] The average of industrialization (measured as the average of the percentage of nonagricultural population) and the percentage of urban population (defined as population living in cities of 20,000 or more inhabitants) are also taken from Vanhanen and are used to approximate the extent to which assets may be mobile.[10] Both axes have been drawn in the reverse order (decreasing in value as one moves away from the origin) so that the high inequality/ high specificity area is in the upper-right corner.

Figure 8.4 plots all civil war onsets (as defined by COW) from 1850 to 1994. The graph shows that most civil wars occur in countries where the agrarian sector is still dominant and land is distributed unequally (basically within the triangle to the right of a diagonal going from no industrialization and less than 50 percent of the land to middle levels of industrialization with no family farms at all). Several cases that are closer to the middle (that is, farther away from the upper-right corner) have considerable oil resources and so conflict there may be related to asset immobility. All in all, the distribution of observed civil war onsets matches quite well the predictions of Figure 8.1.

Figure 8.5 depicts the distribution of guerrilla warfare from 1919 to 1997. The occurrence of guerrillas is more widespread than systematic civil wars but the pattern is still similar: violence is heavily concentrated in unequal agrarian economies.

Civil wars

Although the graphical evidence presented thus far strongly supports the model of the essay, I have not controlled for the impact of important variables in the literature such as per-capita income, population, political regime, geography, and ethnic and religious composition. In Table 8.1 I present results on a multivariate analysis of the factors that may influence the eruption of civil war and guerrilla warfare.

For each type of violence I run three models. The first one includes data prior to 1950 (since 1850 for civil wars and since 1919 for the rest

[8] It varies from countries with 0% of family farms to nations where 94% of the agricultural land is owned through family farms: the mean of the sample is 30% with a standard deviation of 23%. A detailed discussion and description of the data can be found in Vanhanen (1997, 49–51) and the sources quoted therein.

[9] An extensive literature has related the unequal distribution of land to an unbalanced distribution of income. For the period after 1950, and excluding the cases of socialist economies, the correlation coefficient among the Gini index and the percentage of family farms is −0.50.

[10] This average has a mean of 35% and varies from 3 to 99%.

Table 8.1. *Civil wars and guerrilla movements*

	Civil war		Guerrilla warfare			
	Model 1 1850–1994	Model 2 1950–97	Model 3 1950–97	Model 4 1919–97	Model 5 1950–97	Model 6 1950–97
Constant	−1.985*** (0.687)	−3.557*** (0.747)	−3.952*** (1.001)	−2.793*** (0.369)	−3.049*** (0.435)	−2.757*** (0.544)
Lagged dependent variable	2.961*** (0.084)	3.530*** (0.102)	3.487*** (0.106)	1.362*** (0.050)	1.368*** (0.059)	1.213** (0.062)
Percent of family farms t-1	0.004 (0.004)	0.014*** (0.016)	0.020*** (0.006)	0.003 (0.002)	0.002 (0.003)	0.008** (0.003)
Index of occupational diversification t-1	0.005 (0.005)	0.003 (0.006)	0.013* (0.007)	0.005** (0.003)	0.003 (0.003)	0.009*** (0.004)
Family farms t-1* occup. diversif. t-1	−0.025** (0.011)	−0.033*** (0.011)	−0.041*** (0.013)	−0.022*** (0.005)	−0.022*** (0.006)	−0.027*** (0.007)
Log (population) t-1	0.096*** (0.025)	0.160*** (0.034)	0.123*** (0.045)	0.170*** (0.016)	0.155*** (0.019)	0.110*** (0.023)
Log (per cap. income) t-1	−0.162* (0.092)	−0.059 (0.105)	−0.123 (0.119)	−0.026 (0.047)	0.043 (0.060)	−0.072 (0.068)
Democracy t-1	0.148 (0.100)	0.290** (0.114)	0.243** (0.128)	0.173*** (0.056)	0.244*** (0.066)	0.136* (0.072)
Log (percentage mountainous)			0.053 (0.044)			0.073*** (0.025)
Noncontiguous state			0.263** (0.139)			0.431*** (0.076)
Oil exporter			−0.058 (0.175)			−0.073 (0.097)
Ethnic fractionalization			0.643 (0.926)			1.781*** (0.498)

	(1)	(2)	(3)	(4)	(5)	(6)
(Ethnic fractionalization) ^{2}			−0.292			−1.651***
			(0.973)			(0.549)
Religious fractionalization			0.879			0.187
			(0.997)			(0.558)
(Religious fractionalization) ^{2}			−0.577			−0.066
			(1.200)			(0.664)
Percentage of Muslims			0.004*			−0.000
			(0.002)			(0.001)
Percentage of Catholics			0.003			0.002**
			(0.002)			(0.001)
Percentage of Protestants			−0.003			−0.008**
			(0.005)			(0.003)
Growth rate t-2 to t-1			−0.299			−0.068
			(0.744)			(0.438)
Number of observations	8453	4435	4240	6242	4066	3937
Log likelihood	−651.24	−390.23	−365.11	−2006.45	868.80	−1328.40
Prob>chi2	0.0000	0.0000	0.0000	0.0000	0.0000	0.0000
Pseudo R2	0.5832	0.7789	0.7883	0.2344	0.2377	0.2610

Estimation: probit model. Standard errors in parenthesis. ***p<0.01; **p<0.05; *p<0.10.

of violent events) – this dataset maximizes the number of observations, which range from 8,300 to 6,200 country-years, but cannot include variables such as religious composition or geographical structure for which we only have data after World War II. The second model includes data only for the second half of the twentieth century yet employs the same specification used in the first model. The last model adds a whole battery of controls to the second model. Notice that the coefficients remain very stable across the first two models. In the third model, the interactive coefficient and population go up in size – but that change does not affect the thrust of the essay's argument.

For model 1 (employing pre-1950 data) and model 2 (postwar data), the following independent variables are included:

(1) The lagged value of the dependent variable.
(2) The percentage of family farms.
(3) The index of occupational diversification, that is, the average of industrialization and urbanization.
(4) The interaction of the two previous variables, which should capture the theoretical expectations of the model.
(5) The log value of per-capita income. This variable is built with data reported in the Penn World Table 6.1 (Heston *et al.* 2002), covering the period from 1950 to 1999, plus data from Maddison (1995), which provides observations for the period previous to 1950 (essentially for developed countries and some large Asian and Latin American cases), adjusted to make it comparable with the Heston dataset, and some interpolated data from Bourguignon and Morrisson (2002).[11]
(6) The log value of population, taken from Banks (1997).
(7) Democracy. This variable is taken from Boix and Rosato (2001), where all sovereign countries from 1800 to 1999 are coded as either democratic or authoritarian. Countries are coded as democracies if they meet three conditions: elections are free and competitive; the executive is accountable to citizens (either through elections in presidential systems or to the legislative power in parliamentary regimes); and at least 50 percent of the male electorate is enfranchised.

In the third model (of postwar data), the following variables have been added:

(8) Ethnic fractionalization. This measure is computed as one minus the Herfindhal index of ethnolinguistic group shares, with new data gathered and calculated in Alesina *et al.* (2003).

---

[11] For the post-1950 period I use Fearon and Laitin's (2003) definition of per-capita income.

(9) Religious fractionalization, also computed as one minus the Herfindhal index of religious groups, also taken from Alesina *et al.* (2003).

(10) Percentage of Muslims, Catholics, and Protestants, taken from LaPorta *et al.* (1999).

(11) Economic growth rate (in the year before the observed event).

(12) The log of the percentage of the territory that is mountainous.

(13) A dummy variable coded as 1 if oil represents more than one-third of the country's exports.

(14) A dummy variable coded 1 if the state is composed of non-contiguous territories. The last three variables are taken from Fearon and Laitin (2003).

In Table 8.1 civil war and guerrilla warfare are coded as 1 if there was one of these events in place, 0 otherwise. The estimation is done through probit analysis.[12] For the period from 1850 to 1994 (Table 8.1, column 1) I employ data from COW. For the period after 1950 (columns 2 and 3), I employ the dataset from Fearon and Laitin (2003).

As expected from the model, the interactive term of family farms and nonagrarian assets is statistically significant and has a substantial depressing impact on the occurrence of civil wars. A simulation of the results (in column 1, Table 8.1) is shown in Table 8.2. In countries with either less than 20% of the land held by family farms or with an average urbanization and industrialization below 25%, the probability of a civil war onset is more than 5% over the course of a five-year period. As both land equality and industrialization increase, the probability of a civil war declines quickly. In countries where family farms control more than 50% of the cultivated land and average industrialization and urbanization are also over 50%, the probability of a civil war occurring over a period of five years drops below 1%.

Population increases the probability of a civil war onset. For all other variables at their median values, the probability of a civil war erupting increases from 1% in a country of about four million inhabitants to 1.4% in a country of twenty million and 3% in a nation of half a billion inhabitants. The positive effect of population on civil wars even increases once we control for ethnic and fractionalization diversity (column 3, Table 8.1). The conclusion that small countries are less prone to experience political violence than large countries may, however, be deceptive. Consider the following example. Holding other things constant, a country with 100 million inhabitants has a 2% chance of

---

[12] Logit analysis does not change any of the results.

Table 8.2. *Predicted probability of civil war onset over five years by size of agrarian sector and landholding inequality*

		Share of family farms over total cultivated land				
		10	30	50	70	90
Index of	10	0.07	0.07	0.08	0.09	0.10
occupational	30	0.06	0.05	0.04	0.03	0.03
diversification	50	0.05	0.03	0.02	0.01	0.01
	70	0.04	0.02	0.01	0.00	0.00
	90	0.04	0.01	0.00	0.00	0.00

Simulation based on Table 8.1, column 1.

having a civil war in any given year. If we split it into five countries of equal size, the probability that at least one of them falls into a civil war goes up to 7%. Naturally, the scale of the civil war may be bloodier in the larger country – but the actual occurrence of violence is certainly lower for all the population involved.

Democratic regimes slightly increase the probability of civil war onsets (yet the coefficient is only statistically significant in columns 2 and 3; that is, in the postwar period). Per-capita income is statistically insignificant. Industrialization and land inequality are now capturing the part of the variation that other articles modeled through per-capita income and erroneously attributed to state capacity.[13]

Ethnic fractionalization and religious fractionalization are not statistically significant. The proportion of Muslims has a small positive effect on civil wars. In opposition to a substantial literature, neither economic crises nor oil induce more civil wars. Geography has a partial effect: the coefficient of mountainous terrain is positive but not significant; by contrast, noncontiguous states have a stronger chance of facing civil wars.

Guerrilla warfare

Columns 4 through 6 in Table 8.1 examine the covariates of guerrilla warfare. Their results parallel those for civil wars. The effect of inequality and asset specificity is very similar in statistical significance and substantial size for both guerrilla and civil war. Table 8.3 simulates the probability of a guerrilla movement over a five-year period (employing

[13] Dropping the index of occupational diversification (alone and in the interaction) makes per-capita income statistically significant and doubles the size of its coefficient.

Table 8.3. *Predicted probability of guerrilla warfare onset over five years by size of agrarian sector and landholding inequality*

		Share of family farms over total cultivated land (percentiles)				
		10	30	50	70	90
Index of	10	0.20	0.22	0.24	0.25	0.27
occupational	30	0.22	0.20	0.18	0.16	0.15
diversification	50	0.24	0.18	0.14	0.10	0.07
	70	0.26	0.17	0.10	0.06	0.03
	90	0.28	0.15	0.08	0.03	0.01

Simulation based on Table 8.1, column 4.

the results in column 4, Table 8.1). For low levels of family farms and industrialization, the probability fluctuates around 20%. In fact, it increases with each value separately – this may be capturing the fact that societies with family farms may organize more easily. Nonetheless, as both variables increase, the probability drops: it falls below 10% at the median values of both variables and below 5% for values common in developed countries.

Since guerrilla warfare is a far more widespread phenomenon than civil wars, factors other than land inequality and asset mobility must account for the former's higher probability. Per-capita income is again not significant. Although population and democracy raise the eruption of guerrilla movements, their impact is not that different from the effect they had over the likelihood of having civil wars.

Ethnic fractionalization now becomes statistically significant. Its impact is substantial and follows a quadratic form. With all other values at their median, a highly fragmented country (with an index of 0.08, which corresponds to the tenth percentile of the universe of observations) has an annual probability of having a guerrilla movement of about 4.8%. This probability peaks at 8.8% among countries with an ethnic fractionalization of 0.5 (about the sixtieth percentile) and then declines to 5.6% for the most homogenous country in the sample (with an ethnic fractionalization index of 0.93). However, as countries become more industrialized and less unequal, the effect of ethnic fractionalization declines and the difference in violence between balanced countries and either homogenous or very heterogeneous countries narrows significantly. For example, for high levels of equality and development, the probability of a guerrilla starting is 1% for homogenous countries and only 3% for countries with an ethnic fractionalization of 0.5. Given that the impact of ethnic and religious fractionalization on violence vanishes in more equal and developed countries, it is difficult to sustain the hypothesis that ethnic diversity translates automatically into political grievances (and then violence). Although the following point should remain purely speculative, one possibility is that ethnic groups are excellent conveyors of patron–client networks in underdeveloped countries. But that once unequal economic relations and poverty decline, those networks fall in significance and violent conflict lessens as well. Besides ethnic fractionalization, the proportion of Catholics slightly increases and the percentage of Protestants depresses the presence of guerrilla movements.

Not unexpectedly geography plays also a stronger role than for civil wars. Mountainous terrain leads to more guerrilla – with all other parameters at their medians, the probability changes from 6.2% for the minimum value to 8.6% for the fiftieth percentile and to 11.3% for the maximum value. Noncontiguous states are also much more prone to violence: the probability of a guerrilla increases by 8%.

Conclusions

Combining two central strands of the literature on political violence, the literature on material grievances and motivations and recent research on the geographical and organizational opportunities that foster conflict, this chapter offers a model to account for the distribution of civil wars, guerrillas, and rebellious actions across the world. The model is successfully tested with a comprehensive dataset that covers the period after World War II.

Political violence occurs in states in which assets are immobile and unequally distributed. In relatively equal societies, peaceful, democratic means of solving conflict are advantageous to all parties and violence happens with little probability. In economies where wealth is either mobile or hard to "tax" or confiscate, sustained political violence to grab those assets does not pay off since their owners either can leave in response to the threat of confiscation or are indispensable to the optimal exploitation of assets. These two simple parameters (inequality and specificity of assets) capture in a stylized yet robust way the set of intuitions previous scholars have employed to examine the underlying motivations that generate violence, such as the role of inequality or the idea that "lootable assets" correlate with the presence of civil wars. The examination of the existing data on civil wars and guerrilla warfare validates the model of the essay. Spells of organized or systematic political violence in the world tend to cluster in a relatively tight manner in states where both inequality is high and the economy is mainly agrarian.

Besides depicting the motives of political violence, the model incorporates the notion that "opportunities" of an organizational or geographical nature drive the costs of engaging in violence and therefore determine the likelihood with which it will occur (as well as the likelihood with which different types of violence will be employed). Again, this component emerges in the empirics of the essay. Geography matters, although in a less than systematic way. Mountainous terrain enters strongly for guerrilla movements but not for civil wars. Noncontiguous states are in turn more prone to civil wars.

The theoretical and empirical strength of the model, which naturally has to be read in probabilistic terms, has a key advantage. It allows us to think about all the variance that is left unexplained in a fruitful way. This is clear in at least two ways. First, a second look at the visual information conveyed in Figures 8.4 and 8.5 shows that although most cases of "organized" political violence occur within the upper-right corner of inequality and asset specificity, there are a few cases that do not – most of them seem to belong to the cases of "urban terrorism." Second, ethnic and religious traits still play a role, even though it is a diminished one: the positive effect on violence of Catholics and Muslims is very small; the balance of ethnic groups is only relevant for guerrilla warfare when the societies are still agrarian or not very egalitarian. Our theories for those cases are thus far wanting. Naturally, this calls for stepping up our efforts in establishing their theoretical underpinnings.

REFERENCES

Alesina, Alberto, Arnaud Devleeschauwer, William Easterly, Sergio Kurlat, and Romain Wacziarg. 2003. "Fractionalization." *Journal of Economic Growth* 8: 155–194.

Banks, Arthur S. 1997. "Cross National Time Series: A Database of Social, Economic, and Political Data." www.databanks.sitehosting.net.

Boix, Carles. 2003. *Democracy and Redistribution*. Cambridge University Press.

Boix, Carles, and Sebastian Rosato. 2001. "A Complete Data Set of Political Regimes, 1800–1999." University of Chicago.

Bourguignon, François, and Christian Morrisson. 2002. "Inequality among World Citizens: 1820–1992." *American Economic Review* 92 (September): 727–745.

Collier, Paul, and Anke Hoeffler. 1999. "Justice Seeking and Loot-Seeking in Civil War." World Bank. www.worldbank.org/research/conflict/papers/paulnew2.pdf.

  2001. "Greed and Grievance in Civil War." World Bank. www.worldbank.org/research/conflict/papers/greedgrievance_23oct.pdf.

Connor, Walker. 1994. *Ethnonationalism: The Quest for Understanding*. Princeton University Press.

Fearon, James D., and David Laitin. 2003. "Ethnicity, Insurgency, and Civil War." *American Political Science Review* 97 (February): 75–90.

Gurr, Ted. 1973. "The Revolution-Social Change Nexus." *Comparative Politics* 5 (April): 359–392.

Heston, Alan, Robert Summers, and Bettina Aten. 2002. *Penn World Table Version 6.1*. Center for International Comparisons at the University of Pennsylvania (CICUP).

Horowitz, Donald L. 1985. *Ethnic Groups in Conflict*. Berkeley: University of California Press.

Huntington, Samuel. 1968. *Political Order in Changing Societies*. New Haven: Yale University Press.

LaPorta, Rafael, Florencio Lopez de Silanes, Andrei Shleifer, and Robert Vishny. 1999. "The Quality of Government." *Journal of Law, Economics and Organization* 15 (April): 222–279.

Maddison, Angus. 1995. *Monitoring the World Economy, 1820–1992*. Paris: Organisation for Economic Co-Operation and Development.

Meltzer, A. H., and S. F. Richards. 1981. "A Rational Theory of the Size of Government." *Journal of Political Economy* 89: 914–927.

Muller, Edward N. 1985. "Income Inequality, Regime Repressiveness, and Political Violence." *American Sociological Review* 50: 47–61.

Paige, Jeffery M. 1975. *Agrarian Revolution*. New York: Free Press.

Russett, Bruce M. 1964. "Inequality and Instability." *World Politics* 16: 442–454.

Singer, J. David, and Melvin Small. 1994. "The Correlates of War Project: International and Civil War Data, 1816–1992." Correlates of War Project, University of Michigan.

Vanhanen, Tatu. 1997. *Prospects of Democracy: A Study of 172 Countries*. London: Routledge.

Wolf, Eric R. 1969. *Peasant Wars in the Twentieth Century*. New York: Harper & Row.

9 Clausewitz vindicated? Economics and politics in the Colombian war

Francisco Gutiérrez Sanín

[War] ... is a true chameleon ... because it changes its nature a little in each concrete manifestation.

von Clausewitz

Introduction

What is war? Until relatively recently, the answer was coined almost invariably in Clausewitzian terms (von Clausewitz 1982): the continuation of politics by other (violent) means. Then, two new notions challenged – apparently with success – the Clausewitzian canon, at least in regard to civil wars. On the one hand, Mary Kaldor (2001) described contemporary civil conflicts as "new wars" that exhibited a distinct set of features – rent-seeking, strong links with criminal networks, violence against civilians, etc. War, thus, is not what it used to be. "Modern conflict ... challenges the very distinction between war and peace. It takes place typically not between armies, or even between an army of a state and its armed opposition in some easily defined guerrilla movement. The forces of both government and opposition, from Cambodia to Colombia, blend into illicit business and organized crime" (Cairns, quoted in Azam 2002, 131). On the other hand, rational-choice theorists came to the conclusion that, as Keen (2000) has aptly put it, "war is the continuation of economy by other means." Individuals join insurgent groups as maximizers of expected utility, and those (the groups) offer selective incentives to lure the military "work force" into them.

Attractive as they are, both definitions/explanations are reprehensible on many accounts. First, are new wars truly new? Kalyvas (2001) has shown that proximate violence against civilians – neighbors and relatives – has been endemic more or less in all civil wars, as observers have noted from Thucydides on. Certainly the proportion of civilian

I present research results of the project "War, Democracy and Globalization," co-sponsored by the Crisis States Programme. I wish to thank Mauricio Barón, Francy Carranza, Camilo Plata and others for their very valuable input. I use the following sources in the essay: press, judicial proceedings, government documents, interviews, and fieldwork.

casualties shot up from World War I onward, as Kaldor notes, but Polanyi (1992) had shown that the bounds to attacks on civilians and their properties were established only in the mid-nineteenth century and depended on complex and fragile equilibria that soon came apart; the relatively "clean" wars that partially respected civilians and their properties in Europe were a fifty–seventy-year exception, not the historical rule. On the other hand, the most cursory inspection of the Mexican Revolution literature dramatically reveals how fuzzy the frontiers between rebellion and criminality can be (for example Knight 1990) in the "good old times" of "decent clear-cut war," and tens of other precedents can also be found. Indeed, Machiavelli ([1521] 1991, 68) felt the need to craft an aphorism on war and rent-seeking: "la guerre fait les voleurs, et la paix les fait prendre," and Constant (1997) made it the key to his understanding of the Napoleonic wars. In Colombia, the writer Efe Gómez explained war by the desire of mature men to steal cattle, and of young men to steal both cattle and young women. The Hobsbawmian thread on the subject has shown, if anything, that banditism and peasant rebellion form an intricate historical relationship that is anything but new (see for example Hobsbawm 1981 and Gilbert 1990).

Second, precisely because of this, the "quantum" of criminality and politics in a civil war does not sum up to a constant. It is not the case that "more criminal" need be "less political." For Tilly (1985), state building is historically related to war-waging and expansive racketing. Olson's (1993) view seems to be that the state is criminality writ large: the transition from roving bandits to stationary bandits involves new relations and synergies with the population, and ways of appropriation of the territory that are, *in nuce*, forms of stateness. Rebels and states can establish links with organized crime without losing either their identity or their organizational structure, which is, by the way, what happens, *contra* Cairns' quote, in Colombia; but indeed this may be the standard case (Heyman 1999).

Third, there is not a Chinese wall between economics and politics. The business of politics, after all, is largely the aggregation of economic interests. The idea that the quest for a better life with the guerrillas by destitute peasants is identifiable with nonpolitical greed (Collier and Hoeffler 2001) may be simply a wrong operationalization (Cramer 2002; Keen 2000; Gutiérrez Sanín 2004). As soon as individual drives mix with collective action, we are in front of something new, especially if the high risks assumed by warriors are taken into account.[1] The intent

---

[1] The Colombian guerrillas do not offer economic selective incentives: they do not pay salaries, and do not allow their members to loot. The empirical substantiation of this fact is found in Gutiérrez (2004).

of reducing big historical processes to (possibly criminal) individual appetites that demand immediate gratification is, as Cramer (2002) has observed, just another version of vulgar Marxism,[2] and a "case of excessive ambition" (Elster 2000). No sensible microfoundations of war can evade the explanation of why thousands of people become involved in highly trying and hazardous forms of collective action (Olson 1971), many times, as in Colombia, without receiving economic selective incentives to do so.

This takes us to the fourth, and perhaps most fundamental criticism: until now the political economy of war has not been able to account for its *technical* specifics. The idea that efficient, big war machines can be built on the sole basis of material selective incentives misses the very essence of war as a distinct social activity: organizing and managing large-scale violence, killing, and risking your life. This can be seen from two points of view. For the soldiers, rational calculations face incommensurability: warriors are not evaluating the actuarial value of their lives, but the (negative) value they would ascribe to participation in a Russian roulette. For the leaders and officers, individualism is a deplored quality in an army. Strictly individualistic fighters are not prone to organized, sustained efforts, and they will avoid by all means irreparable individual sacrifices for the obtainment of collective goals. This is, however, one of the basic tenets of a good soldier. When dangers loom large, individualistic fighters shirk or desert. Negative incentives to dissuade them from doing so will not work well, because the control structures in all armies, especially in irregular ones, have a limited scope. Cowardice or reluctance diminish *globally* the combat morale of the army, and are dangerously contagious. But combat morale is a decisive variable, especially when there is hand-to-hand fighting. According to Napoleon, "in war, three-thirds [of what matters] are moral forces" (Luvaas 1999, 17). Maslowski (1970, 122) adequately describes combat morale as "the heart of the military machine." For Tolstoy, combat morale boils down to "the greater or less desire to face dangers" (Tolstoy 2006) and so it is able to decide the outcome of battles.[3] Once again, all this is rather venerable common knowledge among military analysts: to have purely greedy soldiers is a "great evil," because they are fixed upon their individual gains, not the global military outcome (Machiavelli [1521] 1991, 193). When the enemy the given army is facing – in the

---

[2] For example, Jacobo Arenas (2000), an outstanding guerrilla ideologue, explained the Colombian conflict in the following terms: the generals earn higher salaries while the country is in war, so they have incentives to behave as hawks.

[3] Not by chance, the willingness to face fatal dangers is a factor practically absent from the contemporary political economy of war.

case of insurgents, the state – has a minimum of organizational structure and technical prowess, strict discipline and engagement are preconditions of survival. No army can last without cultivating gregarious values.

Last but not least, palatable rents are not sufficient to trigger wars (Skaperdas 1992). War is risky, and rational leaders will calculate carefully before starting it (Fearon 1995); it is not unrealistic to imagine situations in which the equilibrium is that the state tolerates the control of huge rents by a private army (or mafia), and the latter renounces challenging the state.[4] Something more than rent-seeking is needed to create an actual war.

None of these objections, however, questions the enormous centrality of rent-seeking in war-waging. They only underscore the impossibility of reducing politics to economics. When (counter)insurgent groups begin their operations they have to promote and fund it. They will be engaged simultaneously in political and economic operations, each one with its own logic and modus operandi. There is no common currency (to use Gigerenzer's [2002] expression) that would allow the researcher, or the social actors that participate in civil strife, to treat the objectives of the contenders – to gather resources and increase the social base of the movement, for example – as a single one. In particular, the equation more resources equals more adherents and sympathies does not hold. Violent rent-seeking can promote or hinder the political objectives of (counter)insurgency.

After presenting this paper at the Yale workshop, several publications that develop similar themes have appeared. I feel particularly near to some of the arguments put forward in the collective volume edited by Duyvesteyn and Angestrom (2005), which makes a strong pledge for coming back to Clausewitz. However, we are still far from a good understanding of the crucial points. If I am allowed a military metaphor, my understanding of the current situation is the following: the concentric attack on the greed and grievance dichotomy has basically broken the front, and now it is difficult to find somebody among the pundits really convinced of it. But two problems remain. First, decision-makers still take it frequently as their conceptual reference frame, despite the fact that even its authors have retreated to more defensible terrain. So it is important to insist on its incorrectness, but also to understand why it seems so commonsensical. It seems that the understanding of contemporary conflicts entails acknowledging their economic dimensions. Second, and most consequential, we do not know very well how life will look after the dichotomy. I would suggest that part of the big constructive

---

[4] Actually, several such situations can be found in Colombia, as will be seen below.

task now is to open the black box of the complex mechanisms that link armed politics and armed economics.

That precisely is the purpose of this essay. I focus on the Colombian war. Certainly, where the conflict is very long, and there is no clear we–them barrier – so that warlords do not only want to exercise violence on the population, but also govern it – it is easier to capture the complexity of the interactions between one and another dimension. I will confine myself here to the simplest aspects of the dynamic tension between the economics and the politics of war. I treat three types of situations:

(a) The attainment of economic goals gets in the way of political ones.
(b) Those "happy" states in which strong synergies can be found: rents buttress political support and vice versa.
(c) Politics harms business, which is obviously – but not exclusively – related to the politicization of crime.

I dedicate a section to each type, considering examples that allow the exhibiting of the mechanisms that generate them. The mechanisms that I describe are anchored on a concrete conflict, but are not idiosyncratic enough, or so I hope, as to be restricted to it.

Economic successes, political defeats

Colombia's main guerrilla, the Fuerzas Armadas Revolucionarias de Colombia (FARC), was evicted from several of its strongholds in the 1980s. This is rather surprising, because it had in those places near-ideal conditions for the development of revolutionary activity: state absence, political support, very strong traditions of social struggle linked to the guerrillas, and even nationalist themes.

The explanation of its disaster may lie in a single word: overtaxation. Take the example of Puerto Boyacá. The FARC found almost no opposition to its entry in the 1970s. It carefully built networks among the poor, but at the same time counted on the leniency of the better-off, who felt that the FARC's firm hand with petty criminals and rustlers suited them well. FARC's revolutionary sermons improved peasant morals, and this was compatible with increased work productivity and public order. Long after, the new bosses – the paramilitary – remembered with nostalgia the "golden age" of FARC's early territorial control. In 1989, for example, Henry de Jesús Pérez declared that the region "had been extremely fertile for the FARC. While the guerrilla had an acceptable behavior, people didn't rebel against it. But in 1979 two new commanders arrived, and then began a policy of aggression against the region."

What did he mean by acceptable behavior? Not angelical, indeed. From the very beginning, the FARC gathered the *vacuna* (vaccine), a racket on livestock farming, that was later extended to other activities. People who did not pay on time, or were very rich, or had connections with "the enemy," were kidnapped. Landlords had to hire workers recommended by the FARC, and this offered the group both support and an invaluable source of information.

But by 1979 there was a qualitative leap, heralded (though not caused by) the arrival of a new commander, Argemiro. The demands of the front on the population sharply increased. The FARC is a very centralized organization, and the center – the *Secretariado* – establishes mandatory quotas of financial and political growth for each front. Following the inertia of its own domination and the demands it got from above, the front started to kidnap key "friends," cattle ranchers that had paid faithfully their *vacuna*, and notables that played a dominant role in the town's social life; extortions and punitive homicides skyrocketed,[5] and affected more and more people. Those better off started to flee, and this had a double impact on the relation between the FARC and the locals: the front translated the weight of its taxation to ever-expanding social layers, and investment fell radically. The initial honeymoon gave way to a widespread and strong disaffection, and when army officers and cattle ranchers took the strategic decision to form a paramilitary group they were backed by a broad sector of the population (Medina Gallego 1990). As the FARC leaders acknowledge, their military defeat was directly linked to the loss of their ties with the population.

The same mechanism can be seen at work one time and another in the most different settings: increasing demands provoke the exodus of the richest, so the guerrilla turns its guns against the middle class and the poor.[6] The tension between the resource-insatiability of the war and

---

[5] Later, in their evaluation of the events, the FARC leaders criticized Argemiro for his highhanded attitude toward the population. But the problem is *structural*: given the huge technological gap between it and the government, the FARC needs to extract regional resources to sustain the war nationally, and thus tends to go overboard.

[6] The epitome of extortion run amok are the so-called *pescas milagrosas*, massive and random kidnappings in the roads by the guerrilla. The *pescas milagrosas* have been one of the many factors that galvanized the middle class against it. But the very poor have also been affected by overtaxing, and they too have rebelled against it. In July 1997, a group of the Front Benkos Biojó of the ELN popped up in Beriguadó y Dipurdú del Guásimo, west of the town of Istmina, in the department of Chocó. They tried to take away food – pigs, chickens, vegetables – from the peasants, but the latter resisted. Four guerrilla members were killed. "The first incident took place when the dwellers of Beriguadó were gathered at a vigil of a deceased man, and three men and one woman from the ELN appeared demanding food. Some of those present at the vigil went to their houses to look for supplies, but other came back with shotguns and put the subversives to flight" (*El*

the limited nature of local-regional rents finally causes a political catastrophe.

The paramilitary also fell victims to the same mechanism, although in a somewhat different form. In 1997, a gathering of cattle ranchers and wholesale merchants of Lebrija – a small town in the northeast of the country – decided to form a *Convivir*. *Convivir* was the name given to security cooperatives fostered by the 1994–1998 government, a very big proportion of which became – or networked with – paramilitary groups. The Lebrija *Convivir* was one of these. Indeed, the original idea came from army officers. In the beginning, everything seemed to work well for the founders. The paramilitary "cleaned" the town of petty criminals, and assassinated several workers who supposedly were "guerrilla informants" (I will come back to this point later on). They also helped notables and politicians with private favors, such as logistic support or intimidation of rival candidates.[7] With time, however, the original funding provided by ranchers and merchants – a quota placed on a bank account and managed by the neighbors' association – became insufficient. The paramilitary group had grown, and needed more resources; it started to sell security more aggressively. The new rules included extraordinary payments, calculated on the number of plants in each rural property or the size of the premises of each owner. Those who were not able or willing to pay were victims of intimidation and aggression. The rich started to flee. Finally, one of the main landowners and founders of the group, who by then was regularly extorted by it, and feeling that the situation had "gone out of control," turned to the military brigade for help; the quotas had reached absurdly high levels and his life was in danger, he said. Very much to its grief, the brigade had to dismantle the group (JP3).[8] In other cases, the people who had initially supported a paramilitary group finally came to the conclusion that it was too burdensome, but were unable to get rid of it (Castro 1996); indeed, the Lebrija *Convivir* was sufficiently small and weak as to be dealt with expediently, but more consolidated paramilitary may remain

Tiempo 1997). Dozens of these events have taken place in the past twenty years. Another way of attacking the problem is noting that overtaxing the rich harms *all* citizens, because it discourages investment. As the rich start to flee, the middle and low segments of the regional society suffer on two accounts: they lose their employment, and start to be targeted as possible contributors.

[7] These rivals were not members of leftist parties.

[8] Characteristically, a *coronel* declared that "some of the rich people of the region asked us to have these groups, to defend their properties, or things related with the guerrilla [*cuestiones de la guerrilla*]." JP refers to the list of judicial proceedings in the references, below.

long periods as a praetorian guard against the will of their original constituencies. However, this makes the territorial control of the group more vulnerable, and it invites new entrants – in several cases, simply rival paramilitary factions.

In sum, the first mechanism that implies paying a high political cost for economic gains is easily understandable: the warlord taxes a given territory so heavily that its carrying capacity is surpassed, so that people flee and/or an armed challenge appears. In the case of the paramilitary of Lebrija, this seems to be a problem of short time horizons and lack of self-restraint. With a less greedy attitude perhaps they may have sustained their key strategic alliance with the notables. Regarding the FARC, we are instead facing a story of local sacrifices to obtain global objectives. The FARC is challenging the state, and there is an enormous technological gap between the former and the latter. The organizational sustainability of the guerrilla depends on its ability to cope with such a gap. In our Puerto Boyacá example, the FARC front was *obliged* to contribute to the general effort of war,[9] because the resources gathered by each well-to-do front are centralized and then redirected by the *Secretariado* to the poorer fronts, military enterprises that are not self-sustainable (urban networks, for example), and coordination structures (so-called interfront and block activities). The case of the guerrilla incurring heavy political losses to obtain economic gains is also related to factors other than the regional–national tension. Illegal businesses do not have independent adjudication mechanisms, so extra-economic arbitrariness always plays a key role in racketing, kidnapping, and collecting quotas from the population: an ideal situation for violent opposition to arise, as Barrington Moore (2000) noted. The *vacuna* and the extortion businesses do not function on the basis of fixed quotas. When a victim fails to pay on time, the quota is increased. Kidnapping apparently works on an equally fuzzy basis; "naughty" victims are punished. People who are slow to react – especially when there is a suspicion that their procrastination is related to some kind of cooperation with the authorities – are imposed higher ransoms to rescue the victim (JP1). Kidnappers rarely seem to have a clear figure in mind when demanding a ransom from the victim's family, and start asking for astronomical sums to "anchor" the negotiation (JP2). Be that as it may, the lack of clear rules is a nuisance in itself and is one of the aspects that most mystifies victims, as it opens the door to sheer arbitrariness.

---

[9] Though of course it can be argued that the FARC leaders were showing also time-related anomalies; had they advanced slower, they could have maintained their territorial control *and* their increasing war effort.

There is another side to the coin. Going too local, and neglecting political objectives, may result in structural collapse. The outcome can hardly be considered idiosyncratic, and should alert against the one-sided economic and/or localistic renderings of armed conflict. Contrary to the standard story of the political economy of war, in Colombia the only organization that offered selective incentives to its warriors – the paramilitary – fell apart; it lasted five years.[10] The paramilitary appeared in the early 1980s as a local answer to subversion, funded by cattle ranchers and drug traffickers, and supported by members of the army and the police (Aranguren 2001; Medina Gallego 1990; Romero 2002; JP4, JP5). As we have seen, they had several successes combating and evicting the guerrillas, but lacked the unity of command that would allow having nationwide coordinated activity. The strongest branch of the paramilitary – the Autodefensas Campesinas de Córdoba y Urabá (ACCU) of the Castaño brothers – started an energetic effort to achieve unity and growth. Both objectives were attained in 1997, when the Autodefensas Unidas de Colombia (AUC) was founded. In the 1990s the paramilitary were the most dynamic group in terms of recruitment and increment of firepower. With very few exceptions, all the regional paramilitary expressions were put under the command of Castaño. These formidable successes gave way, only five years after, to organizational breakdown and disarray. The AUC imploded,[11] the majority of the paramilitary engaged in a reinsertion process, and in at least four cases paramilitary factionalism ended in major internecine war. The paramilitary have been a social success, not an organizational one.

Why has this happened? Three main explanations may account for the phenomenon. First, the AUC was a federation. Contrary to the FARC, the superior command was not in a position to centralize economic or military resources; instead, it had a narrow territorial adscription (Córdoba and Urabá). The territorial units – *bloques*, according to the paramilitary taxonomy – had the power to challenge the center whenever differences around strategy or resource distribution appeared, because they had direct access to the funds provided by "their" landowners, cattle ranchers, and narcotraffickers. Some of the *bloques* had developed very strong ties with the local society (and authorities). These *bloques* were preferred by a broad sector of the deeply parochial notables to the AUC "strangers" of Córdoba and Urabá. There are many examples of this. Take the conflict between the national AUC leader Carlos Castaño and Hernando Giraldo, a paramilitary leader who acts in the north of the

[10] In contrast with thirty-nine-year-old ELN and (at least) forty-one-year-old FARC.
[11] It still exists, but not as a national movement.

country (Sierra Nevada de Santa Marta). By 2000–2001, Castaño had clashed several times with Giraldo. Castaño reproached Giraldo for his too deep involvement in narcotrafficking, his lack of concern for national motives, and his aloofness regarding AUC directives; there were probably distributional conflicts as well. When Giraldo assassinated three members of the anti-narcotics police, and in 2002 became the first Colombian paramilitary targeted for extradition by the United States, Castaño lost his patience and sent a punitive expedition of 200 of his best men to the Sierra. Giraldo calmly declared that he was not afraid of Castaño, and mobilized the population against him; the expedition had to retreat (*Revista Semana* 2002, 40–41; *El Tiempo* 2002, 1–2).[12] Later on Giraldo was partially subdued, and put under the supervision of a Castaño man, Jorge Cuarenta. The latter came to be one of the most powerful strongmen of the Colombian Atlantic Coast, but Giraldo not only continued to enjoy a handsome degree of autonomy, but also survived Castaño, who was killed (allegedly by his brother Vicente's hit men). According to Vicente, Carlos had negotiated Giraldo's head with the US authorities. It is clear that ultimately the centrifugal tendencies of the paramilitary overwhelmed its cohesion.

The individualism of the paramilitary soldiers and officers was one of these powerful centrifugal forces that acted as an organizational dissolver. The paramilitary *bloques* pay their fighters a salary and give the best of them access to narco-rents, which is a nice recruitment incentive, but also:

(a) Fosters distributional conflicts within the organization. The history of armed confrontations between the paramilitary is long and stormy, the last episode being the collision between the *Bloque Centauros* of the AUC and the Autodefensas Campesinas del Casanare, headed by Miguel Arroyave and Martín Llanos, respectively.[13] This struggle has a typically parochialist dimension: Llanos claims to be combating the "invaders" from Córdoba and Urabá, and accused Arroyave of having "bought a *Bloque*" with narco-money.[14]

---

[12] Giraldo still operates in his territory with total impunity. Apparently, the Colombian state has been more impotent than Castaño.

[13] Just before this episode, in the Antioquia department the *Bloque Metro* clashed with the *Bloque Nutibara* of Don Berna, a narcotrafficker who is presently member of the Córdoba-Urabá leadership. The Metro *bloque* claimed that they were against the participation of narcotrafficking in their struggle; paramilitary involved in narco-businesses would not fight subversion, but only make money. Don Berna and his men wiped out the *Bloque Metro*, despite the desperate requests of its commander ("Doble Cero") for government intervention.

[14] Arroyave was eventually killed by his own men.

(b) Discourages combativity, because it focuses the attention of officers and troops on defending and pursuing their own businesses. Internal wars also have a fatal effect on combat morale, as the paramilitary openly acknowledges. Both hard (Spagat *et al.* 2003)[15] and qualitative data show that in the 1990s, the paramilitaries were taking heavy blows from the FARC, which meant the tables were turned in relation to the 1980s.

Last but not least, the involvement of the paramilitary in narco-trafficking and other businesses have caused both economic and political disputes within the top leadership and its immediate network of supporters. Some paramilitary leaders in the mid-1990s were already pursuing an agreement with the Colombian government, and faced the burning problem of what they would do if the US asked for them to be extradited.[16] They thus tried to tone down their participation in narcotrafficking, and even probed US officials with the idea of becoming the forgers of a negotiated massive surrender of narcotraffickers to the US. This caused deep fractures within the paramilitary leadership.[17] At the regional level, the extraction of rents, and the replacement of old owners by new ones – paramilitary commanders and even soldiers rapidly enriched in the midst of war-waging – has been traumatic, and in some regions has weakened the support of the paramilitary among old notables.

Economy aiding politics

The politics and economics of war are also related in several positive ways. First, controlling a business can help the group develop a governance blueprint. The decision of the FARC to admit coca crops in its territories in the late 1970s (Ferro and Uribe 2002) entailed creating a taxation structure, a system of conflict resolution, and a set of initiatives to maintain peasant mores under control. This was generally welcome, frequently also by the well-off. Where the lack of state structures and deeply rooted social ties and the corrosion of the traditional peasant society due to the growth of illegal economies maximally hinder the solution of collective action problems, an external regulator is a source not only of security but also of preciously scarce "social capital." When

---

[15] In the context of our research we built a database of political homicides in Colombia from 1975 until today. It also suggests that in the confrontations between the FARC and the paramilitary since 1990, the latter have gotten the worst of it.

[16] Presently, this constitutes a first order national problem.

[17] It eventually caused the killing of Carlos Castaño, the main AUC leader.

the Colombian state decided to aerially fumigate illegal crops, the FARC opposed the plan, combining economic – defense of the business – and political – articulation and aggregation of the interests of social sectors that make their living in illicit crops – dimensions. In sum, in regions where illegal crops are important, the FARC is playing a threefold political role: it is *replacing* the state; it is *defending* the peasants from the state (for example, from fumigations or indiscriminate repression);[18] and it is defending the peasants *from themselves* (educating them, dignifying their mores, etc.).

In the past section, I spoke about overtaxation. But vendors and buyers are ready to pay taxes – up to a threshold – to a warlord who organizes the illegal market, giving it the minimal conditions for functioning as a bona fide market and preventing raids from third parties. Creating, protecting, and structuring markets – what may be called "peasant liberalism" – is a second way to obtain support through economic activities. Once again, peasant liberalism can be analyzed with the ideas of Moore (2000) on rural rebellion. Moore argued that peasant rebellion was most likely in economic systems where extra-economic coercion played an important role. In the case of Colombia, these are the illegal markets. Defending them from state raids, regulating, and – in a very real sense – creating them (as markets) offers the FARC a window of opportunity to foster rebellion, build a constituency, and make money. Global institutions have pitted state against market, and this fracture has empowered the FARC as an entrepreneur of peasant rebellion *and* as a champion of market economy.

Third – and fairly obviously – the control of economic resources can be transformed into clientelistic politics, both with and without alliances with traditional political parties. Very early, the Ejército de Liberación Nacional (ELN) was supporting electoral barons in Arauca, who in turn favored their constituencies with investments (see Peñate 1991). For example, extortion offers the following opportunities for politicking:

(a) Placing "friends" of the organization in the payroll of the host enterprise. This practice was forced upon banana agro-industrialists in Urabá (FARC and EPL – Ejército Popular de Liberación), cattle ranchers throughout the country (mainly FARC), oil companies (ELN) and gold companies (mainly ELN).[19] Favored friends provide both support and intelligence.

---

[18] This is ambiguous, because there are situations in which the peasants want the presence of the state, while the FARC does not.

[19] According to a government report, in the 1980s the oil company Mannesmann and the ELN had a showdown because the company had a payroll of only 450 employees, and

(b) Sharing spoils with politicians. The governor of Arauca between 1997 and 2000 appears to have systematically funded ELN's initiatives in the department. In 2000, a different faction of a traditional party came to power;[20] it seems to have leaned toward the FARC, and cut the supply to the ELN. The latter – feeling it had been double-crossed – confiscated the ex-governor's livestock. The letter the ex-governor sent to an ELN commander in his defense contained a list that appears to be a nice sample of the type of activities the guerrillas were interested in: "supplies, computers, public works, mobilization, organization, purchase of vehicles and real estate, payment of debts, gasoline, medical treatment ... " (*El Espectador* 2003). Given the country's decentralization, oil companies pay big royalties to departments and municipalities. The ELN and other armed groups not only tax the companies, but milk the municipalities and departments as well; this involves a large-scale operation of embezzlement. In the process, the given politician (be he a mayor or a municipal-department council member) can collect a toll. In other words, the transference of funds to the ELN, the FARC, or the paramilitary groups facilitates the enrichment of several "second-level" rent-seekers. This web of politicians has incentives to cooperate with the given armed group.

(c) As was seen above, putting pressure – many times militarily – on the municipalities, the politicians, or the companies themselves to carry out public works (bridges, roads, etc.). This improves the conditions of some social sectors (possibly at the expense of others).

Sometimes, small-scale operations are equally effective. For example, in some regions the guerrilla front or commander plays the role of a "friendly moneylender," and this builds, or feeds, networks of supporters or sympathizers.

Fourth, and as a variation on the preceding theme, there are some businesses that, by their very nature, can only be developed and managed by an armed group. In such conditions, civilians participate in it as a "friend" or "guest."[21] In other terms, this is not a change of favors for votes, but of favors for support to an armed group. The most obvious and important example is the stealing of oil and gasoline from the

---

the ELN wanted to place more than 700 "friends." As I showed in the first section, the ever-growing dimensions of the war-waging can end with killing the goose with the golden eggs.

[20] Referring to the two big Colombian historical parties, the liberals and conservatives.

[21] Please note the crucial difference with coca crops, where settlers established their business first, and the illegal armies arrived after.

pipelines, by now a huge concern known in Colombia, inexactly but colorfully, as the "gasoline cartel," and basically controlled by the paramilitary.[22] According to government sources, the "cartel" extracts around two and a half million barrels yearly. In Puerto Boyacá, the cartel works in the following manner: two commanders are in charge of the operation. After deciding where the operation will take place, how the profits will be distributed, etc., they encourage groups of civilians to "puncture" the pipeline, paying them a high per diem; they then distribute the fuel through a web of clandestine gas stations (installed in houses, shops, and restaurants), that offer it to the public at half the legal price.[23] All this activity is relatively – i.e., compared to narcotrafficking – low profile and low risk. It is repressed, but it does not entail any international stigma. It is instead a source of immense popularity.[24] Not only do the civilians who participate in the extraction and the illegal distributors have material reasons for gratitude, but also the final consumer (cheaper fuel).

Finally, the guerrillas and the paramilitary have stabilized or reshuffled property rights in Colombia, and, in doing so, they have made both politics and business. This has two distinct dimensions. In some regions of the country, war has a possibly oblique, but distinct link with class struggle. Urabá is an obvious case (García 1996). The armed conflict was juxtaposed with a strong labor–capital struggle, and this motive maintained its centrality until long after the ultimate victory of the paramilitary. With it – the latter say triumphantly – "the relations between capital and labor were pacified, within a general conception of justice and cordiality between workers and bosses" (*El Tercer Actor*).[25] In Lebrija, the *Convivir* started killing not guerrilla collaborators, who were scarce or nonexistent,[26] but workers who had rows and grudges against the notables. This is a standard feature of paramilitary action throughout the country. "When there is security in a zone," concludes Carlos Castaño, "people have the right to their private property, their house,

---

[22] The FARC and ELN also participate, but in the margin; the paramilitary extracts ten times more gasoline than the guerrillas.

[23] In a more traditional fashion, they can collect a quota for the right to puncture the pipeline.

[24] On the other hand, the dispute for the control of the gasoline cartel has caused several scrapes among the paramilitary.

[25] This booklet was one of the key ideological pieces of the paramilitary, crafted by Carlos Castaño and his advisors; it used to be found at www.colombialibre.org/index.php. However, after the demise of Castaño, it was apparently retired from AUC's web page.

[26] The guerrilla had not had a strong presence there since the failed expedition of one of the few FARC splinter groups in 1984.

their car, their motorcycle, without anybody stealing it ... because he has 200 cows or something. And then the land starts to improve, and win value, and schools and roads start to be built, because the State has no fear" (Castro 2003, 219). The second dimension is the provision of security. Killing small-time drug vendors, rapists, and thieves is one of the main activities of *any* Colombian armed group as soon as it becomes dominant in a region. Leftist urban militias, rural guerrillas, the paramilitary in the country and the city, are all intent on extirpating and killing petty criminality. The motivations behind such efforts are variegated, but the consequences are always more or less the same. On the one hand, there is centralization and coordination of criminal economic activities. For example, "cleaning" the neighborhoods from crack retailers may allow the illegal group to seize the distribution networks and increase substantially its participation in the business, as well as its profit margins. Those groups that do provide selective material incentives can use these opportunities to reward effective or loyal members. On the other hand, there is legitimation. Punishing criminals draws heavy popular approval. Actually, in some cases – the leftist militias of Medellín in the early 1990s (see Gutiérrez and Jaramillo 2004) – it was the main source of support. As would befit an Olsonian interpretation of the construction of social order (Olson 1993), in the beginning there was crime, and those who repressed it won the big prize of territorial control.

It must be noted that all these "positive" interactions between economic and political gains can have "negative" side effects. Building patronage networks only makes sense if some people can be excluded. If everybody has unrestricted access, it is impossible to administrate the goods to reward the loyal and chastise the unfaithful. Clientelistic distribution – whether it is managed by a warlord or by somebody else – splits the population into a set of winners and a set of losers. However, then the latter will harbor grievances against the given warlord, which can become sufficiently strong enough to provoke defection (or disloyalty). Governing and taxing can cause widespread disaffection, and invite potential competitors to offer the same services (provision of regulation and security) in better conditions. Managing an illegal business, like the "gasoline cartel," can cause frequent conflicts with the police and the army where they were few or nonexistent before. The provision of security involves killing people, and the families of the victims will be utterly distressed. In this case, even if compliance is relatively broad, social niches of dissatisfaction can end up as a serious source of instability for the warlord, because the *intensity* and *duration* of the preferences of each set of people are asymmetrical: the unhappy are less disaffected, but much more angry than the others are complaisant.[27] Security-selling can also trigger bitter rivalries with friends and allies.[28]

Politics harming business: an example

The Cali Cartel had an "official doctrine" regarding the state: nowhere and never has a criminal group defeated a state deserving of the name. This is why they resorted to infiltration, not to terrorism, to prevent repressive actions against them (Gutiérrez Sanín 2001).[29] The Cali Cartel doctrine can be easily rehashed in rationalistic jargon.[30] To simplify, suppose the state has only two strategies, tolerate or repress. Criminals, on their side, decide to challenge the state or not. The mental representation of the game by the Cartel seems to have been a perturbed and melodramatic version of the Stag Hunt game, as seen in Table 9.1.

The Table of course has only heuristic use, if any. First, note that challenging is suboptimal. As noted above, in an open confrontation, the doctrine held, criminals do not stand a chance. The war that follows will indeed damage the state, but it will harm the narcotraffickers even more.[31] And if the state tolerates, challenging will trigger a public outrage that will increase the probability of retaliation; the gains of the traffickers will not be high if we discount the costs of risk and instability. Additionally, the only Nash equilibrium is "nice": tolerate–not challenge. However, for the state this equilibrium is "risk-dominated" by repressing. The state has much more to lose if it behaves "nicely" and, by the proverbial trembling hand, the traffickers do not. While the Nash outcome is: (a) the state tolerates the control of rents by criminals, and these renounce challenging the state; the risk-dominant outcome

---

[27] I am aware that here I am violating the axiom of interpersonal incomparability of preferences (in this case, of sentiments). The basic underlying idea is the following: diffuse support can be overcome by concentrated odium. I have shown elsewhere that armed actors are quite aware of this. Even then, it could be argued that sometimes even the assassination of relatives receives its share of support (for the case of the militias of Medellín, see Jaramillo *et al.* 1998). However, this appears to happen only in the initial, "heroic" period of inception of the given group; afterwards, these events disappear or become very rare.

[28] For example, at the beginning of the 1980s the FARC and the EPL were competing in the Alto Sinú so enthusiastically for the collection of *vacunas* and the elimination of rustlers, that they had military collisions for this motive.

[29] They were implacable murderers in other domains; their doctrine was a typical result of rational calculation, not of normative behavior.

[30] Of course it was purely instrumental, as it used violence profusely against nonstate actors.

[31] Obviously, this interaction is best represented as a repeated game, but for simplicity I avoid doing so.

Table 9.1. *Coordination game between narcotraffickers and the state*

Narcos/state	Repress	Tolerate
Challenge	(−5,2)	(1,−15)
Not challenge	(−2,3)	(5,5)

The first number is the payoff for the narco-traffickers, the second for the state.

is: (b) the state clamps down on criminals, and the latter yield.[32] Both have a rational flavor. Of course, criminals are vitally interested in producing outcome (a). How can they do it? They can try to increase the cost of repression for the state by threatening a catastrophic scenario in case of war. But this is not credible, as it would be prohibitively expensive for them. Their only other possibility is to decrease the subjectively perceived probability of them challenging. If they signal efficaciously enough that the outcome tolerate–challenge will not take place, they can hope to arrive at the desirable Nash equilibrium. Thus, the traffickers must cultivate their reputation and send clear signals of low-profile, orderly behavior. This means that they will try to pamper politicians and members of the security apparatus, but not enter directly the political realm.

If the doctrine is right, the amount and intensity of *direct* criminal participation in politics in the past twenty years is rather amazing. Mafiosi have created their own political parties, guerrillas, paramilitary groups, and terrorist commands: all related to a few basic motives, such as the struggle against extradition, or against the penal law, or against subversion. The history of the politicization of crime in Colombia is still to be written, but it is clear that, as many narcotraffickers observed immediately, it could be bad for business. If they are a version of the *homo economicus*, a credible enough assumption, why then have they behaved as they have? There are at least three possible answers. First, hyper-rational criminals expect to force equilibrium (a), so they put all their bets on an out-of-equilibrium move (the state represses, but criminals respond) that prohibitively increases the costs of repression and thus makes it highly unlikely: "If you hit us, you will have reason to regret it." It must be noted that increasing the benefits of (a), the

[32] Actually, the transition from equilibrium (a) to (b) is a nice and simple sketch of the Cali Cartel trajectory.

alternative strategy, is much better. On the one hand, retaliating is not (in theory) a credible threat, because it is common knowledge of the state and the criminals that the counter-blows will be unbearable. On the other hand, if criminal rents can be extracted quietly and in an orderly manner, seizing them will be a low priority, especially for a besieged state. And, in effect, semi-legal and/or illegal actors have been able to strike highly politicized regional "peace agreements" with the state's consent (and actual participation; see Gutiérrez and Jaramillo 2003).

Second, criminals may be in a position to transform their economic assets into political capital, and as any other agent they will try to do so. Here the basic intuition is that actors' behavior is governed by inertia and they grab the opportunities that appear without evaluating long-term costs and benefits, which in turn would entail myopia and bounded rationality.[33] As Henry de Jesús Pérez, the paramilitary leader of the 1980s who opposed Pablo Escobar and was finally killed by him, said, "what started as a purely economic criminal problem [the struggle against extradition] ended up as a Peronist type of war, a combination of political movement, class struggle and violence" (*Revista Semana* 1991). Third, the Cali Cartel doctrine was wrong, and the arm of the Colombian state *can* be twisted. If this becomes common knowledge through the setting of numerous precedents, the criminals will have real incentives to become political: through politics they can "move" the line of legality in ways that favor them.[34]

Guerrillas and paramilitary face some of these tensions and dilemmas, although in fairly different ways, because from the very beginning they are challenging or redefining, respectively, the state. For example, the mobilization of the peasantry by the FARC to oppose aerial fumigations in the 1990s resulted in heavy economic losses for coca growers, and ultimately in political losses for the guerrillas as well. The paramilitary have within their leadership large-scale narcotraffickers, so their situation is more complicated. A glimpse of criminal-war dynamics can be caught in the Castaño and don Berna vs. La Terraza conflict. In the late 1990s, Castaño and don Berna co-opted the gang La Terraza of Medellín for the paramilitary cause.[35] They used La Terraza to carry out political killings and establish their control over the city (an account of the process is found in Gutiérrez and Jaramillo 2004). Eventually, La

---

[33] I.e., they start participating in politics unaware that this implies challenging the state; and they indulge in a fight even knowing that they do not have a chance to win it.

[34] I believe it can be shown that *all three* arguments have a role to play in the understanding of the politicization of crime.

[35] La Terraza was actually a huge "meta-gang" that centralized and coordinated the activity of diverse hit men and gangs.

Terraza won autonomy and tried to play its own game; indeed, in the *barrios* of Medellín, the gangs were actively imitating armed political actors and trying to carry out social and communal work (Jaramillo *et al.* 1998). Then came the rupture. The paramilitary accused La Terraza of criminal behavior (not intended as irony) and of causing excessive deaths. The Terraza members retorted by declaring that they had been the authors of several of the most renowned and brutal killings of human rights defenders, but that Castaño had given them the orders. They also denounced Castaño for promising them a narcotrafficking route and failing to fulfill his promise. Finally, the Terraza leaders were killed or put to flight by the paramilitary. Going political had been disastrous for them.

This shows how hazy the crime–political war frontier can be, as Cairns (Azam 2002, 131) and others stress. But at the same time it reminds us that a naive approach to what criminal means is unproductive. One need not be a strong relativist to see that criminality is a category that can actually be the very outcome of political confrontation (Cohen 1996). On the other hand, it appears that it is not that easy, or cheap, to become political. If insurgent groups have been able to remain as structured political actors for decades, investing enormous amounts of resources in typically political activities, the observer would do well to take this datum into account.

Conclusions

To start and sustain their activities, rebels and counterinsurgents have to capture rents. If the war is sufficiently long, this will mean developing large-scale businesses. These involve numerous social actors and create special interests, so they have a dynamics of their own. It is only natural that, past a certain point, (strictly economic) criminals and rebels start to mix, and this will transform both the one and the other.

So far so good. However, this is only part of the picture. "Doing well out of war" is not a novelty but rather one of the few stable traits of the chameleon; it can be found in the Crusades, in the Colombian war, and in practically all events in between. The question is if the political dimensions of armed conflict can be reduced to a pretext for individual enrichment. Such a conjecture could be defensible if war-waging were the way to maximize rents for a set of individuals – soldiers or leaders, for example. But, as seen here, engaging in a political war is not such a good rent-seeking strategy, much less optimal: (a) the resource insatiability of war creates tensions with the population, and warlords will end killing the goose with the golden eggs; (b) rent collection is driven by much shorter time horizons than military strategizing, and so conflicts with it; (c) combat morale and organizational structures cannot be sustained by the unique means of material selective incentives – material incentives can actually corrode organizational structures;[36] and (d) "aggressive politicization" is a prohibitively costly strategy for purely economic criminals. Even in a war with such a degree of criminalization as the Colombian one, cozy rents can harm political success, and going political can be economically counterproductive. Even without taking into account norms or emotions, which I have mainly set aside in this analysis, agents find reasons to sacrifice monetary gains, or even their lives, to political objectives.

A bit more obliquely, all this tends to put into doubt the mechanical divide between economics and politics, as expressed, for example, in the greed and grievance dichotomy. War is a chameleon, and a multi-objective optimization operation. This demands of the analyst an effort to understand the ways in which the economics and the politics of war mix and interact. The Colombian war exhibits a wide gamut of forms of political mobilization, incorporation, and persuasion through economic actions: regulating and structuring markets, aggregating material interests, protecting labor or capital, and redefining the role of the state: it is hard to see in which sense they can be tagged "nonpolitical." All this highlights the importance of identifying the political-economic mechanisms that link nonstate armed groups with specific populations. In sum, it seems that it is time to take politics back in a (partial) vindication of Clausewitz.

REFERENCES

Aranguren, Mauricio. 2001. *Mi Confesión: Carlos Castaño Revela sus Secretos.* Bogotá: Oveja Negra.
Arenas, Jacobo. 2000. *Cese al Fuego: Una Historia Política de las FARC.* Bogotá: Oveja Negra.
Azam, Jean Paul. 2002. "Looting and Conflict Between Ethnoregional Groups: Lessons for State Formation in Africa." *Journal of Conflict Resolution* 46 (1): 131–152.
Castro, Caicedo Germán. 1996. *En Secreto.* Bogotá: Planeta.
    2003. *Sin Tregua.* Bogotá: Planeta.
Clausewitz, Carl von. 1982. *On War,* trans. J.J. Graham. London: Penguin Classics.
Cohen, Stanley. 1996. "Crime and Politics: Spot the Difference." *British Journal of Sociology* 47 (1): 1–21.

---

[36] Put in another way, what works for enterprises does not necessarily work for armies.

Collier, Paul, and Anke Hoeffler. 2001. "Greed and Grievance in Civil War." Working paper, World Bank.

Constant, Benjamin. 1997. *Écrits politiques*. Paris: Gallimard.

Cramer, Christopher. 2002. "Homo Economicus Goes to War: Methodological Individualism, Rational Choice and the Political Economy of War." *World Development* 30 (11): 1845–1864.

Duyvesteyn, Isabelle, and Jan Angstrom, eds. 2005. *Rethinking the Nature of War*. London and New York: Frank Cass.

El Espectador. 2003. "Arauca: Un Ex Gobernador en Problemas." *El Espectador*, October 25: 7-A.

Elster, Jon. 2000. "Rational Choice History: A Case of Excessive Ambition." *American Political Science Review* 94 (3): 685–695.

El Tiempo. 1997. "La Gente se Cansó de la Guerrilla." *El Tiempo*, July 17: 9-A. 2002. "Guerra para en Santa Marta." *El Tiempo*, January 22: 1–2.

Fearon, James. 1995. "Rationalist Explanations of War." *International Organization* 49 (3): 379–414.

Ferro, Juan Guillermo, and Graciela Uribe. 2002. *El Orden de la Guerra: Las FARC-EP: Entre la Organización y la Política*. Bogotá: CEJA.

García, Clara Inés. 1996. *Urabá: Región, Actores y Conflicto 1960–1980*. Bogotá: INER-CEREC.

Gigerenzer, Gerd, and Reinherd Selten, eds. 2002. *Bounded Rationality: The Adaptive Toolbook*. Cambridge, MA: MIT University Press.

Gilbert, Joseph. 1990. "On the Trial of Latin American Bandits: A Reexamination of Peasant Resistance." *Latin American Research Review* 25 (3): 7–53.

Gutiérrez, Francisco, and Ana María Jaramillo. 2003. "Pactos Paradoxais." In *Reconhecer Para Libertar*, ed. Boaventura de Sousa Santos. Rio de Janeiro: Civilizo Brasileíra.
2004. "Crime, (Counter)insurgency and the Privatization of Security: The Case of Medellín, Colombia." *Environment and Urbanization* 16 (2) (October): 1–14.

Gutiérrez Sanín, Francisco. 2001. "Organized Crime and Political Systems." Paper presented at the "Democracy, Human Rights, and Peace in Colombia" conference at the Kellogg Institute, University of Notre Dame, March 26–27.
2004. "Criminal Rebels? A Discussion of Civil War and Criminality from the Colombian Experience." *Politics and Society* 32 (2): 257–285.

Heyman, Josiah. 1999. *States and Illegal Practices*. New York: Berg.

Hobsbawm, Eric. 1981. *Bandits*. New York: Pantheon.

Jaramillo, Ana María, Ramiro Ceballos, and Marta Inés Villa. 1998. *En la Encrucijada*. Medellín: Corporación Región.

Kaldor, Mary. 2001. *Las Nuevas Guerras: Violencia Organizada en la Era Global*. Barcelona: Tusquets.

Kalyvas, Stathis. 2001. "'New' and 'Old' Civil Wars: A Valid Distinction?" *World Politics* 54 (1): 99–118.

Keen, David. 2000. "Incentives and Disincentives for Violence." In *Greed and Grievance: Economic Agendas in Civil Wars*, ed. Mats Berdal and David M. Malone. Boulder, CO: Lynne Rienner.

240   *Francisco Gutiérrez Sanín*

Knight, Alan. 1990. *The Mexican Revolution: Porfirians, Liberals, and Peasants.* Lincoln: University of Nebraska Press.

Luvaas, Jay, ed. and trans. 1999. *Napoleon on the Art of War.* New York: Touchstone.

Machiavelli, Niccolò. [1521] 1991. *Machiavel: L'art de la guerre,* trans. Harvey Mansfield. Paris: Flammarion.

Maslowski, Peter. 1970. "A Study of Morale in Civil War Soldiers." *Military Affairs* 34 (4): 122–126.

Medina Gallego, Carlos. 1990. *Autodefensas, Paramilitares y Narcotráfico: Origen, Desarrollo y Consolidación: El Caso de Puerto Boyacá.* Bogotá: Documentos Periodísticos.

Moore, Barrington. 2000. *Los Orígenes Sociales de la Dictadura y de la Democracia: El Señor y el Campesino en la Formación del Mundo Moderno.* Barcelona: Península.

Olson, Mancur. 1971. *Logic of Collective Action: Public Goods and the Theory of Goods.* Cambridge, MA: Harvard University Press.

———. 1993. "Dictatorship, Democracy, and Development." *American Political Science Review* 87 (3): 567–576.

Peñate, Andrés. 1991. "Arauca: Politics and Oil in a Colombian Province." Master thesis, University of Oxford.

Polanyi, Karl. 1992. *La Gran Transformación.* Mexico: Casa Juan Pablos.

Revista Semana. 1991. "El Enemigo de Escobar." *Revista Semana,* April 16: 14–22.

———. 2002. "No Le Tengo Miedo a Castaño." *Revista Semana,* June 22: 40–41.

Romero, Mauricio. 2002. *Paramilitares y Autodefensas, 1982–2003.* Bogotá: Iepri-Planeta.

Skaperdas, Stergios. 1992. "Cooperation, Conflict, and the Absence of Property Rights." *American Economic Review* 82 (4): 720–739.

Spagat, Michael, Jorge Restrepo, and Juan Vargas. 2003. "The Dynamics of the Colombian Civil Conflict: A New Data Set." http://ideas.repec.org/e/pre46.html.

Tilly, Charles. 1985. "War Making and State Making as Organized Crime." In *Bringing the State Back In,* ed. Peter B. Evans, Dietrich Rueschemeyer, and Theda Skocpol. Cambridge University Press.

Tolstoy, Leo. 2006. *War and Peace.* London: Penguin.

JUDICIAL PROCEEDINGS

JP1. DILIGENCIA DE AMPLIACION DE INDAGATORIA. (SINDICADO EDWIN ANDRES CORTES GARCIA) DELITO SECUESTRO EXTORSIVO RADICACIÓN no. 30.136 – Juzgado de ejecución de penas y medidas de seguridad.

JP2. EXPEDIENTE no. 1374: Folios 39–52 – DELITO: SECUESTRO EXTORSIVO-TRANSCRIPCION MECANOGRAFICA DE LA PRIMERA COMUNICACIÓN QUE HACE UN SUJETO N.N. SECUESTRADOR POR RADIO DE DOS METROS DONDE

DIALOGA CON UN FAMILIAR DEL SEÑOR HENRY ROJAS, EL DIA 100597 A LAS 18:00 HORAS DEL DIA.
JP3. EXPEDIENTE 1770 – JUZGADO DEL CIRCUITO 002 PENAL ESPECIALIZADO DE BUCARAMANGA.
JP4. PROCESO 1589-DELITO: CONCIERTO PARA DELNQUIR-CUADERNO COPIA no. 3.
JP5. PROCESO 1589 (Segunda parte) DELITO: CONCIERTO PARA DELINQUIR CUADERNO COPIA no. 2 SINDICADOS: LUIS ALFREDO RUBIO ROJAS ALONSO DE JESUS BAQUEROA GUDELO (a. VLADIMIR) YAIR GAL KLEIN ARIK PICCIOTO AFER IZHACK SHOSHANNY MERAIOT TZEDAKA ABRAHAMTERRY MELNIK.

10 Articulating the geo-cultural logic of nationalist insurgency

Lars-Erik Cederman

Introduction

As interstate wars become less frequent, academic attention has increasingly shifted to internal conflict. In recent years, an exciting literature on the determinants of civil wars has emerged. Political economists, relying on cross-national statistics and rational-choice modeling, have played a prominent role in this debate. In contrast to most past attempts to account for domestic unrest, they tend to explain outbreaks of civil wars in materialist and logistical, rather than cultural, terms.

There can be no doubt that this kind of analysis has advanced the research frontier considerably. Instead of offering sweeping generalizations based on diffuse and scattered case-study evidence, the political economy literature has brought the phenomenon of civil conflict into sharper focus, thus allowing for a more precise evaluation of competing hypotheses. Still, it would be premature to draw definitive theoretical conclusions from these studies because a considerable gap remains between their macro-level findings and the rationalistic micro-level mechanisms that they posit as explanations.

Questioning these scholars' heavy reliance on materialist factors, this essay proposes alternative causal mechanisms that bring both politics and culture back to the fore. This task calls for deeper and more systemic explanations than those associated with the standard methods and assumptions of microeconomics. Therefore, I rely on computational

Paper prepared for presentation at the Joint Sessions of Workshops, ECPR, Uppsala, April 13–18, 2004, and at the conference on "Order, Conflict, and Violence," Department of Political Science, Yale University, April 30–May 1, 2004. An earlier version of this paper was prepared for presentation at the workshop on "Origins and Patterns of Political Violence I: Violence in Civil Wars," Santa Fe Institute, January 15–19, 2004, and at the Center for the Study of Civil War, PRIO, Oslo, February 12, 2004. I would like to thank the participants of those workshops and Nicholas Sambanis for excellent comments, which have only been partially responded to in this version. Without the computational advice and support of Luc Girardin this paper would not have been possible.

modeling, which is better suited to trace historical path-dependency and to capture intangible entities such as national identities.

Contrary to standard rationalistic assumptions, I show that it is possible to create plausible scenarios in which logistical variables such as state strength and terrain matter, although their effects are primarily mediated through geo-cultural mechanisms. The main goal is to create an artificial world within which peripheral insurgents manage to form coalitions, the effectiveness of which depends on the inclusiveness of their shared national identity. Before creating such interactions in greater detail, however, it is necessary to "grow" a comprehensive, geo-cultural system, which includes geography, political organizations, cultural "raw material," and national identities.

Based on a simple geo-cultural logic, the model generates results that are very similar to those found in Fearon and Laitin's (2003) theory of insurgency, in terms of both state strength and rugged terrain. Unlike the expectations of these authors, however, the model's insurrectional mechanisms hinge directly on national identities, and thus indirectly on the ethnic preconditions of the state in question. To confirm the power of nationalist identity-formation while controlling for materialist factors, I run multivariate regressions on the model's output. This analysis suggests that it is often difficult, if not impossible, to separate political-economy interpretations from constructivist theorizing based solely on quantitative macro-level analysis. Clearly, further empirical investigations will be necessary to resolve this debate.

In the following sections, I review the relevant literature and introduce the four main phases of the computational model. I then present the main computational findings, which are followed by a section that reviews the sensitivity analysis results. A concluding section elaborates the theoretical and empirical consequences of the present study.

The contemporary literature on civil wars

There can be no doubt about the policy relevance of civil wars. Whereas interstate warfare has declined in recent years, intrastate conflict shows few signs of abating (e.g. Gleditsch et al. 2002). It is therefore not surprising that scholars, in both comparative politics and international relations, have joined forces to account for why civil wars break out and why they persist (Lake 2003). Much of this research draws on large-N data from sources such as Gurr's *Minorities at Risk* project (Gurr 1993) and improved, more fine-tuned measurements of internal conflict (Gleditsch et al. 2002).

Marrying such quantitative tools with rational-choice modeling, political economists have been leading efforts to advance candidate explanations along rationalistic lines. These studies tend to ascribe more explanatory power to materialist incentives than to ethnic divisions of the state in question (for a trenchant review, see Sambanis 2004). While several studies have proposed variations on this theme (see e.g. Collier and Hoeffler 2004), a recent article by Fearon and Laitin (2003) stands out as particularly well researched and provocative.

Contending that state strength and the logistical conditions of rebels are the main determinants of the probability of civil war, Fearon and Laitin (2003, 75) define insurgency as "a technology of military conflict characterized by small, lightly armed bands practicing guerilla warfare from rural base areas." Based on this definition, they "hypothesize that financially, organizationally, and politically weak central governments render insurgency more feasible and attractive due to weak local policing or inept and corrupt insurgency practices" (75–76). Furthermore, this logic implies that insurgency should be easier to carry out in rough and mountainous terrain (see also Collier and Hoeffler 2004). More controversially, the authors find that the ethnic composition of the state in question has no impact on the likelihood of conflict.

Fearon and Laitin's article has already attracted considerable attention. As the methodological state of the art, it serves as a useful reference point for critiques and reanalyses. Relying on Bayesian analysis to correct for measurement error, Quinn *et al.* (2004) confirm Fearon and Laitin's contention that weak states are more prone to internal violence, but they also cast doubt on the alleged irrelevance of ethnic diversity. Sambanis (2004) probes Fearon and Laitin's causal reasoning using an impressive series of case studies instead of statistics, but comes to similar critical conclusions by showing that their postulated mechanisms frequently deviate from the empirical record. Most importantly, the tendency to aggregate all instances of civil war into one category obscures the diversity of causal logics, despite the fact that disaggregation demonstrates that in wars over self-determination, ethnic cohesion among peripheral rebels supports collective mobilization against the central government. It is equally plausible that several mechanisms, rational or not, may coexist in the same civil war (Kalyvas 2003; 2006).

What are we to make of this intriguing, if somewhat contradictory, picture? True to their rationalistic inclinations, political economists have relied on rational-choice models as a way to bridge the micro–macro gap. Although there is obviously no complete consensus among these scholars on the postulated mechanisms, their theoretical reconstructions are internally consistent and frequently even elegant. Nevertheless, because of the looseness of the macro-level indicators and proxies used, and without extensive micro-level validation, it would be unwise to place too much confidence in such conjectures. In his review of the literature, Sambanis (2004, 259) summarizes the situation cogently:

The already significant gap between micro-level behavior and their macro-level explanation is magnified when ... micro–macro relationships are studied solely through cross-national statistical analyses. Such studies often overlook information about causal pathways that link individual or group behavior with the outbreak of civil war.

After all, the observed macro-level patterns could have been produced by radically different causal mechanisms, including the cultural ones that Fearon and Laitin downplay. Therefore, it would seem reasonable to heed Sambanis' (2004, 263) call urging researchers to "consider a wider array of micro- and macro-level theories, including ones that explain how emotions, ideology, revenge, or coercion can interact to produce collective action that culminates in a civil war."

Nevertheless, it remains unclear where to turn for alternative theories to fill the conceptual void left by the political economists. Constructivist theory has not managed to live up to the same high standards of internal consistency and systematic validation as have their rationalistic counterparts (Fearon and Laitin 2000). In their preoccupation with mental events rather than with macro-level processes, constructivists have had at least as much trouble advancing complex relational theories as their rationalist colleagues (McAdam *et al.* 2001; Tilly 2003; Cederman 2002b).

My contention is that historical sociology goes a long way toward providing the missing conceptual pieces in the explanatory jigsaw. There are striking parallels between the cases at hand and Rokkan's (1999) classical theory of European state formation and nation building. At the heart of his model is a center–periphery relationship not unlike the one proposed by Fearon and Laitin (2003). Rokkan (1999) insists that "any analysis of variations among political systems must start from notions of territory" and proceeds by specifying his three main building blocks as centers, peripheries, and transactions, with transactions linking the centers to the peripheries. Because transactions have to respect logistical constraints, it is necessary to study the physical, technological, military, economic, and cultural conditions of communication. Even based on this brief enumeration, it is clear that Rokkan's framework manages to avoid the political economists' materialist reductionism. He accomplishes this in part by applying a notion of "peripherality" that means much more than a physical struggle for power. In his more nuanced picture, peripheries are characterized by distance, difference, and dependence:

A periphery is located at some distance from the dominant centre or centres, and its transactions with the latter are fraught with costs. A periphery is also different from the central areas on one or more scores: while the degree of distinctiveness will vary, being to some extent a function of distances and dependence, there will invariably be some minimum level and sense of separate identity. Finally, a periphery is dependent upon one or more centres ... in political decision-making, in cultural standardization, and in economic life. (115)

To say that nation building is important does not mean that one has proposed a full-fledged theory. The strength of Rokkan's approach to system building lies at the macro- rather than at the micro-level. Moreover, his research did not focus on violent conflict as much as on cleavage structures and party politics. In recent years, however, considerable conceptual progress has been made in the study of "contentious politics," both as regards an ontological shift toward relational theorizing and in terms of an increased epistemological emphasis on causal mechanisms as the key to explanation (McAdam *et al.* 2001; Tilly 2003). It is in the spirit of that promising research program that I embark on the task of articulating the geo-political logic of nationalist insurgency.

A computational model of nationalist insurgency

Agent-based modeling has emerged as an increasingly popular complement to conventional, rational-choice methods. By representing distinct actors in their social and often even in their spatial context, this computational technique enables the analyst to represent complex macro-level processes without losing sight of relevant micro-level mechanisms. Moreover, intangible concepts such as culture and social identities that do not easily fit into a rationalistic framework can be readily formalized and integrated into agent-based models (Cederman 1997, chapter 3). As Ian Lustick (2000) puts it:

Difficulties of amassing and manipulating collective identity data into theoretically potent comparisons are among the reasons that agent-based modeling can play an important role in the elaboration, refinement, and testing of the kind of specific and logically connected theoretical claims that constructivists have been faulted for not producing. Because the models are run on computers there is no room for ambiguity in the specification of the model's underlying rules.

This statement describes precisely what this essay aims to achieve, although it is important not to interpret the reference to testing too literally. While it is easy to generate unlimited amounts of "data" with a simulation model, such information should not be confused with real-world evidence. Thus, computational modeling cannot serve as a full-fledged substitute for empirical research. Rather, agent-based models constitute artificial, and indeed simplified, worlds in which the plausibility and consistency of specific causal mechanisms can be evaluated in a more complex context than is possible with standard, rationalistic modeling tools, but they still remain much simpler than the real world. By serving as a stepping stone between micro and macro analysis, such models can help untangle interacting mechanisms that together produce the phenomenon to be explained. This perspective employs a generative research strategy that starts from such patterns and moves backwards in time to the candidate mechanisms that might have generated them (Cederman 2005).

In our case, the main configuration to be reproduced is constituted by the statistical finding that rebellions are most frequent in weak and mountainous states. What would it take to construct a set of plausible, predominantly identity-based mechanisms that can generate such findings without resorting to purely materialist explanations? As indicated in the previous section, any reconstruction of this kind must specify a process of identity-formation that creates the type of center–periphery relationships within which civil wars are likely to occur.

Such configurations feature the following building blocks:

- *Political organizations.* The main protagonists are sovereign states whose centers dominate their peripheries.
- *Terrain.* Interaction proceeds in a realistic space with obstacles, such as mountains and other types of rough terrain.
- *Cultural makeup.* Identity-formation presupposes a multidimensional substrate of cultural traits.
- *National identities.* Nationalist behavior requires identities, which are constituted as combinations of cultural traits.

Needless to say, a model comprising all these components would be very complex. In fact, no existing model combines all these properties in the same framework. Most computational models of cultural politics make no distinction between culture and identity, thus violating a fundamental tenet of constructivist theory. Typically, culture is modeled as fixed and immutable properties that influence behavior (Epstein 2002) or as endogenous vectors whose traits all matter (Axelrod 1997, chapter 7). Identities, however, are more selective, because only politically relevant aspects of culture enter into the power calculus. Allowing for such variation, Lustick's (2000; 2002) agent-based models ABIR and PS-I feature endogenous repertoires composed of sets of identities, but the component identities stand in no specific relationship to each other and thus do not describe a coherent cultural space. Moreover, these and almost all other models of this type fail to provide an explicit representation for formal political organizations or terrain.

Inspired by Bremer and Mihalka's (1977) pioneering computational application to International Relations, I have developed a modeling architecture that is better suited to the research problem studied in this essay (Cederman 1997).[1] Embedded in a dynamic state system populated by formal political organizations, it contains a constructivist logic that represents culture as a tunable attribute space, with identity mappings as schemata based on this substrate (Cederman 1997, chapter 8; 2002a). Once the national identities of the centers and peripheries have been generated, these can be brought to bear on behavior, which allows the model to avoid cultural determinism. What is still missing, however, is a representation of rugged terrain. The current model thus needs to incorporate a topological map beneath its cultural and political representations.

The ruggedness of the artificial landscape is revealed by the three-dimensional snapshot in Figure 10.1. Here state borders appear as lines and the state capitals as half spheres. Both capitals and provinces are marked by colored disks if they possess a national identity. Rebellions are shown as vertical "needles." Interestingly, the projections suggest that most of the fighting takes place in mountainous areas.

While Figure 10.1 helps the reader develop intuition about the model's static structure, it says little about its dynamic properties. As a way to model the prehistory leading up to nationalism, I propose a telescoped, multiphase process that combines various dynamics at different time scales. Complex systems are known to contain processes that operate on vastly different timetables (Simon 1981; Braudel 1980). Although they sometimes last for a long time, civil wars typically outpace nation building. National identities, in turn, usually emerge much faster than the cultural systems within which they are situated.

In order to keep endogeneity within manageable proportions, the multiphased process creates a system that starts with the slowest-moving processes before shifting the focus to faster dynamics. As the faster-moving phases are added, the configurations resulting from the previous phases are held constant. This facilitates the design and calibration of

---

[1] Whereas my first models were based on Pascal, in more recent years, I have relied exclusively on Repast, the leading Java-based package for agent-based modeling (see http://repast.sourceforge.net/). This is the first of my models that has been implemented in a distributed environment developed by Luc Girardin.

t = 1252

Figure 10.1. A 3D-projection of the state system showing rebelling provinces as needles

the framework as well as the tracing of causal pathways that unfold during each stage.

More precisely, the current model features four phases, each corresponding to a distinct set of historical processes.[2] Figure 10.2 provides an overview of how the model's ontological layers are interconnected in each phase, with causal links represented as arrows. Whereas Phase I merely sets up the model structure, the remaining phases simulate historical dynamics. Given the underlying geography, Phase II modifies the state system through state formation and the cultural map through assimilation. During Phase III identity-formation sets in, which introduces a top layer of national identities as cultural coalitions. Nationally determined and other insurgent behaviors are not allowed to occur until Phase IV. It is during this phase that statistical data are collected. In the following, I will describe each phase in greater detail.

Phase I: initialization

The first stage initializes the model by generating three basic ontological building blocks, namely a state system, terrain, and a cultural landscape, all embedded within a square grid. These basic entities are parametric

[2] A detailed specification of the model can be found at www.icr.ethz.ch.

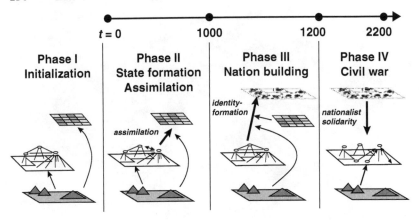

Figure 10.2. The four phases of the model

and result from algorithms that make no claims about achieving realism in terms of the dynamics of the system. Still, the model's parametric nature allows the experimenter to retain full control over the configuration of each component.

First, the initialization routine generates a geographic map that allocates a level of ruggedness to each cell in the grid from zero to max-Rugged = 5. Initially, a tunable number of mountain peaks are distributed randomly across the grid. Then a diffusion process connects these peaks with their surrounding environment, thus creating relatively smooth mountainous terrain that slopes gently down to the plains. Later, these ruggedness levels will be used as weights to slow down interactions between the center and the periphery.

Next, a state system equipped with a tunable number of states (here thirty) is created. Again, the algorithm starts by randomly selecting the same number of sites, from which a recursive process absorbs the surrounding provinces. This accelerated process of geopolitical consolidation is slowed down in mountainous areas, which means that the state borders will respect geographical obstacles at least to some extent. Note that this process is a simplified and drastically compressed version of the more realistic series of conquest in the second phase of the model.

Finally, the initialization phase produces a cultural map that is a multidimensional array that allocates a symbol string to each site of the grid. The algorithm orchestrates a simulated "age of migrations" as occurred in early medieval Europe. As with the previous types of maps, this one starts with a selection of random locations, this time

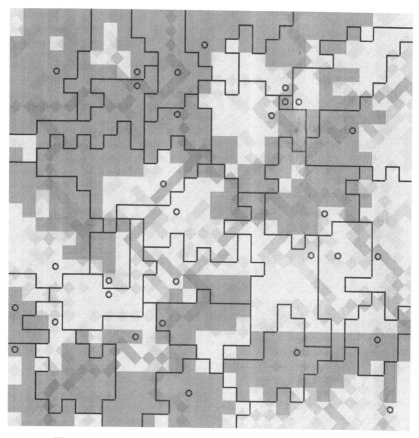

Figure 10.3. The initial state of the system at $t = 0$

corresponding to the homeland of each ethnic community. Each of these ethnic communities is allocated an entirely stochastic symbol string, such as {2 3 1 4 4 2 2 2} with eight traits and four possible values. Two parameters drive this process: the number of ethnic groups numEthnies = 5 that participated in the cultural settling of the landscape and the parameter culturalDrift = 0.1, which defines the cultural differences within each tribe's territory. Cultural drift describes a process of spontaneous change, such as linguistic shifts and religious fragmentation (Axelrod 1997, 170). This entire algorithm, which is also affected by geographic obstacles, guarantees that there will be both dialectal nuances from province to province as well as more abrupt ethnic cleavages that represent linguistic, or even civilizational, frontiers (Rokkan 1999, 172).

Figure 10.3 shows the standard 30×30 grid at time $t = 0$. Each cell possesses a specific level of ruggedness, shown here in dark gray, semi-translucent shading that suppresses minor differences in altitude, which can be seen more clearly in the three-dimensional projection of Figure 10.1. It is obvious that a large part of the grid is mountainous. On top of this geographic map, thirty sovereign states reside, with the black lines corresponding to their borders and the circles to their capitals. In addition, the diagonal gray shadings portray the cultural differences among the local sites. While the darker shades correspond to areas characterized by great cultural differences, the lighter ones refer to "plains" in the cultural landscape.

Phase II: state formation and assimilation

The next phase operates as a geo-cultural "pressure cooker," though at a much slower rate than the first phase. First, because the initial stage does not guarantee that the states are even remotely geopolitically viable, it is important to expose them to some internal and external competition. Once unleashed, the sovereign states will start interacting locally with their immediate neighbors and with their own provinces. This means that both interstate wars and secession can take place, although the latter is less likely because would-be rebels cannot resort to nationalist coordination as in Phase IV.

Interaction can be of two types: either the actors exist peacefully side by side or they engage in combat. Conflict is initiated according to a simple decision rule, which depends on the local balance of power between two parties (see also Cederman 2003). Roughly speaking, the actors play a "grim trigger" strategy with another. This means that they normally reciprocate whatever their neighbors did to them on their respective fronts. But whenever the balance of power in their favor exceeds a preset, stochastic threshold that governs the offense dominance of the system, they launch unprovoked attacks.

Because interactions among states unfold as conventional battles with clearly marked defense lines, the midpoint of the attacker's stochastic threshold is located at 2.5, which requires an actor to be more than twice as powerful as its victim before an unprovoked attack can be launched. This gives the defender a considerable advantage. In internal conflicts, however, the threshold is set to one, because in insurrectional fighting, it is less likely that fixed defense lines will require the aggressor to be decisively superior. In these cases, only the provinces engage in unprovoked attacks, and then always with the aim of breaking out of the state. In view of the dominated peripheries' revisionist interests as opposed to the centers' status-quo orientation, this is a reasonable first approximation. Still, the capitals always fight back when an insurrection erupts.[3]

Identical stochastic criteria govern the outcome of these battles. In interstate wars, a victorious attacker is allowed to absorb the province fought over. If the defending state wins, however, the status quo results. Civil wars always end in secession if the breakaway province prevails; otherwise, there is no change to the geopolitical map.

The system is animated by a primitive resource "metabolism" based directly on territorial size with some stochastic noise added to the extraction process. Crucially, the centers' resource extraction declines as a function of effective distance, discounting for terrain obstacles. Even in the plains, transportation incurs a cost-per-distance unit. In the mountains, however, moving through each site adds a logistical penalty proportional to the roughness of the area. It is convenient to model the logistical constraints with a loss-of-strength gradient (Boulding 1963; Gilpin 1981).[4]

In addition to wars and secessions, this phase also features cultural assimilation by the capitals of the provinces. Although the political and cultural maps produced during Phase I are both influenced by geographical conditions, they are not directly connected. Yet throughout history, states have had various degrees of influence over the cultural makeup of their populations. The assimilation process introduced during this phase proceeds by allowing each capital to assimilate one cultural trait of a province with a constant probability per "visit." In our test run, we will set the assimilation rate assimil at only 0.01, meaning that 1,000 time periods do not suffice to iron out all differences.

Phase III: nation building

Once having created a plausible geo-cultural environment, we are ready to introduce national mobilization. Rather than treating nationalism as a constant "law," I model the phenomenon as a macro-historical process that emerges exogenously in the entire system at a specific point in history. This point occurs at time step 1000 and the process of nation building continues for another 200 time steps.

---

[3] This may be a problematic assumption, because in the real world, many centers choose to make concessions to their peripheral areas, including granting them autonomy arrangements and sometimes even full independence.

[4] The logistical curve slopes gently from 100% extraction at zero distance from the capital down to 30% at large distances. This function also governs power projection of all actors.

In keeping with the multiphase research design, I freeze all previous social configurations, including the state system and the culture map, assuming that they represent slow-moving changes that can be treated exogenously. This means that no interstate warfare or secession can take place during this stage. These simplifications are strictly motivated by the research design rather than by the framework's inherent possibilities.[5] Furthermore, assimilation ceases to operate as well. This allows us to focus entirely on national identity-formation in a stable geo-cultural framework.

In designing the nationalism part of the model, I have striven to stay as close as possible to modern, constructivist theories of nationalism (Cederman 2002b). Most importantly, this modeling extension introduces a fundamental distinction between the underlying cultural landscape and national identities as political coalitions. Although the attribute space has an impact on identity-formation, there is no one-to-one correspondence between culture and national identities, because only politically relevant traits count in national identity-formation (Gellner 1983).

Fortunately, there is a computational solution to this conceptual problem. Letting sets of symbol strings be used in "schemata," John Holland (1995) introduces wildcards (#) for those traits that could be of any value (Cederman 1997, chapter 8; 2002a). For example, the string {4 # # 2 3 # # #} represents an identity template. It is convenient to represent national identities in a similar way. Let us assume that national communities form in the public domain and that states can become members of them as long as their culture strings match them. These constraints generate a hypothetical set of identities to which a given actor could belong.

National identities are represented as distinct groups to which any state or province can belong if the nation's identity matches the actor's own culture. While both capitals and provinces are eligible members of nations, the probability of launching a nationalist movement depends crucially on the geopolitical status of the actor in question. Thanks to their cultural and material resources, capitals have a much higher chance of founding their own nations, but provinces may sometimes create distinct nationalist platforms in opposition to their respective capitals. Indeed, Rokkan (1999, 173) states that "there is an enormous number of distinguishable languages in the world, but only a few of these rate a realistic chance to be transformed into standards of written communication. Such a standard cannot be developed without a center or network, or a

---

[5] In reality, these geopolitical processes are heavily influenced by the onset of nationalism (Cederman 2002a; 2005).

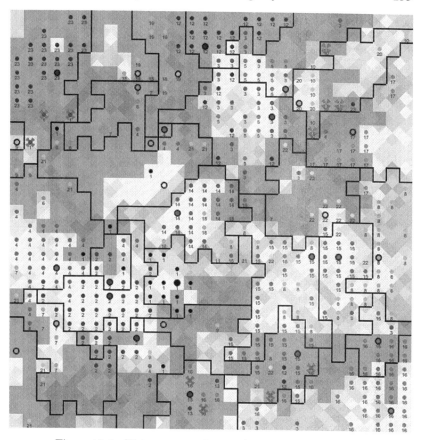

Figure 10.4. The system at time period $t = 1252$

network of centers ... Territorial consolidation increased the opportunities for elite encounters over long distances."

The likelihood of joining an existing nation, however, is quite high,
which reflects the lesser difficulty of identity selection. In addition, all
mobilized actors, whether provinces or capitals, attempt to recruit new
members to their identities by visiting neighboring sites, discounted by
the terrain roughness. Once mobilized, it is assumed that an actor never
loses its national identity.

Figure 10.4 displays the national identities as small disks, comple-
mented with a number beneath each disk corresponding to the respective
nation's index number. It is clear that most capitals have already become
nationally mobilized. In several cases, national communities spill over

state borders. For example, three capitals share the same nation in the southeastern part of the grid (see nation no. 15).

Nearly perfect nation-states appear in the plains. The mountainous regions, in contrast, offer less hospitable conditions to nation builders. As we will see in the next phase, such differences influence the likelihood of civil wars (which are indicated with crosses in Figure 10.4).

Phase IV: civil war

Focusing on internal conflict, the final phase of the model pits provinces against capitals while freezing everything else, including the national identity-formation process of the previous phase. This means that national-identity configurations and the states' outer borders have to remain intact. Culture no longer has any direct impact on the behavior of the model. Having ruled out interstate wars and secession, only rebellions are allowed to occur. Whether the capital or the province prevails, the status quo results, and the rebels are allowed to regroup.

It may seem that this exogenization unduly restricts the analysis, but it makes considerable sense for the period following 1945. With the very important exceptions of imperial collapse associated with decolonization and the disintegration processes that followed the end of the Cold War, secession has been a relatively rare event in post-colonial politics (see e.g. Hechter 1992), especially in post-colonial Africa (Herbst 1989). Likewise, as has already been mentioned, there have been relatively few interstate wars as well. However, the exclusion of these geopolitical transformations should be viewed as a simplifying, analytical assumption rather than as a statement about how the world really is. Moreover, as a first approximation, the model seeks to explain violence leading to secession without attempting to trace the entire process. Of course, endogenous analysis will be necessary in order to reach firmer conclusions about the causal mechanisms behind secessionist violence (cf. Cederman 2005).

This phase retains the mechanism that governs secession attempts in Phase II, though without the geopolitical consequences. While obviously fought interactively between the centers and the peripheries, such conflicts can only be initiated by the provinces in this version of the model. Still, it is assumed that the capitals fight back if attacked. The previous domestic decision-making threshold at one (rather than 2.5) applies to this phase as well. The main difference pertains to the resource calculation of the mobilized provinces. Once it belongs to a nation, a province will attempt to recruit nationalist support from other co-national provinces within the same state. The potential rebel organizes such recruitment campaigns before deciding whether or not to attack the capital. Controlling for how many of these potential recruits can be persuaded to help their co-nationals, the parameter natOblig (with default value 0.5) will determine the stochastic proportion of success.[6] If the total resources of this coalition are large, the province in question will be more likely to trigger a civil war, because nationalist solidarity can shift the balance more decisively in favor of the periphery. Under these circumstances, it is harder for the capital to "divide and rule" within its territory.

If the leading province decides to act, all co-national units that pledge support will make good on their promise.[7] Fighting on multiple fronts will force the capital to redistribute its resources, which in many cases will open the opportunity that other provinces will join the fray, even if they do not belong to the same nation. In some cases, unmobilized actors, who could be bandits or other opportunistic rebels, may decide that the power balance has shifted so much in the rebels' favor that they will also decide to fight the capital.

Combat then proceeds according to the same rules as in Phase II. Depending on the local balance of power for each center–periphery dyad, either the capital or the province prevails. Who wins and how long the fighting lasts are immaterial for the purposes of this essay, because, as already noted, all geopolitical consequences have been inhibited for methodological reasons. What matters here is whether there is fighting at all or not.

Figure 10.4, which marks local battles with crosses, illustrates four civil wars that were ongoing in 1252. The state with a nation no. 23 capital in the northwestern corner of the grid is under attack by three nations no. 1. In the northeastern part of the grid, the state with nation no. 20 as its official identity is fighting a rebellion by four nation no. 10 communities. In addition, two states in the southern part of the grid are also facing challenges from nation no. 16 to their sovereignty.

This particular snapshot suggests that fighting happens predominantly in rugged terrain. Does this pattern hold over time? To find out, we have to study the behavior of the model more systematically. Fortunately, agent-based modeling allows us to rerun history counterfactually as often as we want, and it is to this task that we turn in the next section.

---

[6] In the current configuration, these mobilization attempts are based on a fixed identity. In reality, however, identities often adapt to the center–periphery power balance, with thinner identities becoming selected or chosen should the rebels encounter stiff resistance from the center (see Hannan 1979; Cederman 1997, chapter 8).

[7] This is obviously a questionable assumption that needs to be endogenized in future versions of the model (see Gates 2002).

Replication results

Telescoped histories constitute artificial worlds that can be subjected to controlled experiments. This section applies a combination of experimental and quasi-experimental methods to the system. Relying on the former, the sensitivity analysis in the next section varies several key parameters experimentally. In the current section, which presents results that mimic conventional, quasi-experimental methodology, cross-sectional data are collected and analyzed. I then regress simulated conflict outcomes on the state-level determinants to find out how well each candidate explanation fares. This approach allows us to assess what quantitative analysis would have told us had the model coincided with the real world. Note that the task of measurement is considerably easier in an artificial world, because there is no room for measurement error. Moreover, thanks to the telescoped design, endogeneity becomes more manageable as well.

The research design is simple. For each parameter configuration, thirty runs featuring entire state systems are executed. The replications are based on randomly generated geographical maps with their associated state systems as indicated in Figure 10.2. For each such configuration, the model is run with randomly generated cultural maps. Measurement takes place during Phase IV, which lasts from time step 1200 through step 2200. The number of observations is almost 900, because there are up to thirty states in each of the thirty runs (excluding micro states that are smaller than five units).[8] Regressions are run on all of these observations in a pooled sample. Data on the following variables are collected for each (sufficiently large) state in each run:

- The dichotomous dependent variable *civilwar* is set to one if at least one center–periphery battle occurred within the territory of the state in question throughout the entire Phase IV, otherwise the variable is set to zero. Although this is a crude measure of conflict, the absence of time series means that temporal interdependence can be ignored in the regression analysis.
- The first independent variable *strength* indicates the resource level of each state.
- The second independent variable *ruggedness* measures the average ruggedness level based on the state's entire territory, including the capital and all provinces.

---

[8] This size-related truncation of the sample was introduced to prevent very small states from distorting the effect of the size variable. Otherwise, the findings are reasonably robust to changes in this arbitrary limit.

- The third independent variable *natfrac* refers to a nationalist fractionalization index, computed according to the standard definition $1 - \Sigma p_i^2$ where p_i stands for the proportion of each nationalist group (cf. Fearon 2003 for a discussion of various fractionalization measures).
- The fourth independent variable *natdist* reveals the average terrain-adjusted distance from the capital of all the oppositional nationalist provinces; if there are no oppositional nationalist provinces, the variable is set to zero.

Whereas the first two independent variables focus on materialist properties of states, the last two capture cultural determinants related to national identities. It is therefore possible to separate purely materialist hypotheses from those that also involve an identity-based logic.

Let us start by considering what one would expect from a rationalistic perspective. The hypothesis would be that the first three materialist variables should be significant compared with the nationalist indicators. Indeed, Fearon and Laitin (2003) find that state weakness (operationalized in terms of GDP per capita) and rough terrain are strong predictors of internal conflict.

On the other hand, a relationist interpretation inspired by Rokkan would lead us to anticipate that the last two variables will have a strong impact *independently of the power of the materialist ones*. First of all, the more nationally fractionalized the state, the more opportunities to rebel.[9] This hypothesis goes beyond ethnic fractionalization, which is what Fearon and Laitin (2003) measure. Indeed, nationalism presupposes that nationalist groups exhibit a tendency to form a state rather than to express mere cultural belonging (Weber 1978; Gellner 1983). It is therefore questionable whether Fearon and Laitin really "test" theories of nationalism in their article (Cederman and Girardin 2007). Second, as suggested by Weiner's (1978) "sons of the soil" mechanism, it is not merely the average ruggedness that matters, *but more specifically whether peripheral nationalists can take advantage of rough terrain in their struggle against the center*. Thus, the strategic location of the groups is central in this mechanism.

---

[9] Note, however, that a very high degree of fractionalization may make the task of rebelling harder (see Cederman 1997, chapter 8). I rely on a fractionalization index because it is a standard indicator in the literature, not because I think it is a suitable way to measure the opportunities of collective action in insurgencies. For example, it is clearly problematic that the standard indices are symmetric in that they ignore the distinction between state-controlling groups and the peripheral ones (Cederman and Girardin 2007).

Table 10.1. *Logit regression of simulated data in the default system*

Variable	Model 1.1			Model 1.2		
	coeff.	std.err.	prob.	coeff.	std.err.	prob.
Constant	− 1.114	0.395	0.005	− 3.306	0.533	0.000
State strength	− 0.008	0.001	0.000	− 0.015	0.002	0.000
Ruggedness	0.604	0.112	0.000	0.311	0.151	0.039
Natfrac				6.645	0.639	0.000
Natdist				0.053	0.013	0.000
Log-likelihood	− 424.15			− 302.36		
Sample size	820			820		

To investigate the influence of these factors, I ran multivariate logit regressions with and without the nationalist variables. The column labeled Model 1.1 in Table 10.1 presents the results from a regression that includes only the logistical variables *strength* and *ruggedness*. The Table reveals that both variables are highly significant, with signs in the expected directions. Whereas state *strength* significantly reduces the likelihood of insurgency, the *ruggedness* variable works in the opposite direction: the rougher the terrain, the more likely civil unrest becomes. Based solely on these data, political economists could be forgiven for believing that their theories suffice to account for the behavior of this model.

However, this picture changes drastically when nationalist mobilization is controlled for. Model 1.2 makes clear that the constructivist variables *natfrac* and *natdist* account for much of the variation in conflict behavior. As one might expect, fractionalized states with high *natfrac* scores are especially conflict-prone. On average, peripheral groups that benefit from rough terrain find more opportunities to rebel. Moreover, the nationalists' terrain-adjusted distance from the capital plays a major role, regardless of the state's ruggedness. It seems that the logistical obstacles confronting the center in its exchanges with the periphery have a direct impact on the probability of civil war. Finally, Model 1.2 suggests that the materialist variables remain pertinent, though the significance of the ruggedness variable declines somewhat.

Sensitivity analysis

In view of these findings, it is clear that statistical accounts of the system that incorporate appropriate identity-related variables perform better

Table 10.2. *Logit regression of simulated data for different levels of rugged terrain*

Variable	Model 2.1 (maxRugged = 1)			Model 2.2 (maxRugged = 9)		
	coeff.	std.err.	prob.	coeff.	std.err.	prob.
Constant	−7.090	1.024	0.000	−4.490	0.644	0.000
State strength	−0.008	0.003	0.008	−0.009	0.002	0.000
Ruggedness	1.189	1.039	0.252	0.372	0.267	0.163
Natfrac	6.954	1.136	0.000	5.925	0.642	0.000
Natdist	0.247	0.047	0.000	0.103	0.020	0.000
Log-likelihood	−136.21			−276.02		
Sample size	865			833		

than rely exclusively on materialist ones. But is this general finding robust? To find out, this section presents a preliminary sensitivity analysis. While retaining the default settings of the previous section, I vary one parameter at a time.[10]

Given the telescoped nature of the model, it is important to alter variables belonging to all four phases. This procedure will enhance our confidence in the robustness of the findings across radically different time scales. Let us now consider each of the phases in turn, starting with the most fundamental one.

Variations in Phase I

Empirical scholars can only dream of manipulating environmental background factors, such as terrain. In an artificial world, by contrast, it is just as easy to alter the altitude and shape of mountain chains as it is to change one individual's behavior. Thus, the first series of sensitivity tests entails "lowering" and "elevating" the mountains by running simulations where the maximum ruggedness is one and nine respectively, rather than five as in the default system (see Models 2.1 and 2.2 in Table 10.2).

It is obvious that the two cultural variables remain robust, whereas *strength* is the only materialist variable that remains constant across the test values. Unsurprisingly, reducing the geographic obstacles renders the *ruggedness* variable less significant. For extremely high levels of this

[10] Obviously, a more thorough sensitivity test would have to include combinations of parameter values.

Table 10.3. *Logit regression of simulated data for different numbers of ethnic groups*

Variable	Model 3.1 (numEthnies = 5)			Model 3.2 (numEthnies = 15)		
	coeff.	std.err.	prob.	coeff.	std.err.	prob.
Constant	−3.661	0.536	0.000	−2.611	0.543	0.000
State strength	−0.012	0.002	0.000	−0.013	0.002	0.000
Ruggedness	0.513	0.150	0.001	0.193	0.147	0.188
Natfrac	7.229	0.612	0.000	5.464	0.559	0.000
Natdist	0.015	0.012	0.219	0.031	0.012	0.010
Log-likelihood	−323.93			−312.42		
Sample size	820			820		

variable, the significance also fades. In this case, conflict becomes widespread in the system, because even minor differences in altitude tip the balance in favor of the provinces.

Having studied the effect of changes in terrain, it is now time to introduce variation in the structure of the initial cultural makeup. This is done along two dimensions. First, the number of ethnic communities populating the initial grid is varied (five or fifteen than the default value ten). Second, the rate of cultural drift is varied, which conditions gradual, village-to-village cleavages (here the alternative levels are 0.05 and 0.2 as opposed to the default system's 0.1).

As with the terrain parameter, we find that the more "rugged" the initial cultural landscape, the less internal conflict there is. This effect applies to both ethnic polarity and cultural drift. Thus, there is a strong parallel between cultural and geographic obstacles. Despite these changes, Tables 10.3 and 10.4 suggest that this parameter manipulation makes a rather limited difference in terms of the regression results, although the impact of the *natdist* variable becomes insignificant for small numbers of initial ethnic cores (see Model 4.1). The latter phenomenon can be attributed to the lack of deep identity cleavages dividing multiethnic states. Of the materialist indicators, only state strength exhibits a consistent effect. The ruggedness variable appears to be less robust, typically losing its effect where *natdist* becomes stronger and vice versa.

Variations in Phase II

Having found that the main results are quite robust to limited alterations of Phase I, we now proceed to Phase II, where assimil, the rate of

Table 10.4. *Logit regression of simulated data for different levels of cultural drift*

Variable	Model 4.1 (culturalDrift = 0.05)			Model 4.2 (culturalDrift = 0.2)		
	coeff.	std.err.	prob.	coeff.	std.err.	prob.
Constant	−2.899	0.473	0.000	−2.048	0.586	0.000
State strength	−0.011	0.002	0.000	−0.023	0.003	0.000
Ruggedness	0.249	0.135	0.065	0.276	0.155	0.076
Natfrac	6.228	0.547	0.000	4.390	0.608	0.000
Natdist	0.054	0.012	0.000	0.047	0.013	0.000
Log-likelihood	−348.26			−260.98		
Sample size	820			820		

Table 10.5. *Logit regression of simulated data for different levels of assimilation*

Variable	Model 5.1 (assimil = 0.0)			Model 5.2 (assimil = 1.0)		
	coeff.	std.err.	prob.	coeff.	std.err.	prob.
Constant	−2.532	0.424	0.000	−4.600	1.645	0.005
State strength	−0.009	0.001	0.000	−0.021	0.007	0.002
Ruggedness	0.395	0.121	0.001	0.285	0.417	0.493
Natfrac	4.150	0.456	0.000	16.668	2.599	0.000
Natdist	0.054	0.011	0.000	0.079	0.023	0.000
Log-likelihood	−424.65			−43.22		
Sample size	820			820		

state-led cultural assimilation, plays the main role. What happens if we tune this parameter down to zero from the default value of 0.01? And what are the consequences of increasing this parameter to 1.0? Table 10.5 has the answers to these questions.

This time the behavioral output changes more as a result of these manipulations. Given that the default value is quite low, removing assimilation matters less than accelerating the process to its maximum speed. It should be recalled that the latter configuration produces a cultural "level playing field" within the states, with virtually no deviations from the capitals' culture. Such flat cultural landscapes create almost perfect nation-states, which feature less violent domestic politics. As a result, civil wars become extremely rare, which helps explain the

Table 10.6. *Logit regression of simulated data for different levels of identity exclusiveness*

Variable	Model 6.1 (minNumTraits = 3)			Model 6.2 (minNumTraits = 5)		
	coeff.	std.err.	prob.	coeff.	std.err.	prob.
Constant	−4.586	0.546	0.000	−2.985	0.610	0.000
State strength	−0.010	0.001	0.000	−0.014	0.002	0.000
Ruggedness	0.737	0.153	0.000	0.189	0.168	0.262
Natfrac	7.941	0.630	0.000	6.565	0.662	0.000
Natdist	0.028	0.013	0.029	0.039	0.013	0.002
Log-likelihood	−340.53			−249.70		
Sample size	820			820		

lower significance of the estimates in this case.[11] Despite this fact, the cultural variables remain quite robust. Again, the *ruggedness* variable becomes insignificant at the expense of *natdist*. The state strength variable, on the other hand, retains its significance for the alternative assimilation rates.

Variations in Phase III

The next step of our sensitivity analysis concerns the nation-building phase. I have chosen to control the minNumTraits parameter, which determines the national identities' minimal "thickness." This variable stipulates how many active symbols (rather than wildcards) a national identity needs to hold. The lower the number, the more inclusive the identity, which should facilitate peripheral nationalist mobilization. This expectation is confirmed by the negative correlation between identity thickness and civil war frequencies (not shown in the Table).

In terms of parameter estimates, these limited deviations from the default value minNumTraits = 4 seem to matter little, as shown by Table 10.6. The cultural variables' impact remains quite solid despite some weakness for *natdist* with three traits (see Model 6.1). A similar reduction of significance, though for thicker identities, can be observed

---

[11] Note, however, that assimilation is assumed to happen *before* nationalist mobilization. Once a unit has been mobilized in the model, it cannot be "converted" to a different nation. Deutsch (1953) and many other theorists have hypothesized that centers that attempt to accelerate the assimilation of already mobilized peripheral populations may provoke more, rather than less, civil unrest (see also Cederman 1997, chapter 7).

Table 10.7. *Logit regression of simulated data for different levels of nationalist solidarity*

Variable	Model 7.1 (natOblig = 0.1)			Model 7.2 (natOblig = 1.0)		
	coeff.	std.err.	prob.	coeff.	std.err.	prob.
Constant	−2.877	0.644	0.000	−3.546	0.488	0.000
State strength	−0.025	0.003	0.000	−0.010	0.002	0.000
Ruggedness	0.372	0.174	0.033	0.408	0.140	0.004
Natfrac	5.527	0.714	0.000	6.444	0.573	0.000
Natdist	0.053	0.014	0.000	0.040	0.012	0.001
Log-likelihood	−228.53			−345.85		
Sample size	820			820		

for the materialist variables as well in the case of ruggedness (see Model 6.2).

Variations in Phase IV

We have now reached the last stage, which corresponds to the civil war phase of the research design. At this point, it is appropriate to study the impact of different levels of nationalist solidarity by altering the values of the parameter natOblig both downward to 10% and upward to 100% (see Table 10.7).

The pattern of the previous stages is repeated in this case too. We find that all variables retain their significance, with a slight weakening in the case of ruggedness.

In sum, we have found that the main computational findings reported in Table 10.1 survive a series of robustness tests. Thus, in the absence of a more thorough, combinatorial sensitivity analysis, I conclude that the results are far from "knife-edge." The key materialist and identity-related variables retain their impact across the board, with the occasional exception of ruggedness.

Conclusion

What are the theoretical lessons to be drawn from this essay? Let us start by stressing what it does *not* purport to say. First, it does not claim to have refuted rationalist theories of civil wars. It bears repeating that *the statistical analysis shown above relates to an artificial world, and certainly not to real-world evidence.* In fact, I offer no more micro-level validation than do most political economists, who also usually advance untested (but testable) theoretical interpretations at that level. Nor does this essay argue that the current model offers the best formalization of relational and constructivist theories of national insurgencies. After all, this is the first model of its kind. To my knowledge, geography and identity-formation have never been investigated together in an integrated, dynamic model. Thus, I ask for the reader's patience with the sometimes drastic simplifications introduced.

It is easy to think of important extensions of the model that could bring it closer to the empirical record. One of the most urgent tasks would be to let political and cultural boundaries co-evolve (Cederman 2002b). Fortunately, this can already be done within the current computational framework (Cederman 2002a). Both qualitative and quantitative studies have convincingly shown that ethnic conflict has a tendency to spill over state borders due to irredentism and other diffusion effects (Weiner 1971; Sambanis 2001). Still, sometimes one step backward can enable us to take two steps forward. Despite this obvious loss of realism, the telescoped, phased design of the model introduces a powerful way of handling drastically different time scales without getting swamped by endogeneity.

Another part of the model that calls for elaboration is the behavioral interaction between the center and the periphery. The current specification lets the provinces take the lead, but this obscures an often delicate strategic "dance" going back and forth between the main protagonists, including counterinsurgency initiatives on the part of the capitals. Moreover, the current design stresses opportunity structures rather than actual motivations. Rational-choice theory offers many cues about the micro-foundations of internal conflicts that could be integrated into the current computational framework (see e.g. Gates 2002). Nor is any claim to realism made as regards the clustering of fighting into civil wars, the frequency and duration of which can be validated empirically. More realistic strategies, together with cluster-finding algorithms, could facilitate such measurements, as illustrated by Cederman (2003) in the case of interstate wars.

Having stated what this study does not say, I owe the reader a few final words about what I believe it does contribute to future research. Most importantly, the essay discourages students of civil wars from drawing too far-reaching inferences from political-economy studies such as Fearon and Laitin (2003). While micro-level interpretations of macro-level data are indispensable to most explanations, the current essay illustrates that such mechanisms do not have to be narrowly rationalistic and materialist in the political economists' sense. Moreover, it should be clear that a model with a powerful geo-cultural logic like the one proposed here produces results that at the surface are very hard to distinguish from the expectations of rationalist scholars.

More specifically, two of Fearon and Laitin's (2003) key variables, namely state strength and rough terrain, seem to vindicate their logistical theory of insurrections. If interpreted differently, however, these explanatory factors may turn out to be at least partly driven by mechanisms of nationalist identity-formation. Crucially, the outbreak of violence appears to be linked to the settlement patterns of peripheral nationalist groups. In particular, these groups are predominantly located in rough terrain. Where the center is unable to mobilize more than a limited nationalist following due to logistical constraints, its resistance to insurgencies suffers accordingly. Far from being a matter of ancient, primordialist conditions, nationalist identity-formation only began to evolve over the past couple of centuries, and in many cases, the process began much more recently in conjunction with decolonization.

Rather than imposing a false choice between identity-related and materialist explanations, the computational model offers guidance as to how these mechanisms might be disentangled conceptually. Still, though this is easily done in a computational model, it is much harder to carry out empirically. Fearon and Laitin's (2003) statistical controls for "nationalism theory" fail to grasp the logic of these alternative perspectives, partly because the theories to be refuted are rendered too sweepingly, and partly because the macro-level indicators used are inappropriate (Cederman and Girardin 2007). There is therefore an acute need for better articulated theories of nation building.

The main goal of this essay has been to start closing this gap by proposing candidate mechanisms that can be more readily exposed to empirical testing. Of course, we still have a way to go, both empirically and theoretically, before this can be achieved, but I would argue that the current essay makes some progress in this direction. Fortunately, thanks to the considerable interest that civil wars are attracting, new data are constantly becoming available, especially at the microlevel. Examples include Collier and Sambanis' (2005) systematic series of case studies and Buhaug and Gates' (2002) efforts to use geographic data to pinpoint the exact location of conflict (for a recent review, see Tarrow 2007). It would be very helpful if the conflicting parties could be pinpointed geographically as well, especially in relation to existing communication infrastructures.[12]

---

[12] This is starting to come possible. Cederman et al. (2006) present newly scanned and geocoded data based on the Soviet Atlas Narodov Mira.

Adding a new tool to our toolbox in the study of civil wars, agent-based modeling will help relationist theorists sharpen their hypotheses and test empirical indicators in methodologically underdeveloped areas that have thus far escaped the grasp of conventional approaches. Thanks to their "colonization" of the literature on civil wars, the political economists have raised the explanatory bar considerably. Now the main task is to prevent their methodological advances from leading to premature theoretical closure. After all, much is at stake, and not merely scientifically, but also in terms of policymaking. While factoring in macro-processes may seem defeatist from a policy perspective, it is more likely to lead to more realistic expectations about what is politically desirable and feasible in the short run, and what is not. Failure to see this difference may have serious consequences, as illustrated by the difficulties posed by "nation building" in postwar Iraq. In an era characterized by ambitious democratization projects with uncertain consequences for political mobilization, historical insensitivity and cultural "color-blindness" are likely to worsen the problems of internal violence and terrorism that already haunt the world's most troubled neighborhoods.

REFERENCES

Axelrod, Robert. 1997. *The Complexity of Cooperation: Agent-Based Models of Competition and Collaboration*. Princeton University Press.
Boulding, Kenneth E. 1963. *Conflict and Defense*. New York: Harper & Row.
Braudel, Fernand. 1980. *On History*, trans. S. Matthews. University of Chicago Press.
Bremer, Stuart A., and Michael Mihalka. 1977. "Machiavelli in Machina: Or Politics among Hexagons." In *Problems of World Modeling*, ed. K.W. Deutsch. Boston: Ballinger.
Buhaug, Halvard, and Scott Gates. 2002. "The Geography of Civil Wars." *Journal of Peace Research* 39 (4): 417–433.
Cederman, Lars-Erik. 1997. *Emergent Actors in World Politics: How States and Nations Develop and Dissolve*. Princeton University Press.
——— 2002a. "Endogenizing Geopolitical Boundaries with Agent-Based Modeling." *Proceedings of the National Academy of Sciences* 99 (suppl. 3): 7296–7303.
——— 2002b. "Nationalism and Ethnicity." In *The Handbook of International Relations*, ed. W. Carlsnaes, T. Risse, and B. Simmons. London: Sage, 409–428.
——— 2003. "Modeling the Size of Wars: From Billiard Balls to Sandpiles." *American Political Science Review* 1 (97): 135–150.
——— 2005. "Computational Models of Social Forms: Advancing Process Theory." *American Journal of Sociology* 110 (4): 864–893.
Cederman, Lars-Erik, and Luc Girardin. 2007. "Beyond Fractionalization: Mapping Ethnicity onto Nationalist Insurgencies." *American Political Science Review* 101 (1): 173–185.

Cederman, Lars-Erik, Jan Ketil Rød, and Nils Weidmann. 2006. "Geo-Referencing of Ethnic Groups: Creating a New Dataset." Paper presented at a GROW-Net Workshop, Peace Research Institute Oslo (PRIO), February 10–11.

Collier, Paul, and Anke Hoeffler. 2004. "Greed and Grievance in Civil Wars." *Oxford Economic Papers* 56 (October): 563–595.

Collier, Paul, and Nicholas Sambanis, eds. 2005. *Understanding Civil War: Evidence and Analysis*. Washington DC: The World Bank.

Deutsch, Karl W. 1953. *Nationalism and Social Communication: An Inquiry into the Foundations of Nationality*. Cambridge, MA: MIT Press.

Epstein, Joshua M. 2002. "Modeling Civil Violence: An Agent-Based Computational Approach." *Proceedings of the National Academy of Sciences* 99 (suppl. 3): 7243–7250.

Fearon, James D. 2003. "Ethnic and Cultural Diversity by Country." *Journal of Economic Growth* 8: 195–222.

Fearon, James D., and David D. Laitin. 2000. "Violence and the Social Construction of Ethnic Identity." *International Organization* 54 (4): 845–877.
2003. "Ethnicity, Insurgency, and Civil War." *American Political Science Review* 97 (1): 75–90.

Gates, Scott. 2002. "Recruitment and Allegiance: The Microfoundations of Rebellion." *Journal of Conflict Resolution* 46 (1): 111–130.

Gellner, Ernest. 1983. *Nations and Nationalism*. Ithaca, NY: Cornell University Press.

Gilpin, Robert. 1981. *War and Change in World Politics*. Cambridge University Press.

Gleditsch, Nils Petter, Peter Wallensteen, Mikael Eriksson, Margareta Sollenberg, and Håvard Strand. 2002. "Armed Conflict 1946–2001: A New Dataset." *Journal of Peace Research* 39 (5): 615–637.

Gurr, Ted Robert. 1993. *Minorities at Risk: A Global View of Ethnopolitical Conflicts*. Washington DC: United States Institute of Peace Press.

Hannan, Michael T. 1979. "The Dynamics of Ethnic Boundaries in Modern States." In *National Development and the World System*, ed. J.W. Meyer and M.T. Hannan. University of Chicago Press, 253–275.

Hechter, Michael. 1992. "The Dynamics of Secession." *Acta Sociologica* 35 (4): 267–283.

Herbst, Jeffrey. 1989. "The Creation and Maintenance of National Boundaries in Africa." *International Organization* 43 (4): 673–692.

Holland, John H. 1995. *Hidden Order: How Adaptation Builds Complexity*. Reading, MA: Addison-Wesley.

Kalyvas, Stathis N. 2003. "The Ontology of 'Political Violence': Action and Identity in Civil Wars." *Perspectives on Politics* 1 (3): 475–494.
2006. *The Logic of Violence in Civil Wars*. Cambridge University Press.

Lake, David A. 2003. "International Relations Theory and Internal Conflict: Insights from the Interstices." *International Studies Review* 5 (4): 81–89.

Lustick, Ian S. 2000. "Agent-Based Modeling of Collective Identity: Testing Constructivist Theory." *Journal of Artificial Societies and Social Simulation* 3 (1).

2002. "PS-I: A User-Friendly Agent-Based Modeling Platform for Testing Theories of Political Identity and Political Stability." *Journal of Artificial Societies and Social Simulation* 5 (3).

McAdam, Doug, Sidney Tarrow, and Charles Tilly. 2001. *Dynamics of Contention.* Cambridge University Press.

Quinn, Kevin, Michael Hechter, and Erik Wibbels. 2004. "Ethnicity, Insurgency, and Civil War Revisited." Center for Statistics and the Social Sciences, University of Washington.

Rokkan, Stein. 1999. *State Formation, Nation-Building, and Mass Politics in Europe: The Theory of Stein Rokkan,* ed. Peter Flora. Oxford University Press.

Sambanis, Nicholas. 2001. "Do Ethnic and Nonethnic Civil Wars Have the Same Causes? A Theoretical and Empirical Inquiry." *Journal of Conflict Resolution* 45 (3): 259–282.

2004. "Using Case Studies to Expand Economic Models of Civil War." *Perspectives on Politics* 2: 259–279.

Simon, Herbert. 1981. *The Sciences of the Artificial.* Cambridge, MA: MIT Press.

Tarrow, Sidney. 2007. "Inside Insurgencies: Politics and Violence in an Age of Civil War." *Perspectives on Politics* 5 (3): 587–600.

Tilly, Charles. 2003. *The Politics of Collective Violence.* Cambridge University Press.

Weber, Max. 1978. *Economy and Society: An Outline of Interpretative Sociology.* Berkeley: University of California Press.

Weiner, Myron. 1971. "The Macedonian Syndrome: An Historical Model of International Relations and Political Development." *World Politics* 23 (4): 665–683.

1978. *Sons of the Soil: Migration and Ethnic Conflict in India.* Princeton University Press.

11 Which group identities lead to most violence? Evidence from India

Steven I. Wilkinson

Introduction

In this essay, I use a new dataset I have collected on collective mobilization and collective violence in India from 1950 to 1995 to begin to sketch an answer to three questions.[1] First, empirically I try to establish the patterns of reported ethnic and nonethnic mobilization and violence in India since the 1950s. Is it true that ethnic mobilization and violence in India have become more common, or are scholars such as Paul Brass (1997) correct when they argue that the perceived rise in ethnic mobilization and ethnic violence is merely due to our tendency to pay too much attention to ethnic conflict compared to other kinds of conflict, and to label events as "ethnic" when they are not? Second, is it true, as scholars such as Rabushka and Shepsle (1972) and Elster *et al.* (1998) have argued, that mobilization around ethnic identities is inherently more dangerous than other kinds of political mobilization? By "more dangerous," I should make it clear that I am primarily concerned with the narrow question of whether ethnic mobilization is associated with deadly violence more than other kinds of political mobilization. Third, are some types of ethnic mobilization more damaging to the stability of the state than others? Is it true, for example, that linguistic claims are less dangerous than religious or other types of ethnic mobilization, as Laitin (1999) claims?

My data show that mobilization around ethnic identities, and in particular around religious and caste identities, has been increasing in India, while mobilization around other identities, such as language, has been decreasing. I also find that not all types of ethnic mobilization are equally likely to lead to deadly violence (Rabushka and Shepsle 1972).

---

[1] I thank participants at an SSRC-sponsored conference at the University of Chicago and at a panel at the 2002 APSA convention for their very useful comments on an earlier draft of this essay. At Duke, Camber Warren read the essay and made many good suggestions.

Mobilization around some religious identities, in particular, seems to have a strong positive correlation with deadly violence. Mobilization around the Hindu–Muslim cleavage, for example, seems to be consistently related to deaths. On the other hand, the relationship between mobilization around other ethnic identities and violence seems to be much less clear. Depending on the decade, for example, linguistic mobilization is either negatively related to violence or unrelated to the level of violence. And, depending on decade, mobilization around caste is sometimes positively related to deaths, sometimes negatively.

My finding that linguistic mobilization in India is not positively related to the level of deaths might be seen by some as further support for an intriguing thesis David Laitin (1999) has put forward: that the politics of language are inherently less dangerous than some other forms of ethnic mobilization. I suggest, however, that the negative relationship between linguistic mobilization and deaths in India – and the positive relationship between minority Sikh and Muslim religious mobilization and deaths – is probably due more to specific historical and institutional factors that influence state policy than to any broader structural relationship between identities and violence of the kind Laitin outlines. In particular I highlight the effects of India's struggle for independence on her leaders' post-independence reluctance to accept any demands made on the basis of *minority* religious identities, while accepting those made on the basis of region, language (at least after 1955), or the Hindu religious *majority*. The fact that the Indian state uses force to suppress some types of mobilization, while allowing or even encouraging other types of mobilization (including violence against religious minorities), is the major factor, I argue, in explaining the observed differences in the relationship between different types of mobilization and violence.

This essay is organized into four sections. First, I discuss the general theoretical debates over whether ethnic mobilization is more likely to lead to more violence than other types of mobilization. Second, I introduce my sample data on political mobilization and violence in India from 1950 to 1999. I describe how the data were collected and how I dealt with the problem of how to decide whether ethnicity or some other identity motivated a particular event. Third, I use these data to offer some initial answers to the questions outlined above. I show that ethnic mobilization and ethnic violence have increased both in absolute and in relative terms, and that religious mobilization leads to more violence than other types of ethnic mobilization. Fourth, I consider some of the implications of these data and in particular the question of whether linguistic mobilization is qualitatively different than other kinds of ethnic mobilization.

Is ethnic mobilization different?

Does mobilization around ethnic identities tend to lead to more violence than mobilization around other identities such as class, political party, or social movements?[2] Much theoretical and empirical research suggests that it does. Theoretically, numerous observers have linked ethnic mobilization and high levels of ethnic heterogeneity to higher levels of conflict as well as worse outcomes over a range of economic and democratic variables. In the nineteenth century both Thomas Jefferson and John Stuart Mill argued that multinational states faced particular problems because of the intense nature of ethnic preferences compared to other cleavages.[3] More recently Alvin Rabushka and Kenneth Shepsle (1972, 92) argued that multiethnic polities were particularly prone to breakup because ethnicity tends to drive out other cleavages, and because "democracy, at least as it is known in the West, cannot be sustained under conditions of intense, salient [ethnic] preferences because ... The plural society, constrained by the preferences of its citizens, does not provide fertile soil for democratic values or stability."[4] Elster et al. (1998, 249–251), in their analysis of the post-1990 Eastern European transitions, came to the same general conclusion, arguing that ethnic issues are inherently harder to compromise over than issues of ideology or material welfare, because they are zero-sum, because ethnic groups each represent complete societies (making them less reliant on other groups), and because the long-term stakes in letting the other group win in ethnic conflicts seem so much higher than in distributive or even ideological conflicts. Even those whose research highlights the role that conflict-moderating institutions can play in reducing ethnic violence, such as Donald Horowitz (1985) and Arend Lijphart (1977), accept as their starting point that ethnic mobilization and ethnic conflicts are generally more likely to lead to violence than nonethnic conflicts.

[2] Weber (1978, 389) defines religious groups as "ethnic groups" because of their "subjective belief in their common descent because of similarities of physical type or of customs or both, or because of memories of colonization and migration." See also Horowitz (1985, 50–51).
[3] Thomas Jefferson (1903, 72–73), in his autobiography, wrote that "Nothing is more certainly written in the book of fate, than that these people are to be free; nor is it less certain the two races, equally free, cannot live in the same government. Nature, habit, opinion, have drawn indelible lines of distinction between them." Mill's 1861 work *On Representative Government* lays out many reasons why he thinks multiple "national" identities work against the goal of stable democracies.
[4] Rabushka and Shepsle (1972, 65) assert the preeminence of ethnic cleavages, though they admit, "We are not able to explain its genesis."

Empirically, ethnic mobilization seems to be naturally associated with high levels of violence in many people's minds: we have only to think of recent events such as the Rwanda genocide in 1994, the Chechen and East Timor independence movements, Hindu–Muslim violence in India in 1992–1993 and 2002, and the civil wars and ethnic cleansing in ex-Yugoslavia.[5] Even to casual observers there seem to be far fewer instances of similar large-scale deadly conflicts along nonethnic lines. This general sense that ethnic mobilization is more dangerous than other types of mobilization has also been driven by the (apparently) robust finding by scholars that countries with higher levels of ethnic hetero-geneity have higher levels of violence and instability in general than more homogenous states (Easterly and Levine 1997; Gurr 1993; Gurr and Moore 1997).

Some observers also suggest that, within the broad category of "ethnic" mobilization, mobilization around *particular* ethnic identities such as language or religion might lead to higher levels of violence than mobilization around others, such as caste or tribe. Historically, many political scientists took the view that linguistic mobilization was espe-cially dangerous. For instance, Mill ([1861] 1991, 230) argued that a high degree of *linguistic* heterogeneity was a more serious problem for a country's unity than other types of ethnic heterogeneity. The political scientist Carl Buck (1916, 49) argued that language was the element of nationality to which people were "most fanatically attached." And in the 1950s, many analysts of Indian politics argued forcefully that linguistic conflicts, which had led to large-scale instances of violence in southern India in the early part of the decade, were most likely to lead to the breakup of India and other Asian states (Harrison 1960, 56; see also Windmiller 1954).[6]

More recently, however, scholars have tended to argue that religious mobilization is especially prone to conflict. Some highlight the willing-ness of religious adherents to kill for a cause (or rewards in the afterlife) or focus on the specific nature of particular religious traditions in terms of their capacity to generate intense loyalty and conflict (Stark 2001). Scholars in political science, however, generally highlight the organiza-tional aspects of religious practice that give religious leaders a greater capacity to mobilize around religious identities than ethnic entrepreneurs

---

[5] The past two decades have seen a massive increase in research on ethnic and religious violence. A search for the words "ethnic violence" in the full text of sociology and political science articles in the Jstor database done on April 13, 2004 found only 12 articles from 1960 to 1980, but 120 in the period from 1980 to 2004.

[6] Harrison's pessimistic view of India's ability to handle its linguistic conflicts was first published in the journal *Foreign Affairs* in the late 1950s.

who mobilize around other identities. Laitin (1999, 10–13), for instance, argues that political entrepreneurs in linguistic groups face collective-action problems when seeking to "recruit warriors to fight on their behalf" because individual members of the group have an incentive to defect and because "language groups never have organizational hierarchies with powers to police members." Religious groups, by contrast, have organizational hierarchies that can monitor members and they are willing and able to use sanctions against those members who "defect." Another factor Laitin (1999, 19–23) identifies that predisposes religious conflicts to have higher levels of violence than linguistic ones is that "language shift takes generations, and it is impossible for a state to impose a new language of education, administration or certification without a long lead time." This reduces the short-term costs to the minority group of changes in policy, and therefore lessens the likelihood of violence.

The empirical basis for our belief that ethnic mobilization is more dangerous than nonethnic mobilization or that particular identities might be more associated with violence than others is weaker than we might think. One weakness is that much of our existing data on the prevalence of conflict was collected in research projects that viewed "ethnic" and "ethnic conflict" as self-evident and highly important categories worthy of detailed inquiry, and therefore tended not to collect data on other identities, other forms of mobilization, or other forms of conflict. The Minorities at Risk (MAR) dataset, for example, which is widely used in large-N studies of violence, selected cases of repression against minorities but not, until recently, against nonethnic groups.[7] Because datasets on collective violence contain very little information on nonethnic forms of mobilization or identity they are arguably biasing their findings toward ethnic answers. We simply cannot tell from existing data, for example, whether ethnic cleavages are more important than other kinds of cleavage in explaining support for public goods provision or levels of violence, so it might plausibly be the case that once we introduce party, ideology, and class-cleavage data some impressive findings about the relationship between ethnic mobilization and variables such as public goods provision or levels of violence might evaporate. Stathis Kalyvas (2001; 2002), for example, in one of the few empirical studies that has carefully compared ethnic and nonethnic mobilization and patterns of violence, found no significant differences in terms of violence between areas where participants in the Greek Civil War were mobilized on ethnic grounds and those areas where they were not.

---

[7] *Minorities at Risk Dataset Users Manual* Version .899.

A second reason why our assumptions about the relationship between ethnic mobilization and violence might be wrong is that there are real problems with much of the "hard" data that have been used in the past decade to demonstrate a positive statistical association between ethnic heterogeneity and violence. Most of the criticism of these data, in particular the widely used Ethnolinguistic Fractionalization Index (ELF), which provides a cross-national measure of ethnic diversity, has focused on measurement problems, in particular the way in which ethnolinguistic fractionalization fails to capture multiple levels of ethnic identity and changes in ethnic identity over time.[8] An even more serious objection, in my view, is the fact that levels of ethnic heterogeneity are endogenous to processes of state formation and state building, raising the strong possibility that the statistical associations between heterogeneity and violence of the type that Easterly and others describe might be spurious. Homogenous states are, after all, multiethnic states that have been made homogenous. The France of 1860 described by Eugen Weber (1976, 67) in *Peasants into Frenchmen*, for example, was highly heterogeneous, with no French spoken at all in 25 percent of the country's communes and around half of schoolchildren speaking no French or only a little. But following the mid-nineteenth century, there was a century of nation building carried out through the introduction of mass education and conscription, improvements in infrastructure, and a massive increase in state employment and regulation. The fact that France was homogenous in terms of the ELF measure in 1960 is a reflection of this state building and modernization, which forced some and encouraged others to assimilate to a French identity after 1860. It is at least plausible that it is long-term differences in these (omitted) modernization and state-building variables, rather than something intrinsic to ethnic identity, that is responsible for much of the observed relationship in large-N studies between ethnic heterogeneity and violent conflict.

A third reason that ought to make us question structural relationships between particular types of mobilization and violence is that we can point to significant empirical exceptions to almost any structural generalization we want to put forward. For example, the case of the Czech–German conflict in the nineteenth century seems to disprove many of the distinctions we might want to draw about the collective-action

---

[8] See e.g. Dan Posner and David Laitin (1999), "Constructing Ethnic Fractionalization Indices," available at www.duke.edu/web/licep/1/posner/laitinposner.pdf, as well as Dan Posner (2000), "Measuring Social Identities," presented at LiCEP 2 and available at www.duke.edu/web/licep/2/posner/posner.pdf.

problems faced by political entrepreneurs who mobilize groups on the basis of language as opposed to religion, and about the potential of linguistic mobilization to lead to violence. In nineteenth-century Bohemia and Moravia, German and Czech linguistic associations effectively policed their respective groups and used various means to prevent individual members from defecting in just the same way that Laitin describes as characteristic for religious groups. Recent research by Jeremy King (2002), for example, shows how German-language associations in the town of Budweis threatened individuals with boycotts and the loss of employment if they defected to the Czech-language camp. Mark Cornwall (1994) describes the same intense competition between Czech- and German-language organizations on the "language-border" around Jihlava, especially just before the decennial census during which citizens had to declare their linguistic allegiance. In 1896–1897, 1905, and 1908, intense linguistic mobilization by Czechs and Germans led to large-scale riots in Prague and other towns in Bohemia (Cohen 1975, 448–453).

To give another example, this time from India, the events of the immediate post-partition period seem to show that linguistic transitions can in fact be much more rapid and therefore threatening to minorities than we might think. In August 1947, when India was partitioned, much of the local administration in north Indian cities was still being conducted in the Urdu language and script. In the United Provinces (the present-day state of Uttar Pradesh), for example, nine out of ten reports filed in the police department in July 1947 were written in Urdu, the remainder being written in English and Hindi.[9] But once India became independent, Hindi-language majorities throughout northern India passed Hindi-only laws and told government Urdu-speaking employees to learn the Hindi language and script within two to six months or else be dismissed.[10] Some employees were dismissed, while others successfully made the switch to Hindi, which replaced Urdu in official use by the beginning of 1948. Other similar examples of quick, brutal language transitions, which precipitated mass layoffs of those who spoke the newly disfavored language, are the post-1919 transitions in Czechoslovakia,

---

[9] Uttar Pradesh State Archives, "Police Reorganisation Committee." File 640/46. Lucknow, Home Police Box 373. Of 3,267 cases filed in the northern range in July 1947, 2,889 (88%) were in Urdu, 39 (1%) in English, and 339 (10%) in Hindi.

[10] For instances of this policy being imposed in the towns of Bareilly, Jhansi, and Varanasi, see *The Pioneer* (October 6, 1947; November 5, 1947). This switch was not easy. Hindi is written in the Devanagiri script and draws heavily on Sanskrit vocabulary (which gives literate Hindus, whose sacred texts are in Sanskrit, an advantage), while Urdu draws heavily on Persian vocabulary and is written in a modified version of the Arabic script.

where Czechs discriminated against German speakers, and Romania, where Hungarians were discriminated against by Romanians (Wingfield 1989; Gower 1937, 27–29).

A new dataset on collective mobilization and collective violence in India

To try to assess the relationship between different types of mobilization and violence, this essay employs a new dataset on group mobilization in India since 1950. My research design for this paper tries to correct for what I regard as two problems with existing datasets on ethnic mobilization and violence. First, most large-N studies of ethnic violence tend to select and code events for inclusion based on their high value on the dependent variable. Large datasets on ethnic mobilization and ethnic violence, in other words, often contain data on only those events in which ethnic mobilization has led to large-scale ethnic violence.[11] Nonviolent cases, or cases of nonethnic mobilization and violence, are typically excluded. This selection bias makes it impossible to find out whether ethnic violence is a normal or a highly unusual outcome of ethnic mobilization. It also makes it impossible to find out how ethnic mobilization and ethnic violence differ compared to other types of mobilization and violence, and to find out how various types of violence have increased or decreased over time.[12]

To address this issue, at least as far as violence in India is concerned, I collected a systematic sample of newspaper reports of all incidents of ethnic and nonethnic mass mobilization and group violence in India since Independence. In this essay, I present some preliminary results from this dataset, based on a random data sample of 1,080 days from 1950 to 1995.[13] By collecting information about all the demonstrations, processions, strikes, and various other forms of political mobilization that we know can lead to violence, my aim is ultimately to determine whether, and under what conditions, specific types of mass mobilization lead to violence.[14] By collecting information on all the different kinds of

---

[11] See e.g. the data on race riots in Spilerman (1971) and the Varshney–Wilkinson Hindu–Muslim riot data in Varshney (2002) and Wilkinson (2004).

[12] For a discussion of selection bias, see Geddes (1990, 131–150).

[13] Data are currently being collected for the 1996–2000 period.

[14] Of course the data I collect here are not reflective of all the times that mobilizations do not happen, such as the many times that curfews are imposed or processions banned. It is simply impossible to generate such a database unless one could gain access to local police station records – and even then there would be questions about the validity of the records, because it is well known that police record-keeping in India is subject to several sources of bias, which I discuss in Appendix A in Wilkinson (2004).

mass mobilization – e.g. linguistic, economic, women's movements, union, political party – we can also get a better sense of the identities, once mobilized, that are most likely to be associated with violence.

The source for my data sample is the Mumbai (Bombay) edition of *The Times of India (TOI)*, India's oldest and most respected English-language daily newspaper. My method – explored in greater detail in an appendix to this essay – is to carry out a random sample of all incidents of political mobilization and violence reported in *The Times of India* on 240 selected days in each decade. To avoid biasing the sample, I selected a random sample of two days in each month in each year, rather than taking the easier route of selecting one month in each year.[15] This is because we know that some types of mass mobilization and violence in India take place disproportionately in some months. For example, union, civic, and political-party protests over electricity and water shortages take place largely during the summer, when these shortages are most acute.

How good a source is *The Times of India*? The paper offers a good reputation for reliability, unrivaled historical coverage (it was founded in 1838), and good all-India coverage, because it is part of a major media group with offices and correspondents throughout India. Moreover, unlike the prominent regional-language dailies such as the Hindi paper *Amar Ujala*, whose archive I used in 1995, the *TOI*'s back issues are complete and widely available in Western libraries. The *TOI* probably over-reports low-violence events from Mumbai, where it is published, from the state of Maharashtra (of which Mumbai is the capital), and from Gujarat, which was joined to Maharashtra in the state of Mumbai prior to 1960. But large-scale mobilization and any incidents in which deaths occur seems to be well covered. A study I conducted in 1997 found that *The Times of India* provides more complete data on Hindu–Muslim riots in the northern state of Uttar Pradesh than the source usually regarded as authoritative: the Government of India's own reports to the Indian Parliament. In a cross-check of 1970 to 1993 reports on Hindu–Muslim riots in the state of Uttar Pradesh, I found that the *TOI* listed fifty-eight riots not covered in the government reports. Thirty-seven riots are covered by both sources, and only seven riots were listed in the government reports but not by the *TOI*.[16] None of this is meant to suggest

---

[15] Selecting one month per year would have been easier as a practical matter, despite the greater number of days, because it would have required using only two rolls of microfilm per year, rather than twenty-four. For a discussion of sample bias, see Keohane *et al.* (1993, 29–30).

[16] For full details of this cross-check, which was used to check the reliability of a dataset I collected jointly with Ashutosh Varshney, see Appendix A in Wilkinson (2004).

that the newspaper is a perfect source. It is not, and in a perfect world it would be preferable to use a larger sample of newspapers, perhaps incorporating sources from all the thirty-three major languages of India and from each of the twenty-nine states. As a starting point, however, I believe *The Times of India* offers broader and more detailed coverage of political mobilization and political violence in India since 1950 than any other single source.

The second major problem that I try to address is one of throwing away too much information on the multiplicity of identities around which people mobilize. How do I decide which demonstrations, strikes, and acts of violence are motivated by which ethnic or nonethnic identities, when multiple motivations (political party, religion, caste) may be reported for the same event? The usual approach to being confronted with three or four possible motivations for violence, and the approach Ashutosh Varshney and I used when we compiled our 1950–1995 dataset on Hindu–Muslim violence,[17] is to develop coding rules that determine which of several possible interests or identities was the *most* important in motivating a particular violent event. For example, where the Indian press reported unspecified "group clashes" in connection with events that we believed indicated Hindu–Muslim conflict, such as "cow-slaughter" or "music in front of mosque," we coded the violence as a definite Hindu–Muslim riot. Where, on the other hand, a report mentioned "group clashes" in connection with the demolition of a nonreligious building, we coded the event as "weak" likelihood. Other data-collection efforts, such as the Minorities at Risk project, employ similar coding rules to determine whether particular group conflicts are motivated by "indigenous peoples," "ethno-classes," "militant sects," or "communal contenders."[18]

In this essay I try to incorporate more of the information that we presently exclude about the multiple motivations and identities involved in group mobilization. First, I record (as dummy variables) every reported instance of every type of group mobilization in India, including strikes, processions, party rallies, violent demonstrations, and organized physical attacks. Then I record *all* the reported motivations for each demonstration or act of violence. If a procession in Mumbai, for example, was organized by the Communist Party around women's issues, I list it as being motivated by two identities: "women's rights" and "political party." I code a demonstration led by a Congress Party-affiliated trade union against a

---

[17] The dataset is used in Varshney (2002) and Wilkinson (2004).
[18] The codes for the MAR dataset are available at www.bsos.umd.edu/cidcm/mar/cbwebpg.htm.

cut in food subsidies as having three motivations: "political party," "union," and "economic." And a demonstration by the Hindu nationalist Bharatiya Janata Party against cow-slaughter is given the labels "religion" and "political party."[19] For each event I record in a spreadsheet the type of mobilization (demonstration, violent demonstration, strike, procession, and attack), and the number of deaths, injuries, and arrests caused by each mobilization.

This method does have some limitations, for example if we want to find out whether a particular ethnic or nonethnic identity is the primary cause of a demonstration, strike, or riot. But if, as is the case in this study, our aim is to find out about broader patterns of mobilization and conflict *over time*, and about differences between different types of ethnic mobilization, then the method offers some advantages. Because we exclude none of the information about mobilizing identities, we should be able to get a clearer picture of how aggregate patterns of political mobilization (both ethnic and nonethnic) have changed over time.

Some descriptive statistics on patterns of mobilization and violence in India

In my 1,080-day sample from 1950 to 1995, *The Times of India* reported 2,979 mobilizations: meetings, attacks, violent demonstrations, processions and strikes. These events led to 6,832 deaths and 7,606 injuries. As we can see from Figure 11.1, the number of mobilizations per year, averaging 41 in the 1950s and 33 in the 1960s, increased to 77 in the 1980s and 110 in the 1990s, a rate of increase slightly less than that of India's population. Meanwhile the average number of deaths per year in the sample rose from 13 in the 1950s and 11.7 in the 1960s, to 183 in the 1970s, 132 in the 1980s, and 573 in the 1990s, far outstripping the threefold increase in India's population since Independence in 1947.

How did the types of reported identities invoked by Indians to press their demands change from 1950 to 1995? There has been a shift, as we can see in Table 11.1, in the balance between economic mobilizations – those made on the basis of union membership or economic interest – and those made on the basis of ethnic identities such as caste, religion, or tribe. The number of times economic identities were invoked exceeded ethnic claims in the 1950s and also in the 1960s and 1970s, the latter an

---

[19] The variables "religion" and "caste" are then subcategorized so that we can tell which religious groups or castes were involved. My hope in the future is to examine the question of whether and why particular caste or religious identities are prone to higher levels of violence than others.

Table 11.1. *Broad patterns of ethnic and nonethnic mobilization,*
1950–1995

Decade	Total number of mobiliza- tions	Total number of ethnic identities reported in mobiliza- tions	Total number of all economic identities reported in mobiliza- tions	Total number of all social movement identities reported in mobilizations	Total deaths	Total injuries
1950s	411	122	127	5	130	637
1960s	326	75	123	2	117	1180
1970s	820	83	345	17	1833	2261
1980s	765	317	178	24	1317	2119
1990–95	657	389	105	21	3435	1409

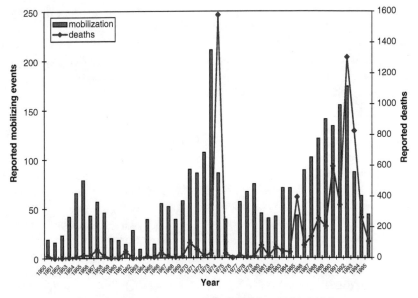

Figure 11.1 Mobilizing events and deaths, 1950–1995

era in which Prime Minister Indira Gandhi polarized politics along
the rich–poor dimension by promising mass nationalizations, help for
the poor, higher taxes, and an end to "princely privilege." But in the

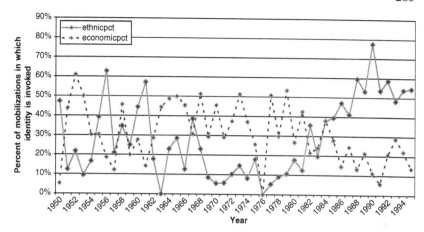

Figure 11.2 Demands framed in ethnic or in economic terms,
1950–1995

1980s and 1990s ethnic identities have been invoked much more
than economic. The number of social movements – a category that
includes women's movements, peace movements, and environmental
movements – has registered a slow, steady increase since the 1950s but
the total percentage of reported mobilizations around these identities
still seems to be very small. Environmental issues, for example, were
invoked in zero mobilizations in the 1950s and 1960s, twice in the
1970s, once in the 1980s, and eight times in the 1990s.

In Figure 11.2 we can see that in the 1950s and 1960s, there was
significant variation from year to year in whether ethnic claims or economic claims accounted for a larger proportion of identities invoked in
meetings, demonstrations, strikes, processions, and attacks. In the 1970s
and the beginning of the 1980s, economic mobilizations still accounted
for considerably more mobilizations than ethnic claims. But from around
1984 on, ethnic mobilizations and ethnic claims have become increasingly
dominant in India's public sphere.

Within the broad category of "ethnic mobilization," there has also
been a change in *which* ethnic identities are invoked, as we can see in
Table 11.2 and Figure 11.3 below. Caste, which motivated only 3% of
all events in the 1950s, is mentioned in 12% of events, and accounts for
20% of all reported ethnic identities, up from 10% in the 1950s and 7%
in the 1960s. Language, on the other hand, which was reported as an
identity in sixty-one mobilizations in the 1950s – when there were several movements to create linguistic states from the colonial-era state

Table 11.2. *Reported number of times specific identities or aims were invoked in each decade, 1950–1995*

	1950s	1960s	1970s	1980s	1990–1995
Agricultural	38	4	14	18	2
Caste	12	5	22	37	76
Revolutionary	0	2	34	0	14
Hindu–Muslim	15	5	13	15	58
Hindu religion	6	8	1	3	9
Muslim religion	0	8	14	0	97
Language	61	30	12	3	5
Nationalist	21	15	23	5	12
Party	141	82	178	112	180
Protest against official actions	24	36	31	4	55
Regional	17	42	53	226	19
Religion (unspecified)	7	1	10	43	1
Separatist	85	51	51	220	226
Students	37	86	138	67	72
Tribal	16	14	4	13	42
Economic	127	123	345	178	105
Protest against central government's misuse of powers	6	1	1	2	3
Sikh and Hindu versus Sikh	17	5	6	202	108
Environmental	0	0	2	1	8
Peace	0	1	3	17	7
Women/Gender	3	1	10	3	5
Disabled	1	0	2	3	0

boundaries India had inherited – had dropped to only three mobilizations in the 1980s and five in the 1990s. The big growth (see Table 11.2 and Figure 11.3) has been in mobilizations along religious grounds, such as Hindu mobilizations or mobilizations around Muslim identity (the latter has been especially important in the long-running insurgency in Kashmir). Sikh identities were also increasingly invoked in the 1980s and 1990s, the cause and result of the 1981–1994 insurgency by Sikh separatists, which led to an estimated 25,000 deaths.

In Table 11.2 we can also see that separatist mobilizations, which briefly fell in the 1960s after India defused several linguistic separatist movements by creating new states, have sharply increased again in recent decades, as other groups have sought their own states using the

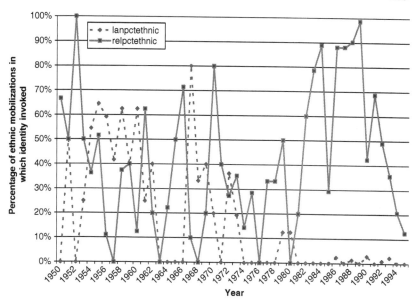

Figure 11.3 Linguistic versus religious mobilization as %
of all ethnic mobilization

constitutional norms and procedures established in the 1950s. Other
movements, for example around student issues or those organized by
political parties, have remained more stable.

The level of reported mobilizations has also been uneven across states
(Table 11.3). Using as a (very rough) indicator the ratio of mobilizations
to state populations, we can see that several states have had much higher
ratios of mobilizations to their 2001 populations than others: Delhi,
Goa, Jammu and Kashmir, Punjab, and Rajasthan all have had a ratio of
mobilizations to their 2001 population of under 1:100,000.[20] Several
other states – Tripura, Mizoram, Manipur – have ratios between
1:100,000 and 1:200,000. The high rates of mobilization in most of
these states can be explained by their separatist movements, with states
in the northeast (Tripura, Mizoram, Manipur) and north and northwest
of the country (Punjab, Jammu and Kashmir) having all had large-scale
insurgencies demanding independence, greater autonomy, or a separate

[20] I recognize that this is a rough and ready estimate and that it would be better to
calculate the mobilization rate using decadal census figures, because (among other
reasons) violence in one decade might also affect the population level of a state in the
next census.

Table 11.3. *State totals of mobilization, 1950–1995*

State	Population (2001)	Deaths	Injuries	Mobilization	Ethnic identities	Economic	Ratio of mobilization to 2001 population
Andhra Pradesh	75,727,541	203	266	130	8	21	582,519
Assam	26,638,407	193	189	69	26	15	386,063
Bihar	109,788,224	259	352	172	49	49	638,303
Delhi	13,782,976	1002	346	438	67	204	31,467
Goa	1,343,998	1	4	17	2	2	79,058
Gujarat	50,596,992	427	520	132	50	24	383,310
Haryana	21,082,989	644	175	61	21	19	345,622
Himachal Pradesh	607,7248	0	50	8	3	1	759,656
Jammu and Kashmir	10,069,917	351	1045	140	102	7	71,927
Karnataka	52,733,958	148	308	88	27	35	599,249
Kerala	31,838,619	20	206	76	13	27	418,929
Madhya Pradesh	81,181,074	191	268	83	18	26	978,085
Maharashtra	96,752,247	876	1190	275	60	145	351,826
Manipur	2,388,634	78	102	13	5	1	183,741
Meghalaya	2,306,069	0	21	4	1	1	576,517
Mizoram	891,058	14	5	5	5	2	178,211
Nagaland	1,988,636	81	7	26	24	2	76,486
Orissa	36,716,920	7	117	42	12	10	874,212
Punjab	24,289,296	961	327	378	314	18	64,257
Rajasthan	56,731,220	55	110	74	16	28	76,663
Sikkim	540,493	0	0	2	0	0	270,246
Tamil Nadu	62,110,839	122	356	102	41	34	608,929
Tripura	3,191,168	51	92	21	11	2	151,960
Uttar Pradesh	174,532,421	623	1071	377	85	107	462,950
West Bengal	80,221,171	189	437	209	16	91	383,833

Table 11.4. *Percentage of mobilizations around particular
identities in which deaths or injuries occurred*

	Total mobilizations in which identity invoked	Percentage of mobilizations in which deaths occurred	Percentage of mobilizations in which injuries occurred
All economic mobilization	878	7%	8%
All social movements	69	3%	10%
All mobilizations	2979	23%	17%
Ethnic	986	46%	20%
Specific identities			
Agricultural	76	7%	4%
Caste	152	16%	18%
Revolutionary	50	70%	22%
Hindu–Muslim Polarization	106	60%	37%
Hindu	27	11%	15%
Linguistic	111	4%	6%
Nationalist	76	1%	4%
Political party	693	15%	20%
Protest versus officials	150	8%	19%
Regional	357	50%	17%
Religion (unspecified)	62	23%	37%
Sikh	338	82%	14%
Student	400	6%	15%
Tribal	89	39%	17%
Protest vs. center	13	0%	0%

state for their group within the Indian union. Rajasthan has not had a
separatist movement itself, but it suffered during the Punjab insurgency
in 1981–1994, when many Sikh militants carried out operations within
the state, which is adjacent to Punjab. The remaining state, Delhi, has
such high rates of mobilizations because, as the national capital, it
attracts demonstrators and meetings from all over India.

Just looking at the total numbers of deaths and injuries that occur when
some identities are invoked rather than others (Table 11.4) immediately
suggests that some kinds of ethnic mobilization in India might indeed be
more related to violence than others. Agricultural movements, nationalist
demonstrations and meetings, and linguistic movements and protests

against central government actions rarely or never seem to have led to deaths and injuries. Certain ethnic identities, on the other hand, seem to be invariably associated with high levels of deaths or injuries: Of reported mobilizations around Sikh identities, 82% led to deaths and 14% injuries, while Hindu–Muslim polarization led to deaths in 60% of reported cases and injuries in 37%. Caste movements, on the other hand, led to deaths in 16% of cases, and injuries in 18% of cases, a much lower level than for other ethnic identities.

To investigate the relationships between mobilization around particular identities and violence I conducted a very preliminary statistical analysis of the data, using a negative binomial regression, with fixed effects for each state. The total sample ($n = 2,979$) used in these regressions represents the total number of reported mobilizing events in the years 1950–1995. The dependent variables in the regression results presented in Table 11.5 are the log of the number of deaths in each event (*logdeaths*) as well as the absolute number of deaths.

The basic regression results using the pooled 1950–1995 sample (Table 11.5) indicate that first, ethnic mobilization in general seems to be associated with more deaths than other types of mobilization, such as mobilization around economic or social movement issues (columns 1 and 2). Second, within the broad category of ethnic mobilization particular mobilizing identities – especially those associated with religious mobilization – do indeed seem to be associated with higher levels of casualties than others (columns 3 and 4). Mobilization around Hindu–Muslim issues is positively related to deaths, even when we control for state fixed effects. Mobilization around Sikh and Muslim identities and around "tribe" and "caste" also seems to be positively related to the level of deaths when we adjust for clustering on state. Only mobilization around language seems to be negatively related to the level of casualties.

Many of these observed relationships in the pooled sample, however, break down when we run the same regressions on subsets of the data. In Table 11.6 I present a summary of the results when I ran the same regressions found in the first column of Table 11.5 separately for each of the five decades in the sample. Mobilization around Hindu–Muslim issues is still positively related to deaths in four out of the five decades, and language is negatively related to deaths in three decades (not related in one and positively related in one). Several of the other ethnic identities show much more variation, however: caste, for instance, was negatively related to violence in the 1960s and 1990s but positively related in the 1950s and 1980s. Mobilization around "Hindu" issues such as the reform of personal laws is negatively related to deaths in

Table 11.5. *Mobilizing identities and deaths, 1950–1995*

	(1)	(2)	(3)	(4)
			logdeaths	deaths
Caste			0.338	0.096
			(0.195)*	(0.327)
Economic			− 0.537	− 0.920
			(0.306)*	(0.430)**
Hindu–Muslim			2.033	3.329
			(0.260)***	(0.398)***
Hindu			− 0.248	− 0.097
			(0.713)	(0.722)
Language			− 1.595	− 1.756
			(0.755)**	(0.498)***
Muslim			1.021	0.750
			(0.290)***	(0.299)**
Party			− 0.674	− 0.885
			(0.154)***	(0.222)***
Protest versus			− 0.916	− 0.526
officials			(0.465)**	(0.757)
Region			0.516	0.392
			(0.358)	(0.347)
Religion			− 0.040	− 0.561
			(0.463)	(0.392)
Sikh			1.307	1.110
			(0.208)***	(0.169)***
Student			− 1.658	− 2.070
			(0.370)***	(0.346)***
Tribal			0.786	0.576
			(0.311)**	(0.300)*
Union			− 1.240	0.682
			(0.363)***	(0.560)
Anti-center			− 20.412	− 14.680
			(0.427)***	(0.424)***
Aggregated	1.569***	2.178***		
ethnic	(0.253)	(0.327)		
Aggregated	− 0.465	1.397**		
economic	(0.296)	(0.657)		
Aggregated	− 0.655	0.962		
social movement	(1.097)	(1.038)		
Constant	− 2.194***	− 0.722***	− 1.445	0.329
	(0.249)	(0.254)	(0.236)***	(0.200)
Observations	2943	2943	2943	2943

Robust standard errors in parentheses
*significant at 10%; **significant at 5%; ***significant at 1%.

Table 11.6. *Summary of decade by decade regressions on the relationship between mobilizing identities and deaths*

	(1) 1950s logdeaths	(2) 1960s logdeaths	(3) 1970s logdeaths	(4) 1980s logdeaths	(5) 1990s logdeaths
Caste	1.806 (0.811)**	−17.304 (0.545)***	−0.895 (1.111)	1.148 (0.425)***	−1.093 (0.935)
Economic	0.183 (1.065)	0.559 (0.505)	−0.805 (0.652)	−0.310 (0.671)	−1.204 (0.804)
Hindu–Muslim	1.559 (0.713)**	2.914 (0.401)***	−15.852 (0.549)***	1.970 (0.841)**	1.928 (0.373)***
Hindu	−14.983 (0.754)***	−17.834 (1.012)***	2.646 (0.494)***	−15.589 (0.628)***	−0.514 (0.787)
Language	−0.241 (0.922)	−17.050 (0.792)***	−15.334 (0.676)***	−15.165 (0.745)***	2.265 (1.215)*
Party	−0.710 (0.790)	−0.337 (1.184)	−0.117 (0.510)	−0.312 (0.310)	−0.770 (0.164)***
Protest versus officials	−0.087 (0.946)	−0.199 (0.782)	−15.523 (0.537)***	−15.190 (0.578)***	−0.773 (0.661)
Region	−14.165 (0.630)***	−17.051 (0.765)***	−15.811 (1.148)***	0.910 (0.379)**	−1.674 (0.947)*
Religion	−14.950 (0.732)***	−18.050 (1.328)***	0.775 (1.023)	0.032 (0.431)	−18.692 (1.881)***
Sikh	−14.559 (0.820)***	−17.315 (1.360)***	−15.918 (0.608)***	−15.429 (0.584)***	1.073 (0.352)***
Student	0.238 (0.322)	1.552 (1.467)	−0.996 (0.541)*	−1.587 (0.748)**	−1.692 (0.734)**
Tribal	0.483 (0.761)	1.287 (1.349)	−0.038 (1.076)	0.804 (0.282)***	0.729 (0.474)
Union	0.564 (0.624)	−1.634 (0.792)**	−0.708 (0.784)	−2.209 (0.796)***	−1.427 (0.755)*
Anti-center	−14.512 (0.726)***	−17.930 (1.052)***	−15.859 (0.917)***	−15.429 (0.808)***	−14.257 (1.282)***
Revolution		−18.222 (2.144)***	0.702 (0.419)*		0.130 (0.545)
Muslim		0.480 (1.646)	−15.976 (0.613)***		0.869 (0.342)**
Constant	−2.883 (0.773)***	−2.083 (1.226)*	−1.704 (0.494)***	−1.534 (0.378)***	−1.040 (0.346)***
Observations	400	318	809	760	656

Note: "Muslim" dropped in regressions for 1950s and 1980s because of co-linearity.
– No statistically significant relationship
*significant at 10%; **significant at 5%; ***significant at 1%.

three of the five decades, positively in one (the 1970s), and has no statistically significant relationship in the 1990s.

Making sense of the patterns

How can we explain the fact that religious mobilization around Hindu–Muslim issues and Sikh and Muslim identities is positively related to deaths in the pooled sample while linguistic mobilization is negatively related? One interpretation would be that this result confirms the hypothesis that some kinds of ethnic identities, once mobilized, have structural characteristics that simply make them less likely to lead to ethnic violence than conflicts over religion. Religious identities are just more likely to lead to violence than mobilization over economic issues or language.

More likely, in my view, is that there is nothing intrinsic about particular identities that leads to religious mobilization being associated with high levels of violence while linguistic mobilization should be negatively related or unrelated to violence. The positive relationship between religious mobilization and violence in India, and the negative relationship between linguistic mobilization and violence, I think, is probably better explained by a historical-institutionalist argument that accounts for why the state at some times regards some ethnic-mobilizing identities as illegitimate, and therefore uses force against them, while taking a relatively benign view of other ethnic demands.

A plausible historical-institutional explanation of why religious identities are more likely to lead to violence in India than linguistic ones would highlight the British government's "divide and rule" technique of institutionalizing religious identities through the pre-1947 electoral system (with separate electorates for Hindus and Muslims) and the resulting struggle between the Congress Party and the Muslim League prior to Independence.[21] The political competition prior to Independence and the religiously based partition of India in 1947 are highly significant because they gave India's post-independence leaders a profound suspicion of any minority claims made against the state on the basis of religion. Consequently, as the work of Paul Brass (1974) explores in great depth, the post-1947 Indian state has been much more willing to acknowledge claims made on the basis of language than those made on the basis of a religious identity. Successive Indian governments, Brass (1974, 17) shows, have decided that "regional demands based on

---

[21] This historical-institutional argument is, in some respects, similar to the one Laitin (1986) himself offers to explain the absence of religious conflicts in Nigeria.

language and culture will be accommodated, but that regional demands which are explicitly based on religious differences will not be accepted."

The contrasting example of Pakistan emphasizes that there is no necessary connection between particular identities and deadly violence. In 1947 the same independence process that produced an Indian government intransigent over the issue of religion produced a Pakistan government intransigent over the issue of the official language. The Pakistan government, largely because of the symbolic role played by Urdu in India during the struggle between the Congress and the Muslim League prior to 1947, was uncompromising over the dominant status of the Urdu *language*, even as it was relatively conciliatory to the state's *religious* Shi'i minority. In the late 1940s and early 1950s Pakistani governments imposed Urdu on the country's 54 percent Bengali-speaking majority, precipitating large-scale language riots in East Pakistan in 1952 and the imposition of emergency rule on that Bengali-speaking province (Noman 1990, 30). While religion has been most associated with violence in post-independence India, until recently more violence in Pakistan has been over language.

Within India, the fact that the post-independence state has been so profoundly suspicious of minority religious mobilization (due to partition) has meant that the Indian government has met quite moderate demands in recent years by the Sikh majority in the state of Punjab and the Muslim majority in the state of Jammu and Kashmir in a quite different way than it has approached the linguistic demands of the Tamil and Telegu speakers in southern India. Laitin, Brass, and many other scholars have pointed out that the Indian state's approach to linguistic demands has been generally conciliatory since the 1950s, and these conflicts have consequently led to very little violence. Rather than employing a similar policy of negotiation and compromise with regard to the Sikh and Kashmiri Muslim demands, however, Indian governments have suppressed them by dismissing state governments that oppose the will of the center, supporting local strongmen and, when all else fails, sending in the army and paramilitary forces. Some of this resistance is no doubt connected to the fact that both states lie on the sensitive border with India's strategic enemy, Pakistan, and the history of Pakistani claims to Kashmir in particular is too well known to need retelling here. Through their intransigence, successive Indian governments have therefore driven many Sikhs and Kashmiris to join armed militant organizations. The attacks launched by these organizations, and the counterattacks launched by the government, have been responsible for most of the upsurge in deadly violence in India in the 1990s.

The fact that state policies change over time (because different coalitions privilege different sets of identities that they regard as legitimate or think they stand to gain from if the identities are institutionalized and mobilization around them is allowed) and in different Indian states would also help explain why minority religious identities such as Sikhism and Islam as well as other identities such as caste are positively associated with violence in India in some decades and not in others (Table 11.6).

There is nothing, it seems to me, in the intrinsic character of the demands being made by India's religious minorities that accounts for the high level of violence in these conflicts. The relationship between identities and violence is best explained by the composition of the ruling government coalition, the identities it prefers to highlight, and its ready use of repression against religious minorities it regards as threatening. The fact that several ethnic identities (caste, Muslim) flip signs from positive to negative during the 1970s, for example, is largely a function of the years 1971–1977, during which Indira Gandhi's Congress Party dominated the center and the state governments both suppressed religious and caste mobilization, especially during the 1975–1977 emergency, and put forward social policies that were explicitly designed to help "the poor" rather than specific caste or religious groups.

Why has Hindu–Muslim mobilization been consistently related to deadly violence? The key fact to note here is that virtually all these instances of violence are the outcome of Hindu mobilization against members of the Muslim minority, often with a clear political purpose. My own work has shown that Hindu politicians foment violence in close seats in order to polarize voters and win elections (Wilkinson 2004). Because Hindus are a majority of the population, Indian governments have in most cases been loath to use violence against people who claim to represent "Hindus," lest they alienate large numbers of Hindu voters. Numerous riot commission reports and independent studies have shown that the overwhelming proportion of deaths in these riots are due to state firing on minorities and to members of the majority community being allowed to attack and kill members of the minority community, often for personal, political, and economic reasons. There is clear evidence that virtually all instances of anti-Muslim violence in post-independence India have been facilitated by state complicity, either by delaying ordering the police to intervene or (as in Gujarat in 2002) by actively encouraging riots in order to solidify the Hindu majority by increasing the salience of a Hindu identity (Wilkinson 2004, chapter 2). The fact that the state treats majority religious identities very differently from minority religious identities is also borne out by the fact that mobilization around specifically "Hindu" identities, such as demands for the reforms of Hindu personal laws, are also negatively related to violence in the pool and four out of the five decades by decade regressions.

Fully testing the effects of particular state incentives to mobilize around particular identities in India, and testing for which identities are likely to lead to violence, represent a formidable challenge, however, because government in India is in reality not a single "state," but rather the product of central government actions in New Delhi interacting with those of the twenty-eight different state governments, each of which has its own particular coalitions and incentives. All these states and their incentives would need to be coded over time, I argue, to fully understand the patterns of mobilization and violence. I have done this in Wilkinson (2004) for the single factor of Hindu–Muslim violence but to do it for all identity mobilizations would clearly be a huge task.

Implications

Much of this essay makes the relatively obvious point that expanding the amount of information we collect, especially about the multiple ethnic identities that may motivate any particular instance of political mobilization, makes for more nuanced and reliable results. Systematically gathering data on mobilizations that do not lead to violence as well as those that do helps us to pin down those ethnic identities that are the most likely to threaten security and stability. And collecting information on nonethnic group mobilization as well as ethnic mobilization can help us, in the future, to develop better models of how ethnic mobilization varies and interacts with other types of mobilization, such as economic, agrarian, or social movements.

But two points that are implicit in this essay are less obvious, and bear restating. First, large-N studies that operationalize ethnic identities and ethnic conflict need to include variables that capture the state incentives for individuals to mobilize around one ethnic identity rather than another. Large-N studies that treat a state's ethnic groups as forever fixed – as Ordeshook and Shvetsova (1994, 108) put it, as an "exogenous variable" – are making a fundamental mistake.[22] The fact that the Indian state established large-scale caste quotas in employment in the 1970s and 1980s gave caste-based claims upon the state legitimacy that surely

[22] Ordeshook and Shvetsova (1994, 108) argue, in their study of the effects of ethnic fractionalization on the number of parties, that "social heterogeneity (with the possible exception of religion) is not a product of individual choice – rather, it is better portrayed as an exogenously determined social state."

helps account for the increase in caste-based identities and caste mobilization in India in the 1990s. Similar state incentives in India and elsewhere need to be measured and controlled for. In future revisions of this essay I hope to develop ways of testing to see whether policy changes in India over the past fifty years that we would expect to lead to a change in group identities actually had the predicted effect. In general I expect that for those periods in which the central government policy is to permit mobilization along certain identities, and to offer incentives such as education or job preferences or new federal states to those groups that do so, we would see an increase in mobilization along these identities but a decrease in the deaths associated with them. This is because the state and its agents will be reluctant to use serious force against people whose mobilizing identity is generally accepted by the state as legitimate. For periods in which the central government does not accept mobilization along a particular identity as legitimate, we would expect to see a decrease in the number of mobilizations but an increase in violence.

One way of measuring this would be to include dummy variables to reflect periods when the state is determined to be encouraging or dis-couraging mobilization along particular identities. For language for example we would expect more deadly violence associated with lin-guistic mobilization prior to the States Reorganization Commission's 1955 report, which for the first time accepted the principle of linguistic reorganization as generally valid for all regions of India, than after the 1955 report.

The second point is that any large-N effort to determine whether mobilization around one type of ethnic identity is inherently more likely to cause violence than others needs also to control for the state's dis-criminatory attitude toward some types of ethnic mobilization. India discriminates against religious mobilization compared to linguistic mobil-ization, while Pakistan in the 1950s and 1960s discriminated against language rather than religion. We need to capture these state preferences in our large-N studies if we are ever to get a more definitive answer than I have provided here to the tantalizing question of whether some forms of ethnic mobilization are indeed more dangerous than others.

APPENDIX

Coding rules for dataset on mobilization in India

A.   Sources
- A random sample of two days from each month in the Mumbai edition of *The Times of India* from 1950 to 1998. A sample of days from each month was chosen in preference to a random sample from each year or

decade because we know that mobilization and violence tend to cluster in some months – especially summer months – rather than others, and we therefore want representative coverage. The dates to check are generated using the random number generator in Excel, generating a number each month between 1 and 28, 29, 30, or 31 depending on the month and whether it is a leap year or not.

- If in doubt, photocopy more pages than you think you will need, so that later we can go through and recode the data.

B.   *Which events should be entered?*

- First, note that we only include events that have taken place, not those that are planned but have not yet taken place, and not those that were planned in the past but were blocked by local officials. For example in 1953 there is a report that the District Magistrate for Moradabad banned a planned Jana Sangh procession in support of Jammu Praja Parishad: *TOI*, March 28, 1953.
- Include all instances of group mobilization and violence by nonstate actors reported to have taken place during the seven days prior to the date of publication. By a "group" mobilization we mean any collective action reported to involve four or more people. As a practical matter, reports in which a collective noun such as "group," or "militants," or "union members" is used are assumed to meet this threshold. Wherever possible list the number of participants in the mobilization in the appropriate column. By "nonstate" we mean action by a party, social organization, farmers' organization, separatist militants, women's organization, etc. For example the Independence parades in New Delhi in January 1960 don't count, nor do the state-sponsored activities in April 1960 to celebrate the founding of the new state of Gujarat. Walkouts by MPs in the Lok Sabha would not count, nor would a behind-closed-doors meeting.
- *What happens if, over several months, we get separate daily reports of the same months-long strike or separatist violence? Are these the same event or several events?* The coding rule is that you should enter these as if they were separate events.

C.   *Categories recorded*

- **Year, month, date**. Records the year, month, and date in which a mobilizing event or instance of violence actually took place, rather than the date on which it was reported. Months are reported as numbers (1–12) rather than words. All events within previous month reported.

- **Location**. Record the state under "state" and put the town, village, etc. in the notes. Where you do not know the state, enter the reported town or village under "state" so that we know to go back and reenter.

Type of mobilization

Record the nature of the group activity, whether a demonstration, strike, procession, violent demonstration, or attack. If violence is reported, then record the nature of the group activity that preceded the act of violence.

Distinctions between the various types of mobilization are as follows:

- **Demonstration** – a peaceful mass protest. This category includes the Hindi terms *satyagraha* (defined by McGregor [1993, 978] as "organized, non-violent protest having a political aim; non-violent resistance; civil disobedience"), and *dharna* (McGregor 1993, 524 "sitting constantly at the door of a person whose attention one is demanding [as that of a debtor, or of one from whom a favor is sought]" or "picketing").
- **Procession** – a mass protest or regularly scheduled mass event (such as a religious festival) that follows a set route through a town's streets.
- **Strike** – an organized work stoppage either by a union or by the local citizenry. Often the Hindi term *hartal* is used in newspaper reports, which McGregor (1993, 1056) defines as "1. passive resistance (specif. shutting the shops of a market). 2. a strike."
- **Violent demonstration** – a mass protest in which demonstrators initiate violence, for example by throwing objects, committing arson, or forcing others to close their shops or remain trapped in their place of work. This category includes the Hindi term *gherao*, which McGregor (1993, 292) defines as "besieging or blockading, especially of the house or office of an official, to gain political or other demands."
- **Attack** – use this label for reports where no demonstration, strike, procession, or violent procession preceded an act of violence.
- **Festival** – where no procession involved, such as Holi.

Arrests, casualties
- Record the number of arrests, injuries, and deaths due to a specific instance of group mobilization. Where several different totals are given in different reports, use the lowest. Where arrest totals and casualty totals are given for mobilizations in several towns or districts then average them. Where arrest totals are given use lowest total. In the case of injuries and deaths, record the combined injuries and deaths suffered by the police *and* by the demonstrators. When injuries or

casualties are listed as "several" enter "3" and note in notes. When newspaper reports specify "hundreds" or several "thousands" enter as "300" or "3000" and record this in notes.

Mobilizing identity

Record *all* the identities that are reported as mobilizing an event. Use the following categories:

- Union – workplace complaints, strikes
- Protest versus officials – object is not to change government policy but to protest against official high-handedness, brutality, corruption, or incompetence.
- Economic – note that this is general economic protest rather than specific union-related protests.
- Agrarian
- Caste
- Economic (union, class, economic interest group). Note that when entering subfields, there is a distinction between action taken by unions and that taken by employers and by economic interest-group agitations – so factory owners, lockouts or lorry owners' actions are not union action but economic action. As long as you enter notes we can then go back through and recode if necessary.
- Language
- Nationalist – either patriotic or a demonstration against a foreign country such as Pakistan.
- Political party
- Protest against government actions or government negligence – the key here is that the protest not just be against the policy, but against the poor or corrupt quality of actions/implementation.
- Regional/secessionist
- Religion (disaggregate by which religions involved)
- Social movement (prohibition, environment, disabled, women's groups, peace groups)
- Students
- Tribe
- Unknown

In some cases you as a coder will probably suspect that other identities will be involved than those reported. For example, in March 2, 1972 *TOI* there is a clash mentioned between Congress and Akali Dal supporters. You as a coder may believe that behind this party clash may be a clash between Sikhs and Hindus; however, you should enter only the party identities that are reported, as these other identities are not listed in the newspaper report.

REFERENCES

Brass, Paul. 1974. *Language, Religion and Politics in North India.* Cambridge University Press.

1997. *Theft of an Idol: Text and Context in the Representation of Violence.* Princeton University Press.

Buck, Carl. 1916. "Language and the Sentiment of Nationality." *American Political Science Review* 10 (February): 44–69.

Chandra, Kanchan. 1999. "Ethnic Bargains and Group Instability." Unpublished draft prepared for the SSRC-Macarthur Foundation workshop on "The Impact of Ethnic Politics on Democratic Stability," Chicago, May 19–21.

Cohen, Gary Bennett. 1975. "The Prague Germans, 1861–1914: The Problems of Ethnic Survival." Ph.D. dissertation. Princeton University.

Cornwall, Mark. 1994. "The Struggle on the Czech–German Language Border, 1880–1940." *English Historical Review* 119 (433): 914–951.

Easterly, William, and Ross Levine. 1997. "Africa's Growth Tragedy: Policies and Ethnic Divisions." *Quarterly Journal of Economics* 112 (4): 203–250.

Elster, Jon, Claus Offe, and Ulrich K. Preuss. 1998. *Institutional Design in Post-Communist Societies: Rebuilding the Ship at Sea.* Cambridge University Press.

Geddes, Barbara. 1990. "How the Cases You Choose Affect the Answers You Get." *Political Analysis* 2 (1): 131–150.

Gower, Robert. 1937. *The Hungarian Minorities in the Succession States.* London: Grant Richards.

Gurr, T. R. 1993. *Minorities at Risk: A Global View of Ethnopolitical Conflicts.* Washington DC: United States Institute of Peace.

Gurr, T. R., and Will H. Moore. 1997. "Ethnopolitical Rebellion: A Cross-Sectional Analysis of the 1980s, with Risk Assessments for the 1990s." *American Journal of Political Science* 41 (4): 1079–1103.

Harrison, Selig R. 1960. *India: The Most Dangerous Decades.* Princeton University Press.

Horowitz, Donald L. 1985. *Ethnic Groups in Conflict.* Berkeley: University of California Press.

Jefferson, Thomas. 1903. "Autobiography." In *The Writings of Thomas Jefferson,* vol. I, ed. A. Lipscomb. Washington DC: Thomas Jefferson Memorial Association of the United States.

Kalyvas, Stathis. 2001. "The Dynamics of Violence in Civil War: Evaluating the Impact of Ethnicity." Unpublished manuscript.

2002. "The Logic of Violence in Civil War: Ethnic and Non-Ethnic Civil Wars." Unpublished manuscript.

Keohane, Robert, Gary King, and Sidney Verba. 1993. *Designing Social Inquiry: Scientific Inference in Qualitative Research.* Princeton University Press.

King, Jeremy. 2002. *Budweisers into Czechs and Germans: A Local History of Bohemian Politics, 1848–1948.* Princeton University Press.

Laitin, David D. 1986. *Hegemony and Culture: Politics and Religious Change among the Yoruba.* University of Chicago Press.

1999. "Language Conflict and Violence: Or, the Straw that Broke the Camel's Back." Working Paper 1999/137. Madrid: Instituto Juan March, Centro de Estudios Avanzados en Ciences Sociales.

Lijphart, Arend. 1977. *Democracy in Plural Societies: A Comparative Exploration.* New Haven: Yale University Press.

McGregor, R. S. 1993. *The Oxford Hindi–English Dictionary.* Oxford University Press.

Mill, John Stuart. [1861] 1991. *Considerations on Representative Government.* Buffalo, NY: Prometheus Books.

Noman, Omar. 1990. *Pakistan: A Political and Economic History since 1947.* London: Kegan Paul.

Ordeshook, Peter C., and Olga V. Shvetsova. 1994. "Ethnic Heterogeneity, District Magnitude and the Number of Parties." *American Journal of Political Science* 38 (1): 100–123.

Rabushka, Alvin, and Kenneth A. Shepsle. 1972. *Politics in Plural Societies: A Theory of Democratic Instability.* Columbus, OH: Charles E. Merrill.

Spilerman, Seymour. 1971. "The Causes of Racial Disturbances: Tests of an Explanation." *American Sociological Review* 36: 427–442.

Stark, Rodney. 2001. *One True God: The Historical Consequences of Monotheism.* Princeton University Press.

Varshney, Ashutosh. 2002. *Ethnic Conflict and Civil Life: Hindus and Muslims in India.* New Haven: Yale University Press.

Weber, Eugen. 1976. *Peasants into Frenchmen: The Modernization of Rural France 1870–1914.* Stanford University Press.

Weber, Max. 1978. *Economy and Society: An Outline of Interpretive Sociology*, vol. I, ed. Guenther Roth and Claus Wittich. Berkeley: University of California Press.

Wilkinson, Steven I. 2004. *Votes and Violence: Electoral Competition and Ethnic Riots in India.* Cambridge University Press.

Windmiller, Marshall. 1954. "Linguistic Regionalism in India." *Pacific Affairs* 27 (4): 291–318.

Wingfield, Nancy Merriwether. 1989. *Minority Politics in a Multi-National State: The German Social Democrats in Czechoslovakia.* Boulder, CO: East European Monographs.

12   Order in disorder: a micro-comparative study of genocidal dynamics in Rwanda

Scott Straus

Introduction[1]

The 1994 Rwandan genocide, in which between 500,000 and 800,000 civilians were killed in three months, is one of the most important cases of ethnic violence since the Cold War. In the past decade, much has been written about the genocide, and Rwanda has come to hold a key place in many university syllabi. Yet the analytic discussion about the dynamics driving the genocide remains fairly narrow. Most analysis focuses on the history of ethnic-identity formation in the country, on the planning for genocide by national-level hard-liners, and on the diffusion of racist propaganda, principally through the radio. The focus, in short, is on the top – on the genocide's "master narratives" and on the most powerful military and political elites in the country who ordered and executed the extermination campaign directed against Rwanda's Tutsi minority.[2]

What remains underexplored is genocide at the micro level. By this I mean a number of different dimensions of the violence, but principally the processes and dynamics that led the violence to spread throughout the country and that led so many Rwandans with no prior history of violence to take part in the killing. We know that hard-liners in the capital called on the population to destroy the "Tutsi enemy," but we do not know very well how and why that message succeeded – and with such alacrity. That gap in evidence and understanding would be important for any case of violence, but the lacuna is particularly significant in the Rwandan case

[1] This essay is drawn in large measure from chapter 3 of my book (Straus 2006). Parts of the chapter are reprinted with the generous permission of Cornell University Press. The chapter has received helpful comments from Scott Gehlbach, Stathis Kalyvas, David Leonard, Hanna Pitkin, Ben Valentino, Michael Watts, and Libby Wood. Research for this project has been generously supported with grants from the National Science Foundation, the Social Science Research Council, and the United States Institute for Peace. All views contained herein are my own.
[2] On the importance of distinguishing between "master" and "local" narratives, see Kalyvas (2003).

where the violence engendered large-scale civilian participation and took hold in almost all areas of the country, which is 95 percent rural. Thus, how and why did top-down orders to kill the Tutsis become a nationwide genocide?

The existing literature on the genocide indicates two possible models for how the violence spread to local areas. The first might be called a hierarchy model. In this model, the violence is presented as "efficient" and "machine"-like, and the planning for it is called "meticulous."[3] Rwanda's state plays a central role in this story, and the administration's centralized, even "totalitarian," character is emphasized.[4] The second, less common version of events might be called an outbreak model. In this model, the violence is presented as a chaotic "explosion" of hatred in the context of state "collapse."[5] The central images are of marauding, machete-wielding militias and racist radio broadcasts whipping a susceptible public into a fever of killing. Neither model is fully developed. Rather, these are two nascent images of how violence disseminated to rural areas in a literature that underreports on that question. A central task for advancing research on the Rwandan genocide is to develop a better understanding of how violence spread.

This essay takes one step in that direction. The essay reports findings from a micro-comparative study conducted in Rwanda in 2002. During the genocide, there was variation at the local level in terms of timing and mobilization. In some areas violence started immediately after the Rwandan president was assassinated on April 6, 1994. In other areas, violence started two weeks later. In some areas, local administrative officials launched the killing; in other areas, nonofficial local elites bypassed local authorities to lead the violence; and in still other areas, the military dominated. In one area under government control, genocidal violence did not occur. To examine variation systematically, I selected five communes (an administrative unit roughly equivalent to a town) that exhibited some differences in how the violence started.[6] In each commune, I interviewed

---

[3] For an example of violence as "efficient," see Power (2002, 334) and Melvern (2004). For an example of the "machine" metaphor, see Pottier (2002, 31).

[4] For an example of the claim of Rwanda's "totalitarian" state, see Scherrer (2002, 109); Melvern (2000, 24); Twagilimana (2003, 161); and Gourevitch (1998). For examples of references to how the genocide was "meticulously" or "scrupulously" planned, see African Rights (1995, xix) and Organization of African Unity (2000, 8).

[5] For examples where "collapse" is the central idea, see Zartman (1995, 4); journalists quoted in Power (2002, 355–356); and Diamond (2005, 328).

[6] Prior to and during the genocide, the commune was the most significant administrative unit in Rwanda. In 1994, there were 145 communes in the country; communes averaged 182 square kilometers and more than 50,000 inhabitants.

a cross-section of inhabitants who were present during the genocide: perpetrators, survivors, current and formal local officials, church leaders, bystanders, and anyone else who could describe how the violence started in their communities. In the main, the essay reports and analyzes the findings from this research.

The micro-comparative analysis reveals important dimensions of Rwanda's genocidal violence. First, perpetrators are not all alike; the micro-comparative analysis shows that the category of "perpetrators" needs disaggregating. Second, neither the hierarchy nor the outbreak model sufficiently describes the onset and progression of violence. The central dynamic, I argue, concerns securing power in a period of acute crisis. In this context, the order to kill the "Tutsi enemy" – the order emanating from the hard-liners who controlled the central state in this period – functioned as a basis for authority, one that local actors could use to gain or protect power. Once a coalition of local actors using this basis for their authority (that is, adopting a policy of killing) consolidated control, they in turn mass mobilized Hutu men, which resulted in rapid and participatory massacres.

Micro-comparative analysis

Giti

Giti commune is the one commune under government control where genocide did not take place in 1994.[7] However, there is no *a priori* reason why this should have been the case. The commune was proximate to the capital, which is where the genocide started in April 1994. The commune was supportive of the ruling MRND Party, whose leaders fomented the killing. Prior to the genocide, the burgomaster had distributed firearms as part of a civil defense program, and a system of nightly civilian defense patrols had been instituted – both of which, in other areas, are commonly interpreted as indicators of planning for genocide. The commune had domestic refugees or internally displaced persons (IDPs), and all radio stations could be heard in the commune – again, both of which are generally seen as triggers of the genocide. The commune had normal levels of education and population growth rates,

---

[7] Interviewed for this case study were the burgomaster during the genocide; the burgomaster immediately after the genocide; the current mayor of Rwamiko (the commune of Giti no longer existed in 2002 as it was fused with another and renamed); a former sub-prefect who is from Giti; the current police inspector; two survivors; two current *conseillers*; one former *conseiller*; a current school director; and one perpetrator chosen randomly (from neighboring Rutare commune).

according to former officials. The economy was peasant-based, without factories or any large-scale commercial centers. If anything, the commune was marginally poorer than most and entirely rural; in 1994, it had neither electricity nor phone lines.

At the same time, Giti had an above-average concentration of Tutsi – 25–30 percent of the population, according to the former burgomaster – and much intermarriage. Many inhabitants spoke of a culture of tolerance in the area. Indeed, although the ruling MRND was dominant, political-party contests prior to the genocide were, by all accounts, not violent and the burgomaster, Edouard Sebushumba, was considered a moderate. The commune was not home to armed youth from the *interahamwe* (a youth wing of the political party that later morphed in some areas into an armed militia). Many rural elites lived in Kigali, and some were associated with the moderate wing of the opposition MDR Party. However, moderate politicians, a lack of irregulars, and a high Tutsi concentration were not anomalous; those conditions existed in many areas throughout Rwanda, and especially in the south.

But there was no genocide in Giti. On April 6, when President Juvénal Habyarimana was killed, which was the trigger for the genocide, the burgomaster knew there would be trouble. "Fear took hold of me," Sebushumba told me in an interview. "I said that the consequences would be bad. A president who died! One expected something terrible." Almost immediately, he saw houses burning in a neighboring commune, but he decided he would try to prevent violence from breaking out in Giti. "One cannot fight for one's country by killing people," he said. Also true is that the burgomaster did not face a strong internal challenge to his authority. He said that he and other powerful local-level officials in the commune "spoke the same language" and a rival from the rural elite did not make an early bid for control. Still, "a tension in the population" existed, and some wanted violence to erupt, he said. On April 8, youth slaughtered cattle belonging to Tutsi – often an early act of violence, according to Sebushumba. But the burgomaster arrested them and multiplied nightly patrols to prevent further breakouts. Still, he said, "It was nearly finished. If things had continued, I could have lost control."

The critical change that stopped the violence from taking hold was the arrival of RPF rebel troops. Although the troops did not set foot in the Giti commune headquarters for another week, they arrived in neighboring Rutare commune the night of April 9, and knowledge of their presence was widespread in Giti on April 10. Just knowing the RPF troops had arrived and had stopped the violence in Rutare was enough to calm the situation and block a dynamic of violence from taking hold in Giti, according to several survivors and former officials.

As will be shown below, although the outcome in Giti was anomalous, its early dynamics were not. They resemble the dynamics in many other communes where local officials hesitated or resisted the violence immediately after President Habyarimana was killed. The critical difference that stopped a genocidal dynamic from taking hold in Giti was the RPF arrival, which calmed the situation. The rebels' arrival in the area was not apparently an attempt to stymie violence there. Rather, Giti and its surrounding areas lay on the route that the rebels took from their main northern positions and the capital Kigali. As the rebels advanced toward the capital, they entered the region where Giti is located, thus short-circuiting the dynamics that led to genocide. Elsewhere where the RPF did not arrive quickly, the dynamics were different. In these other locations – as we shall see – rather than moderates succeeding to hold power, as Sebushumba did in Giti, the balance shifted to those who adopted killing as a policy, thereby leading to massacres.

Gafunzo

Gafunzo is more developed than Giti: in 1994, the commune had one major and several small commercial centers, a major parish (Shangi), and electricity and phone lines.[8] Politically, the commune was divided between the ruling MRND Party and the opposition MDR Party. The commune did not have military-trained party militia, though both the MRND and MDR had active youth wings. According to the burgomaster, Tutsi were 12 percent of the population and intermarriages were common. Yet an estimated 6,000–6,800 Tutsi were killed in Gafunzo during the genocide.

The violence started immediately after Habyarimana's assassination. The first targets were opposition political-party leaders. On the night of April 7 and morning of April 8, the MDR and PL Party leaders in the commune, a Hutu and a Tutsi respectively, were attacked and killed. The early message to Hutu and Tutsi alike was that the violence was between parties. "We heard there was fighting between the MDR and the MRND," summarized one Hutu man not implicated in the killings. In short, inhabitants of the commune knew that violence had begun; were aware of a present danger; and in general were conscious of a

---

[8] Interviewed for this case study were five sentenced perpetrators, chosen randomly; the former burgomaster; a former *conseiller*; two former soldiers (both sentenced in prison, one refused to speak); the current mayor (in 2000 burgomasters were renamed mayors); a current *conseiller*; the commune head of IBUKA; a former *conseiller* and survivor; the former MDR commune president; three Hutu men who did not participate in the genocide; and two members of the clergy.

confused and unsettled national and local situation. But the early violence was not clearly anti-Tutsi. Indeed, survivors and perpetrators alike
report that in several sectors, Hutu *conseillers* (local government officials)
organized patrols to fight possible intruders. As in many other areas
throughout Rwanda during this period, the patrols were composed of
both Hutu and Tutsi men. But the climate changed rapidly. By April 9,
key members of the rural social elite as well as a posse of armed reservists
and former soldiers had taken control and were leading widespread violence against Tutsi. By April 10, they had initiated a genocidal dynamic
throughout the commune.

Interviewed in prison, the burgomaster, Charles Karorero, maintained
that, since his authority was already weakened in multipartyism and since
he was ill in early April, he had no control over what happened. He said
he called a security meeting for all *conseillers* and other rural social elite
on April 8, but only two *conseillers* came. Karorero also said he deployed
communal police and gendarmes to a church where Tutsi congregated,
but both forces ultimately were overpowered. (These claims were corroborated.) On balance, though, the burgomaster appears not to have
made a concerted effort either to prevent or to promote the violence, at
least publicly. As such, his role is best described as passive – a response
that allowed pro-violence forces to take control.

Judging from interviews with perpetrators, survivors, and Hutu non-
participants, two groups formed. The first was composed of rural social
elites, some of whom were family relations of the burgomaster. The
second group consisted of former soldiers and army reservists, in par-
ticular one named "Pima." As violence spread through the commune,
Tutsi fled to government offices, to Shangi, and to neighbors' homes.
But the attacks followed them there. According to several witnesses,
Pima led the first large-scale attack on April 11 at a sector headquarters.
Then on April 14, he led an even larger-scale attack on Shangi, which
Tutsi, police, and gendarmes posted there resisted with some success.
However, the final blow in the commune came from the outside. Further
south in the prefecture, Yusuf Munyankazi – an MRND stalwart and
militia leader who headed an agriculture association prior to the genocide – led attacks in several communes, according to numerous witnesses. On April 27, Yusuf – as he is known – arrived in Gafunzo with
several busloads of armed militias. According to several accounts,
Yusuf's team easily overwhelmed the resistance and decimated the Tutsi
population at the parish. Witnesses and survivors describe a scene of
unbelievable horror, of death all day and night.

In retrospect, the mobilization outline seems to be the following.
Although from a distance the pattern seemed to be administrative-led

genocide, closer analysis shows that the top officials' primary response was passivity. Some *conseillers* organized early resistance while others did not, but none emerged in my research as an active promoter of violence. The burgomaster was publicly absent for all of April. With the early attacks on the opposition, the leaders of those groups were absent too. Thus, the early days of violence appear to be characterized by an initial gap in social authority, confusion, and fear – a short rupture. That gap in turn opened what I would call a "space of opportunity," used by a pro-MRND rural social elite working with a nucleus of military-trained individuals. All this points to a pattern also seen elsewhere: a nucleus of rural social elite working with aggressive thugs who pressured others to participate. Once that basic configuration formed, genocidal violence was swift and devastating.

How different were the processes of violence in Giti and Gafunzo? Although the outcome differed immensely, the early processes had similarities. In Giti, the burgomaster acted in a timely fashion against the violence, while in Gafunzo he was passive. In both areas, the violence turned toward genocide several days after President Habyarimana was killed. In Giti, the burgomaster did not face a strong internal challenge from the rural social elite, but in Gafunzo a rural social elite moved quickly to occupy the space left publicly void by the turmoil and the burgomaster's inaction. In Giti, aggressive youth were at first controlled; in Gafunzo, the aggressive youth were soldiers and reservists who dominated others. In Giti, the RPF arrived before the dynamic could change. In Gafunzo, the violence went unchecked until late April when a leading source of regionwide violence reinforced it. But the key difference in early dynamics is the degree of contestation for social control. In Giti, the burgomaster chose to resist violence, and he had effective control. In Gafunzo, the burgomaster chose passivity, but several poles of competing social power existed. The opposition fled, and the pro-regime forces – some aligned with the burgomaster – took center stage and promoted genocide.

Kayove

Kayove is about 50 miles north of Gafunzo is the hilly lakeside commune of Kayove, in Gisenyi Prefecture.[9] Rich in coffee and strongly

---

[9] Those interviewed for this case study include ten confessed sentenced perpetrators chosen randomly; a former *conseiller* accused of genocide; a former vice-president of the *interahamwe*; and four alleged aggressive killers (in prison); the current mayor (returnee); the current head of IBUKA for the commune and current district administrator (survivor); a businessman (survivor); a current *conseiller* (survivor); the former MRND

supportive of President Habyarimana, Kayove had a smaller concentration of Tutsi than Giti or Gafunzo, estimated at around 10 percent. The reconstruction of early genocidal dynamics in Kayove is distinguished by several remarkable sources. First, there are letters from former *conseillers* written to the burgomaster during the genocide. Second, the MRND Party leadership in Kayove is not implicated in the genocide – a very rare occurrence in Rwanda – and some can be interviewed. And third, one of the most active genocide leaders is open and articulate about what he did and why, and I interviewed him over the course of three days. Overall, the pattern of mobilization in Kayove appears to be a rural social elite, working with party and other aggressive youth, initiating a genocidal uprising against Tutsi and intimidating anyone who tried to stop them. The burgomaster's role is disputed. Some claim he orchestrated all that happened from behind the scenes, but closer examination suggests he took a position of tacit acceptance.

By all accounts, the violence started on April 7 in numerous sectors and spread to all but one by April 8. In the holdout sector, Hutu and Tutsi, with the *conseiller*'s encouragement, mounted a joint defense against attacks from other sectors. They succeeded until April 10, when the burgomaster came and, according to two witnesses, claimed he could do nothing to halt the violence. In a different sector, the burgomaster claimed the same. According to the former MRND secretary:

At 10 am on the 7 I saw a band of people … They had killed three people at the school … I went to see the burgomaster about the situation. I met him near the school. He had a vehicle. There were two gendarmes and two communal police with him. I told him the situation. He said, "What can we do? I can do nothing." And the fighting continued … The *interahamwe* passed everywhere. If they found you, no matter whom they found, they took you by force. They were crazy in the head.

By this account and others, the burgomaster's main public course of action was to claim powerlessness. In so doing, the burgomaster tacitly accepted the attacks. However, judging from perpetrator testimony and from the *conseiller* letters, the officials' authority was, in fact, violently challenged. Let us start with the key perpetrator mentioned earlier, a former national ballet dancer from a well-connected family:

It was Wednesday in the night [of April 6]. A veterinarian, a neighbor, came to tell me that he just heard the radio that Habyarimana had been shot. Me, in my

president; the former commune accountant now head of Gacaca; the commune's burgomaster from 1982 to 1993 (the burgomaster during the genocide was still in Congo when I did field research); a *conseiller* during the genocide not accused of genocide; a former teacher; and several members of the clergy.

mind I understood the Tutsis were responsible. I was angry, and I said to myself, "It is true. The Tutsis are mean." And I said everything that people say about them is true. I went to the cabaret [a local bar]. I found that the peasants had set up roadblocks. It was then they said, "No Tutsi can remain in our sector." That is what they decided at this meeting at this roadblock; it was like a meeting; there were a lot of people. Those they found this day they did not kill. It was the 7. The 8, we heard that a woman had been killed; we heard in the other sectors people were being killed. So we too attacked those who were our neighbors.

Over the next seven days, he said he led a group ranging between 300 and 500 people that killed all but one of the 17 Tutsis in the sector and 1 Hutu. Describing himself as "a terrorist," he said only 5 men did the actual killing, including a former soldier and a former prisoner who had been released. Asked about those who did not participate, he cited an example:

Our *conseiller* refused to help us, saying that he could not tolerate people being killed. So we went to look to kill him. We could not find him ... The *conseiller* had fled to the burgomaster. When the burgomaster brought him with the gendarmes, we threw rocks at the vehicle.

When interviewed, the *conseiller* in question corroborated this account, describing how he repeatedly fled and hid during the course of the genocide.

The dynamic here is that the rural elite and peasants took control; they initiated violence against Tutsis; they overpowered local officials; they threatened to kill anyone who resisted. The same pattern is evident in other sectors. Several *conseillers* wrote to the burgomaster during the genocide, pleading for help. In one sector, the *conseiller* described how an army sergeant, a reservist, and two state agents, one of whom was armed, led an attack on April 7. The attack killed the man of the household, but the survivors fled to the *conseiller*'s home. Writing on April 8, the *conseiller* pleaded for help:

I gave them money, but they would not leave me alone. They searched the whole house and found there [name withheld] and certain members of his family. They took them by force and beat them with gun butts. Mr. Burgomaster, I am asking you to help us quickly because if this continues, no one will remain. I am weakened, I am afraid.

In retrospect, the pattern of mobilization in Kayove was not substantially different from those in the communes examined above. In all, President Habyarimana's death and the onset of violence in the capital Kigali and the commune environs unsettled existing power relationships and created a space of opportunity. When those heeding the call to kill Tutsis controlled the balance of power, genocidal violence began immediately. In Kayove, that process happened extremely rapidly, but what particularly distinguishes the commune is that MRND Party leaders and officials held the moderate position. Unthreatened by the opposition, MRND Party leaders and officials did not immediately see a need to use violence in order to secure their positions. The call to violence – the new genocidal order – thus resonated most strongly with the rural social elite, members of whom quickly mobilized and achieved dominance. Where the MRND faced a serious challenge – as in Gafunzo – party leaders and officials seized on violence to protect their authority. In Kayove, the formal party challenge did not exist, so the MRND authorities were slow to mobilize, letting the call to violence fall to an insurgent rural social elite. This dynamic again points to the way in which power was in play during this period, and how promoting violence was a means by which to establish power in an unstable environment.

Kanzenze

Outwardly, the genocidal dynamic in Kanzenze looks quite different from those in the other communes examined because of the military's role there, but on closer inspection, as will be shown, the similarities are greater than the differences.[10] Kanzenze is an hour's drive southeast of Kigali. Numerous sources report a nearly equal Hutu/Tutsi ratio in the commune prior to the genocide. Politically, the MRND controlled the leading administrative posts in the commune, but the opposition PL and MDR political parties had substantial support. The key factor that distinguishes this commune from others is the regional presence of a large military camp, called Gako.

Both perpetrators and survivors agree that the first killing occurred on the night of April 8, when soldiers from Gako killed a Tutsi businessman and threatened other rural Tutsi elites. Before then and especially in the two days following, the climate in the commune was tense. The insecurity and violence prompted some Tutsi civilians to flee to at least two major hilltops in the commune, Kayumba and Rebeho. Both survivors and perpetrators report skirmishes between these groups and Hutu in the vicinity. The change came on April 10 and 11, and all accounts assign a decisive role to the Gako soldiers. The existing evidence

[10] Those interviewed for this case study include the former assistant burgomaster, the former *interahamwe* president, a reservist, two other perpetrators in prison, the current mayor, two other current commune authorities, IBUKA head in the commune (who also is a communal authority), a current councilor (also a survivor), four Tutsi survivors, and a nonparticipating Hutu.

suggests that the local military camp commander initiated the attacks, whether independently, on orders from Kigali or from local officials – or some combination thereof.

The discussion below benefits from the testimony of two active killers in the commune, interviewed separately. The first is an army reservist and activist from the hard-liner CDR Party; the second is an *inter-ahamwe*.[11] Both admit to, and are widely credited with, being among the foremost attackers in the commune. According to the reservist, the order to kill Tutsi civilians came from officers in the camp on April 10:

> The lieutenant gave an order for revenge. We had to kill the enemy. The Tutsis had killed the president. We had to kill the Tutsis.

In the interview, the reservist emphasized that the entire ethnic group – all its members – were defined as the enemy. The reservist said that the military strategy was to contact civilian officials, who in turn would mobilize the Hutu population. Soldiers considered the local population "intelligence," he said, meaning they used civilians to find out where Tutsi were located. Numerous perpetrators from the communes surrounding the camp report a similar process, in which soldiers arrived and either summoned local authorities to mobilize the population or did so themselves.

The *interahamwe* perpetrator gave a slightly different, but not inconsistent account. He said he was summoned to a meeting at the commune offices on April 10. In the meeting, he said, a military general from Kigali took the floor and said that, in response to the resumption of hostilities and the president's assassination, the Tutsis had been declared the enemy. According to the *interahamwe*, the general ordered the commune authorities to participate in the annihilation of the enemy. A regional official was there, as was the burgomaster. Both, according to the perpetrator, reiterated the message. The logic, he said, was:

> The enemy attacked the country. They were *Inkotanyi* [a synonym for the RPF rebels]. They said we had to defend ourselves. If not, they could kill us.

Everyone understood this to mean that Tutsis had to be killed, the *interahamwe* perpetrator said. After the meeting concluded, the burgomaster ordered a local businessman to hand out machetes to the local youth; the perpetrator himself got one, he said. Violence started the next day.

On April 11, perpetrators, bystanders, and survivors all report, busloads of soldiers descended on Kanzenze. Working in conjunction with

[11] The CDR was a minority, but extremist party that was openly racist against Tutsi.

interahamwe and other Hutu men, the soldiers led an attack on Kayumba, the first of a series of large-scale attacks in the commune. Tutsi surviving this attack and others fled to churches, the commune offices, and a cultural center. Attacks against these gathering points and another place followed through April 16, all with significant military involvement. Each attack resulted in a major massacre, similar to the one attributed to Yusuf in Gafunzo described above.

Prior to the genocide, the burgomaster, Bernard Gatanazi, was considered by most to be a moderate. But several perpetrators and survivors report Gatanazi's direct, active encouragement of the violence. One survivor recalled a change in the burgomaster's behavior after he returned from a meeting in Kigali on April 7: "Before, he was a friend," he said. "But Thursday, after his return, he was very angry. He wouldn't talk to you." But Gatanazi was not alone. Perpetrators and survivors alike claim that the CDR commune president (a businessman), the MDR president (a businessman), and the MRND president (the commune's agricultural officer) all encouraged the violence. The lone Hutu elite political-party member who opposed the genocide, it appears, was the opposition PSD Party leader. A Hutu, he was killed along with his Tutsi wife, according to two survivors. PL supporters – generally Tutsi – also were targeted.

In retrospect, the onset dynamics in Kanzenze are not a major departure from the other communes analyzed so far. In the first three days, fear and confusion prevailed. Tutsi fled and some Hutu attacked. However, the course of violence was not yet set. The tipping point came on April 10 with the military's aggressive entry into the civilian arena. The military's entry into the arena appears to have had several effects. For the burgomaster, whose participation was directly demanded, a passive response was no longer possible. If he had opposed, he would have lost power and probably his life. If he accepted, he retained his position. For the other rural elite, the military backing of civilian authorities left little opportunity for political maneuver or a local power struggle. In short, the military set the dynamics within the commune, as it did in other locations throughout the country. Where soldiers entered into the civilian arena and promoted violence against the "Tutsi enemy," that entry swiftly determined the balance in favor of genocide.

Musambira

Outwardly, again, the pattern of genocidal violence in Musambira commune looks different, and the violence started later in the commune, as it did throughout southern Rwanda.[12] But closer inspection shows that while the shift to widespread genocidal violence took longer to materialize – for reasons that will be explored below – the pattern of violence was similar to what occurred elsewhere.

Musambira is in Gitarama Prefecture, southwest of Kigali, and strongly supportive of the opposition MDR Party. Although precise details about the preexisting ethnic population are not available, the commune had a sizable Tutsi population and much intermarriage – on a scale comparable to Giti. Not apparently particularly wealthy, Musambira had a commercial center on a par with the main centers in Kayove and Gafunzo, though larger than Giti's and marginally smaller than Kanzenze's. About a year prior to the genocide, a new burgomaster was elected: Justin Nyandwi, a young former teacher from the moderate wing of the MDR Party.

By all accounts – from perpetrators, survivors, Hutu bystanders, and current authorities – Nyandwi mobilized people to prevent violence from spreading to the commune in the first days after President Habyarimana's death. Nyandwi himself said:

People knew there were killings in Kigali. With our prefect, we took the decision to thwart the killings, to repulse them, and each commune organized to do this.

In the first week, the strategy worked for Musambira. Even so, Nyandwi described a harrowing experience when he traveled to Kigali.

On the 10th, a friend came to my place. He told me his brothers were in danger. I thought I should do something to save them. I went to Kigali, but I was arrested at a roadblock ... They told me a lot of things: that I was against the *interahamwe*, that I had a conflict with the president of MRND. They decided to kill me and my three policemen.

Nyandwi and his companions were brought to a pit where the dead were thrown, the former burgomaster told me. He described a scene of horrific violence and said he expected to die. But, he said, a police commander there intervened; the commander recommended calling Gitarama to verify if Nyandwi really was the burgomaster of Musambira (he had been accused of being an RPF infiltrator). That was done, and the commander released the Musambira team the following day. On his way back, Nyandwi stopped to see the burgomaster of Runda, a friend, to inform him of what had happened. However, Nyandwi said his colleague's authority had been compromised. In the early days, the Runda burgomaster

---

[12] Those interviewed for this story include four perpetrators selected randomly, the former burgomaster, the former sub-prefect (both sentenced prisoners), a detainee accused of being an active participant, the current mayor, two current *conseillers*, the current IBUKA head in the commune, and the commune's elected Gacaca president.

had imprisoned people who had started killing. But, Nyandwi said, a militia leader had come from Kigali and forcibly released the detainees. An even more devastating event, he said, occurred the following week:

I continued to struggle ... The week of the 11th, there were *interahamwe* incursions. There was also a very serious incident for me. The population killed an *interahamwe* and that was very expensive for me. On RTLM [a private radio station broadly supportive of the national-level hard-liners], it was said I was killing *interahamwe* and helping Tutsis. That was repeated many times. It was the 14th. The population [in the commune] began to be afraid, calling a bur-gomaster an enemy! ... It was grave for me. The population helped me, but the police began to be scared. They asked, "What will we do?" I tried to calm them. We continued all the same, up until the 20th.[13]

In fact, the balance of power had begun to shift slightly earlier. Three main changes occurred. First, on the 18th, a meeting was held with the other burgomasters in Gitarama, with the prefect, and with the prime minister, in which the latter threatened to replace burgomasters who resisted the violence.[14] In Mugina, a neighboring commune, the bur-gomaster who had opposed the violence was killed that day or the fol-lowing one.[15] Second, soldiers arrived in Musambira on the 19th, killed Tutsis, and ordered peasants to continue killing. And third, the dynamic in neighboring Taba commune changed.

Regarding the soldiers' arrival, three interviewed witnesses said sol-diers stopped on the main road and threatened to kill Hutus who did not take part in killing Tutsis. One perpetrator said:

I was on the road. A soldier came. He said, "Others have killed the Tutsis and you, you are like that [doing nothing]! If you don't kill them, I will begin on one side without leaving a house – I will kill everyone" ... The war had not yet started in Musambira ... I was with delinquents. They profited by taking cows and looting.

As for Taba, the burgomaster there, Jean-Paul Akayesu, apparently changed his position on April 19 (see below). On that date, according to several sources, Akayesu entered Musambira looking for someone who supposedly was plotting to kill him. The incursion generated insecurity in Musambira, and Tutsi also began fleeing from Taba to

[13] Interviews with others in the commune have corroborated key elements of this story: that Nyandwi led resistance against killing; that there were incursions; that an attacker (here called an *interahamwe*) was killed; and that Nyandwi was denounced on RTLM. Given the private nature of what happened to Nyandwi in Kigali, I have not been able to corroborate this aspect of the story. However, nothing I have heard calls it into question.
[14] See International Criminal Tribunal for Rwanda (ICTR), "The Prosecutor versus Jean-Paul Akayesu Case No. ICTR-96-4-T," 32. www.un.org/ictr/english/judgements/akayesu.html.
[15] As footnote 14 and also corroborated in the interview with Nyandwi.

Musambira. Nyandwi tried to calm the situation on the 20th, he told me, but when he returned, his wife told him men dressed in military uniform were looking for him. Having been threatened already and with his control already tenuous, Nyandwi concluded that soldiers had come to kill him. He decided to flee, first to the prefect's house and from there to others' homes.[16]

Immediately after Nyandwi fled, by all accounts, a Musambira native on the MRND national committee, Abdulraham Iyakaremye, took control of the commune. Prior to the genocide, Abdulraham was a director of an agricultural association. After taking control, Abdulraham established a "security crisis committee" that had representatives in every sector. According to several accounts, the representatives were ordered to mobilize the population for nightly patrols, which became attacks on Tutsi. At first, only men were targeted; the killing of women was ordered later. Several Hutu – perpetrators and nonperpetrators – said the pressure to participate was intense.

In retrospect, the main difference in Musambira was that the antiviolence forces remained active longer than in the other areas examined. The question is, why? The answer seems to lie in the politics of the area. By and large, the peasants, the rural social elite, the administrative officials, and the prefectural authorities were all solidly in the opposition. On April 7 in Kigali, the first attacks were against MDR politicians from the south, and those promoting the violence did so on behalf of Habyarimana and the MRND. Thus, the call to violence did not resonate in Musambira – at first. Nyandwi did not face a strong local challenger (Abdulraham appears not to have been a resident in the commune prior to April 20); the burgomaster did not face initial military pressure or an initial attack from a neighboring commune. Nyandwi was thus able to remain in effective control and maintain a plurality of force against violence. However, his authority was challenged at the national level – the prime minister threatened those who resisted the violence; soldiers invaded the commune; and violence began in neighboring Taba. The final blow was the arrival of soldiers who sought him out. With these, the balance of power tipped; the burgomaster gave up; and the genocide began.

The dynamics in neighboring Taba commune make for an instructive comparison.[17] The burgomaster, Akayesu, was the first convicted

---

[16] Current authorities, survivors, and perpetrators corroborated this story.

[17] Although I interviewed several perpetrators from Taba, the key source of information for the following discussion comes from a decision from the International Criminal Tribunal for Rwanda that found Akayesu, Taba's burgomaster, guilty of genocide.

perpetrator at the International Criminal Tribunal for Rwanda (ICTR); therefore there is a well-documented public record of what happened in Taba. Akayesu's case resembles Musambira's with only one key difference. Like Musambira, Taba was an MDR stronghold, and until April 18, by all accounts, Akayesu tried to prevent violence.[18] As in other places, Tutsi conducted night patrols with Hutu until April 18, and a concerted attempt was made to ward off incursions.[19] But on April 18, according to numerous witnesses and in the opinion of the ICTR chamber, a "marked change" occurred.[20] According to the ICTR's findings, Akayesu switched to cooperating with the militia and adopted a pro-genocide position. In the words of the chamber, Akayesu "called on the population to unite and eliminate the sole enemy: accomplices of the *Inkotanyi*."[21] Widespread violence started immediately.

What prompted the switch? Akayesu claims variously that he was "overwhelmed," that he lost control, and that he was coerced.[22] But closer inspection suggests that as the balance shifted toward violence at a certain point Akayesu chose to adapt, to switch his own position. Up until April 18, as in Musambira, Taba faced incursions and influxes of Tutsis fleeing from elsewhere in the country. These probably weakened his authority, but Akayesu had the support of prefectural authorities and seemingly did not face a strong rural elite challenge. But on April 18, two external conditions changed. First, the prime minister threatened noncompliant burgomasters, as seen above. Second, violence became widespread on April 18 in another neighboring commune, Runda.[23] Moreover, pro-violence forces appear to have arrived from Kigali. On April 19 – after resisting violence – Akayesu appeared before a crowd beside an *interahamwe* waving a document given to him that he said showed how the RPF and local accomplices were plotting to kill Hutu and seize power.[24] In short, the pattern is similar to elsewhere: once the balance of power shifted toward the violence position, the burgomaster faced a new choice: switch, remain passive, or flee. Musambira's burgomaster fled; Mugina's was killed; Akayesu switched.

---

[18] See ICTR, "The Prosecutor versus Jean-Paul Akayesu," 31, 32, 37 (on Akayesu's attempts to prevent violence) and 35 (on MDR's strength).

[19] On trying to stop incursions, see ICTR, "The Prosecutor versus Jean-Paul Akayesu," 31; on Hutu and Tutsi patrols, see 51.

[20] ICTR, "The Prosecutor versus Jean-Paul Akayesu," 31.

[21] ICTR, "The Prosecutor versus Jean-Paul Akayesu," 52.

[22] See ICTR, "The Prosecutor versus Jean-Paul Akayesu," 32, 51.

[23] ICTR, "The Prosecutor versus Jean-Paul Akayesu," 36.

[24] ICTR, "The Prosecutor versus Jean-Paul Akayesu," 43, 51.

Dynamics of violence

The micro-comparative study reveals important but often over-looked dimensions of the violence during the genocide. First, the micro-comparative study shows that the category of "perpetrators" should be disaggregated at the local level. At the top were influential rural elites who organized, legitimized, and directed the killing within their communes. The composition of rural elites varied across locations, but they were primarily administrative officials and well-educated Rwandans with high social status in their locations. Next were a relatively small group of aggressive and often young men – political-party youths, unemployed youths, "delinquents," army reservists, former soldiers, and policemen. These aggressive men killed and, working with the rural elite, mobilized as many adult Hutu males as possible to join the attacks. They were the elites' principal enforcers. Finally, there was a large group of mostly male civilians, who ultimately made up the largest portion of attackers – the rural elite and aggressive young men recruited them to join the killing. In short, the micro-comparative study helps us see the dynamics among perpetrators.

Second, the micro-comparative study reveals significant intra-ethnic competition for power and some Hutu resistance to anti-Tutsi violence. The Hutu response to the onset of genocide was not uniform. The period was one of confusion, uncertainty, and fear after a presidential assassination and during a civil war. That disorder unsettled existing power structures and created an opening whereby rural social elites could jockey for control. In some areas – as in Musambira and in Giti – rural elites rallied their supporters to prevent attacks from other Hutus outside their commune. In other areas – as in Kayove – a forceful alliance of Hutus directly launched attacks on Tutsi and bypassed their local authorities. The micro-comparative study shows how power was in play in this period: *intra-Hutu* struggles for power were a central dynamic as a precursor to the violence against Tutsis.

Third and crucially, the micro-comparative study provides a different model of how violence spread than exists in the current literature. The violence neither flowed "efficiently" from the center to the periphery through established administrative hierarchies. Nor did the violence "explode" chaotically.

On the one hand, crisis and disorder unsettled existing power structures in this period. Prior to April 1994, there had been a period of political change and regime transition in Rwanda. The country was undergoing a two-twin process of civil war and the end of one-party rule. But the catalyst of dramatic change in April 1994 was President

Habyarimana's assassination, the subsequent killing of Hutu political leaders in Kigali, and the renewed onset of civil war, which had been nominally suspended until the president's assassination. These processes destabilized the country – they produced a climate of crisis, confusion, and fear – and in turn created a "space of opportunity" at the local level, as described above. Order had been ruptured, and power was indeterminately held. As such, an opportunity existed for influential actors at the local level to take charge, to establish control in a period of wartime disorder.

On the other hand, the hard-liners in the capital tied to the ruling party declared war on the "Tutsi enemy." They did so almost immediately after President Habyarimana's assassination. Their call to war against Tutsis galvanized local actors throughout the country, who in turn promoted violence in the name of the state and the law. In this way, genocidal killing became a means by which to claim or defend power. The micro-comparative study shows that wartime disorder and competition for power were integral to why local elites and aggressive young men adopted the call to kill Tutsis as their own. In the context of an acute emergency, with old institutions of authority already compromised and with war on the horizon, killing Tutsis became a means by which to claim or defend power. Killing Tutsis became a basis of authority, and, moreover, the most powerful institutions in the country, the military and the national government, appeared to back this genocidal course of action.

This dynamic of order and disorder helps explain the onset variation at the local level. In some areas, the balance of power lay with the pro-violence position: when the call from the top rang out, there was a plurality of force on the ground ready to comply. These areas tended to be areas where the hard-liners within the MRND had strong support. In Kayove, for example, the strong pro-violence position came from the rural elite, the aggressive thugs, and others in the commune. In Kanzenze, however, the strong pro-violence position came from the local military. In these areas, the consolidation of power by pro-violence forces was swift, and violence quickly became the new basis of order, "the law" as perpetrators often recalled. A dichotomous, us-or-them logic based on alliance to the genocidal program followed. All Hutu men were pressured to participate, while all Tutsi were targeted for murder. The local authorities, in particular the burgomaster, either were part of the coalition launching the violence or remained passive. In the latter case, key members within the rural elite would move in to assume control.

However, in other areas, the balance lay initially with the anti-violence position or was unclear. The areas initially opposing the violence tended to be areas of strong opposition support or areas with moderate political leaders where the calls to violence by the MRND hard-liners who controlled the central government found little resonance. Here, burgomasters responded by trying to prevent a breakout of violence or by remaining passive, as they did in Giti, Musambira, and Taba. However, the balance shifted over time. The change could come from a military or militia incursion, an invasion from a neighboring commune, or direct pressure from prefectural or national authorities. But the change also could be subtler: houses could burn on a neighboring hill, refugees could flee into the community, or a rival could begin consolidating power. At this stage, violence looked inevitable. Burgomasters in turn faced a second choice: switch to a pro-violence position, remain passive, or flee. Once the pro-violence position was consolidated, mass mobilization of Hutu and mass violence against Tutsi swiftly followed.

More undoubtedly can be said about the micro-comparative evidence. But at a minimum, the study indicates a set of nested dynamics that ultimately led to violence starting throughout the country. The critical dynamics that led to the onset of genocide were not about "meticulous planning" at the local level. The violence did not spread efficiently or always through established administrative hierarchies. Nor was the violence chaotic – those who promoted the violence acted in the name of authority and the law. Nor, for that matter, is ethnicity a sufficient explanation for why so many Rwandans took part in the killing. Inter-ethnic enmity and racist indoctrination do not appear to have prompted individuals to join the killing campaign. Rather, the foremost dynamic concerned individuals' relations to power in a wartime, emergency period. In the period after the presidential assassination, national leaders declared war on the Tutsi enemy; in so doing, killing Tutsi became the new "law" – a new basis for authority. Such a call in turn triggered an unfolding set of choices for individuals at the local level. When the new "law" finally succeeded in gaining enough adherents to become the dominant position in particular communities, individuals had to arrange accordingly. Many faced a credible choice between perceived in-group sanction and out-group violence. Many chose the latter – but the dynamics driving that choice were less about hatred and dehumanizing indoctrination and more about insecurity, relationships to power, and, in some cases, intra-ethnic coercion.

The micro-comparative study on its own does not resolve how and why genocide happened in Rwanda. But the study helps peer into what is often a black box – the processes and dynamics that led to violence starting at the local level. The study reveals the importance of a play between order and disorder, between a national-level policy of killing and a period of war and acute uncertainty. These elements of order and disorder were essential to why genocidal violence spread so thoroughly and so swiftly throughout the country.

REFERENCES

African Rights. 1995. *Rwanda: Death, Despair, and Defiance*, 2nd edn. London: African Rights.
Diamond, Jared. 2005. *Collapse: How Societies Choose to Fail or Succeed.* New York: Viking.
Gourevitch, Philip. 1998. *We Wish to Inform You that Tomorrow You Will Be Killed with Your Families.* New York: Picador.
Kalyvas, Stathis. 2003. "The Ontology of Political Violence." *Perspectives on Politics* 1 (3): 475–494.
Melvern, Linda. 2000. *A People Betrayed: The Role of the West in Rwanda's Genocide.* London: Zed Books.
2004. *Conspiracy to Murder: The Rwandan Genocide.* London: Verso.
Organization of African Unity. 2000. *Rwanda: The Preventable Genocide: Special Report of International Panel of Eminent Personalities to Investigate the 1994 Genocide in Rwanda.* www.africa-union.org/Offical_documents/reports/Report_rowanda_genocide.pdf.
Pottier, Johan. 2002. *Re-Imagining Rwanda: Conflict, Survival and Disinformation in the Late Twentieth Century.* Cambridge University Press.
Power, Samantha. 2002. *"A Problem from Hell": America and the Age of Genocide.* New York: Public Affairs.
Scherrer, Christian. 2002. *Genocide and Crisis in Central Africa: Conflict Roots, Mass Violence, and Regional War.* Westport, CT: Praeger Publishers.
Straus, Scott. 2006. *The Order of Genocide: Race, Power, and War in Rwanda.* Ithaca, NY: Cornell University Press.
Twagilimana, Aimable. 2003. *The Debris of Ham: Ethnicity, Regionalism, and the 1994 Rwandan Genocide.* Lanham: University Press of America.
Zartman, I. William. 1995. "Introduction: Posing the Problem of State Collapse." In *Collapsed States: The Disintegration and Restoration of Legitimate Authority*, ed. I. William Zartman. Boulder, CO: Lynne Rienner.

13 Sexual violence during war: toward an understanding of variation

Elisabeth Jean Wood

While sexual violence occurs in all wars, its extent varies dramatically. During the conflict in Bosnia-Herzegovina, the sexual abuse of Bosnian Muslim women by Bosnian Serb forces was so systematic and widespread that it comprised a crime against humanity under international law. In Rwanda, the widespread rape of Tutsi women comprised a form of genocide, according to the International Criminal Tribunal for Rwanda. Yet sexual violence in some conflicts is remarkably limited despite other violence against civilians. Even in some cases of ethnic conflict, sexual violence is limited; the conflicts in Israel/Palestine and Sri Lanka are examples. Some armed groups, such as the Salvadoran and Sri Lankan insurgencies, appear to effectively prohibit their combatants engaging in sexual violence against civilians.

The form of sexual violence varies as well. In some conflicts, it takes the form of sexual slavery; in others, state agents engage in sexualized torture of persons suspected of collaborating with insurgents; in others, combatants target women of particular groups during ethnic or political cleansing; in still others, individuals engage in it opportunistically; and in some conflicts, all or nearly all forms occur. In some wars, women belonging to particular groups are targeted; in others, the attacks are much less discriminate. In some wars, only females are targeted; in others, males are as well. Some acts of wartime sexual violence are committed by individuals; many are committed by groups. Some acts occur in private settings; many are public, in front of family or community members.

I am grateful for research support from the Yale University MacMillan Center for International and Area Studies and the Santa Fe Institute, and for research assistance from Margaret Alexander, Laia Balcells, Karisa Cloward, Kade Finnoff, Amelia Hoover, Michele Leiby, Amara Levy-Moore, Meghan Lynch, Abbey Steele, and Tim Taylor. I also thank the many people who commented on earlier versions, particularly Jeffrey Burds, Christian Davenport, Anna Grzymala-Busse, Amelia Hoover, Magali Sarfatti Larson, Meghan Lynch, Daniel Posner, David Plotke, Michael Ross, Jessica Stanton, and Jeremy Weinstein. This essay draws on an earlier essay, which was published in *Politics and Society* 34 (3) (2006): 307–341.

In some settings, wartime sexual violence appears to magnify existing cultural practices; in others, patterns of sexual violence appear to be innovations. In some conflicts, the pattern of sexual violence is symmetric, with all parties to the war engaging in sexual violence to roughly the same extent. In other conflicts, it is very asymmetric as one armed group does not respond in kind to sexual violence by the other party. Sexual violence often increases over the course of the conflict; in some conflicts, it decreases.

Sexual violence varies in extent and form among civil wars as well as interstate wars, among ethnic wars as well as nonethnic, and among secessionist conflicts (Wood 2006). Despite the challenges to gathering data on this sensitive topic, the variation does not appear to be a product of inadequately reported violence: there are well-documented cases at the low end of the spectrum of sexual violence as well as the high end. The variation has not been adequately explained in the literature. Initial works emphasized the ubiquity of sexual violence, with little attention to variation (Brownmiller 1975; Enloe 1983). Subsequent literature focused on sexual violence in Bosnia-Herzegovina and Rwanda, as human rights advocates and legal scholars sought to hold perpetrators of widespread sexual violence responsible under international law. This project joins recent works that analyze wartime sexual violence more comparatively (Enloe 2000; Sharlach 2000; 2001; Green 2004; Bloom [no date]; and Leiby [in press]), but significantly deepens the analysis by including cases where sexual violence is anomalously low or sharply asymmetric.

Recognizing the variation in the frequency and form of wartime sexual violence has important policy implications. In particular, if there are armed groups that do not engage in sexual violence despite other forms of violence against civilians, then rape is not inevitable in war as is sometimes claimed, and we have stronger grounds for holding responsible those armed groups that do engage in sexual violence. Understanding the determinants of the variation in sexual violence may help those UN officials, members of nongovernmental organizations, government, military, and insurgent leaders who seek to limit sexual violence and other violations of the laws of war.

In accordance with recent international law, by *rape* I mean the penetration of the anus or vagina with any object or body part or of any body part of the victim or perpetrator's body with a sexual organ, by force or by threat of force or coercion, or by taking advantage of a coercive environment, or against a person incapable of giving genuine consent (ICC 2000, Article 8(2) (e) (vi)-1). Thus rape can occur against men as well as women. *Sexual violence* is a broader category that includes rape, nonpenetrating sexual assault, mutilation, sexual slavery, enforced prostitution, enforced sterilization, and forced pregnancy. (Sexual violence differs from the broader category of gender violence in that the latter includes violence that occurs because of the victim's gender without necessarily including sexual contact.)

Focusing on sexual violence against civilians by combatants, I first summarize patterns of variation in form and extent across several war settings. In particular, I document the absence of sexual violence in some conflicts and on the part of some groups. After discussing the methodological challenges to gathering and analyzing sexual violence data, I argue that the subject merits further comparative analysis because sufficiently large variation occurs across well-documented cases. I then assess whether the causal mechanisms identified in the literature (often implicitly) explain the variation. In the conclusion, I sketch an analytical framework for the study of sexual violence as part of armed groups' repertoires of violence and suggest several avenues of research that should contribute to scholarly understanding of sexual and other forms of violence.

Selected cases contrasting high, low, and asymmetric prevalence of sexual violence

In this section, I describe the pattern of sexual violence in several wars, including interstate as well as civil wars, ethnic as well as nonethnic conflicts, and wars in which sexual violence was very prevalent and where it was not. I begin by discussing cases in which the prevalence of sexual violence was high before turning to cases where it was low.

World War II

As the Soviet army moved westward onto German territory in early 1945, large numbers of women were raped (Naimark 1995, 69–140). While the earlier Soviet offensives in Romania and Hungary had seen widespread rape of civilian women (particularly after the siege of Budapest), the practice intensified as the army moved into East Prussia and Silesia. Although women of various ethnicities were raped in the course of looting of villages and cities, German women were particularly targeted. In German villages in East Prussia, "it was not untypical for Soviet troops to rape every female over the age of twelve or thirteen" (Naimark 1995, 72; see also 74). Naimark notes the contrast between the "exemplary" behavior of Soviet troops in Bulgaria and the generally better behavior toward Polish and other Slavs with the looting and rape that occurred in Germany and Hungary, both non-Slavic groups (1995, 106–107).

As the Soviet army moved westward toward Germany, propaganda posted and distributed along the way as well as official military orders encouraged soldiers to take revenge and punish Germans broadly speaking, not just soldiers. On the eve of the offensive into Poland, the orders to the First Belorussian Front included, "Woe to the land of the murders. We will get our terrible revenge for everything." On the eve of crossing into East Prussia, the orders included, "On German soil there is only one master – the Soviet soldier, that he is both the judge and the punisher for the torments of his fathers and mothers, for the destroyed cities and villages … 'remember your friends are not there, there is the next of kin of the killers and oppressors'" (quoted in Naimark 1995, 72).

As the Soviet army occupied Berlin in late April and early May 1945, thousands of women and girls were raped, often by several men in sequence, often in front of family or neighborhood, sometimes on more than one occasion. Soldiers sometimes detained a girl or woman for some days in her home or elsewhere and subjected her to repeated rape. Even after occupation became more institutionalized, Soviet soldiers continued to rape girls and women. Sexual violence gradually subsided as occupation authorities realized the harm being done to the Soviet postwar political project and gradually instituted stronger rules against fraternization in general and rape in particular.

This is a relatively well-documented case: historians draw on a wide range of sources including Soviet military and secret police reports, military reports, wartime memoirs and diaries, and German hospital and police records (many women did report the incidents). Even in this case, however, the frequency of rape – even in Berlin itself – is difficult to establish.[1] The best estimate appears to come from the two main Berlin hospitals: staff members estimated the number of rape victims as between 95,000 and 130,000 (Beevor 2002, 410). Taking 100,000 as a rough estimate of the number of victims and 1,500,000 as the number of

---

[1] Potential sources to establish the prevalence of sexual violence in Berlin are the records of women requesting abortions. While abortion was technically illegal, authorities suspended the law in the case of rape by foreigners; permission was granted to nearly all cases in the district whose records were analyzed by Atina Grossman (1997). Given that 90 percent of pregnancies stated to be the result of rape were aborted (Grossman 1997, 50), the prevalence could be estimated if either those districts were known to be representative or the records for all districts were preserved. However, that does not appear to be the case (Grossman 1997, 33, fn. 2).

women in Berlin at the time implies a prevalence (victims/female population) of roughly 6 percent.[2]

This is an unusual case in that the response of the leadership to widespread sexual violence was recorded. Naimark documents the tolerance of sexual violence against civilians on the part of the Soviet command structure, from field officers to Stalin himself, who responded to complaints from East Prussia with, "We lecture our soldiers too much. Let them have some initiative," and to those from German socialists with, "In every family there is a black sheep … I will not allow anyone to drag the reputation of the Red Army in the mud" (1995, 71).

The sexual violence by Soviet troops appears to be an exercise in collective punishment and perhaps the taking of victor's spoils. Did the Soviet troops engage in such widespread sexual violence in retaliation for sexual violence by German troops? The extent of sexual violence by German troops occupying Eastern Europe appears to have been widespread in some areas according to recent research in newly available archives (Burds 2009). According to Wendy Jo Gertjejanssen (2004), German soldiers raped girls and women of various ethnicities, including Jews, despite regulations against sexual relations with non-German women.[3] Much sexual violence appears to have taken the form of forced prostitution as many girls and women were forced to serve in military brothels in cities and field camps. While some volunteered to serve in the brothels as a way to survive in the dire circumstances of the occupation, others were forced to serve under threat of death or internment. Gertjejanssen (2004, 220) estimates that at least 50,000 women and girls served in military brothels throughout the Reich. German military authorities also organized brothels in labor and concentration camps, which were visited by favored prisoners, guards, and occasionally officers. Some girls and women were forced to serve in these brothels, others when offered the choice of internment or service in the brothels, chose the latter. Women and girls in privileged sectors of the camp (where they retained their own clothes and hair and mingled with the guards) suffered occasional rape (Rees 2005, 236–238). The scale of sexual violence in the concentration and labor camps (aside from the sexual humiliation of forced undressing and the violence against homosexuals, which often took the form of medical experiments)

[2] The incidence of rape (incidents/population) would be much higher than the prevalence (victims/population) given the pattern of gang rapes and multiple incidents suffered by the same person.

[3] See also Friedman (2002, chapter 2). The German military treated rape of civilians by German soldiers on the eastern front much more leniently than on the western front where military courts imposed significantly more severe punishment (Beck 2002).

appears to have been limited, as the number of women in the brothels appears to be a small fraction of the number interned in the camps.[4]

Massive sexual violence also occurred in the Pacific theater. The "rape of Nanjing," the widespread violence by Japanese soldiers in the environs of the Chinese city of Nanjing for eight weeks beginning December 13, 1937, included extensive sexual violence. According to Iris Chang (1997), 20,000 to 80,000 women and girls were raped and then executed; that is, 8 to 32 percent of the approximately 250,000 female civilians present in the city at the time of the takeover.[5] Among them were prepubescent girls, pregnant and elderly women, and Buddhist nuns; most were summarily executed afterward. Sexual violence in Nanjing also included various forms of sexual abuse of men, including rape, the forcing of men to have intercourse with family members or the dead, and the forcing of celibate men to have intercourse.

One result of the negative international publicity in the wake of the violence in Nanjing was the widespread implementation of the so-called "comfort women" system of military-organized and controlled brothels that accompanied Japanese forces (Goldstein 2001, 367).[6] According to a 1993 study by the Japanese government that included a review of wartime archives and interviews with both military personnel and former "comfort women," more than 200,000 women from across East and Southeast Asia were recruited by force and deception to serve as on-call prostitutes subject to immediate violence if they resisted. In establishing the "comfort stations," Japanese officials sought "to prevent anti-Japanese sentiments from fermenting [*sic*] as a result of rapes and other unlawful acts by Japanese military personnel against local residents in the areas occupied by the then Japanese military, the need to prevent loss of troop strength by venereal and other diseases, and the need to prevent espionage" (Japanese Cabinet Councillors' Office on External Affairs 1993, 14).[7] Most of the comfort women were between fourteen and eighteen years old, and most were Korean. According to the Korean Council for the Women Drafted for Sexual Slavery by Japan (cited in

---

[4] Based on Gertjejanssen's description of the camp brothels, I estimate the number to have been between 1,000 and 10,000.

[5] Chang draws on a wide range of documents, including the diaries and reports of international observers who remained in Nanjing throughout the violence, as well as some interviews. It is not clear how Chang arrives at this estimate.

[6] The system was begun in 1932 but expanded extensively in the aftermath of Nanjing.

[7] "On the Issue of Wartime 'comfort women'" by the Japanese Cabinet Councillors' Office on External Affairs, August 4, 1993 (E/CN.4/1996/137, 14), cited in UNESCO 1998 (Appendix: 9[a]). The precise number of women forced to serve as military sexual slaves is not well documented as the Japanese destroyed many of the documents in 1945.

Hyun-Kyung 2000, 17–19), perhaps a third of them died in the course of the war.

Bosnia-Herzegovina

Sexual slavery was also a prominent form of sexual violence in the conflict in the former Yugoslavia in the early 1990s. According to a European Union investigation, approximately 20,000 girls and women suffered rape in 1992 in Bosnia-Herzegovina alone, many of them while held in detention facilities of various types (Goldstein 2001, 363; Enloe 2000, 140).[8] According to the UN Commission of Experts to investigate violence in the former Yugoslavia, the "vast majority of the victims are Bosnian Muslims and the great majority of the alleged perpetrators are Bosnian Serbs" (UNSC 1994, Annex IX.I.C). The history of violence in the district of Foča illustrates a common pattern in this conflict (UNSC 1994; Barkan 2002). Before the conflict began, Muslims comprised 58% of the residents. From March to September 1992, Muslim girls and women were subjected to rape in the forests, in their homes, in detention centers, and in private flats. Of the sixty three cases of rape and sexual assault in Foča compiled by the commission, about 55% took place in detention centers, including the local high school, a gym, and the workers' barracks of a hydroelectric plant under construction. In such centers, members of the various Bosnian Serb forces walked in, chose from among the girls and women there, and raped them either on the premises or in nearby flats. Many of the women and girls endured gang rapes, repeated over days or weeks.

The most authoritative investigation of sexual violence in the former Yugoslavia was carried out by a UN commission (UNSC 1994, see especially Annex IX). The commission drew on two sources of evidence. The first was their analysis of tens of thousands of allegations contained in documents from a wide variety of sources from which the commission

---

[8] Twenty thousand girls and women comprise 2.1% of female Muslims in prewar Bosnia-Herzegovina of all ages (calculated from Federal Office of Statistics data for 1991). The UN Special Rapporteur of the Commission on Human Rights (cited in Salzman 2000, 76) initially made a lower estimate of 11,900 rapes, based on 119 pregnancies resulting from rape that were aborted in six major medical centers (the rapporteur assumed a rate of pregnancy after rape of about 1%). However, as Salzman points out, on the one hand many women were raped more than once and others had no access to medical facilities and induced abortion themselves, abandoned the child, or kept the child. On the other hand, many pregnant women who sought abortions did not indicate that pregnancy originated in rape. On balance, Salzman argues that the number of pregnancies was likely significantly higher than 119 and he concurs with the 20,000 estimate (76–77, 63).

distilled 1,100 reported cases of rape and sexual assault (eliminating duplicate and unspecific allegations), including 800 identifiable victims, 700 named alleged perpetrators with another 750 identifiable, and 162 detention sites (UNSC 1994, Annex IX.I.A). Representatives of the commission also carried out interviews with 223 people who were victims of or witnesses to sexual violence in Bosnia-Herzegovina (UNSC 1994, Annex IX.A).

The commission identified several distinct patterns of sexual violence, by individuals and small groups in conjunction with looting and intimidation of the targeted group, in conjunction with fighting, often including the public rape of selected women in front of the assembled population after the takeover of a village, against some women and girls held in detention or collection centers for refugees, in sites for the purpose of rape and assault where all women were assaulted frequently, apparently for the purpose of forced impregnation (women were told that was the case and pregnant women were sometimes held past the point when an abortion was possible), and in detention sites for the purpose of providing sex. Sexual violence against men of various ethnicities (castration, being forced to perform fellatio or to have intercourse in front of guards), while much less frequent than that against women, also occurred in camps and detention centers (examples given include camps run by Serbs, Muslims, and Croats).

Among the characteristics stressed by the commission were an emphasis on shame and humiliation (many assaults occurred in front of family or in public), the targeting of young girls and virgins along with educated and prominent female community members, and sexual assault with objects. Moreover,

In both custodial and noncustodial settings, many victims report that the alleged perpetrators stated that they were ordered to rape and sexually assault the victims, or that they were doing it so that the victims and their families would never want to return to the area. Also, every reported case occurred in conjunction with an effort to displace the civilian population of a targeted ethnic group from a given region. (UNSC 1994, Annex IX.I.C)

For example, the commission interviewed nineteen women from Kotor Varos, of whom six had been raped, and most gang-raped by guards in a sawmill that had served as a temporary collection center. One woman was told by a rapist that he wanted to try a Muslim woman and that she should be honored; a second woman was told that he would make "Cetnik babies" in Muslim and Croat women; a third woman was told by a rapist that he had been ordered to do so (UNSC 1994, Annex IX.A III.A.2).

The commission concluded that while some cases were the result of the actions of individuals or small groups acting without orders, "many more cases seem to be part of an overall pattern. These patterns strongly suggest that a systematic rape and sexual assault policy exists, but this remains to be proved" (UNSC 1994, Annex IX "Conclusions"). In drawing this conclusion, the commission relied on the fact that a majority of the cases (600 of the 1,100) occurred against people in detention, that similar patterns of sexual violence occurred in noncontiguous areas, and that sexual violence was often simultaneous with military action or activity to displace certain civilian populations.

While not explicitly stated in the report, the inference is clear that the commission believed it probable that rape comprised part of the systematic ethnic cleansing on the part of the Bosnian Serb forces.[9] Direct evidence that Bosnian Serb and possibly Serbian forces planned a campaign of sexual violence as part of the ethnic cleansing of Serbian areas of the former Yugoslavia is lacking, but may emerge as the various trials at the International Criminal Tribunal for the Former Yugoslavia continue.

Sierra Leone

Sexual violence during the war in Sierra Leone, in contrast to Bosnia-Herzegovina, did not involve explicit ethnic targeting.[10] According to the Truth and Reconciliation Commission of Sierra Leone, sexual violence was carried out "indiscriminately on women of all ages, of every ethnic group and from all social classes" (TRC [Sierra Leone] 2005, chapter 3b, par. 282). The commission found that "all of the armed factions, in particular the RUF and the Armed Forces Revolutionary Council, embarked on a systematic and deliberate strategy to rape women and girls, especially those between the ages of ten and 18 years of age, with the intention of sowing terror amongst the population, violating women and girls and breaking down every norm and custom of traditional society" (TRC [Sierra Leone] 2005, par. 298). The commission noted that some armed groups targeted young women and girls

---

[9] Of course one reason the ethnic violence in the former Yugoslavia seemed troubling to many observers was the fact of significant intermarriage before the war: from 1981 to 1991, 18.6 percent of new marriages in Bosnia-Herzegovina were inter-ethnic (1991 census figures, Enloe 2000, 142).

[10] In the testimonies compiled by Human Rights Watch and Physicians for Human Rights, victims reported perpetrators wanting sex with a virgin, wanting a new wife, to send a message to the government, and so on, but do not report perpetrators stating a wish to have sex with or to punish a person of particular ethnicity or religion.

presumed to be virgins (see also HRW 2003a), as well as those girls and women associated with other armed groups. The sexual assault of post-menopausal women broke a particular cultural taboo against sexual activity among this group. On occasion, rebels broke other taboos as well, forcing male family members to rape female family members or to watch them dance naked or be raped by others (TRC [Sierra Leone] 2005, chapter 3b, pars. 292–296; HRW 2003a, 35–42). However, the commission did not analyze patterns of sexual violence in detail and therefore makes a less compelling case for sexual violence as a systematic strategy than that advanced by the commission for the former Yugoslavia, which laid out specific patterns not easily accounted for except by such a strategy.

Sexual violence was widespread among those internally displaced by the war. According to a survey of 991 internally displaced women carried out by Physicians for Human Rights, 9% of the respondents had suffered sexual assault during the ten years of the war (Amowitz *et al.* 2002, Table 2).[11] Of the respondents who were sexually assaulted, 89% reported being raped and 33% reported being gang-raped (Amowitz *et al.* 2002, Table 3). Of the human rights abuses suffered by household members, 40% were alleged to have been carried out by the rebel group Revolutionary United Front (RUF), 34% by unknown groups, 16% by unspecified rebels, and 4% by mixed groups (Amowitz *et al.* 2002, Table 2).

Sexual violence in Sierra Leone was also extremely brutal (HRW 2003a). Gang rapes often took the form of very young victims enduring rape, with rebel combatants lining up to take turns. Many of those who suffered sexual assault did so on multiple occasions. The extreme violence with which girls and women were raped often resulted in severe bleeding, tears in the vagina, anus, and surrounding tissue, long-term bleeding and incontinence, and sometimes death.[12]

A particular form of sexual violence in Sierra Leone was the detention of girls and women, often for long periods of time, as slaves serving and sexually servicing a rebel camp or a particular rebel (TRC [Sierra Leone]

---

[11] The survey design combined systematic random sampling and cluster sampling in four locales representing 91% of the internally displaced population. The estimated prevalence rate appears to be several times higher than the peacetime rate (the estimated lifetime prevalence of nonwar related sexual violence is 9.0%; Amowitz *et al.* 2002, 518).

[12] See PHR 2002, chapter 4 and HRW 2003a, chapter V. According to Physicians for Human Rights, girls and women who undergo female genital cutting are at increased risk for genital trauma and related complications after rape (PHR 2002, 49). Human Rights Watch (2003a, 24) reports that 90 percent of females in Sierra Leone undergo female genital cutting.

2005, chapter 3b, 299–311). In some cases, they underwent forced marriage with a particular person. Of the internally displaced women who suffered sexual assault, 33% of the respondents were abducted, 15% were forced to serve as sexual slaves, and 9% were forced to marry a captor (Amowitz *et al.* 2002, Table 3). Escape was reportedly very difficult, and attempts were severely punished. At war's end some "wives" were not willing or able to leave their spouses.[13]

Other cases in which sexual violence appears to be very prevalent include the present conflict in Darfur, Sudan, where rape occurs frequently in the context of the campaign by militias and government forces to punish villages thought to be associated with rebel groups (Amnesty International 2004; Médecins Sans Frontières 2005; International Commission of Inquiry on Darfur 2005). During the genocide in Rwanda, some Tutsi girls and women (as well as, in much fewer numbers, Hutu women thought to support Tutsis) suffered rape and mutilation before their execution. Estimates of the prevalence of sexual violence in Rwanda vary widely, but appear to merit inclusion in the high prevalence category (African Rights 1994; Human Rights Watch 1996; Sharlach 1999).

Given the high prevalence of sexual violence in these very different conflicts, one might conclude that sexual violence inevitably accompanies war. However, the following cases in which the incidence of sexual violence is remarkably low or sharply asymmetric compared to the above demonstrate that such a conclusion is incorrect.

Israel/Palestine

In the Israeli–Palestinian conflict, also an ethnic conflict characterized by the increasing separation of ethnically defined populations, sexual violence appears to be extremely limited. While the forced movement of Palestinians out of some areas in 1948 was accompanied by a few documented cases of rape (Morris 2004), at present neither Israelis nor Palestinians carry out sexual assaults despite the killing of Israeli civilians by Palestinian groups and of Palestinian civilians by Israeli security forces. In December 2003, I asked representatives of three human rights organizations (two Israeli and one Palestinian) whether they believed sexual assault was occurring but was not reported, or was not in fact taking place. They independently and unanimously stated that they

---

[13] Forced marriages in the sense of marriages of girls without their consent, often at a very young age, were common in Sierra Leone before the war but required permission of the girl's family (HRW 2003a, 17, 23–24).

received information for almost no cases of sexual assault and that they believed they would hear of it occurring as they did receive reports of lesser instances of sexual harassment (for example, during pat-down searches at checkpoints). It could be the case that the intensive international monitoring of the conflict deters the practice of sexual violence, but both sides do not appear much deterred in their other practices despite their frequent condemnation by international actors.

Sri Lanka

Like Bosnia-Herzegovina, Sri Lanka is also a case of a secessionist ethnic conflict, but in Sri Lanka the level of sexual violence appears to be significantly less and is also highly asymmetric. When it does occur, it has generally been wielded by government forces against women associated with the insurgency. Police, soldiers, or security forces occasionally subject displaced Tamil women and girls to various forms of sexual assault, including gang rape and rape with foreign objects, after their arrest or detention at checkpoints, sometimes on the grounds that they or family members are suspected members of the Tamil insurgency (Amnesty International 1999; 2002; United Nations Development Fund for Women 2005). Various human rights groups report that sexual torture by police and security forces against male and female political and criminal detainees occurs frequently (Wood 2009). Sexual violence against Tamil women by government forces is one reason girls and women volunteer to fight with the insurgents (Alison 2003). Of particular interest is the relative absence of sexual violence against civilians by the Tamil insurgent group, despite their inflicting frequent civilian casualties during attacks on non-Tamil villages, assassinations of political and military leaders, and their forcing non-Tamil populations to leave areas of their control, as in 1990 when 90,000 Muslims were forced to leave the Jaffna peninsula on extremely short notice (Wood 2009). Despite the frequent recruitment by force of girls as combatants, the group does not appear to engage in sexual abuse within its own ranks (HRW 2004; United Nations Development Fund for Women 2005).

El Salvador

Sexual violence during the civil war in El Salvador, a nonethnic conflict pitting a leftist insurgency against an authoritarian government, was one-sided, and very low in comparison to Bosnia-Herzegovina and Sierra Leone. Government soldiers and security forces occasionally engaged in sexual violence, including gang and multiple rapes, against some suspected insurgent supporters (including some men) detained in both official and secret detention sites. Government forces carried out sexual violence while on operations early in the war. For example, according to Mark Danner (1994), some of the nearly one thousand people killed by the Salvadoran military at El Mozote in 1981 were raped. And two of the four US churchwomen detained and killed by National Guardsmen in 1980 were raped. The final report of the UN-sponsored Truth Commission mentions only one incident of rape, carried out by government forces in a village in eastern El Salvador in 1981. However, the unpublished annex to the commission's report discussed sexual violence in some detail (TC [El Salvador] 1993, Anexos. Vol. II, 8–10, 15). The majority of incidents reported took place in the first few years of the war; all were reported to have been carried out by state forces or agents. Sexual violence appears generally to have varied over time with other forms of violence against civilians, steeply decreasing after 1983 in response to the US conditioning its military aid on improved human rights performance. No incidents of sexual violence in the Annex were attributed to the insurgent force. In the human rights and ethnographic literature analyzing the conflict, there are very few reports of sexual violence by insurgent forces against civilians (Wood 2003, chapter 4). Sexual violence in the Salvadoran conflict was thus asymmetric, distinctly low compared to other cases, and declined over the years of the war.

Summary of observed patterns

Sexual violence in these cases appears to vary substantially in prevalence; in form; in who is targeted (all women, girls and men as well as women, or particular persons, perhaps members of an ethnic outgroup); in whether it is exercised by combatants from a single party or more generally; whether it is pursued as a strategy of war; where it occurs (in detention, at home, or in public); in duration; whether it is carried out by a single perpetrator or by a gang; whether victims are killed afterward; and whether its incidence varies with other forms of violence against civilians or occurs in a distinct pattern. In some wars, armed groups "mirror" the use of sexual violence by committing their own; in other wars, such tit-for-tat retaliation does not occur. In some conflicts, sexual violence increases over time, in others it declines.

The type of war (at the broadest level) does not explain the variation even among these few cases. Sexual violence varies in prevalence and form among civil wars as well as interstate wars, among ethnic wars as well as nonethnic, among genocides and ethnic-cleansing cases, and among secessionist conflicts. Nor does the prevalence of sexual violence simply reflect the intensity of conflict: the prevalence of sexual violence in Bosnia-Herzegovina was remarkably high compared to the frequency of lethal violence, while it is disproportionately low in Israel/Palestine and sharply asymmetric in El Salvador and Sri Lanka.

Challenges to documenting wartime sexual violence

Before continuing, however, a preemptive concern must be addressed. Perhaps the variation described above is merely an artifact of inadequate knowledge about the empirical patterns present in each case. The reported variation may reflect different intensities of domestic and international monitoring of conflicts rather than different prevalence rates; violence in some regions appears to garner more international attention than others.

Even in peacetime and even in countries with well-developed infrastructure and liberal norms, the methodological challenges to gathering data concerning sexual violence are serious. For example, what counts legally as "rape" varies significantly among US states depending on whether it is narrowly defined as forced penetration of the vagina by a penis or more broadly to include anal penetration and vaginal penetration by other objects, and whether rape requires forcible compulsion or merely lack of consent (Tobach and Reed 2003, Tables 5.1 and 5.2). The definitional ambiguity is still greater across societies; for example, societies differ in whether rape is considered possible between husband and wife. In some cultures, coerced vaginal penetration may be socially condoned in particular situations, with the result that an incident that would count as rape in other societies would not be considered as such.[14]

Whether persons who have suffered some form of sexual violence are willing to report it, whether to health workers, to police, to ethnographers, or in surveys, also varies substantially across societies. One reason that many do not do so, even in societies with liberal sexual norms, is that they feel shame and fear stigmatization. In most societies, male victims of sexual violence appear to be particularly reluctant to report it. And in societies where abortion is illegal, female victims of rape who abort may be particularly reluctant to report rape.

---

[14] For example, in some societies, sexual access to women is granted to guests, brothers, or other associates of the husband (and the women are beaten or killed if they refuse). And in some societies, female transgression of social norms (such as women seeing ceremonial artifacts strictly reserved for males) is punished by rape, sometimes group-rape in a public place (Rozee 1993, 507–508).

These challenges are of course compounded during war when surveys are generally absent, police and health services are disrupted, and families and social groups are displaced and dispersed. The fear of reprisal for reporting sexual violence is likely greater in war settings, particularly if the perpetrator or his group is still present. Increased political polarization may intensify partisan bias in the reporting of human rights violations – even by nonpartisan organizations – as violence and displacement may isolate some populations from services and intensify the counting of incidents in others. The destruction of rural infrastructure may reinforce urban bias. International organizations that document human rights violations tend to have limited resources and as a result focus their investigations on particular cases. And because many of the physical injuries sustained during sexual assault are to soft tissue, sexual violence does not always leave an observable trace in the long-run forensic record. As a result, the exhumation of massacre sites may not document sexual violence unless it took the form of mutilation, dismemberment, or involved guns, knives, or other weapons likely to remain evident for many years.

However, the disruption of war may also increase reporting. Sexual violence in the context of political conflict may be more likely to be reported as the stigma felt by its victims may be less, and displacement from home communities may loosen traditional norms and lessen the likelihood of reprisal. Health services may be more available, not less, to populations that fled to urban areas or in some refugee camps, compared to their place of origin. Human rights groups, women's organizations, and medical service groups may emerge or command more resources in wartime, enabling the compiling of reports and patterns and facilitating investigation by international commissions and human rights groups. Perhaps due to the strengthening of international norms against sexual violence during war, recent truth commissions tend to document sexual violence more carefully than earlier commissions. Medical surveys are one way to estimate the prevalence of sexual violence; respondents in at least some cultures are willing to answer questions concerning sexual violence in a medical context, if given sufficient privacy (Amowitz et al. 2002; Physicians for Human Rights 2002). However, there are particular challenges of using medical data to estimate prevalence rates of violence, including the difficulty of estimating prevalence in home areas based on prevalence in refugee camps (e.g. the dead are missing from the camp sample; see Hagan et al. 2006).

Another challenge to analyzing variation in wartime sexual violence is the fact that levels of sexual violence vary across countries in peacetime, making more difficult the interpretation of the wartime variation.

Evidence for peacetime variation comes from studies that draw on two very different methodologies. The United Nations Interregional Crime and Justice Research Institute uses crime victimization surveys in many countries to compile cross-national data on rates of sexual assault. In developing-country capital cities, five-year prevalence rates in the mid-1990s for sexual assault varied between 0.83%, the average for the three cities at the low end (Manila, Gaborone, and La Paz) and 6.60% for the three cities at the high end (Rio de Janeiro, Tirana, and Buenos Aires), about eight times as high (WHO 2002, Table 6.1, 151).[15] In industrialized countries, estimated annual rates of sexual assault also vary, between 0.13 at the low end (the annual average for Japan, Ireland, and Scotland) and 1.03 at the high end (for Sweden, Finland, and England), with the high rate again about eight times as high as the low rates (Kesteren *et al.* 2000, Appendix 4, Table 6, 188–189).[16]

Despite these empirical challenges, the variation in sexual violence is sufficiently well documented across enough wars and armed groups to suggest that it is real and not solely an artifact of bias in reporting and observation or a reflection of variation in peacetime levels. The variation in frequency among conflicts and among groups within a conflict appears to be large, with well-documented cases at both ends of the frequency spectrum. At the high end of the variation are some of the best-documented cases, for example Bosnian Serb forces in Bosnia, for which it is difficult to imagine a significantly lower rate given the numerous and mutually corroborating reports from dozens of investigations. And at the low end of the spectrum, it is difficult to imagine a high rate of sexual violence in the Israeli–Palestinian conflict going unreported, given the density of nongovernmental human rights organizations and the intensity of international scrutiny of both parties' behavior. In some conflicts, the pattern of sexual violence is highly asymmetric, with a high proportion attributed to one party to the war. Not only does the prevalence vary significantly, the particular pattern of sexual violence does as well, which gives additional analytical traction. Finally, for some of the cases (World War II and Bosnia-Herzegovina, for example) it is evident that sexual violence was much more prevalent

---

[15] For developing countries, the data are compiled from face-to-face surveys in the capital city; there is apparently no correction for possible rural–urban differences other than for variation in household size. Given the challenges to compiling comparable sexual violence data, I average across the lowest and highest three cities.

[16] For industrialized countries, the surveys are national samples and done by phone (with the exception of Malta). The high reported rates in Sweden and Finland probably reflect high rates of binge alcoholism, with attendant violence, or higher rates of reporting sexual assault, and a more inclusive definition of "assault."

during the war than before. And in cases where it is unclear whether it was more prevalent during war than during peacetime, the form of sexual violence changed during war, as in the case of sexual slavery in Sierra Leone.

Explaining variation in wartime sexual violence

Several causal mechanisms that might explain the observed variation appear (often only implicitly) in the literature on sexual violence during war. In this section I assess whether these mechanisms in fact do so. Candidate explanations for the variation also come from the recent literature on mechanisms of collective violence (for a more detailed discussion, see Wood 2006).

Opportunity

One hypothesis, often implicit, is that the oft-observed increase in sexual violence during war reflects increased opportunity. Institutions of social control are often weaker in war, particularly when young combatants fight far from their home, communities are scattered to distinct areas, norms of respect for elders are undermined by new sources of authority such as guns, and armed groups loot kitchens for supplies. This approach implies that the pattern of sexual violence should mirror those of other forms of violence (because opportunity to loot and rape is also opportunity to kill), that combatants should not target civilians of a particular ethnicity (unless opportunity depends directly on ethnicity), and that sexual violence should be higher on the part of groups that loot provisions.

Some studies weakly confirm these implications. Neil Mitchell and Tali Gluch (2004) found that prevalence of sexual violence was significantly correlated with the presence of war. However, their finding was based on data for only one year and relied on a crude coding of limited human rights sources, principally State Department human rights reports. Madeline Morris (1996) found that the rates of rape by male US military personnel in World War II were three to four times *higher* than the rate by male civilians of the same age. (In contrast, military rates during peacetime were significantly lower than civilian rates.) Sexual violence in some conflicts does appear to vary with other forms of violence, the frequency increasing and decreasing in the same patterns across time and space.

More generally, however, variation in opportunity does not account for the observed variation in sexual violence. Many armed actors target particular groups in patterns not explained by opportunity; in both

Bosnia-Herzegovina and Rwanda, perpetrators had roughly equal access to civilians of various ethnicities yet targeted particular ones. The Salvadoran insurgency depended closely on residents of contested areas for supplies yet to my knowledge there are no documented instances of rape by insurgents of civilians. And sexual violence does not always vary with other forms of violence; the Sri Lankan and Colombian insurgencies appear to strictly limit sexual violence but engage in other forms of violence against civilians. To my knowledge, no one has systematically compared patterns of different forms of violence by the same group.

Incentives

A distinct approach argues that wartime experience increases individual incentives to engage in sexual violence. There are several versions of this argument. (See Wood 2006, 17–19 and Goldstein 2001 for consideration of biological versions.) Some scholars interpret wartime increases in sexual violence to the breakdown of patriarchal institutions during war (Brownmiller 1975; Enloe 1983). Just as lynchings of African-Americans increased in the US South after the ending of slavery in the aftermath of the Civil War, when patriarchal institutions weaken, violence to enforce gender boundaries increases. Arguments based on patriarchal social relations imply that sexual violence should be more prevalent in wars in which traditional gender norms are more disrupted. But in many civil wars, gender roles become less polarized because village hierarchies break down as the population disperses and women take on tasks normally carried out by men. It does not appear to be the case that sexual violence is higher when traditional norms are more disrupted. Contrary to the patriarchal thesis, in some conflicts patriarchal relations are so disrupted that there are significant numbers of female combatants in insurgent factions. Rather than the predicted high rates of sexual violence, rates appear to have been very low in two such cases: Sri Lanka and El Salvador. And women sometimes participate in sexual violence as in Rwanda, where women sometimes incited men to rape, and in the sexual humiliation of men detained by US forces in Iraq, Guantánamo, and Afghanistan. Nor does the argument account for the targeting of enemy civilians (Skjelsbaek 2001).

A second argument that does account for such targeting is that of revenge: combatants target enemy civilians with violence in revenge for the violence suffered by their community. However, why revenge takes the form of sexual rather than other kinds of violence is usually not explained. Sexual violence is sometimes said to occur in retaliation for sexual violence previously suffered (or rumored to suffer) by co-ethnics, but as our cases showed, some armed groups do not respond in kind to sexual violence.

The militarized masculinity approach (Morris 1996; Goldstein 2001) does account for the targeting of enemy women and men, and with specifically sexual violence. In order to persuade men to fight and endure the hardships of war, societies develop members willing to stand fast under fire, usually via the development of sharp distinctions between genders: to become men, boys must become warriors. Leaders persuade soldiers that to be a real man is to assert a militaristic masculinity, with the result that soldiers represent domination of the enemy in highly gendered terms and use specifically sexual violence against enemy populations. Moreover, bonding among members of the small unit – the loyalty that enables warriors to fight under the terrifying conditions of war – also takes gendered forms, reinforcing the militaristic masculinity of training.

Wartime memoirs from some conflicts (for example, memoirs by US soldiers who served in Vietnam) offer anecdotal support for this approach. Particular types of small unit bonding such as joint visits to brothels may play a role in the frequent occurrence of gang rapes in wartime. However, if this approach is to explain *variation* in wartime sexual violence, armies should promote different notions of masculinity, with armies that emphasize more militaristic notions of manhood responsible for higher levels of sexual violence. I am not aware of systematic comparisons of military training, norms, and practices across state militaries; the variation in sexual violence among state militaries appears significantly greater than the surprisingly limited variation in their training. Moreover, the militaristic masculinity approach does not specify well what mechanism underlies its link to sexual violence, whether armies inculcate new norms, provide incentives to reward compliance without internalization, or recruit only those attracted to militaristic practices. To my knowledge, no one has systematically evaluated these relationships. There are obvious exceptions to the claimed relationship: the Salvadoran insurgency, one of the two most militarily effective guerrilla armies in Latin America, had little record of sexual violence despite their highly militarized notion of masculinity.

Perhaps variation in sexual violence is better addressed by variation in military discipline than training and socialization. I return to this issue below.

Sexual violence as instrumental for the group

In the explanations based on increased opportunity and incentive, sexual violence occurred for reasons of individual gratification or as a byproduct

of supposedly necessary training. In contrast, some armed groups promote (or tolerate) sexual violence as an effective means toward group
goals. While strategic sexual violence may not be explicitly ordered, it is
(at least) tolerated; if any punishment occurs it is symbolic and limited,
clearly for external consumption rather than deterrence. Such violence
appears to take two broad forms. The first is sexual torture and/or
humiliation of persons detained by an armed group. The second is
widespread sexual violence as a form of terror or punishment targeted at
a particular group, which frequently takes the form of gang (and often
public) rape, usually over an extended period of time, most notoriously as
part of some campaigns of "ethnic cleansing," to force the movement of
entire populations from particular regions claimed as the homeland, and
as part of some genocides.

The conditions for such instrumental promotion of sexual violence are
not well identified in the literature. Some authors suggest particular
cultural beliefs provide the relevant condition: where armed groups
understand sexual violence as a violation of the family's and community's honor, they are likely to engage in sexual violence as a weapon of
war (Enloe 2000). However, this appears to predict significantly more
sexual violence than is in fact observed as such beliefs are present in
many societies where massive sexual violence has not occurred, as in Sri
Lanka, El Salvador, and Colombia. Moreover, such broad notions of
cultural proclivity do not account for cases where one party to the war
promotes sexual violence while the other does not. In addition, most
instrumentalist accounts do not adequately address whether sexual
violence is in fact a strategy enforced by the military hierarchy or is a
norm that has diffused across an armed group, one not particularly
endorsed by leadership. Goals may diverge widely between leaders of an
armed group and individual members (Kalyvas 2003), resulting in a
potential gap between measures advocated at the top and priorities
among small units on the ground.

Sanctions against sexual violence

The effectiveness of an armed group's command and control structure is
particularly important for the effective prohibition of sexual violence.
An armed group's leadership may prohibit it for strategic, normative,
or practical reasons (Wood 2006). If an organization aspires to govern
the civilian population, leaders will probably attempt to restrain combatants' engagement in sexual violence against those civilians (though
perhaps endorsing it against other civilian groups) for fear of undermining support for the coming revolution. Similarly, if an armed group

is dependent on civilians, leaders will probably attempt to restrain sexual violence against those civilians.

Reasons for prohibiting sexual violence may reflect normative concerns as well as practical constraints. Members of a revolutionary group seeking to carry out a social revolution may see themselves as the disciplined bearers of a new, more just social order for all citizens; sexual violence may conflict with their self-image. A norm against sexual violence may take a distinct form; sexual violence across ethnic boundaries may be understood by leaders or combatants as polluting the instigator rather than humiliating the targeted individual and community. New social norms against the use of particular forms of violence and in favor of others may also be actively cultivated by an armed group as a matter of strategy or principle. The Salvadoran insurgency attempted to shape individual longings for revenge toward a more general aspiration for justice because revenge-seeking by individuals would undermine insurgent discipline and obedience (Wood 2003). Despite systematic celebration of martyrdom in pursuit of victory, the insurgency did not endorse suicide missions and explicitly prohibited sexual violence. In contrast, the Sri Lankan insurgency carries out suicide bombing and, arguably, shapes desires for revenge toward that end, yet does not engage in sexual violence toward civilians despite its practice of ethnic cleansing.

Dependence on international allies may also constrain sexual violence if those allies have normative concerns about such violence. Even if neither the armed group nor its sponsor is itself normatively concerned, it may seek to avoid criticism by international human rights organizations.

An army for whom females comprise a high fraction of combatants may also be constrained in its use of sexual violence. This is suggested by the empirical pattern that female-intensive insurgencies in El Salvador, Sri Lanka, Peru, and Colombia appear to carry out less sexual violence. However, the mechanism is not clear, and these insurgencies share other characteristics as well, such as an unusual degree of internal discipline.

For the case of both promotion and prohibition of sexual violence, whether an armed group effectively enforces strategies decided on by the leadership depends on the group's internal discipline. The use of violence poses dilemmas to principals whose agents prefer a level or type of violence distinct from theirs (Mitchell and Gluch 2004; Hoover 2006; Kalyvas 2003). For example, when an armed group prohibits sexual violence based on practical constraints, if combatants do not themselves feel the direct causal pinch of the constraint, whether it in fact constrains depends on the degree of discipline within the organization. Many armies probably prohibit sexual violence yet do not in fact discipline soldiers who commit it. However, under some, possibly rare conditions, the prevalence of sexual violence may be low without relying on the hierarchical discipline of the armed group, namely when combatants themselves have internalized norms against sexual violence or if small units share such a norm and may therefore effectively enforce the norm.

Other mechanisms

The emerging literature on violence during war has identified a number of mechanisms thought to shape patterns of violence. Stathis Kalyvas (2006) argues that the killing of civilians reflects attempts by armed actors to deter civilians from collaborating with the other party. According to Jeremy Weinstein (2006), armies whose members have easy access to resources such as abundant lootable natural resources will attract opportunistic rather than idealistic recruits and will be less likely to constrain their use of violence against civilians compared to armies that depend on the voluntary provision of services by civilians. Charles Tilly (2003) identified a number of mechanisms (such as group boundary activation and maintenance, signaling spirals, and alliance building by brokers) that escalate violence. Scott Straus (2006) argues that perpetrators of genocidal violence in Rwanda acted out of long-standing patterns of obedience to authority, backed up by credibly coercive threats. These mechanisms may contribute to an explanation of the observed variation in sexual violence but do not themselves explain it. Sexual violence often has the effect of sharpening group boundaries and is often carried out by armed groups that rely on lootable resources. And in cases where armed groups effectively implement strategies either promoting or prohibiting sexual violence, obedience to authority may play a role. However, although sexual violence occasionally takes the form of punishment of enemy collaborators, it appears to be rare. In particular, the mechanisms do not explain why some armed groups effectively prohibit sexual violence on the part of the combatants. For example, the Colombian leftist insurgent groups appear not to follow Weinstein's pattern; despite their reliance on revenues from coca paste and kidnapping, they engage in relatively little sexual violence against civilians compared to other armed groups (HRW 2003b).

Conclusion: a research agenda

The literature on sexual violence during war has yet to provide an adequate explanation for its variation across wars, armed groups, and units. While many authors have distinguished between opportunistic and strategic sexual violence, the empirical pattern of variation is wider, including wars where sexual violence is remarkably low on the part of one or more parties to the conflict. In the light of comparative analysis, we do not adequately understand the conditions under which armed groups provide effective sanctions against their combatants engaging in sexual violence or those under which groups effectively promote its strategic use. To conclude, I offer suggestions for further research on the patterns and sources of variation.

In research on sexual violence, scholars should disaggregate our analysis to focus on distinct types of sexual violence (or combinations thereof) as the underlying mechanisms generating high or low prevalence may be different for each type. Major sub-types should include sexual torture (including of men), sexual slavery, sexual violence (particularly rape) in the context of ethnic or political cleansing (rape and displacement; rape and genocide), sexual violence (particularly rape) as collective punishment, and opportunistic rape. Some work has already been done along these lines (see Enloe 2000; Sharlach 2001; Lilly and Marshall 2000).

Whether or not an armed group engages in sexual violence in general and particular forms in particular should be understood as a question about the groups' *repertoire* of violence, by which I mean the analogue for violence of Charles Tilly's notion of the repertoire of collective action. This broader concept suggests several avenues of research. While focusing on the variation in sexual violence, this essay has also shown that the repertoire of violence varies across conflicts and armed groups, and may vary across units within a group. More specifically, the repertoire of a particular group may be constant over time and space, with the relative incidence of different forms of violence remaining approximately the same. In other cases, the repertoire may not be constant, as when co-variation occurs for some but not all kinds of violence; for example, if disappearances and executions rise and fall together but sexual violence remains constant. Whether a group's repertoire is a product of its own strategy (if it has one) or of its strategic and military interaction with other parties to the war likely varies across time and cases (Hoover 2006).

An obvious implication is that scholars should collect and code for all kinds of violence, not just lethal violence. However, we do not yet understand the selection issues that underlie observed data. For example, is an incident of rape more likely to be counted if accompanied by lethal violence (there is a body to be examined) or less (human rights groups may only record the death)?

To understand the repertoire of violence, I suggest that armed groups (both state and nonstate) should be approached as complex organizations that (in a particular setting, with more or less success) define opportunities, enforce specific norms, shape particular incentive structures, embrace some strategies and condemn others. In focusing on why violence sometimes but not always takes sexual form, we should not assume that male combatants will rape given the opportunity; rather, the sexual aspect of violence should be explained, not presumed. This approach suggests a focus on four units of analysis and their interrelationships: the armed group leadership, its hierarchy, the small unit in which combatants have face-to-face relations, and the individual combatant.[17]

Key to explaining the observed variation are the conditions under which armed groups, small units, and individuals develop sanctions and norms that effectively endorse or constrain combatants' engagement in sexual violence. The distinction between leaderships that endorse sexual violence as an effective form of terror against or punishment of a targeted group and those that do not is of course essential. Patterns of violence also depend, however, on whether the armed group provides effective incentives that promote sexual violence or sanctions that prohibit it. If there are no effective sanctions either promoting or discouraging sexual violence (either because the group does not have an explicit policy or because there is no effective enforcement of that policy), the degree of sexual violence engaged in by combatants depends on whether the group has access to civilians (as when it loots kitchens and fields for food) or not, and whether small units promote norms prohibiting or endorsing sexual violence, and whether individuals have such norms.

Norms and practices should not be assumed to be static; rather, they must be understood as evolving over the course of conflict. Individual combatants enter an armed group with (possibly heterogeneous) norms, preferences, and cultural practices concerning sexual violence. The initial socialization in their small unit, the brutalizing processes of witnessing, enduring, and wielding violence, and the pressure to conform to the evolving practices of their unit may reshape those norms, preferences and practices in fundamental ways. The extent of opportunistic sexual violence depends on the absence of sanctions and norms (on the part of the armed group, the small unit, or the individual) that effectively prohibit it and on proximity to potential victims. Where individual and small-unit norms prohibit sexual violence, perhaps on the grounds that it is polluting to the perpetrator, sexual violence will not occur even if a

---

[17] See Hoover (2006) for analysis of how repertoires of violence can be understood via principal agent models in which elites (the principals) have distinct preferences than do combatants (the agents) for different types of violence.

unit has ready access to civilians and even if the armed group does not punish those who engage in it.

This approach suggests a number of hypotheses that might guide scholarly research (see also Wood 2006, 330–335). First, where armed groups depend on the provision of support (supplies, intelligence) from civilians *and* aspire to govern those civilians, they do not engage in sexual violence against those civilians if they have a reasonably effective command structure. For example, leftist insurgencies in Latin America, which typically have intensive socialization processes and effective command structures, engage in little sexual violence against civilians, with the exception of Peru's Sendero Luminoso.

Second, where norms held by individual combatants and small units, either condemning or approving sexual violence, are the same and are also endorsed by the armed group's leadership, sexual violence by that group will be either very low or very high, respectively. Specifically, where armed groups reinforce cultural taboos against sexual contact with the potential target populations, sexual violence against that population will be low; in the absence of such taboos, where armed groups promote sexual violence, violence will be high. There was relatively little sexual violence (apart from sexual humiliation) in the labor and concentration camps of Nazi Germany. The high marriage rate among ethnic groups before the conflicts in Bosnia-Herzegovina and Rwanda, according to this hypothesis, facilitated the widespread sexual violence during the conflicts.

Third, if an armed group prohibits sexual violence against a particular population, the less effective the military discipline of the group, the more likely combatants are to engage in sexual violence (unless they hold particularly strong norms against it). Thus ill-disciplined militias, ill-trained armies of conscripts, poorly trained military police, and little-supervised service troops are more likely to engage in sexual violence than well-trained troops (in the absence of a policy promoting sexual violence). The challenge in conducting research on military discipline is of course to do so without the tautology of the kind that occurs when an absence of discipline is inferred from a pattern of violence against civilians.

This approach raises questions as well. To what extent is sexual violence accounted for by a breakdown in command-and-control structure and morale versus a change in norms on the part of combatants? What accounts for the emergence of an organizational structure strong enough to enforce strategic decision by the leadership? How and why do small-unit norms evolve that enable sexual violence by its members? In what conditions does military victory, on the one hand, and military stalemate, on the other, contribute to sexual violence? To what extent do international norms and law constrain the practice of sexual violence? Why are men targeted in some settings but not in others?

There are other puzzling patterns that researchers might address. Armed groups with a high proportion of female combatants engage less in sexual violence; potential explanations include the disruption of male bonding practices in small units, the more general undermining of patriarchal role models that support sexual violence, or a group ideology that both encourages girls and women to join and discourages sexual violence. Democracies rarely engage in widespread sexual violence and generally punish rape for personal gratification, but limited sexual violence is sometimes endorsed in practice. What constrains democracies, and why do those constraints not prohibit all forms of sexual violence?

More broadly, the following avenues of research may contribute to addressing the overall puzzle of variation in sexual violence.

More research is needed to better document variation in the patterns of sexual violence across conflicts, including those analyzed here. In particular, because the cases were chosen for their variation in sexual violence, additional research is needed to estimate the relative frequency of occurrence of different patterns in the actual universe of cases.

Scholars should not neglect "negative cases" of groups or conflicts where sexual violence does not occur (or occurs at low levels) as they should illuminate cases where it does. Of particular interest are those conflicts where one party does not "mirror" the use of sexual violence by another party to the war and conflicts where sexual violence seems anomalously low in the light of high rates in similar conflicts. This essay suggests a key distinction among such negative cases, whether sexual violence does not occur due to effective sanctions against it, individual norms against it, small-unit norms against it, or because the group has little access to civilians. In particular, a comparison of the working of ideological and religious or other cultural mores against sexual violence might shed light on the character of many armed groups. However, establishing the operative force of such mores poses a particular methodological challenge, namely, how to establish the causal force of a stated norm or sanction independently of the observed presence or absence of sexual violence.

Such research requires access to detailed local sources, which is not always possible during or in the aftermath of war. However, wars differ in the availability of such records and the possibility of extended local field research. Fortunately, it is precisely such negative cases for which local research may be possible.

To explore the force of potential causal processes, within-case contrasts should be explored as the simplest way to control for many otherwise confounding variables. This approach is already proving very rich for the study of violence and participation in civil war, including in Greece (Kalyvas 2006), Rwanda (Straus 2006), Peru (Weinstein 2006), and El Salvador (Wood 2003). Ideally, one could compare patterns of sexual (and other) violence not just between factions and over time, but across sub-units of the armed factions, thereby clarifying the causal force of factors at different levels. The extent to which sexual violence varies with other forms of violence should also be analyzed as a way to identify particular strategies and norms of violence. A particularly interesting case would be that of US forces in Vietnam if relevant documents exist and could be declassified. Comparing patterns of sexual violence in different colonies of the same empire would also be an illuminating variation on this research design.

The small-group dynamics that lead to unit norms promoting or constraining the occurrence of sexual violence appears a promising avenue of research. Relevant factors include recruitment of individuals who endorse the group norm and conformity to the norm once the individual is a member of the group. For example, there may be systematic differences between armed groups that rely on mercenaries, career professionals, and conscripts. In particular, the extent to which military training practices differ among armies in the degree of brutalization of recruits and in the activities to build bonds between members of the small units could be a fruitful avenue for further exploration. Comparison to small-group dynamics in other settings where group sexual violence sometimes occurs, such as fraternities, urban gangs, and sports teams, may prove fruitful.

A related agenda that would be very illuminating is the study of perpetrators of wartime sexual violence. Although such research would be difficult to carry out for human subject concerns as well as practical reasons, it may not be impossible. Scott Straus (2006) was able to interview a particular subset of perpetrators of the Rwandan genocide: those who had been convicted, had confessed, and had been sentenced.

Another avenue of research would focus more explicitly on dynamic interactive mechanisms. For example, patterns of sexual violence might be fruitfully analyzed with a model based on positive feedback mechanisms that amplify small initial differences between groups, units, or sites and result in large differences in the prevalence and form of sexual violence. Such models may illuminate the diffusion of decentralized norms that condone sexual violence, for example. One such mechanism is escalating revenge: if a member of one party commits sexual violence against a member of another group, a member of the other may retaliate in ways leading to a spiral of sexual violence. Or epidemiological models might be productive, in which if some members of a small group commit sexual violence, other members of that small group may do so as well; once that small group does, neighboring units may join in, leading to widespread sexual violence by that party to the war. In both cases the dynamic processes explaining the escalation or dampening of violence will be characterized by tipping points such that seemingly small differences in the causes of violence would account for large differences in the consequences.

The ongoing brutality in Darfur reminds us that sexual violence remains a horrifying aspect of war, one that occasions great suffering on the part of civilians – particularly women and girls – trapped in conditions of insecurity and terror. Yet, rape is not inevitable in war, as this essay's emphasis on negative and asymmetric cases has illustrated. Understanding the determinants of the variation in sexual violence may help those UN officials, members of nongovernmental organizations, government, military, and insurgent leaders who seek to limit sexual violence and other violations of the laws of war.

REFERENCES

African Rights. 1994. *Rwanda: Death, Despair and Defiance*. London: African Rights.

Alison, Miranda. 2003. "Cogs in a Wheel? Women in the Liberation Tigers of Tamil Eelam." *Civil Wars* 6 (4): 37–54.

Amnesty International. 1999. *Sri Lanka: Torture in Custody*. www.amnestyusa. org/countries/sri_lanka/reports.do.

  2002. *Sri Lanka: Rape in Custody*. www.amnestyusa.org/countries/sri_lanka/reports.do.

  2004. *Sudan, Darfur: Rape as a Weapon of War: Sexual Violence and its Consequences*. AI: London.

Amowitz, Lynn L., Chen Reis, Kristina Hare Lyons *et al*. 2002. "Prevalence of War-Related Sexual Violence and Other Human Rights Abuses among Internally Displaced Persons in Sierra Leone." *Journal of the American Medical Association* 287 (4): 513–521.

Barkan, Joanne. 2002. "As Old as War Itself: Rape in Foca." *Dissent* (Winter): 60–66.

Beck, Birgit. 2002. "Rape: The Military Trials of Sexual Crimes Committed by Soldiers in the Wehrmach, 1939–1944." In *Home/Front: The Military, War and Gender in 20th Century Germany*, ed. Karen Hagerman and Stefanie Schuler-Springorum. New York: Berg.

Beevor, Antony. 2002. *The Fall of Berlin 1945*. New York: Penguin.

Bloom, Mia. N. d. "War and the Politics of Rape: Ethnic versus Non-Ethnic Conflicts." Unpublished manuscript.

Brownmiller, Susan. 1975. *Against Our Will*. New York: Ballentine.

Burds, Jeffrey. 2009. "Sexual Violence in Europe in World War II, 1939–1945." *Politics and Society* 37.

Chang, Iris. 1997. *The Rape of Nanking: The Forgotten Holocaust of World War II*. New York: Penguin.

Danner, Mark. 1994. *The Massacre at El Mozote*. New York: Vintage Books.

Enloe, Cynthia. 1983. *Does Khaki Become You? The Militarization of Women's Lives*. Cambridge, MA: South End Press.

———. 2000. *Maneuvers: The International Politics of Militarizing Women's Lives*. Berkeley: University of California Press.

Friedman, Jonathan C. 2002. *Speaking the Unspeakable: Essays on Sexuality, Gender, and Holocaust Survivor Memory*. Lanham, MD: University Press of America.

Gertjejanssen, Wendy Jo. 2004. "Victims, Heroes, Survivors: Sexual Violence on the Eastern Front During World War II." Ph.D. dissertation, University of Minnesota.

Goldstein, Joshua A. 2001. *War and Gender: How Gender Shapes the War System and Vice Versa*. Cambridge University Press.

Green, Jennifer L. 2004. "Uncovering Collective Rape: A Comparative Study of Political Sexual Violence." *International Journal of Sociology* 34 (1): 97–116.

Grossman, Atina. 1997. "A Question of Silence: The Rape of German Women by Occupation Soldiers." In *West Germany under Construction: Politics, Society, and Culture in the Adenauer Era*, ed. Robert G. Moeller. Ann Arbor: University of Michigan Press.

Hagan, John, Heather Schoenfeld, and Alberto Palloni. 2006. "The Science of Human Rights, War Crimes, and Humanitarian Emergencies." *Annual Review of Sociology* 32: 329–349.

Hoover, Amelia. 2006. "Disaggregating 'Violence' During Armed Conflict: Why and How." Unpublished manuscript, Yale University.

Human Rights Watch [HRW]. 1996. *Shattered Lives: Sexual Violence During the Rwandan Genocide and its Aftermath*. New York: HRW.

———. 2003a. "We'll Kill You if You Cry." *Sexual Violence in the Sierra Leone Conflict* 15 (1A). New York: HRW.

———. 2003b. *You'll Learn Not to Cry: Child Combatants in Colombia*. New York: HRW.

———. 2004. *Living in Fear: Child Soldiers and the Tamil Tigers in Sri Lanka* 16 (13 C). New York: HRW.

Hyun-Kyung, Chung. 2000. "Your Comfort versus My Death: Korean Comfort Women." In *War's Dirty Secret: Rape, Prostitution, and Other Crimes Against Women*, ed. Anne Llewellyn Barstow. Cleveland, OH: The Pilgrim Press.

International Commission of Inquiry on Darfur. 2005. *Report of the International Commission of Inquiry on Darfur to the United Nations Secretary-General*. UN: Geneva. www.un.org/news/dh/sudan/com_inq_darfur.pdf.

International Criminal Court [ICC]. 2000. *Elements of Crimes*. UN Doc. PNICC/2000/1/Add.2.

Japanese Cabinet Councillors' Office on External Affairs. 1993 (E/CN.4/1996/137). In UNESCO, *Contemporary Forms of Slavery: Systematic Rape,*

Sexual Slavery and Slavery-like Practices During Armed Conflict, Appendix 9(a) (E/CN.4/Sub.2/1998/13, 1998).

Kalyvas, Stathis. 2003. "The Ontology of 'Political Violence': Action and Identity in Civil Wars." *Perspectives on Politics* 1 (3): 475–494.

2006. *The Logic of Violence in Civil War*. Cambridge University Press.

Kesteren, J. N. van, P. Mayhew, and P. Nieuwbeerta. 2000. *Criminal Victimisation in Seventeen Industrialised Countries: Key Findings from the 2000 International Crime Victims Survey*. The Hague: Ministry of Justice, WODC.

Leiby, Michele. In press. "Wartime Sexual Violence in Guatemala and Peru." *International Studies Quarterly*.

Lilly, J. Robert, and Pam Marshall. 2000. "Rape – Wartime." In *The Encyclopedia of Criminology and Deviant Behavior*, ed. Clifton D. Bryant. Oxford: Brunner-Routledge.

Médecins Sans Frontières. 2005. *The Crushing Burden of Rape: Sexual Violence in Darfur*. Amsterdam: MSF.

Mitchell, Neil, and Tali Gluch. 2004. "The Principals and Agents of Political Violence and the Strategic and Private Benefits of Rape." Paper presented at the annual meeting of the American Political Science Association, Chicago.

Morris, Benny. 2004. *The Birth of the Palestinian Problem Revisited*, 2nd edn. Cambridge University Press.

Morris, Madeline. 1996. "By Force of Arms: Rape, War, and Military Culture." *Duke Law Journal* 45 (4): 651–781.

Naimark, Norman M. 1995. "Soviet Soldiers, German Women, and the Problem of Rape." In *The Russians in Germany: A History of the Soviet Zone of Occupation, 1945–1949*. Cambridge, MA: The Belknap Press of Harvard University Press.

Physicians for Human Rights [PHR]. 2002. *War-Related Sexual Violence in Sierra Leone*. Boston: PHR.

Rees, Laurence. 2005. *The Nazis and the "Final Solution."* London: BBC Books.

Rozee, Patricia D. 1993. "Forbidden or Forgiven? Rape in Cross-Cultural Perspective." *Psychology of Women Quarterly* 17: 499–514.

Salzman, Todd. 2000. "Rape Camps, Forced Impregnation, and Ethnic Cleansing." In *War's Dirty Secret: Rape, Prostitution, and Other Crimes Against Women*, ed. Anne Llewellyn Barstow. Cleveland, OH: The Pilgrim Press.

Sharlach, Lisa. 1999. "Gender and Genocide in Rwanda: Women as Agents and Objects of Genocide." *Journal of Genocide Research* 1 (3): 387–399.

2000. "Rape as Genocide: Bangladesh, the Former Yugoslavia, and Rwanda." *New Political Science* 22 (1): 89–102.

2001. "Sexual Violence as Political Terror." Ph.D. dissertation, University of California, Davis.

Skjelsbaek, Inger. 2001. "Sexual Violence and War: Mapping out a Complex Relationship." *European Journal of International Relations* 7 (2): 211–237.

Straus, Scott. 2006. *The Order of Genocide: Race, Power, and War in Rwanda*. Ithaca, NY: Cornell University Press.

Tilly, Charles. 2003. *The Politics of Collective Violence*. Cambridge University Press.

Tobach, Ethel, and Rachel Reed. 2003. "Understanding Rape." In *Evolution, Gender, and Rape*, ed. Cheryl Brown Travis. Cambridge, MA: MIT Press.

Truth Commission [TC] for El Salvador. 1993. *From Madness to Hope: The 12 Year War in El Salvador. Report of the Truth Commission for El Salvador.* Reprinted in *The United Nations and El Salvador, 1990–1995.* The United Nations Blue Books Series, vol. IV. New York: United Nations.

Truth and Reconciliation Commission [Peru]. 2003. *Final Report.* www.cverdad.org.pe/ingles/ifinal/index.php.

Truth and Reconciliation Commission [TCR] of Sierra Leone. 2005. *Final Report.* http://trcsierraleone.org/drwebsite/publish/index.shtml.

UNESCO. 1998. *Contemporary Forms of Slavery: Systematic Rape, Sexual Slavery and Slavery-Like Practices During Armed Conflict.* E/CN.4/Sub.2/1998/13.

United Nations Development Fund for Women. 2005. *Gender Profile of the Conflict in Sri Lanka.* www.womenwarpeace.org/sri_lanka/sri_lanka.htm [updated on October 31, 2005].

UNSC. 1994. *Rape and Sexual Assault. Annex IX of the Final Report of the United Nations Commission of Experts Established Pursuant to Security Council Resolution 780 (1992).* S/1994/674/Add.2 (vol. V).

Weinstein, Jeremy. 2006. *Inside Rebellion: The Politics of Insurgent Violence.* Cambridge University Press.

Wood, Elisabeth Jean. 2003. *Insurgent Collective Action and Civil War in El Salvador.* Cambridge University Press.

2006. "Variation in Sexual Violence During War." *Politics and Society* 34 (3): 307–341.

2009. "Armed Groups and Sexual Violence: When is Wartime Rape Rare?" *Politics and Society* 37.

World Health Organization [WHO]. 2002. "Sexual Violence." Chapter 6 of *World Report on Violence and Health.* Geneva: WHO.

14 "Military necessity" and the laws of war in Imperial Germany

Isabel V. Hull

One of the chief ways in which states have tried to order, that is to limit, the violence of war is through law. The international law of war grew out of customary practices developed by armies as they clashed on the field. There were three great periods when these customs were codified into written law: the seventeenth century (done by individual writers, most notably Hugo Grotius), the late nineteenth/twentieth centuries (done by international conferences), and the late twentieth/twenty-first centuries (done by international conferences, judicial extension, the establishment of international courts, and of the International Court under international auspices). This essay examines the second period, when a fundamental disagreement occurred between Imperial Germany and most other Western states over whether war could be limited at all. That disagreement, which had profound effects on how war was actually prosecuted, hinged on the definition of military necessity.

The term "military necessity" is a technical phrase of international law and custom coined to describe the spheres and circumstances in which lethal force or destruction may lawfully occur in time of war. Military necessity has a long history, yet it has been surprisingly little studied.[1] In the late nineteenth and early twentieth centuries it was especially controversial because, as nations codified custom into written law, they successively narrowed the meaning of military necessity. Imperial Germany battled against this development. It claimed wide latitude for military necessity – so wide as to cancel out law altogether, contemporary observers from other countries charged. The effects of Germany's understanding of military necessity in World War I, well known at the time, are currently being rediscovered and reevaluated by historians. This essay examines the German view and asks: how did it develop, what were its essential characteristics, why did it remain so

---

[1] Rodick (1928, chapter 6) is devoted to military necessity. The most thorough modern account is McCoubrey (1991, 215–255). See also Best (1980) and Messerschmidt (1996, 191–230).

adamantine against the strong international tide, and, finally, did it represent a conservative attachment to an older interpretation or rather an alternative, modern concept that recognized and developed further extreme potentials in modern warfare?

The development of military necessity in international law

The first codifier of the international law of war, Hugo Grotius, might be read as permitting everything in a just war: "the steps that are necessary [to a lawful end], *necessity* being taken not in physical exactness but morally, we have a right to use" (1853, 295–296). But in fact Grotius recognized several limits to military necessity, even in just wars. Four limits are particularly important to note: (1) the danger must be real, vital, and imminent; (2) the claimer of necessity must exercise proportionate, i.e., limited force in countering the threat; (3) not every means was permitted even then (for example, using poisoned weapons or engaging in assassination); and (4) restitution for damages was required (Rodick 1928, 6). None of the writers in the just war tradition (which defined the early modern period), nor even those often interpreted to have criticized them, such as Machiavelli, believed that military necessity was unlimited. They all believed in the rule of proportionate force and most held to the other three limits as well (Rodick 1928, 1–25). Emmerich de Vattel (1797, 346–347), writing at the end of the eighteenth century, is typical in establishing the principle of military necessity and then immediately modifying it. In his third book, on the international laws of war, he wrote:

The Whole is to be deduced from one single principle, – from the object of a just war: for, when the end is lawful, he who has a right to pursue that end, has, of course, a right to employ all the means which are necessary for its attainment ... [Two sentences later, he continues:] The lawfulness of the end does not give us a real right to any thing further than barely the means necessary for the attainment of that end ... Right goes hand in hand with necessity and the exigency of the case, but never exceeds them ... We may choose such methods as are the most efficacious and best calculated to attain the end in view, provided they be not of an odious kind, or unjustifiable in themselves, and prohibited by the law of nature.

The just war/natural law framework waned in the nineteenth century, ironically just as the real spurt in codifying and defining the laws of war took place, after mid-century. The Paris conference of 1856 began a series of international meetings which discussed, drafted, and finally produced widely ratified written codes of positive law reflecting what the participants understood as the hitherto unwritten customs governing warfare. The Geneva Convention of 1864 on the treatment of wounded and sick soldiers, was followed by meetings at St. Petersburg (1868), Brussels (1874), Oxford (1880), and then the two Hague conferences (1899 and 1907) out of which came the authoritative Hague Rules of Land Warfare, which most European states, including Germany, ratified. Indispensable to the international discussions was the first national manual of war law drafted for the Union in 1863 by Francis Lieber.

There has been much speculation about why the spurt of codification happened when it did and whether the modern, mid-nineteenth-century doctrine of national sovereignty retarded or furthered its progress (Brownlie 1963, 49; Best 1980, 48, 135–140). For our purposes, it is important to recall several features of codification. First, it was not a matter of civilian jurists versus hard-nosed military men. There were many practical reasons for officers to desire clear, positive (i.e. written) rules of warfare. They were especially enthusiastic about safeguards for themselves, as the popularity of the Geneva Convention among the military attests. But officers were instrumental in driving the process forward. St. Petersburg in 1868 was an entirely military gathering (Garner 1920, 15). Lieber's *Instructions* were revised by officers before they were issued (Rodick 1928, 2). And each nation sent strong military contingents to the conferences. Second, the purpose of codification was not to outlaw war, or make it impossible to wage, but to curb the widely feared tendency of wars to drift toward gratuitous excess. And, third, the delegates did not seek to expand law by innovative legislation, but to set down the customary limits currently practiced by armies in the field. Codification was thus not a dizzy, humanitarian bubble (as cynics claimed) but a practical attempt by practitioners of war, lawyers, and statesmen to clarify the rules by which states fought each other.

How did military necessity figure in the codification process? We should begin with Lieber, whose *Instructions* served as the basis for subsequent drafts of war law and whose work set down the customs of war as they were understood in 1863.[2] Lieber began by defining military necessity (which most codes thereafter failed to do). "Military necessity, as understood by modern civilized nations, consists in the necessity of those measures which are indispensable for securing the ends of the war, and which are lawful according to the modern law and usages of war"

---

[2] See comment by editors to Francis Lieber, Instructions for the Government of Armies in the United States in the Field, General Orders No. 100, 24 April 1863, in Schindler and Toman (1988, 3).

(Art. 14). Like all the international jurists before him, Lieber thus limited military necessity to those methods permitted by positive law and unwritten usages or customs. Within those limits, military necessity had a relatively wide berth:

Military necessity admits of all direct destruction of life or limb of *armed* enemies, and of other persons whose destruction is incidentally *unavoidable* in the armed contests of the war; it allows of the capturing of every armed enemy, and every enemy of importance to the hostile government, or of peculiar danger to the captor; it allows of all destruction of property, and obstruction of the ways and channels of traffic, travel, or communication, and of all withholding of sustenance or means of life from the enemy; of the appropriation of whatever an enemy's country affords necessary for the subsistence and safety of the army, and of such deception as does not involve the breaking of good faith either positively pledged, regarding agreements entered into during the war, or supposed by the modern law of war to exist. Men who take up arms against one another in public war do not cease on this account to be moral beings, responsible to one another and to God. (Art. 15; emphasis in original)

Military necessity is thus the basis on which war can be fought at all. It permits the killing of soldiers and the unavoidable killing of civilians, property destruction, infrastructure destruction or curtailment, requisitions, and deception. But Lieber is cautious in appending to this list the admonition that war does not annul a soldier's moral obligations. In the next, and final, explicit article on military necessity, Lieber set down its absolute limits:

Military necessity does not admit of cruelty – that is, the infliction of suffering for the sake of suffering or for revenge, nor of maiming or wounding except in fight, nor of torture to extort confessions. It does not admit of the use of poison in any way, nor of the wanton devastation of a district. It admits of deception, but disclaims acts of perfidy; and, in general, military necessity does not include any act of hostility which makes the return to peace unnecessarily difficult. (Art. 16) (in Schindler and Toman 1988, 3)

Here, Lieber sums up three points of custom: nothing in excess of what the object demands is lawful; some methods are absolutely forbidden, even in the direst necessity; and the touchstone for deciding difficult cases is peace, not war. That is, again like most writers on international law, Lieber was concerned to break the cycle of violence, to prevent it from ratcheting upwards until mutual hatred and distrust blocked peace.

Lieber mentions military necessity in four other articles, as well, setting the template for all later codes. All four articles deal with non-combatants: the retention of native civil and criminal codes of the occupied zone, martial law, bombardment of fortified areas (where civilians normally also lived), and the seizure or destruction of private property.[3] The intent in each case was to encourage moderation but at the same time to acknowledge that moderation might not be possible. So, for example, Lieber advocates prior warning before bombardments, so that noncombatants, "especially the women and children," may leave, but adds, "it is no infraction of the common law of war to omit thus to inform the enemy. Surprise may be a necessity" (Art. 19).

Lieber's work makes clear that the difficult areas for interpreting the sway of military necessity all involved the impact of war on non-combatants. That remained the case down to the World War and beyond. Johann Caspar Bluntschli, professor of law at the university of Heidelberg, published a draft manual of the laws of war, which he hoped would be used by the armies of the German states as they prepared to fight each other in 1866. Like Lieber, Bluntschli mentioned military necessity only in connection with civilians. Necessity permitted the killing of enemy civilians in occupied areas who passed information to the enemy, the destruction or seizure of private property, the burning of houses, destruction of crops and vineyards, and the devastation of a country's communication and transportation infrastructure (Bluntschli 1866).[4] The Brussels Declaration of 1874 also used military necessity, or phrases like "as far as possible," to denote potential exceptions to the requirement to restore public order and safety and to retain native civil law in the occupied zones, to refrain from destroying or seizing private property, or raising money and services from the occupied (in Schindler and Toman 1988, 25–34).[5]

The manual produced in 1880 by the Institute of International Law at Oxford, *The Laws of War on Land*, expanded the areas in which military necessity or an equivalent phrase was specifically mentioned, and again all save one of them dealt with noncombatants. Added to the list of the Brussels Declaration were: the evacuation of medical personnel, sparing buildings of cultural or religious value, destroying municipal (as opposed to state) property, the raising of contributions, and reprisals (which could also be levied against military personnel) (in Schindler and Toman 1988, 34–48). By the time of the Oxford Manual the phrase "if possible" appeared more frequently than "military necessity," presumably because codification was no longer in the negative mode of clearing territory over which military necessity could rule, but in the positive mode of restricting more and more areas to unlimited military sway. Whereas governments had signed (but not ratified) the Brussels Declaration, the

---

[3] Arts. 3, 5, 19, and 38, respectively.   [4] Arts. 120, 139, and 149, respectively.
[5] Arts. 2, 3, 13.g, and 40, respectively.

Oxford Manual was a private endeavor offered as a model for national war manuals. All these precedents, however, laid the groundwork for the first Hague conference in 1899, which produced the first widely ratified international rules of war.

Military necessity was hotly debated at the Hague conference. The importance of the issue had become clear at the latest in 1874 at the Brussels conference when disagreement between Germany and the rest of the delegates over how far military necessity permitted reprisals threatened to end a conference that, until then, had been conducted in "perfect harmony."[6] At the Hague, Germany took up the cudgels again. Its military delegate, Col. Groß von Schwarzenberg, wanted the military necessity exception to be entered into virtually every article. When he insisted that the words "as far as military necessities permit" be inserted into Art. 38, which protected "family honor and rights, and the lives and property of [civilian] persons" in the occupied zone, Belgian's representative replied that it was "contrary to the spirit of the Brussels draft to introduce into the different articles a special clause relating to the necessities of war. It is impossible to admit the destruction of human rights as a legal thesis although recourse is occasionally had thereto if necessary" (Scott 1920, 488). This colloquy pitted military necessity directly against "human rights," and it underscored the difference between the majority of delegates, who considered military necessity to be exceptional, and the German representatives, who felt it suffused every aspect of war.

In the end, how the Hague delegates handled the issue determined how it has been interpreted ever since. First, they did not define military necessity. That omission reflected, but also encouraged, controversial interpretations and left Lieber's definition the most cited instance. Second, and most important, the delegates twice inserted military necessity into the preamble. The first mention referred to "the purpose

---

[6] The words of the British delegate, cited in Best (1980, 348). The phrase "military necessity" did not appear in the draft article on reprisals, but the words "as far as possible," and "in extreme cases," show that that was the issue. The articles, which were dropped due to the disagreement, read: "Art. 69: Reprisals are admissible in extreme cases only, due regard being paid, as far as shall be possible, to the laws of humanity, when it shall have been unquestionably proved that the laws and customs of war have been violated by the enemy ... " Art. 70 required that reprisals be proportionate to the offense, and Art. 71 that they be conducted only upon the order of a commanding officer. Reprisals exposed the punitive (as opposed to war-functional) aspect of military necessity. Reprisals remained a major area of disagreement between Imperial Germany and most other nations, and revealed Germany's fundamentally different view of international law. A number of the most serious violations of the Hague Rules in World War I, such as the use of gas or unrestricted submarine warfare, were justified as reprisals against allegedly previous infractions by the Allies and as necessary to win the war.

of modifying [the] severity" of the laws and general customs of war "as far as possible." The other stated that the wording of the rules "has been inspired by the desire to diminish the evils of war so far as military necessities permit [and] are destined to serve as general rules of conduct for belligerents in their relations with each other and with populations" (Scott 1915, 100–101). This phrase came to be interpreted as meaning that military necessity had already been taken into account in all the articles that followed. We will return to this important matter below. Finally, the delegates nonetheless did mention military necessity specifically in several articles, following the pattern since Lieber. With the exception of the article on ruses, all the places where military necessity or a phrase like "as far as possible" occurred dealt with civilians (destroying or seizing property, notifying people of bombardment, sparing cultural buildings, restoring public order, keeping native laws, raising taxes and extraordinary levies, demanding personal services and requisitions, and paying for these with real currency) (Scott 1915).[7]

The Hague Rules of Land Warfare that emerged out of the negotiations in 1899 were not innovative. They reflected the consensus that had emerged among most nation-signatories about what was legal in wartime (Garner 1920, 21). In 1907 the British international jurist John Westlake laid down what has become the dominant modern view regarding military necessity. He wrote that because military necessity appeared in the preamble, it had already been factored into the articles and could not be discounted a second time. Military necessity therefore could not be used as an argument to break those rules (Westlake 1907, 57, 115–117; Spaight 1911, 8; Garner 1920, 282; Oppenheim 1958, 233; Downey 1953, 262; Rodick 1928, 59–61). Positive law cannot be broken by military necessity. At most, military necessity could be invoked as an exceptional excuse regarding those articles in which it was specifically mentioned. More and more that excuse has been taken to mean the physical impossibility of fulfilling the rule. McCoubrey states the modern view: "Military necessity is a doctrine within the laws of armed conflict which recognises the potential impracticality of full compliance with legal norms in certain circumstances, and, accordingly, may mitigate or expunge culpability for prima facie unlawful action in appropriate cases of armed conflict" (1991, 240).

This narrow construction of military necessity was not universal prior to 1914, but it was dominant. It was the overwhelming consensus among English-language writers, and there were some German jurists

[7] Arts. 24, 23.g, 26, 27, 43, 48, 49, 51, and 52, respectively.

who agreed with them.[8] But a far larger, and more influential, number of German international lawyers held the opposing view (Garner 1920, 196–197). In 1922 the German Federal Court upheld their opinion, ruling that "the right of a belligerent state to self-preservation goes before all treaties and the state may in the case of an emergency diverge from the rules of land warfare" (Germany, Reichsgericht 1931, 179). German legal handbooks did not recognize the narrow construction as dominant until the 1960s (Tobler 1961, 351–353; Berber 1969, 78).

The German view of military necessity

The German understanding of military necessity first became visible as a set of practices in the 1870–1871 war against France. After winning a stunning battlefield victory that, in the Prussian General Staff's opinion, ought to have led France to capitulate, the French threw off their defeated government and hastily raised new armies to carry on the fight. Lacking adequate troops successfully to occupy the unruly French districts and frustrated by its inability to end the war, Germany introduced desparate measures. It forced civilian notables to act as hostages on threatened trains (thus reintroducing a practice that had all but disappeared); it burnt down whole villages where it suspected civilians had engaged in fighting or near where acts of sabotage had occurred; it levied huge, punitive "contributions" on localities; it requisitioned whole areas into impoverishment; it threatened noncombatants with death for refusing to cooperate in aiding the occupation against France, or as reprisal against *francs-tireurs*; it forced locals to act as guides against their own country; it bombarded Paris, etc. Criticism was immediate, and not limited to Frenchmen or jurists. Foreign diplomatic observers protested, as did the commander of Britain's Staff College, who labeled Germany's methods a "system of terrorism" (Best 1980, 194). Debate at the Brussels conference in 1874 centered on Germany's controversial actions in 1870–1871; the acrimony nearly destroyed the conference (Best 1980, 348). It was *ex post facto* and in response to the critical uproar that the German position gradually was articulated.

In a lengthy, two-part article entitled "Military Necessity and Humanity, a Critical Essay," General Julius von Hartmann in 1876 distilled the principles behind Germany's acts in the Franco-Prussian war, all of which he defended. His remarks accorded closely with those of General Staff Chief Helmuth von Moltke, at the time, and they were taken by influential German jurists to represent the expert, military

---

[8] Scott and Garner (1918, 8) list von Bar, von Liszt, and Wehberg.

opinion on the subject (Moltke 1992; Lueder 1889a, 256–257; 1889b, 378).[9] Contemporary English-speaking jurists considered Hartmann archetypical of the German viewpoint (Garner 1920, 4, 279, 328; Munro *et al.* 1917, 6).

For Hartmann (1877–1878), military necessity *was* the law of war. He wrote, "the grand goal of war [is] the *defeat of the enemy's power, the overcoming of his energy, the mastery of his will.* This *one* goal commands absolutely; it dictates law and regulation. The concrete figure of this law appears in the form of *military necessity*" (453–454, emphases in original). The kind of law Hartmann meant was not positive law, but a determinant, natural process. His "military realism," as he called it, regarded "the entire construction of war from the war apparatus to its use in the most extensive way as an entirety growing out of the innermost nature of war, regulated and functioning in its specific particularity according to military necessity" (120–121). According to Hartmann, war cancels peace and all its principles. "War, compared to peace, is thoroughly *abnormal* . . . it is an exceptional state [*Ausnahmezustand*] because it abjures in its inmost nature the bases on which civilization and culture rest, the laws according to which they develop, and in their stead it returns to conditions which grant to individual energy and power [*Macht*] unlimited justification" (123). Therefore, "once war has started, then only the requirements of military necessity are operative" (471).

In place of law, which Hartmann regarded as an external, necessarily vain attempt to mitigate a natural force, he opined that only the civilized inclinations of individual commanders and the discipline of their troops might limit military necessity. Whether they succeeded depended on reciprocity. But the emotional dynamics loosed by war, its existential character as a matter of life and death, and in the modern period its character as a "people's war," always threatened to pull war into the spiral of excess. Tellingly, Hartmann (1877–1878, 88) approved of those international agreements, like the Geneva Convention, designed to help wounded or captured soldiers or to clarify the conditions of battle (uniforms, rules for parliamentarians and for capitulations, and the like). But further attempts at codification he interpreted as unrealistic efforts to thwart military necessity. The Brussels Declaration, he wrote, "is generally unacceptable."

---

[9] Lueder (1889a) cites Hartmann as his authority on the (approved) use of "terrorism" against occupied civilians and on the precedence of military necessity over law. On Hartmann's importance, see Best (1994, 145–146) and Messerschmidt (1996, 196).

Hartmann reasoned entirely from within the military framework. Professional military goals determined how he understood the nature of war. The "self-preservation" that most jurists took to legitimate military necessity mutated in Hartmann's mind into the mere need to achieve victory. "Unlimited freedom of military action in war is the one imperative precondition for military success" (Hartmann 1877–1878, 88). Once success replaced self-preservation, however, military necessity became limitless. Foreign critics focused on this point. Writing after the World War, Garner (1920, 195) observed that "the German doctrine of military necessity embraces more than the right of self-preservation and includes acts of mere military interest, utility, and convenience." If this doctrine were accepted, Westlake (1907, 117) argued, then "the most elementary restraints on war, which have been handed down from antiquity, are not safe."

Nevertheless, Hartmann's military interpretation became the template most eminent German jurists used in their texts on the laws of war. So, for example, Christian Meurer (1907, 14) defined military necessity like this: "The law of war is not contravened if the action is necessary to support the troops or to repel a danger to them and cannot be accomplished in any other way, or is necessary to execute or achieve the success of an enterprise of war that is not otherwise illegal." Or, C. Lueder (1889a, 186), after a nod to proportionality, continued: "therefore the nature and essence of war is *unlimited force* [*Gewalt*], the dominion of the sword and of military necessity, which alone set its limits regarding the goal of war and for which alone the highest powers of the state take responsibility." Lueder (1889a, 256) summed up the German position with the phrase: "when the exception [i.e. war] occurs, following its nature it cancels law, and *Kriegsraison* has precedence over *Kriegsmanier*." *Kriegsraison* meant military necessity following from the logic or goal of war, while *Kriegsmanier* meant the (limiting) customs, or laws of war. Lueder (1889a, 254) apologized for his antiquated wording, but claimed these were technical terms stretching back to the beginnings of international custom/law.

Foreign critics stamped Lueder, Meurer, and the rest as militarists who fatally weakened the mitigating power of law. But that judgment is too simple. Lueder (1889a, 257) was at pains to argue that a "true conflict" between law and military necessity rarely occurred. Meurer (1907, 247) insisted that necessity trumped law only in "a true emergency": "Military necessity requires an emergency which in normal war situations is not present. That which leads more quickly or easily to the goal is not on that account already necessary." The German jurists whom foreign critics most vociferously attacked were in fact trying to save international law by making it palatable to military men; otherwise, they feared, armies would disregard it altogether. Lueder (1889a, 262–263, 275) pleaded:

in the interests of the further development of the law of war it is devoutly to be wished that international lawyers ... should not rush one-sidedly forward without hearing the important demands of the military on international law; at the same time, military and state practitioners should no more than is necessary reject [the views of] international lawyers. Both must work hand in hand.

German jurists were fighting a much more powerful current of military influence and prestige than was true in other countries. The military view defined the discourse in Germany, significantly restricting the reception of the new direction in codification.

The German view of military necessity is not only, or even mainly, visible in legal books. It permeated Germany's international relations – for example, in the obstructionist and almost paranoid instructions to the German delegates to the 1899 Hague conference (Dülffer 1981, 108–120; Stenzel 1973, 21, 29; Zorn 1915, 77–79) or in the satisfaction with which General Erich von Gündell, Germany's military delegate to the 1907 Hague conference, noted Kaiser Wilhelm's attitude "of indifference, which I anticipated and desired." Gündell noted also the German strategy: "In general we follow the tactic, as long as we can, of not fighting dizzy pacifist suggestions if other states are already doing so." Altogether Gündell chafed at the "lukewarm, overcivilized surroundings" of the conference (Gündell 1939, 107, 98, 99).

Apparently, none of the signatories to the Hague Rules of Land Warfare did an especially good job of drilling their officers in the code, but Germany was conspicuous in its neglect: from 1907 to 1911, for instance, the teaching plan at the War Academy devoted no time at all to the subject (Stenzel 1973, 36–37). Of the twenty instruction manuals the postwar Reichstag investigating committee examined, only one devoted a chapter to international law (Germany, Parliament 1927, 36). And whereas other nations' armies drafted their manuals to take the Hague Rules of Land Warfare into account, Germany did not; in fact, Germany did not compile an official manual at all. In Britain and France, the drafters of these manuals were all, as Lieber had been, international lawyers. The officer detailed by the General Staff to write the only officially issued handbook that existed by 1914, Major Rudolf von Friederich, was not.[10] After the war, Friederich explained that his

---

[10] Only a manual issued by the (Prussian) War Ministry would have been truly official. Foreign observers could imagine neither that Germany had no official manual, nor that

task was to compile a practical guide for officers that reflected "the current general opinion in the war literature." He used his own and the General Staff's library. He knew of the Hague Rules (which Germany had ratified with only one reservation[11]), but frequently did not follow them, apparently because the "current general opinion" he found in the German literature did not reflect them.[12] Friederich (Germany, Großer Generalstab 1902, 48, 62, 63, 16, 31) not surprisingly recapped Hartmann's arguments and concluded that military necessity annulled written law (not merely custom). *Kriegsbrauch* also departed from the Hague Rules on the following points: enemy civilians could be forced to give militarily relevant information, requisitions from occupied civilians were unlimited, collective fines were still permitted, prisoners of war could be killed as security risks or if they could not be fed, and "spies" could be killed without trial.

Kriegsbrauch was not exceptional. Most of Imperial Germany's practical manuals displayed the same ignorance or rejection of the writ of positive law in wartime, or they focused so single-mindedly on the military tasks at hand as to leave the impression that no other consideration must be allowed to interfere.[13] The practical manuals are significant, because in the end it is less important what German representatives wrote or said than what German officers (and soldiers) did. Or perhaps it is more accurate to say that what was written and taught accurately reflected the actual practices of 1870–1871 (and thereafter) which almost everyone defended before the chorus of critics. Thus, for Imperial Germany practice set principle.

The centrality of recent war practices to the German understanding of military necessity makes the work of J. M. S. Spaight especially interesting for us. Spaight was one of the few jurists, then or now, who took seriously the truism that international law comes from actual practices in

---

Major Friederich was unlearned in law, so they assumed that *Kriegsbrauch* was authoritative and that Friederich was the General Staff's "Jurist" (Spaight 1911, 7, 89, 406; Garner 1920, 4, 328; Scott and Garner, 1918).

[11] Germany's reservation concerned Art. 44 prohibiting an occupying power from forcing civilians to take part in military operations against their own nation (Scott 1915, 132).

[12] After the war, Friederich told the Reichstag that he had not known of the Hague Rules, yet he refers to them numerous times in *Kriegsbrauch*: 3, 7, 14, 15, 18, 21, 24, 31, and 67. See also his testimony in Germany, Parliament (1927, 27–28).

[13] For example, the *Kriegs-Etappenordnung* (Prussia, War Ministry 1914) that regulated the occupied zones violated the Hague Rules on several points, while the *Feld-Dienstordnung* (Prussia, War Ministry 1908), the practical handbook for all soldiers, did not prepare troops at all for encounters with civilians or prisoners. See Garner (1920, I:6 n. 1). Both the French and British manuals were based on the Hague Rules and both instructed officers in great detail about how to minimize civilian hardship in war (Jacomet 1913; Edmonds and Oppenheim 1912).

wartime (abbreviated as "usage" or "custom"), as well as from positive laws or treaties, or from "the laws of humanity, and the requirements of the public conscience."[14] Spaight's (1911) compendious and influential *War Rights on Land* therefore surveyed what armies actually had done in wars since the Napoleonic period. Consequently, Spaight's conclusions about what was permissible were much closer to the German view than were those of his non-German contemporaries. It is all the more significant, then, to observe the discrepancies between what Spaight's practice-oriented conservatism found common usage, on the one hand, and German actions and subsequent justifications, on the other.[15] If I may try the reader's patience with one last list, the German military invoked military necessity to negate accepted custom and, after 1907, positive law in these areas: poisoning wells, killing prisoners of war for reasons of convenience, denying quarter, devastating a land in order to harm its economy or finances, devastating a land to terrorize its noncombatants into compliance, claiming occupation when one's forces were too weak to establish actual authority, bombarding without notification (a change since Lieber's time), expansively using the label "spy," forcing noncombatants to act as guides (illegal after 1907), using forced oaths to substitute for effective occupation, raising unlimited requisitions and contributions (even if the population should starve), using the same for combat rather than strictly for administrative purposes, using forced civilian labor for "warlike operations," and levying unlimited collective punishments (Spaight 1911, 84, 89, 112, 131, 113, 375, 122, 327–328, 173, 208–209, 368–369, 373, 383–384, 388–390, 396, 405, 403, 408). To this list I would add, though Spaight disagreed, the latitudinarian use of the rubric "war treason" to require extreme obedience from occupied enemy civilians (Spaight 1911, 334–335).

The significance of this list, beyond its sheer length, is twofold. First, it cites actual practices, not theoretical musings. Furthermore, these practices regularly recurred in Germany's wars from 1870–1871 through World War I and beyond, in Europe and in the colonies. Thus, these practices describe a military-institutional pattern. Second, this list is broader than the rubrics in which international law conventionally recognized a potential loophole thanks to military necessity. Noncombatants surely bore the brunt of the excessive force excused here, but poisoning wells, killing prisoners of war, denying quarter, and

---

[14] This is the famous phrase written by the Russian jurist Fedor Martens and incorporated in 1899 into the preamble of the Hague Rules (Scott 1915, 102).

[15] The following list recounts military actions in 1870–1871 and 1914–1918, the latter of which Spaight could not have known, of course.

causing extreme devastation were methods of fighting, not solutions to problems of occupation. In other words, military necessity operated more deeply and broadly in the German army than was true for its counterparts. It was an ubiquitous feature of the assumptions behind German war conduct (*Kriegführung*).

The German view of military necessity: conservative or revolutionary?

It is important to know if the Imperial German understanding of military necessity indicated a conservative clinging to principles being steadily abandoned by the progress of legal codification, or whether Imperial Germany was exploring new, even revolutionary, terrain. The antique epithet by which the German position was known, "Kriegsraison geht vor Kriegsmanier," made it appear that this view of military necessity was old. However, the eminent (British) international jurist Georg Schwarzenberg (1968, 136), after searching the "comprehensive collection of articles of war in *Corpus Juris Militaris* (1724)," concluded that the idea was "of more recent vintage."[16]

If Germany's view was not ancient, it is still possible that it was merely traditional; Germany might have simply stayed still while the international community moved on, whittling military necessity down to a thinner and thinner exception as it went. International law did indeed develop during codification. A number of acts permitted in Lieber's manual of 1863 were already outlawed in 1899, and several more joined the forbidden list by 1907.[17] Chief of Staff Moltke's famous, skeptical reply to Prof. Bluntschli was therefore not as peculiar when he wrote it in 1880, before international codification was successfully under way, as it would have been twenty years later, after the conclusion and widespread ratification of the Hague Rules of Land Warfare (Moltke 1992, 633–634).

Despite the gradual narrowing of military necessity during codification, however, the German view was clearly novel. It did not merely resist the pull of modern development, it broke radically with the traditional understanding of military necessity as that had existed at least since Grotius. Indeed, the German interpretation negated the defining

---

[16] Felix Dahn used the old term in his 1870 work on the laws of war, but I do not know when it was used for the first time (1870, 3–4).

[17] Concerning bombardments without warning, unlimited requisitions, and impressing guides: see Lieber, Arts. 15, 19, and 93 (in Schindler and Toman 1988). On changes in 1907: see Westlake (1907, 268–270).

characteristics of the traditional definition. Six points strike me as critical to characterizing the new position.

(1) Military necessity was no longer the unfortunate exception in the law of war, it was the law of war. The exception had become the rule (Hartmann 1877–1878; Scott and Garner 1918, 4; Garner 1920, 197). Once war began, its putative nature dictated the permissible. After World War I had amply demonstrated where this conviction led in practice, Elihu Root (President of the American Society of International Law) remarked, "Either the doctrine of *kriegsraison* must be abandoned definitely and finally, or there is an end of international law, and in its place will be left a world without law, in which alliances of some nations to the extent of their power enforce their ideals of suitable conduct upon other nations" (Downey 1953, 253).

(2) The Imperial German interpretation of military necessity made it strong enough to break even absolute, positive laws that had always stood as inviolate, regardless of circumstance or necessity. Well poisoning is a particularly striking example, since it stood since time immemorial under the absolute ban on using poison in warfare. In 1915, as British forces invaded Southwest Africa, the German *Schutztruppe* poisoned wells in their arid colony. The commander in charge defended the action as legal because it was not done secretly and, he argued, poisoning merely "effect[ed] a change in the natural condition of the water in order to deprive the enemy of the use of this means of existence." The governor of Southwest Africa, defending the poisoning, thereupon dubbed water a "war material" (Garner 1920, 289–290).[18] A method of fighting that focused on depriving the enemy of the "means of existence" converted practically everything into "war material," and, thus, practically everything became a legitimate military target.

(3) From this expansionary tendency it is clear that the German viewpoint did not and could not distinguish noncombatants from soldiers. Hartmann (1877–1878, 127) wrote that an army "must absolutely assume" solidarity between civilians and their army, and thus, "one is not in a position to distinguish between armed foes and peaceful inhabitants." For Moltke (1992, 634), "all the sources of aid for the enemy government" were fair game for use or destruction. Following these guidelines, Lueder (1889b, 469, 475) first affirmed that civilians deserved protection as "subjects of law,"

---

[18] Germany poisoned wells during the retreat of 1917 in northern France.

but then promptly negated their rights, including protection from forced labor and unlimited requisitions, because "in cases of conflict, military necessity has precedence, indeed, so absolutely, that all other rules, rights, objections, and considerations are subordinate." The German armies in World War I continued the practices of 1870–1871 regarding instrumentalizing civilians. Many observers still find the erasure of noncombatant status the most important consequence of the German view of military necessity and the one most at variance with the principle since the early modern period that, to quote Vattel (1797, 352), "we have no right to maltreat their persons, or use any violence against them, much less to take away their lives. This is so plain a maxim of justice and humanity, that at present every nation, in the least degree civilized, acquiesces in it."[19]

(4) As military necessity swelled, it also obliterated the old, universally recognized doctrine of proportionality. That view had held that the exceptional action must be tailored (and thus limited) to the specific circumstances that permitted its use. But in a world in which the exception was the rule and in which success, not the higher standard of self-preservation, was the test, military necessity would be constantly invoked (as it was in World War I). Thus, the limiting factors inherent in any specific situation vanished. Moreover, the logic of German war doctrine ran directly counter to proportionality. The methods of warfare adopted under Moltke and retained and perfected thereafter called for "victory of annihilation" (*Vernichtungssieg*) achieved by overwhelming force concentrated in an offensive battle (and, if necessary, relentless pursuit), in order to end the war quickly. The *Vernichtungsgedanke* encouraged the greatest use of force and it aimed at the utter destruction of the enemy (regardless of the war's political goal, which would have introduced proportionate calculations, as Clausewitz had written [Clausewitz 1968, 105]). The standard German goal to "destroy" the enemy overshot the legitimate aim of war as it was enunciated in 1868 at St. Petersburg and repeated verbatim at Brussels in 1874 and in the Oxford Manual: "The only legitimate end that States may have in war being to weaken the military strength of the enemy" (in Schindler and Toman 1988, Art. 3).

(5) As the limits that the international law tradition had built into military necessity fell away, the path to the spiraling use of reciprocal

---

[19] See also Westlake (1907, 115–117), Stenzel (1973, 32), Best (1976, 120–135).

force opened with its threat of the resort to methods "which make the return to peace unnecessarily difficult," as Lieber had warned (in Schindler and Toman 1988, Art. 16). In the Wilhelminian period, peace steadily receded as the goal of war. Peace was replaced by complete military victory, at best, or at worst, by armed security in the form of preparation for the next inevitable war. This had not been true in 1870. Even a fire-eater like Adolf Lasson (1871, 73), one of the first to justify philosophically Bismarck's "blood and iron" methods, believed that "even in the midst of war one recognizes the enemy as one's equal with whom one would soon like to live in peace." By September 1914 Chancellor Theobald von Bethmann Hollweg envisioned peace "for all imaginable time" – a total peace dictated to the rest of Europe by complete German military victory. When that victory eluded their grasp, the goal for most German military leaders became to ensure a good starting position for the next war.[20]

(6) The final novel aspect of the Kaiserreich's view of military necessity was that it was increasingly anticipatory. Recall, legal tradition required the danger to be real, vital, and immediate. In 1842 this principle was clearly enunciated by US Secretary of State Webster in a dispute with Great Britain, the "Caroline" incident. The power claiming military necessity, Webster wrote, would have to show "necessity of self-defence, instant, overwhelming, leaving no choice of means, and no moment for deliberation" (in Brownlie 1963, 37). The Wilhelminian citation of military necessity rarely fulfilled these conditions. Perhaps the most famous example was the violation of Belgian neutrality in August 1914 on the (false) assumption that France was about to do so itself.[21] Or perhaps it is Chief of Staff Helmuth von Moltke (the younger) (in Wieland 1984, 7), who already on the second day of war claimed the situation "a matter of life and death" and so excused what he termed Germany's "brutal" military actions against Belgium. "The grave situation in which the fatherland finds itself," he said, "makes the use of every means that can harm the enemy a duty." Similarly, the adoption of gas warfare, clearly outlawed in the Hague Rules, occurred before the trench stalemate in the west had solidified and made it "necessary," and the same could be said for the adoption of unrestricted submarine

---

[20] For 1918: see Klein (1968–1969, 228, 239). This position was already widespread among the officer corps in 1915: see Hohenborn, diary entry November 1, 1915 in Wild von Hohenborn (1986, 92–93); Tirpitz (1919, 484).

[21] See Garner's discussion (1920, 188–191).

warfare in 1915, before the British blockade was truly effective. The rest of the World War is replete with similar examples of this pattern.[22]

The extreme practices that triggered Germany's new view of military necessity arose in 1870 to meet the unexpected challenges posed by democratic warfare, the nation in arms. It became a trope of German conservative, military, and international-legal writing to blame the use of excessive force on the passions provoked by popular participation. Hartmann (1877–1878, 462; emphasis in original) was typical in claiming that "the mob [*Menge*], as soon as its passions awaken, uses force against force, and the unpredictability of its excesses [*Ausschreitungen*] can only be tamed if very drastic measures are used against their paroxysm ... When a people's war breaks out, *terrorism* becomes a militarily necessary principle."[23] Against this menace writers deployed the ideal of the well-disciplined, professional standing army. It is difficult to overlook the analogy between the Prussian army's old, domestic job of securing monarchy and conservative order against the people and this new myth of the professional army driven to extremes by the undisciplined mob. The year 1870 made clear, and Moltke ultimately admitted as much, that the old virtues of the Prusso-German army could not defeat a fully mobilized republic (Förster 1999, 352). In another sense, then, the new, expansionary idea of military necessity was the response of an anti-democratic institution to the potential of warfare waged by democratic or republican states.

The Imperial German military thus developed an alternative to the emerging international order. It trusted that the expertly directed use of extreme violence would provide more security (and ultimately order of a stringently military kind) than that promised by the international legal order. It risked the possibility that violence, unleashed from the limits of law, might be impossible to curb, even by the (military) experts in wielding controlled violence.

The Wilhelminian alternate, expansionary view of military necessity has been interpreted in several ways. Geoffrey Best (1980, 48, 130, 143) sees Germany as merely farther along a spectrum of views common to large states with standing armies. He reads international law in the late nineteenth century as having been militarized by these powers' insistence that law should defer more to military considerations. Best's view is close to that of Manfred Messerschmidt (1996, 191–192), who

---

[22] These are analyzed in Hull (2005).

[23] On popular passions encouraging more extreme wars, see Moltke (1992, 633–634), Lueder (1889b, 387), Meurer (1907, 55), Lasson (1871, 66, 73–74).

interprets the Kaiserreich's exaltation of military necessity as a reflection of the hypertrophic state sovereignty characteristic of Germany's late emergence as a unified state under Bismarck, and thus as an extreme instance of the phenomenon of state building. The contemporary ideologies of Social Darwinism and imperialism certainly also contributed to justifying and supporting extreme constructions of military necessity. A full account of Imperial Germany's convergence with and divergence from the Western international community on the issue of law versus permitted violence would require an elaborate comparison. In the remaining pages, I want to shift the focus from the superstructural level (of state sovereignty) and from the intentional level (of ideology) to the prosaic, organizational-cultural level of the military itself, where I believe most of the actual development of the Wilhelminian view of military necessity took place.

The Wilhelminian experiment in controlled violence developed from practices, methods, and techniques developed in wartime and honed inside the military institution until they became an almost unconscious part of Imperial German military culture. They became self-replicating and self-radicalizing. This process was made possible and later encouraged and ossified by Germany's political structure. These were complex developments, but I will offer a brief sketch of them in order to show how such a radical alternative to the international legal consensus might occur and how impossible was the attempt to use violence to limit itself.[24]

Military necessity and military culture

Like later historians, many contemporary, non-German critics focused on ideology and traced the Imperial German view of military necessity back to Carl von Clausewitz. They quoted his dismissive phrase concerning "self-imposed restrictions, almost imperceptible and hardly worth mentioning, termed usages of International Law, [that] accompany [war] without essentially impairing its power" (Clausewitz 1968, 101; Garner 1920, 4, 328; Munro *et al.* 1917, 5). They neglected to notice that this phrase occurs at the very beginning of Clausewitz's treatise, in which he explores "absolute" war, that is, war as it would be without intervening circumstances to limit or shape it. His point was that international law did not affect the inner nature of warfare. The rest of Clausewitz's hefty volume is devoted to real war, which "is subjected to conditions, is controlled and modified" by these, and thus rarely if ever

[24] For a complete discussion, see Hull (2005).

approaches the pristine, absolute state of unlimited violence. It is true that Clausewitz was uninterested in international law, but in my view that is because his subject was what he regarded as the intrinsic qualities of war and national politics and the forces they unleashed; he understood international law as an extrinsic factor.

Too much emphasis has been placed on the intellectual origins of Imperial Germany's understanding of military necessity, and not enough on its practical origins. These lay on the battlefield in the early 1860s when Helmuth von Moltke demonstrated how effective the full concentration of unfettered violence could be in destroying the enemy's force. Moltke's methods became key to the development of the new conception of military necessity. Complete destruction of the opposing army came to be defined as the goal of war (this is the *Vernichtungsgedanke*). The *Vernichtungsgedanke* held great appeal because it solved Prussia's recurrent military dilemma: how to win wars against larger, more financially secure powers (Showalter 1990, 66). By using unlimited, focused means of destruction against the enemy's army, one might hope to defeat it before it could mobilize its greater resources (Förster 1994).

As the French uprising of 1870 showed, battlefield victory did not automatically mean winning the war. Nonetheless, the General Staff clung to the *Vernichtungsgedanke* because it produced impressive, practical results in combat and because it seemed like the best hope for dealing with Germany's nightmare, the two-front war. *Vernichtung* was the centerpiece around which German training, doctrine, and institutional habits and basic assumptions accreted. The resulting military culture preserved the *Vernichtungsgedanke* from criticism and enacted its precepts (and their powerful implications) whenever Germany went to war.[25]

As the *Vernichtungsgedanke* shaped, and was shaped by, Germany's military culture, it acquired specific characteristics that encouraged every engagement to go to extremes. Accomplishing the total destruction of the enemy seemed to require the offensive, which is riskier and more costly in human terms than the defensive. It demanded at once great numbers of troops, but also speed and expert coordination. To fulfill these requirements, the system of "mission tactics" was developed, which gave greater latitude to junior officers in executing plans. With their greater responsibility came a greater burden of success and the institutional expectation that officers would always go beyond what was

[25] The formation and operation of Imperial Germany's military is the subject of Hull (2005).

necessary, or even reasonable, to achieve the goal. The difficulties in achieving a victory of annihilation encouraged the claim that only military experts could run war, and that the only considerations that counted were military ones.

Almost every aspect of Imperial Germany's military culture increased the intensity of warfare: not just the intensity of numbers or firepower, but more important, the intensity of risk, the heightened expectations, the quick tempo, the demanding timetable of the plan for the single battle of annihilation, the cleft between the impossible goal and the inadequate logistics to achieve it, the willingness to sacrifice one's own troops and to instrumentalize civilians, the inability to conceive of anything less than total success or to recognize defeat. In short, the Imperial German military became a machine for producing military necessity. It planned for, anticipated, and actually created situations where everything was at stake from the very first blow. The dire straits of its own creation made it seem that military necessity was the ubiquitous condition of war.

The subjective conviction that military necessity operated everywhere presented a problem for international law. In 1948 the International Military Tribunal (in Draper 1973, 136) observed, regarding "re List and others," a case of claimed military necessity in World War II, that "we are obliged to judge the situation as it appeared to the defendant at the time." Subjective convictions count in law. But what to do when situations of military necessity, as they are perceived by the perpetrators, are systemically produced? Germany's contemporary critics typically believed that "the systematic application of scientific inhumanity," as they called it, was more self-conscious than it probably was in fact (Scott and Garner 1918, 9, 13). Precisely because many of the Kaiserreich's worst military policies emerged almost automatically from its institutional assumptions and apparatus, they seemed to officers compulsory and were therefore all the more impervious to criticism or correction. So, for example, despite thunderous external censure and even some internal criticism of the massive destruction of northern France during Germany's strategic retreat in 1917, the same commanders and decision-makers undertook the same measures in 1918. That wave of gratuitous destruction practically stopped the armistice. One of the few instances where Germany reversed a policy adopted because of putative military necessity concerned the Belgian deportations of 1916–1917. The decision to stop them was possible because the military leadership agreed that they had failed, not because of the international uproar or the resulting loss of Germany's international prestige. Functional, directly military reasons were the only ones strong enough to bend military necessity to the limits imposed by law.[26]

It was not merely organizational-cultural blindness that shielded the extreme view of military necessity from criticism – it was increasingly upheld from outside the military, too, by elements of Germany's political culture which multiplied and strengthened over time. Bismarck's constitution had intentionally protected the military from critical scrutiny, and the domestic role of the army as bulwark of the monarchy against liberals and social democrats insulated it further. Growing militarism among bourgeois civilians encouraged them to embrace rather than criticize the extreme view of warfare, and in the measure to which they elevated the army to the preeminent national institution, they correspondingly increased the pressure on it to achieve huge, easy victories. After 1897, Germany's risky foreign policy created exactly the circle of superior enemies that confirmed the military in its belief that all war was existential and that only extraordinary measures stood a chance of victory. Under these political circumstances, the Wilhelminian view of military necessity hardened. It mutated from a mere justification for extraordinary actions into a set of basic assumptions about the nature of war and national survival. It became untouchable. In the World War the Wilhelminian experiment in violence ran its full course to self-destruction.

Epilogue: World War I

Germany invoked military necessity from the first day of the war. It is not too much to say that Germany fought the World War under the sign of military necessity. It determined all those features of war conduct which were most controversial, costly, and in the end fatal to Germany: the violation of Belgian neutrality, the "Belgian atrocities," the complete instrumentalization of occupied civilians (leading to partisan resistance movements in the east and to international censure in the west), the Belgian (and many other) deportations, gas warfare, unrestricted submarine warfare (which led to American intervention and German loss of the war), the total destruction of northern France in the areas of Germany's retreat in 1917, the purposive destruction of northern France and Belgium in the fall of 1918 (which led directly to the demand for reparations after the war), the proposed total subordination of

---

[26] And even these did not suffice to convince German leaders to try energetically to stop the genocide of the Armenians by Germany's ally, Turkey, in World War I. Turkey's claim of military necessity stopped every real protest. See chapter 11 in Hull (2005).

374   *Isabel V. Hull*

civilian life in Germany to the military (visible in the Hindenburg Program of 1916), the reluctance to distance itself publicly from the genocide of the Armenians done by its Turkish ally, and the plans in the autumn of 1918 to fight on even to Germany's own complete destruction (*Endkampf*).[27] Every one of these actions was not only justified in terms of military necessity, but they were conceived of and acted on out of the assumptions about the nature of war, self-preservation, the just use of extreme force, and consequent military duty, that had developed under this rubric.

After the war, the Reichstag asked Chancellor Bethmann Hollweg why he had acquiesced in the military's absurd and illegal plan to deport Belgian civilians to work in German munition plants. He told them:

it was even for the Imperial Chancellor a matter of immense difficulty, if not of impossibility, to do away with a measure concerning which the military authorities said: "If this measure is not carried out, we shall simply be unable to win the war."

He continued:

To me, too, from the standpoint of statesmanship, these deportations were unwelcome to the greatest degree. The military branch claimed that they were matters of necessity, regulations resulting from a forced situation, essential for the purpose of carrying out the Hindenburg program, required in order to carry it out at all. So far as I know, it was not possible to carry out this program even then; but the argument of inexorable military necessity always confronted me. (German National Consituent Assembly 1923, 419, 412)

Military necessity, the doctrine which Imperial German military culture had developed to free the army from the fetters of international law, had become Germany's straitjacket.

REFERENCES

Berber, Friedrich. 1969. *Lehrbuch des Völkerrechts*. Munich: C. H. Beck.
Best, Geoffrey. 1976. "How Right is Might? Some Aspects of the International Debate about How to Fight Wars and How to Win Them, 1870–1918." In *War Economy and the Military Mind*, ed. Geoffrey Best and Andrew Wheatcroft. London: Croom Helm, 120–135.
    1980. *Humanity in Warfare: The Modern History of the International Law of Armed Conflicts*. London: Methuen.
    1994. *War and Law since 1945*. Oxford University Press.
Bluntschli, Johann Caspar. 1866. *Das moderne Kriegsrecht*. Nördlingen: C. H. Beck.

[27] Hull (2005) treats these issues in detail in chapters 9–12.

Brownlie, Jan. 1963. *International Law and the Use of Force by States.* Oxford University Press.

Clausewitz, Carl von 1968. *On War,* trans. J. J. Graham. London: Penguin Books.

Dahn, Felix. 1870. *Das Kriegsrecht: Kurze, volksthümliche Darstellung für Jedermann zumal für den deutschen Soldaten.* Würzburg: A. Stuber.

Downey, William Gerald, Jr. 1953. "The Law of War and Military Necessity." *American Journal of International Law* 47 (2): 251–262.

Draper, Col. G. I. A. D. 1973. "Military Necessity and Humanitarian Imperatives." *Revue de Droit Militaire et de Droit de la Guerre* 12: 129–143.

Dülffer, Jost. 1981. *Regeln gegen den Krieg? Die Haager Friedenskonferenzen 1899 und 1907 in der internationalen Politik.* Berlin: Ullstein.

Edmonds, Colonel J. D., and Lassa Oppenheim. 1912. *Land Warfare: An Exposition of the Laws and Usages of War on Land, for the Guidance of Officers of His Majesty's Army.* London: HMSO.

Förster, Stig. 1994. "The Prussian Triangle of Leadership in the Face of the People's War: A Re-Assessment of the Conflict Between Bismarck and Moltke, 1870/71." In *On the Road to Total War: The American Civil War and the German Wars of Unification, 1861–1871,* ed. Stig Förster. Cambridge University Press.

1999. "Dreams and Nightmares: German Military Leadership and the Images of Future Warfare, 1871–1914." In *Anticipating Total War: The German and American Experiences, 1871–1914,* ed. Manfred F. Boemeke, Roger Chickering, and Stig Förster. Cambridge University Press, 343–376.

Garner, James Wilford. 1920. *International Law and the World War.* London: Longmans, Green, & Co.

German National Constituent Assembly. 1923. *Official German Documents Relating to the World War,* 2 vols, trans. Division of International Law Carnegie Endowment for International Peace. Oxford University Press.

Germany, Großer Generalstab. 1902. *Kriegsbrauch im Landkriege.* Vol. XXXI: *Kriegsgeschichtliche Einzelschriften.* Berlin: E. S. Mittler.

Germany, Parliament. 1927. *Völkerrecht im Weltkrieg.* In *Dritte Reihe,* vol. IV of *Das Werk des Untersuchungsausschusses der Verfassungsgebenden deutschen Nationalversammlung und des deutschen Reichstages 1919–1928, Verhandlungen/Gutachten/Urkunden,* ed. Eugen Fischer, Berthold Widmann, and Johannes Bell. Berlin: Deutsche Verlagsgesellschaft für Politik und Geschichte.

Germany, Reichsgericht. 1931. *Die Entscheidungen des deutschen Reichsgerichts in völkerrechtlichen Fragen 1879–1929.* Fontes Juris gentium, Series A, Section 2, vol. 1, ed. Ernst Schmitz. Berlin: Carl Heymann Verlag.

Grotius, Hugo. 1853. *Grotius on the Rights of War and Peace: An Abridged Translation.* William Whewell. Cambridge University Press.

Gündell, Erich von. 1939. *Aus seinen Tagebüchern: Deutsche Expedition nach China 1900–1901, 2. Haager Friedenskonferenz 1907; Weltkrieg 1914–1918 und Zwischenzeiten,* ed. Walter Obkircher. Hamburg: Hanseatische Verlagsanstalt.

Hartmann, Julius von. 1877–1878. "Militärische Nothwendigkeit und Humanität: ein kritischer Versuch." *Deutsche Rundschau* 13: 111–128 and 450–471; 14: 71–91.

Hull, Isabel V. 2005. *Absolute Destruction: Military Culture and the Practices of War in Imperial Germany*. Ithaca, NY: Cornell University Press.

Jacomet, Robert. 1913. *Les lois de la guerre continentale*. Paris: Fournier.

Klein, Fritz, ed. 1968–1969. *Deutschland im Ersten Weltkrieg*, 3 vols. Berlin: Akademie-Verlag.

Lasson, Adolf. 1871. *Princip und Zukunft des Völkerrechts*. Berlin: Wihelm Hertz.

Lueder, C. 1889a. "Krieg und Kriegsrecht im Allgemeinen." In *Handbuch des Völkerrechts*, vol. 4, ed. Franz von Holtzendorff. Hamburg: A. G. Richter, 169–367.

1889b. "Das Landkriegsrecht im Besonderen." In *Handbuch des Völkerrechts*, vol. 4, ed. Franz von Holtzendorff. Hamburg: A. G. Richter, 371–545.

McCoubrey, H. 1991. "The Nature of the Modern Doctrine of Military Necessity." *Revue de Droit Militaire et de Droit de la Guerre* 30 (1–4): 215–255.

Messerschmidt, Manfred. 1996. "Völkerrecht und 'Kriegsnotwendigkeit' in der deutschen militärischen Tradition." In *Was damals Recht war ... NS-Militär- und Strafjustiz im Vernichtungskrieg*, Manfred Messerschmidt. Essen: Klartext, 191–230.

Meurer, Christian. 1907. *Die Haager Friedenskonferenz*, vol. II: *Das Kriegsrecht der Haager Konferenz*, 2 vols. Munich: J. Schweitzer.

Moltke, Helmuth von. 1992. *Moltke: vom Kabinettskrieg zum Volkskrieg: eine Werkauswahl*, ed. Stig Förster. Bonn: Bouvier.

Munro, Dana C., George C. Sellery, and August C. Krey, eds. 1917. *German War Practices, Part 1: Treatment of Civilians*. Washington DC: US Government.

Oppenheim, Lassa. 1958. *International Law: A Treatise*, vol. II, 8th edn, ed. H. Lauterpacht. London: Longmans, Green.

Prussia, War Ministry. 1908. *Felddienst-Ordnung*, ed. War Ministry Prussia. Berlin: E. S. Mittler.

1914. *Kriegs-Etappen-Ordnung (K. E. O.) (12 March 1914) (D. V. E. Nr. 90)*. Berlin.

Rodick, Burleigh Cushing. 1928. *The Doctrine of Necessity in International Law*. New York: Columbia University Press.

Schindler, Dietrich, and Jiri Toman, eds. 1988. *The Laws of Armed Conflicts*. Geneva: Henry Dunant Institute.

Schwarzenberg, Georg. 1968. *International Law as Applied by International Courts and Tribunals*, vol. II: *The Law of Armed Conflict*. London: Stevens and Sons.

Scott, George Winfield, and James Wilford Garner, eds. 1918. *The German War Code Contrasted with the War Manuals of the United States, Great Britain, and France*. Washington DC: Committee on Public Information.

Scott, James Brown, ed. 1915. *The Hague Conventions and Declarations of 1899 and 1907, Accompanied by Tables of Signatures, Ratification and Adhesions of the Various Powers and Texts of Reservations*. Oxford University Press.

1920. *The Proceedings of the Hague Peace Conferences; Translation of the Official Texts; the Conference of 1899*. Oxford Univerity Press.

Showalter, Dennis. 1990. "German Grand Strategy: A Contradiction in Terms?" *Militärgeschichtliche Mitteilungen* 48 (2): 65–102.

Spaight, J. M. 1911. *War Rights on Land.* New York: Macmillan.

Stenzel, Ernst. 1973. *Die Kriegführung des deutschen Imperialismus und das Völkerrecht: zur Planung und Vorbereitung des deutschen Imperialismus auf die barbarische Kriegführung im ersten und zweiten Weltkrieg, dargestellt an den vorherrschenden Ansichten zu den Gesetzen und Gebräuchen des Landkrieges (1900–1945).* Berlin: Militärverlag der Deutschen Demokratischen Republik.

Tirpitz, Alfred von. 1919. *Erinnerungen.* Leipzig: K. F. Koehler.

Tobler, Achim. 1961. "Kriegsnotwendigkeit." In *Wörterbuch des Völkerrechts,* 2nd edn, ed. Hans-Jürgen Schlochauer. Berlin: Walter de Gruyter, 351–353.

Vattel, Emmerich de. 1797. *The Law of Nations, or, Principles of the Law of Nature, Applied to the Conduct and Affairs of Nations and Sovereigns.* London: G. G. and J. Robinson.

Westlake, John. 1907. *International Law: Part II: War.* Cambridge University Press.

Wieland, Lothar. 1984. *Belgien, 1914: die Frage des belgischen "Franktireurkrieges" und die deutsche öffentliche Meinung von 1914 bis 1936.* Frankfurt/Bern/New York: Peter Lang.

Wild von Hohenborn, Adolf. 1986. *Briefe und Tagebuchaufzeichnungen des preußischen Generals als Kriegsminister und Truppenführer im Ersten Weltkrieg,* ed. Helmut Reichold and Gerhard Granier. Boppard a.R.: Harald Boldt.

Zorn, Philipp. 1915. *Die beiden Haager Friedenskonferenzen von 1899 und 1907.* In *Handbuch des Völkerrechts,* vol. V, part 1, ed. Fritz Stier-Somlo. Stuttgart: W. Kohlhammer.

15   Preconditions of international normative change: implications for order and violence

Jack L. Snyder and Leslie Vinjamuri

The pace of change is accelerating in international politics, yet social science remains a notoriously poor guide to understanding and shaping it. The waning of sharp military rivalries among the great powers, America's unprecedented position of material dominance, its struggle against hydra-headed terrorist networks, and the rise of global advocacy politics suggest that the basic shape of the international order is changing. Old conceptions of international order and the role of violence in it have been overtaken by events. However, new visions of international order that are prominent in the academy and in the world of affairs often misunderstand the relationship between material and normative change. People who act on these mistaken assumptions may unintentionally hinder the achievement of their goals of peace and democracy.

According to the realist school of international relations, which dominated American academic thought for half a century, politics among states is ordered only in the thin sense that their struggle for security in international anarchy recurrently produces balance-of-power behaviors, such as the formation of military alliances against strong, threatening states. Realists portray this order as timeless, changing only in its details since Thucydides, depending on the number of great powers and the ebb and flow of their relative strength (Waltz 1979; Mearsheimer 2001).

In today's unipolar circumstances, where American power cannot be balanced in the traditional sense, many prominent international relations scholars still adopt a state-centered power-politics framework as a starting point, though not necessarily the end point, of their analyses. Even Robert Jervis, whose main contributions have focused on the ways that leaders misperceive the strategic problems they face, argues that "the forceful and unilateral exercise of US power is not simply the byproduct of September 11, the Bush administration, or some shadowy neoconservative cabal – it is the logical outcome of the current unrivaled US position in the international system" which permits the US to indulge its nightmarish fears and its Wilsonian hopes (Jervis 2003, 84, 86).

Realists' unchanging assumptions about international power politics have come under sharp challenge from diverse quarters in academic and policy circles. Social constructivists and principled activists, for example, argue that the familiar game of international power politics is not based on some inexorable, timeless logic, but was constructed at a particular moment in time out of the discourse of state sovereignty and *raison d'état*. Anarchy, they say, was what states made of it. Consequently, the norms that constitute international relations can be remade through campaigns of principled persuasion spearheaded by transnational activist networks. If more benign ideas and identities are effectively spread throughout the globe by cultural change and normative persuasion, then "ought" can be transformed into "is": support for warlike dictators can be undermined, perpetrators of war crimes and atrocities can be held accountable, benign multicultural identities can be fostered, and international and civil wars will wane (Finnemore and Sikkink 1998, 916; Risse and Sikkink 1999; Wendt 1999, 141, 37–378; Ruggie 1998, 199).[1]

Not only human rights activists, legalists, and social constructivists see international order as a norm-guided project for social change. The highest officials of the Bush administration argued that power politics must serve the agenda of democratic idealism. President Bush, in his preface to the September 2002 National Security Strategy Memorandum that laid out the doctrine of preventive attack that subsequently justified the Iraq war, stated: "the United States enjoys a position of unparalleled military strength," which creates "a moment of opportunity to extend the benefits of freedom across the globe. We will actively work to bring the hope of democracy, development, free markets, and free trade to every corner of the world" (Office of the President 2002, 1–2). The text of the strategy document itself pulls the concept the "balance of power" inside-out and conflates it with ideological expansionism: "Through our willingness to use force in our own defense and in the defense of others, the United States demonstrates its resolve to maintain a balance of power that favors freedom" (Office of the President 2002, 29). In explaining the new strategy, National Security Advisor Condoleezza Rice mused about the theoretical debates of her erstwhile days as a Stanford international relations professor, remarking that power-political realism and idealism should not be seen as alternatives (Rice 2002). Paul Wolfowitz and the neoconservative proponents likewise saw

---

[1] These scholars adhere to the constructivist approach to the study of international politics, but not all constructivists are so clearly wedded to this transformative political agenda. For more qualified views, see Katzenstein (1996, 536–537) and Owen (1997, 232–235).

the Iraq war as the opening round of a campaign to overturn prevailing political patterns in the Arab world and generate momentum toward democracy there (Herrmann 2004, 191–225).

Many activists, legalists, and constructivists share this urge to use coercive power to bring about change in the international order. Secretary of State Madeleine Albright justified the Kosovo war as, above all, a human rights necessity. Samantha Power's prize-winning book on America's repeated failures to prevent genocide helped galvanize a generation of idealistic activists to jawbone in favor of humanitarian military interventions (Power 2002). Constructivist international relations scholar John Ruggie worked in support of the war effort as an advisor to the UN Secretary General Kofi Annan. In constructivist accounts of international change, the main aim of transnational activists' normative persuasion campaigns is often to convince powerful states to use their leverage to coerce rights abusers (Keck and Sikkink 1998; Risse and Sikkink 1999).[2]

Each of these schools of thought gets part of the story right – and part of it dangerously wrong. The traditionalist realists, most of whom spoke out against the 2003 attack on Iraq, are right in insisting that any worldview and any policy derived from it must start with a realistic appreciation of the positional interests of entrenched powers, especially states. However, they are wrong insofar as they underrate the role of normative convictions in constituting social orders and in promoting change in them. Liberal activists and constructivists have made that point well, but their theory of normative change is too voluntarist and lacks an understanding of the preconditions needed to sustain change. The Bush administration war hawks were right that American power is crucial to the fate of normative change in international relations, but their strategies were likely to be counterproductive in bringing about the goals they claimed to seek.

What then might be a better-grounded approach to understanding the potential for change in the international order and the role in it of political violence?

First, in the period before a hoped-for change, the norms needed to bring about the change should be understood as aspirations, as standards outlining what might be achieved after a great deal of hard work and subtle politicking (Beitz 1979). They should not be understood legalistically, as if they were unconditional rights in need of immediate and universal enforcement regardless of the political consequences.

---

[2] Bukovansky (2002) explores changing bases of legitimacy as a power resource.

Second, the potential for normative change should be assessed in light of the material, political, and institutional preconditions for it. Any normative aspiration – democracy, human rights, justice – is only as good as the soil that is available to nurture it. Typically, this requires the existence of favorable (or at least permissive) material conditions, a powerful coalition of global and local actors with an interest in bringing it about, and the construction of institutions with the administrative capacity to give real effect to the norms. Normative persuasion may help to shore up these preconditions and consolidate them once they are in place, but it cannot create them out of whole cloth.

Third, sequence matters in effecting normative change. Generally, the creation of a powerful reform coalition internationally and locally must be the first step. It does no good and may even do harm to try to implement aspirational norms if they are supported only by weak institutions and fragile coalitions. In the short run, aspirational norms may have to be put on hold in order to pursue the pragmatic political maneuvers that are needed to neutralize potential spoilers and strengthen coalitions for reform (Stedman 1997).

Fourth, the promotion of normative change is a strategic interaction. Would-be norms exist in a crowded field. They must contend with prevailing traditional norms, with other new candidate norms, and with powerful, self-interested actors that seek to evade being bound by any norms other than ones that are temporarily convenient. New norms may be threatening to powerful actors, who will respond with their own normative countercampaigns and perhaps even with violence. Norms entrepreneurs should make sure that they can win normative battles – or at least contain the damage from the possible backlash – before they start the fight.

To show how this general argument might apply to concrete items on the agenda of international normative change, I will briefly examine the issues of democracy promotion and of justice for perpetrators of atrocities.

Democracy promotion and the democratic peace

One of the few points that the Bush administration and the principled activists agree upon is that the assertive promotion of democracy is a good idea.[3] In particular, both argue that democracy and free speech are pillars of peace, and therefore to promote peace, promote democracy. Of course, this is in principle. In fact, the Bush administration was rightly

---

[3] This section draws on Snyder (2002).

worried about the consequences for inter-ethnic relations of holding early elections in Iraq. The occupation authorities shut down newspapers that spread falsehoods that inflamed Iraqis to resist the occupation. This is the kind of problem that the US is likely to face wherever it tries to install democracy in countries that lack a strong reform coalition and useable institutions for the rule of law.

It is true that no two mature democracies have ever fought a war against each other. The basic workings of this democratic peace rely on supports in the material, institutional, and cultural domains. The absence of war between mature democracies depends on the material motivation of the average member of society to avoid needless death and impoverishment (goals widely if not universally shared across cultures), political institutions that predictably empower the median voter, and a set of cultural symbols sanctifying civil rights, free speech, and electoral legitimacy in ways that underpin those institutions, facilitate peaceful bargaining, and establish a nonthreatening, "in-group" identity among democratic states. The democratic peace works best when these material, institutional, and cultural elements are all in place (Russett 1993; Owen 1997).

Moreover, democracy itself has material preconditions. Adam Przeworski finds that transitions to democracy are almost always successfully consolidated in countries with a per-capita annual income above $6,000 in 1985 constant dollars, whereas democratic transitions almost always suffer reversals below $1,000, with a very few exceptions, such as India (Przeworski *et al.* 2000, chapter 2). These economic levels may to some degree be proxies for closely related factors such as literacy and the development of a middle class. Between those levels, consolidation seems to depend on a number of institutional preconditions, such as the strength of the rule of law and the development of civil society organizations (Linz and Stepan 1996, 7–15). The fact that these material and institutional preconditions often arise along with symbols and ideas supportive of democracy does not mean that democratic culture can somehow be a substitute for those conditions. Not surprisingly, Western jawboning in favor of free speech, fair elections, and human rights has borne little fruit in countries that lack these preconditions (Carothers 1999). There is no cultural shortcut to a global democratic peace.

Proponents of democratic transformation are often too direct and nonstrategic in their approach to achieving their objectives. For example, Thomas Carothers notes that the typical "strategy" of democracy assistance efforts is to generate a checklist of the attributes of mature democracies, and then mount parallel programs to try to install each of them in the targeted country right away. This approach is flawed because it pays insufficient attention to interaction effects between these efforts, issues of sequencing and preconditions, strategic responses from resistant actors, and other negative feedback effects.

Demanding a democratic transition and accountability to international human rights norms can be risky in settings that lack even the rudiments of the rule of law or the material resources needed to sustain an independent civil society and media. In such settings, transformative projects may unleash a populist form of mass politics at an inopportune, premature moment, when elites threatened by such changes can exploit social turmoil by playing the ethnic card. Thomas Risse and Kathryn Sikkink (1999) acknowledge that there may be a backlash phase in response to efforts to press dictators to accept human rights norms, but they portray this as a transitory delaying tactic. In fact, coercive persuasion that skips over the needed material and institutional preparatory steps may trigger costly setbacks that could have long-term consequences. Untimely voting demanded by the international community in such places as Burundi in 1993 and East Timor in 1999 has led directly to hundreds of thousands of deaths and refugees (Lund et al. 1998). Arguably, it has also led to the deepening of ethnic and social cleavages and to the tainting of democratic remedies.

The risk of such backlashes may be increasing. The "third wave" of democratization, already eroding in some places, consolidated democratic regimes mainly in the richer countries of Eastern Europe, Latin America, Southern Africa, and East Asia (Diamond 1996). A fourth wave would have to take on harder cases: countries that are poorer, more ethnically divided, and starting from a weaker base of governmental institutions and citizen skills. In facing this challenge, culturally creative activists and thinkers may play an important role in changing behavior in the international system, but they must do so within a context that is structured by the system's material and institutional possibilities.

Justice for perpetrators of atrocities

Advocacy groups such as Human Rights Watch and Amnesty International have made a historic contribution to the cause of international human rights by publicizing the need to prevent mass atrocities such as war crimes, genocide, and widespread political killings and torture.[4]

---

[4] For elaboration on the arguments in this section, see Snyder and Vinjamuri (2003/2004). On the advocacy community, see Clark (2001). On international human rights law, which applies to all people at all times, and international humanitarian law, which concerns the actions of combatants during military conflict, see Best (1994).

However, a strategy that many such groups favor for achieving this goal – the prosecution of perpetrators of atrocities according to universal standards – risks causing more atrocities than it would prevent, because it pays insufficient attention to political consequences.[5] Recent international criminal tribunals have failed to deter subsequent abuses in the former Yugoslavia and Central Africa. Because tribunals, including the International Criminal Court (ICC), have often failed to gain the active cooperation of powerful actors in the United States and in countries where abuses occur, it is questionable whether this will succeed as a long-run strategy for international change unless it is implemented in a more pragmatic way.

Amnesties, in contrast, have been highly effective in curbing abuses when implemented in a credible way, even in such hard cases as El Salvador and Mozambique. Truth commissions, another strategy favored by some advocacy groups, have been effective mainly when linked to amnesties, as in South Africa. Simply ignoring the question of punishing perpetrators – in effect, a *de facto* amnesty – has also succeeded in ending atrocities when combined with astute political strategies to advance political reforms. In Namibia, for example, a formal amnesty for all political prisoners was extended *de facto* to become a general amnesty.

The shortcomings of strategies preferred by most advocacy groups stem from their flawed understanding of the role of norms and law in establishing a just and stable political order. Like some scholars who write about the transformative impact of such groups, these advocates believe that rules of appropriate behavior constitute political order and consequently that the first step in establishing a peaceful political order is to lobby for the universal adoption of just rules (Finnemore and Sikkink 1998, 898; Roth 2001). This reverses the sequence that is necessary for the strengthening of norms and laws that will help prevent atrocities.

Justice does not lead; it follows. A norm-governed political order must be based on a political bargain among contending groups and on the creation of robust administrative institutions that can predictably enforce the law. Preventing atrocities and enhancing respect for law will frequently depend on striking politically expedient bargains that create effective political coalitions to contain the power of potential perpetrators of abuses (or so-called spoilers). Amnesty – or simply ignoring past

---

[5] On proposals for international tribunals, see Kritz (1996) and Minow (1998), as well as the numerous publications by Human Rights Watch, Amnesty International, and the Coalition for International Justice. See also the sources cited in the balanced critical commentary in Bass (2000, 284–310).

abuses – may be a necessary tool in this bargaining. Once such deals are struck, institutions based on the rule of law become more feasible.[6] Attempting to implement universal standards of criminal justice in the absence of these political and institutional preconditions risks weakening norms of justice by revealing their ineffectiveness and hindering necessary political bargaining. Although the ultimate goal is to prevent atrocities by effectively institutionalizing appropriate standards of criminal justice, the initial steps toward that goal must usually travel down the path of political expediency.

The social psychologist Tory Higgins posits three different logics whereby a person may decide on the rightness of a choice of action: whether it follows right principles, whether it leads to the right outcome, and whether it feels right given the person's current emotional state (Higgins 2000; Camacho et al. 2003). These correspond to the logics of appropriateness, consequences, and emotions that reflect the prevailing range of views on justice for perpetrators of atrocities.

These logics are ideal types. The strategies adopted by real political actors inevitably include a mix of these elements, as do those advocated by scholars. For example, human rights "norms entrepreneurs" argue not only that following their prescriptions is morally right; they also claim that these principles are grounded in a correct empirical theory of the causes of behavior and will therefore lead to desirable outcomes (Finnemore and Sikkink 1998, 896–899). Thus, even arguments based on the logic of appropriateness usually also make claims about consequences (Schultz 2001).[7] Conversely, proponents of the logic of consequences might argue that bargains based on the expediency of power and interest are often a necessary precondition for creating coalitions and institutions that will strengthen norms in the long run. For example, in September 2002, the UN administrator for Afghanistan, Lakhdar Brahimi, resisted calls from outgoing Human Rights Commissioner Mary Robinson to investigate war crimes by key figures in the UN-backed government of Hamid Karzai on the grounds that such investigations would undercut progress toward peace and stability (Burns 2002). In short, all three logics are concerned with reducing the chance of future atrocities, and consequently it is justifiable to compare the validity of their empirical claims (Finnemore and Sikkink 1998, 910–914).

---

[6] On institutionalization of the rule of law as a precondition for successful human rights promotion, see Putnam (2002) and Ignatieff (2001, 25, 40).
[7] Schultz is the executive director of Amnesty International USA. On a philosophical plane, see Nagel (1988, 60).

The logic of appropriateness

Martha Finnemore and Kathryn Sikkink, leading social-scientific scholars studying human rights, adopt a social-constructivist definition of a norm as "a standard of appropriate behavior for actors with a given identity" (Finnemore and Sikkink 1998, 889). Norms, for them, imply a moral obligation that distinguishes them from other kinds of rules. In this constructivist view, norms do more than regulate behavior; they mold the identities of actors, define social roles, shape actors' understanding of their interests, confer power on authoritative interpreters of norms, and infuse institutions with guiding principles (Finnemore and Sikkink 1998, 913; Wendt 1999).[8] In this sense, norms – and discourse about what norms ought to be – help to constitute social reality. Powerful states and social networks matter, too, but principled ideas and arguments often animate their actions. In that sense, world society is what its norms make of it.

According to this perspective, norms entrepreneurs attempt to persuade others to accept and adhere to new norms; targets of persuasion respond with arguments and strategies of their own (Finnemore and Sikkink 1998, 914). Persuasion may work through any of several channels, including logical arguments about consistency with other norms and beliefs that the target already adheres to, arguments from legal precedent, and emotional appeals (Finnemore and Sikkink 1998, 912–913). Once persuasion has succeeded in establishing a norm within a social group, norm entrepreneurs seek to promote conformity with the norm by "naming and shaming" violators, to use the terminology of constructivist theorists and human rights activists (Keck and Sikkink 1998, 16–25).

Finnemore and Sikkink conceive of the process of normative change as a three-stage "cascade." First, norms entrepreneurs use their organizational platforms to call attention to issues by naming, interpreting, and dramatizing them. Second, once these entrepreneurs achieve widespread success in their campaign of persuasion, a tipping process pushes the norm toward universal acceptance as international organizations, states, and transnational networks jump on the bandwagon. This occurs in part because of these actors' concern to safeguard their reputation and legitimacy, and in part because processes of socialization, institutionalization, and demonstration effects convince people that the rising norm is a proper one. In the third stage, the logic of appropriateness is so deeply imbued in law, bureaucratic rules, and

---

[8] Nagel (1988, 913); more generally, see Wendt (1999).

professional standards that people and states conform unquestioningly out of conviction and habit (Finnemore and Sikkink 1998, 904–905).

Constructivist social scientists have written little that directly applies the logic of appropriateness to the study of judicial accountability for war crimes or genocide (Lutz and Sikkink 2000, 644). Nonetheless, NGOs and legalists advocating war crimes tribunals implicitly hold to the constructivist theory. These activists assume that efforts to change the prevailing pattern of social behavior should begin with forceful advocacy for generalized rules embodied in principled institutions, such as courts.

Proponents of war crimes prosecutions have long been prone to exaggerate the centrality of rule following in ordering world politics. Judith Shklar's (1964) book discussing the Nuremberg and Japanese war crimes trials charged some of their proponents with excessive, apolitical legalism, which she defined as "the ethical attitude that holds that moral conduct is to be a matter of rule following, and moral relationships to consist of duties and rights determined by rules" (Shklar 1964, 1). Contemporary activists argue that handing down indictments and holding trials strengthen legal norms even when perpetrators are hard to arrest and convict. Many of them favor generalizing norms through such measures as universal jurisdiction for prosecuting war crimes and crimes against humanity (Roth 2001). They also encourage setting up judicial institutions that will embody the norm of accountability, such as the ICC, even when its short-term effect is to reduce the chance that a powerful, skeptical actor such as the United States will cooperate with the implementation of the norm.[9]

In the realm of international criminal justice, the logic of appropriateness generates several predictions. None of them has been supported by evidence from recent tribunals.

First, as norms of criminal accountability for war crimes and other violations of international humanitarian and human rights law begin to cascade, the notion of individual responsibility should gain international momentum. Local actors, not just proponents in the advanced liberal democracies, should increasingly blame atrocities on individuals (e.g. specific Serbian leaders), not collectivities (e.g. the Serbian ethnic group as a whole). In fact, the Hague Tribunal's indictments and trials have been polarizing in Serbia and Croatia, and local trials overseen by international authorities in Kosovo have spurred resentment and violence. The political parties of two war criminals on trial at the Hague, Slobodan Milosevic and Vojeslav Seselj, made a strong showing in the December 2003 Serbian parliamentary elections, unseating the incumbent

---

[9] For historical background, see Weschler (2000) and Scheffer (2000).

liberal government by running against the tribunal's interference with Serbian sovereign rights.

Second, if the vast majority of individuals worldwide accept the basic principles of the laws of war and prohibitions against genocide and torture, then prevailing practices should tip in favor of a universal system of international criminal justice. In this view, changes in behavior follow the adoption of new beliefs about appropriate standards of behavior. In fact, the prevailing pattern of political power and institutions shapes behavior in ways that are difficult to change simply through normative persuasion. For example, an extensive survey commissioned by the International Committee of the Red Cross (ICRC) shows that large majorities of people in powerful democracies and in conflict-ridden developing countries agree that it is wrong to target civilians for attack or to engage in indiscriminate military practices that result in widespread civilian slaughter (Greenberg Research 1999). However, the vast majority of those polled were not participating as fighters in the conflicts. Respondents who said they were participants in the conflict or who identified with one side expressed significant reservations about the laws of war. The report finds that "the more conflicts engage and mobilize the population," as in Israel and Palestine, "and the more committed the public is to a side and its goals, the greater the hatred of the enemy and the greater the willingness to breach whatever limits there exist in war" (Greenberg Research 1999, 32). Moreover, "weak defenders feel they can suspend the limits in war in order to do what is necessary to save or protect their communities" (Greenberg Research 1999, 33). Despite the convergence on abstract principles, these data imply that one person's terrorist is often another's freedom fighter.

Third, as the norm is embodied in institutions like the war crimes tribunals for Yugoslavia and Rwanda and the ICC, it should begin to have some deterrent effect (Kritz 1999). In fact, the indictments and trials initiated by the Yugoslav and Rwanda tribunals failed to deter the Srebrenica massacre, the ethnic cleansing of Kosovo, atrocities involving Hutu and Tutsi in eastern Congo, let alone subsequent atrocities in other parts of the globe, such as East Timor, that failed to be impressed by the example of the Hague's justice.

Human rights abusers – such as repressive states, extremist factions, and warlords – stand outside of any normative consensus, whether global or local. They need to be deterred through the predictable application of coercive force. The problem is, however, that they are often too powerful to deal with simply as criminals. Indeed, they can sometimes be indispensable allies in efforts to bring war criminals to justice. For example, the 2001–2002 US war against the terrorist-harboring Taliban would have been infeasible without the self-interested participation of the Afghan Northern Alliance, whose own leadership was earlier responsible for horrendous crimes in the Afghan Civil War in the 1990s. Strategies that deal with rights abusers on a political rather than criminal basis may be indispensable for the advancement of the international justice project itself, let alone other practical objectives, including national self-defense.

In such circumstances, legalists need to exercise prosecutorial discretion: A crime is a crime, but not all crimes must be prosecuted (Roth 2001, 153). Such choices, however, risk putting judges and lawyers in charge of decisions that political leaders are better suited to make. For example, the investigations of the International Criminal Tribunal for Yugoslavia (ICTY) have complicated a peace settlement between the Macedonian government and ethnic Albanian former guerrillas accused of committing atrocities.[10] The settlement granted these rebels an amnesty except for crimes indictable by the international tribunal. The ICTY's decision to investigate rebel atrocities led the guerrillas to destroy evidence of mass graves, creating a pretext for hard-line Slavic Macedonian nationalists to renew fighting in late November 2001 and to occupy Albanian-held terrain.[11]

In sum, the logic of appropriateness and the theory of norms cascades capture the mind-set and strategies of advocates of international criminal accountability. However, this social-constructivist theory of normative change fundamentally misunderstands how norms gain social force. As a result, legalist tactics for strengthening human rights norms can backfire when institutional and social preconditions for the rule of law are lacking. In an institutional desert, legalism is likely to be either counterproductive or simply irrelevant.

The logic of consequences

Drawing on the work of James March and Johan Olsen (1989, chapter 2), Finnemore and Sikkink (1998, 7) distinguish between the logic of appropriateness and the logic of consequences. Whereas Finnemore and Sikkink place the former at the center of their analysis, our approach emphasizes the latter. The logic of consequences assumes that actors

[10] "Macedonia Bolsters Albanian Rights: After Constitutional Change, Amnesty Is Declared for Former Rebels." *International Herald Tribune*, November 17–18, 2001.
[11] Garton Ash (2001); "Macedonia Is Seeking Control of Land Harboring Ex-Rebels." *New York Times*, November 26, 2001, sec. A, column 1, 11.

try to achieve their objectives using the full panoply of material, institutional, and persuasive resources at their disposal. Norms may facilitate or coordinate actors' strategies, but actors will follow rules and promote new norms only insofar as they are likely to be effective in achieving substantive ends, such as a reduction in the incidence of atrocities.

If norms are to shape behavior and outcomes, they must gain the support of a dominant political coalition in the social milieu in which they are to be applied. The coalition must establish and sustain the institutions that will monitor and sanction compliance with the norms. Strategies that underrate the logic of consequences – and thus hinder the creation of effective coalitions and institutions – undermine normative change.

This perspective has important implications for rethinking strategies of international criminal justice. Sporadic efforts by international actors to punish violations in turbulent societies are unlikely to prevent further abuses. Deterrence requires neutralizing potential spoilers, strengthening a coalition that supports norms of justice in the society, and improving the domestic administrative and legal institutions that are needed to implement justice predictably over the long run. Meeting these requirements must take precedence over the objective of retroactive punishment when those goals are in conflict. Where human rights violators are too weak to derail the strengthening of the rule of law, they can be put on trial. But where they have the ability to lash out in renewed violations to try to reinforce their power, the international community faces a hard choice: either commit the resources to contain the backlash, or else offer the potential spoilers a deal that will leave them weak but secure. Efforts to prosecute individuals for crimes must also be sensitive to the impact of these efforts on relations between dominant groups in a future governing coalition. Where trials threaten to create or perpetuate intra-coalition antagonisms in a new government, they should be avoided.

According to the logic of consequences, decisions about prosecution should be weighed in light of their effects on the strengthening of impartial, law-abiding state institutions. In the immediate aftermath of a state's transition to democracy, such institutions may already be capable of bringing rights abusers to trial, as for example in Greece following the collapse of the junta in 1974. However, in transitional countries that are rich in potential spoilers and poor in institutions, such as contemporary Indonesia, the government may need to gain spoilers' acquiescence to institutional reforms, especially the professionalization of police and military bureaucracies and the development of an impartial legal system. In these cases, decisions to try members of the former regime should be weighed against the possibly adverse effects on the strengthening of institutions. Trials may be advantageous if they can be conducted efficiently, strengthen public understanding of the rule of law, add to the institutional capacities of domestic courts, help to discredit rights abusers, help to defuse tensions between powerful groups in society, and produce no backlash from spoilers. Where these conditions are absent, punishment for the abuses of the former regime may be a dangerous misstep and should be a low priority.

The main positive effect of truth commissions has probably been to give political cover to amnesties in transitional countries with strong reform coalitions. In South Africa, for example, the truth commission recommended amnesties for the vast majority of the perpetrators who testified. In El Salvador, the truth commission helped to discredit the appalling practices of the former regime, but its release triggered a blanket amnesty for both government and rebel perpetrators (Hayner 2001, 101–105).

The international criminal justice regime should permit the use of amnesties when spoilers are strong and when the new regime can use an amnesty to decisively remove them from power. Deciding what approach to adopt in a particular case requires political judgment. Consequently, decisions to prosecute should be taken by political authorities, such as the UN Security Council or the governments of affected states, not by judges who remain unaccountable to both domestic electorates and international politicians.

Nonetheless, purely pragmatic approaches are inadequate if they do not address the long-term goal of institutionalizing the rule of law in conflict-prone societies. Opportunistic "deals with the devil" are at best a first step toward removing spoilers from positions of power so that institutional transformation can move forward. Institution building must begin with the strengthening of general state capacity and then move on to regularize the rule of law more deeply. Both amnesties and trials require effective state institutions and political coalitions to enforce them. Without those conditions, neither approach is likely to succeed. In cases where legal accountability is not barred by the danger of backlash from spoilers, trials should be carried out through local justice institutions in ways that strengthen their capacity, credibility, and legitimacy. When international jurists must get involved, mixed international–domestic tribunals, such as the one in Sierra Leone, are preferable to strictly international bodies like the ICC.

In short, the logic of consequences generates the following empirical predictions: When a country's political institutions are weak, forces of reform there have not won a decisive victory, and potential spoilers are strong, while attempts to put perpetrators of atrocities on trial are likely to increase the risk of violent conflict and further abuses, and therefore hinder the institutionalization of the rule of law.

The logic of emotions

A third approach to dealing with past atrocities and preventing their recurrence reflects the logic of emotions. Scholars and advocates suggest that eliminating the conditions that breed atrocities depends on achieving an emotional catharsis in the community of victims and an acceptance of blame by the perpetrators. Without an effort to establish a consensus on the truth about past abuses, national reconciliation will be impossible, as resentful groups will continue to use violence to voice their emotions. For these reasons, proponents of truth commissions stress the importance of encouraging perpetrators to admit responsibility for their crimes, sometimes in exchange for amnesty (Rotberg and Thompson 2000).

Some proponents of the logic of emotions speak in the language of psychotherapy (Pupavac 2001). Others ground their arguments in evolutionary biology, claiming that the emotional aspects of reconciliation are central to social cohesion. For example, an important study by William Long and Peter Brecke contends that successful civil war settlements tend to go through a trajectory that starts with truth telling and limited justice, culminates in an emotionally salient call for a new relationship between former enemies, and sometimes accomplishes a redefinition of social identities (Long and Brecke 2003, 31). One problem with their research design, however, is the difficulty of knowing whether the emotional theater of reconciliation is causally central to establishing peace or whether it is mainly window dressing that makes political bargaining and amnesties more palatable to the public.

Approaches based on the logic of emotions locate the solution to human rights abuses at the popular level. Reconciliation, in this view, resolves conflict because it reduces tensions between peoples, not between elites. However, elites, not masses, have instigated many recent ethnic conflicts with high levels of civilian atrocities. Solutions that mitigate tensions at the mass level need to be combined with strategies that effectively neutralize elite spoilers and manipulators (Kaufman 2001).

No one contends that emotion should be entirely removed from an analysis of the politics of punishing atrocities. Emotion plays some role in both the logic of appropriateness and the logic of consequences. Finnemore and Sikkink (1998), for example, discuss the importance of emotional appeals in proselytizing for new norms. Likewise, in the logic of consequences, the goals of political action are valued in part for emotional reasons (Elster 1999). Many people worldwide, including those who have experienced atrocities firsthand, feel that judicial punishment is intrinsically satisfying, even apart from any effect that trials may have in deterring future abuses (Liberman 2003). Nonetheless, few would want to base a global strategy of justice simply on the emotional satisfactions of retribution. The logic of emotions is useful to the extent that it can be integrated into a broader approach that has as its principal aim the prevention of future abuses.

Conclusion: the potential for transforming contemporary anarchy through culture

The radical constructivist notion that anarchy is nothing more than ideas, culture, and identity "almost all the way down" is just as misleading as the hyper-realist notion that the unchangeable situation of anarchy will always make life nasty, brutish, and short, regardless of anarchy's institutional and cultural content. Those who seek to transform the culture of contemporary anarchy need to work within an existing material and institutional setting that may enable, derail, or pervert efforts to promote change. Efforts to force the pace of change risk unintended consequences that could wind up hindering change and increasing its costs.

Understanding the relationship between "is" and "ought" should indeed be a central task of contemporary international relations scholarship. While undertaking that task, however, it is important to avoid taking a one-dimensional, voluntarist view of behavior in anarchy that could make more likely the kinds of outcomes that principled scholars and serious-minded practitioners want to avoid.

REFERENCES

Bass, Gary Jonathan. 2000. *Staying the Hand of Vengeance: The Politics of War Crimes Tribunals*. Princeton University Press.
Beitz, Charles R. 1979. *Political Theory and International Relations*. Princeton University Press.
Best, Geoffrey. 1994. *War and Law since 1945*. Oxford: Clarendon.
Bukovansky, Mlada. 2002. *Legitimacy and Power Politics*. Princeton University Press.
Burns, John F. 2002. "Political Realities Impeding Full Inquiry into Afghan Atrocity." *New York Times*, August 29: 5.
Camacho, Christopher, E. Tory Higgins, and Lindsay Luger. 2003. "Moral Value Transfer from Regulatory Fit: 'What Feels Right *Is* Right' and 'What

Feels Wrong *Is* Wrong.'" *Journal of Personality and Social Psychology* 84 (March): 498–510.

Carothers, Thomas. 1999. *Aiding Democracy Abroad.* Washington DC: Carnegie Endowment for International Peace.

Clark, Ann Marie. 2001. *Diplomacy of Conscience: Amnesty International and Changing Human Rights Norms.* Princeton University Press.

Diamond, Larry. 1996. "Is the Third Wave Over?" *Journal of Democracy* 7: 20–37.

Elster, Jon. 1999. *Alchemies of the Mind: Rationality and the Emotions.* Cambridge University Press.

Finnemore, Martha, and Kathryn Sikkink. 1998. "International Norm Dynamics and Political Change." *International Organization* 52 (Autumn): 887–917.

Garton Ash, Timothy. 2001. "Is There a Good Terrorist?" *New York Review of Books,* November 29: 30–33.

Greenberg Research. 1999. *The People on War Report: ICRC Worldwide Consultation on the Rules of War.* Geneva: International Committee of the Red Cross, October. www.icrc.org/icrceng.nsf.

Hayner, Priscilla B. 2001. *Unspeakable Truths: Confronting State Terror and Atrocity.* New York: Routledge.

Herrmann, Richard K. 2004. "George W. Bush's Foreign Policy." In *The George W. Bush Presidency,* ed. Colin Campbell and Bert Rockman. Washington DC: CQ Press, 191–225.

Higgins, E. Tory. 2000. "Making a Good Decision: Value from Fit." *American Psychologist* 55 (November): 1217–1230.

Ignatieff, Michael. 2001. *Human Rights as Politics and Idolatry,* ed. Amy Guttman. Princeton University Press.

Jervis, Robert. 2003. "The Compulsive Empire." *Foreign Policy* 137 (July/August): 82–87.

Katzenstein, Peter. 1996. *The Culture of National Security.* New York: Columbia University Press.

Kaufman, Stuart J. 2001. *Modern Hatreds: The Symbolic Politics of Ethnic War.* Ithaca, NY: Cornell University Press.

Keck, Margaret, and Kathryn Sikkink. 1998. *Activists Beyond Borders: Transnational Advocacy Networks in International Politics.* Ithaca, NY: Cornell University Press.

Kritz, Neil J. 1996. "Coming to Terms with Atrocities: A Review of Accountability Mechanisms for Mass Violations of Human Rights." *Law and Contemporary Problems* 59 (Autumn): 127–152.

    1999. "War Crime Trials: Who Should Conduct Them – and How." In *War Crimes: The Legacy of Nuremberg,* ed. Belinda Cooper. New York: TV Books.

Liberman, Peter. 2003. "Crime, Punishment, and War." Paper presented at the annual meeting of the American Political Science Association, Philadelphia, Pennsylvania, August 28–31.

Linz, Juan J., and Alfred Stepan. 1996. *Problems of Democratic Transition and Consolidation.* Baltimore: Johns Hopkins University Press.

Long, William J., and Peter Brecke. 2003. *War and Reconciliation: Reason and Emotion in Conflict Resolution*. Cambridge, MA: MIT Press.

Lund, Michael, Barnett Rubin, and Fabienne Hara. 1998. "Learning from Burundi's Failed Democratic Transition, 1993–1996." In *Cases and Strategies for Preventive Action*, ed. Barnett Rubin. New York: Century Foundation.

Lutz, Ellen, and Kathryn Sikkink. 2000. "International Human Rights Law and Practice." *International Organization* 54 (Summer): 633–651.

March, James P., and Johan Olsen. 1989. *Rediscovering Institutions: The Organizational Basis of Politics*. New York: Free Press.

Mearsheimer, John. 2001. *The Tragedy of Great Power Politics*. New York: Norton.

Minow, Martha. 1998. *Between Vengeance and Forgiveness: Facing History after Genocide and Mass Violence*. Boston: Beacon Press.

Nagel, Thomas. 1988. "War and Massacre." In *Consequentialism and Its Critics*, ed. Samuel Scheffer. Oxford University Press.

Office of the President. 2002. *National Security Strategy of the United States*, September. www.whitehouse.gov/nsc/nss.html.

Owen, John. 1997. *Liberal Peace, Liberal War*. Ithaca, NY: Cornell University Press.

Power, Samantha. 2002. *A Problem from Hell: America and the Age of Genocide*. New York: Basic.

Przeworski, Adam, Michael E. Alvarez, José Cheibub, and Fernando Limongi. 2000. *Democracy and Development: Political Institutions and Well-Being in the World, 1950–1990*. Cambridge University Press.

Pupavac, Vanessa. 2001. "Therapeutic Governance: Psycho-Social Intervention and Trauma Risk Management." *Disasters* 25 (December): 358–372.

Putnam, Tonya. 2002. "Human Rights and Sustainable Peace." In *Ending Civil Wars: The Implementation of Peace Agreements*, ed. Stephen John Stedman, Donald Rothchild, and Elizabeth Cousens. New York: Lynne Rienner, 237–272.

Rice, Condoleezza. 2002. "Dr. Condoleezza Rice Discusses President's National Security Strategy." Wriston Lecture, Waldorf Astoria Hotel, New York, October 1. www.whitehouse.gov/news/releases/2002/10/20021001-6.html.

Risse, Thomas, and Kathryn Sikkink. 1999. "The Socialization of International Human Rights Norms into Domestic Practices." In *The Power of Human Rights: International Norms and Domestic Change*, ed. Thomas Risse, Stephen C. Ropp, and Kathryn Sikkink. Cambridge University Press, 1–38.

Rotberg, Robert I., and Dennis Thompson, eds. 2000. *Truth vs. Justice: The Morality of Truth Commissions*. Princeton University Press.

Roth, Kenneth. 2001. "The Case for Universal Jurisdiction." *Foreign Affairs* 80 (September): 150–154.

Ruggie, John. 1998. *Constructing the World Polity*. London: Routledge.

Russett, Bruce. 1993. *Grasping the Democratic Peace*. Princeton University Press.

Scheffer, David J. 2000. "The U.S. Perspective on the ICC." In Sewall and Kaysen, eds., 115–118.

Schulz, William F. 2001. *In Our Own Best Interest: How Defending Human Rights Benefits Us All*. Boston: Beacon Press.

Sewall, Sarah B., and Carl Kaysen, eds. 2000. *The United States and the International Criminal Court*. New York: Rowman & Littlefield.

Shklar, Judith. 1964. *Legalism*. Cambridge, MA: Harvard University Press.

Snyder, Jack. 2002. "Anarchy and Culture: Insights from the Anthropology of War." *International Organization* 56 (Winter): 7–46.

Snyder, Jack, and Leslie Vinjamuri. 2003/2004. "Trials and Errors: Principle and Pragmatism in Strategies of International Justice." *International Security* 28 (Winter): 5–44.

Stedman, Stephen John. 1997. "Spoiler Problems in Peace Processes." *International Security* 22 (Fall): 5–53.

Waltz, Kenneth. 1979. *Theory of International Politics*. Reading, MA: Addison-Wesley.

Wendt, Alexander. 1999. *Social Theory of International Politics*. Cambridge University Press.

Weschler, Lawrence. 2000. "Exceptional Cases in Rome: The United States and the Struggle for an ICC." In Sewall and Kaysen, eds., 85–114.

16 Promises and pitfalls of an emerging research program: the microdynamics of civil war

Stathis N. Kalyvas

The study of civil war ranks among the most notable developments in political science during the last decade. Several important papers have been published in this period and the field has witnessed an important shift toward cross-national, large-N econometric studies (e.g. Collier and Hoeffler 2004; Fearon and Laitin 2003), following a previous shift from the case-study format to that of theoretically informed studies (Wickham-Crowley 1992; Skocpol 1979; Scott 1976; Eckstein 1965).

However, despite these advances much remains to be understood. On the one hand, the conceptual foundations of our understanding of civil wars are still weak (Kalyvas 2001; 2003; Cramer 2002); on the other hand, econometric studies have produced very little in terms of robust results – the main one being that, like autocratic regimes (Przeworski *et al.* 2000), civil wars are more likely to occur in poor countries. The problems of econometric studies are well known: their main findings are incredibly sensitive to coding and measurement procedures (Hegre and Sambanis 2006; Montalvo and Reynal-Querol 2005; Sambanis 2004b); they entail a considerable distance between theoretical constructs and proxies (Cederman and Girardin 2007; Fearon *et al.* 2007) as well as multiple observationally equivalent pathways (Kalyvas 2007; Humphreys 2005; Kocher 2004; Sambanis 2004a); they suffer from endogeneity (Miguel *et al.* 2004); they lack clear microfoundations or are based on erroneous ones (Cramer 2007; Kalyvas and Kocher 2007b; Gutiérrez Sanín 2004); and, finally, they are subject to narrow (and untheorized) scope conditions (Wimmer and Min 2006).

In response to these problems, a new research program has emerged: the microdynamics of civil war. It calls for the systematic collection of data at the subnational level and its sophisticated analysis. Compared to the macro level, a subnational focus offers the possibility of improving data quality, testing microfoundations and causal mechanisms, maximizing the fit between concepts and data, and controlling for many variables that can be held constant. Inspired by pioneering research on political violence and contention – whether quantitative (Tong 1991; Greer 1935), ethnographic (Wood 2003; Brass 1997), or mixed-method (Wilkinson 2004; Gould 2003; Varshney 2002; Petersen 2001; Tarrow 1998; Tilly 1978) – this research program is presently in full bloom.[1]

These studies address a variety of questions (e.g. patterns of conflict, dynamics of violence, logic of recruitment and displacement, processes of demobilization, effects of civil war), focus on several units of analysis (e.g. events, localities, organizations, individuals) and geographical regions (e.g. Colombia, Greece, Sierra Leone, Rwanda), spring from different disciplines (e.g. political science, sociology, economics), and rely on diverse methods (e.g. individual surveys, human rights datasets, archival research, GIS or Geographic Information Systems), but they do share a distinct outlook, namely the systematic application of social scientific methods at a level of analysis and on a type of problem where such methods did not traditionally enjoy much purchase.

Clearly, this is a very exciting development which has already begun to deepen our understanding of civil conflict and mass violence. At the same time, however, like any such program, it entails certain compromises. The most obvious ones are the sacrifice of a measure of external validity to gain more internal validity and the exclusion of those macro processes that cannot be analyzed at the micro level. These compromises are often accompanied by a pronounced lack of clarity on scope conditions, and a tendency, sometimes, toward reckless extrapolation from the micro to the macro level.

Besides these somewhat inherent "structural" compromises, the incipient microdynamics literature is characterized by recurrent flaws that can be addressed and corrected. Here, I focus on two such flaws. The first one is the use of overaggregated variables. One would not expect this to be a problem in micro-level research, yet it turns out to be. A combination of insufficient theorization, superficial engagement with the case at hand, and reliance on off-the-shelf datasets leads to the use of variables that are insufficiently or inadequately disaggregated. These practices lead to the reproduction of problems encountered in the macro-literature such as the absence of clear microfoundations, the distance gap theoretical constructs and proxies, and the inability to

---

[1] A very partial listing would include recent works such as: Arjona and Kalyvas (2006); Barron *et al.* (2004); Blattman and Annan (2007); Deininger (2004); Deininger *et al.* (2004); Guichaoua (2007); Humphreys and Weinstein (2006); Weinstein (2007); Verwimp (2003; 2006); Kalyvas (2006); Kalyvas and Kocher (2007a; 2007b); Kocher (2004); Restrepo *et al.* (2004); Straus (2006); Trejo Osorio (2004), and Viterna (2006). Much more work is currently underway.

adjudicate between observationally equivalent causal mechanisms. The second flaw is the frequent omission of what turns out to be a key factor shaping the dynamics of civil war, namely territorial control. I show why territorial control matters and demonstrate how its omission biases the results of econometric analysis.

I proceed in two steps. First, I discuss three recent papers that in many ways exemplify the micro-level turn – at least in its more "economistic" manifestation. These papers use extensive subnational data to quantitatively analyze the dynamics of the civil war in Nepal. Also known as the Maoist insurgency, this conflict, presently in remission, lasted for about ten years (1996–2006) and cost over 13,000 lives. In spite of their important contributions, these papers suffer from the problems described above. Second, I turn to my own quantitative study of the dynamics of violence in the Greek Civil War and replicate it in order to show how insufficient disaggregation and the omission of territorial control from the analysis bias the results – and hence how these problems may be likewise biasing the results presented in the three papers on Nepal.

The Maoist insurgency in Nepal: a critical review

The first paper to focus on the Nepal insurgency using district-level data was published in 2005 by S. Mansoob Murshed and Scott Gates. Their dependent variable, *conflict intensity*, is proxied by fatality data. These data, collected by Shobha Gautam and published in 2001 by the Institute of Human Rights Communication Nepal (IHRCON), include the number of homicides in each of the seventy-five districts of Nepal from the start of the war, in 1996, up to 2001. From this dataset, Murshed and Gates generate a single fatality indicator per district for the entire period. They then find that the intensity of the conflict, as measured, is a function of two types of inequality: asset inequality (proxied by landlessness) and horizontal income inequality (proxied by a human development index for each district which includes life expectancy, education, and road density). Districts with high values of landlessness and low values of the HDI are found to have experienced higher fatality rates. An additional finding is that hilly terrain is associated with higher levels of violence. Finally, the main negative finding is that the presence of natural resources (which are not plentiful to begin with in Nepal) is associated with lower fatality rates. The authors conclude by suggesting that inequality causes civil war, a claim associated with the "grievance theory" of civil war onset, which has not fared well in the cross-sectional econometric literature.

The second paper, published in 2006 by Alok K. Bohara, Neil J. Mitchell, and Mani Nepal, also uses violence as a proxy for conflict intensity, but pays some attention to violence *per se,* and especially the relation between incumbent and insurgent violence. The paper focuses on three causal variables: poverty, political participation, and social capital. The data on violence come from a different source than those used in the previous paper: the Informal Sector Service Center (INSEC), a human rights NGO which published them in 2003. Violence is much more disaggregated: by actor (state and insurgents) and by time (the models are run on three time periods: 1997–2001, 1997–2002, and 1997–2003). The main findings are that geography (hilly terrain) and rurality (captured by population density) are powerful predictors of violence, whereas participation in elections and "social capital," as proxied by the number of civic organizations, reduces the levels of violence. Ethnicity and, contrary to the previous paper, poverty are found to have no effect on the levels of violence. Furthermore, insurgent and incumbent violence seem to interact with each other.

Finally, the third paper by World Bank economists Quy-Toan Do and Lakshmi Iyer, initially circulated in 2006 and revised in 2007, relies on the same INSEC dataset but takes better advantage of its rich data. The authors normalize the district-level fatality counts, disaggregate them into four yearly counts (1999, 2002, 2003, 2004), and analyze data on insurgent abductions. The most important predictors of violence in this paper are geographical factors, namely elevation and forested areas (which explain about 25 percent of the total variation), and poverty. Prewar poverty levels are also a significant predictor of violence, whereas sociopolitical variables such as the prevalence of advantaged castes, and caste or linguistic polarization, do not significantly increase the intensity of the conflict. Some variables, such as caste polarization, literacy rates, or infrastructure, matter in some specifications but not others. The authors conclude that development indicators are more robust predictors of conflict compared to political factors such as caste and ethnicity (described in the paper as "diversity factors"). Of particular importance is the fact that the disaggregation of the fatality data into yearly counts yields an important finding: there is considerable variation in the significance of the key causal factors across time. For example, whereas poverty and literacy are significant until 2003, they cease to be significant in 2004, a fact suggesting that the war is moving from more to less poor areas; in other words, war is a dynamic rather than a static process.

Clearly, all three papers go a long way toward improving our understanding of the dynamics of civil war. Nevertheless, there are problems. While all three papers converge in ascribing causal significance to geographical factors, especially hilly terrain, they diverge in their assignment of causal significance for almost every other variable, i.e. poverty, class, caste and ethnic polarization, participation, or social capital. Furthermore, the interpretation of their findings is loose. The reason, I contend, is related to the fact that while the empirical focus of these papers is unmistakably turned toward the micro level, their conceptual and theoretical focus is almost exclusively derived from the macro-level literature. These papers refer almost exclusively to the macro-literature on civil war onset, as if empirical findings on violence at the district level in Nepal could be extrapolated to civil war onset at the cross-national level and vice versa. In other words, there is a mismatch between their micro-level empirical focus and their macro-level conceptual and theoretical focus. This mismatch is reflected in five specific problems: (a) problematic proxies, (b) observational equivalence, (c) endogeneity, (d) overaggregation, and (e) omitted variable bias.

Problematic proxies

At its heart, the problem of the distance between concepts and empirical proxies is theoretical. A common problem in many studies on civil war, aptly illustrated by the three Nepal papers, is the conflation of two related, yet distinct, concepts: war/conflict on the one hand, and violence on the other.

Although war is defined as collective violence, the dynamics of violence and the dynamics of war are analytically distinct – and more so in civil wars compared to interstate ones. An obvious example of the perils of such a conflation is the use of fatality counts as a proxy for the intensity of a conflict. In a civil war, the absence of fatalities from a particular location may be indicative of two distinct (even opposite) states of the world: either a total state monopoly of violence (which is what most studies assume is the case) or a total absence of the state. This is the case for two reasons: primarily because the absence of the state in a civil war context does not necessarily signify the prevalence of anarchy understood as the absence of any order; and secondarily because, *contra* Hobbes, anarchy may not necessarily entail mass violence. A common state of affairs is instead the emergence, in a country undergoing a civil war, of an alternative state, one fully controlled and administered by

rebels in so-called liberated zones – or "base areas" to use Maoist par-
lance. Such zones are often violence-free because violence there is off the
equilibrium path (Kalyvas 2006).[2] The emergence of such zones is a
testament of the state's inability to defeat the rebels and is compatible
with a view of a civil war as being intense. In other words, the absence of
violence from a specific area cannot be assumed to indicate the reduction of a conflict's intensity.

This point holds an additional implication. Insofar as the emergence
of rebel-held zones is typically the crucial factor that fuels the expansion
of the war in neighboring areas, the intensity of the conflict in these
districts cannot be attributed exclusively to factors that are *only* present
in that district. However, all these papers share the fundamental
assumption that the conflict in a given district is *solely* related to factors
that are district-specific.

Observational equivalence

A second problem is observational equivalence. Consider the finding
that poverty is positively correlated with high fatalities, which points to
several observationally equivalent mechanisms, each with different theoretical and policy implications. It may be, for instance, that insurgents
recruit poor individuals who join to seek justice (the "grievance theory"
of civil war); or that individuals in poor areas (which is not the same
as saying poor individuals) see joining as a job in places where job
opportunities are nonexistent (the "greed theory" of civil war); or that
the government invests more resources to prevent the conflict in
wealthier areas which is why the conflict is "fully expressed" in the rural
countryside; or that the opportunity costs of violence are lower for the
state in poor areas; or that people in poor areas may be less able to
protect themselves from violence, including its "collateral damage"
dimension. Of the three Nepal papers, Do and Iyer's stands alone in
recognizing several possible observational pathways, though it acknowledges its inability to distinguish between them. The other two papers
are much less forthcoming in recognizing this problem.

Endogeneity

Endogeneity is a significant problem in all three studies, most notably in
Bohara *et al.*'s paper. For example, they use turnout in the May 1999

---

[2] I have also argued that high levels of contestation are associated with low levels of violence,
which undermines proxying conflict by violence even more. See Kalyvas (2006).

elections to measure participation and find that it predicts lower rates of fatalities, which is to say that districts with low turnout in these elections have lower levels of violence. Obviously, with an ongoing war and with the Maoists openly denouncing the political process, the incidence of lower turnout in conflict-affected areas should not be surprising. However, there are exceedingly strong grounds to believe that the direction of causality flows from the conflict to turnout rather than the other way around. The same is likely the case for their indicator of social capital which is based on an index of social organizations compiled in the Nepal Living Standard Survey (NLSS) conducted in 1995–1996, again while the war was ongoing. It is not clear that organizations can operate freely in the midst of war, yet this would not mean that the presence of associations inhibits conflict. Note that this is also a measurement problem as the conflict must have affected the process of data collection; it is unlikely that the enumerators of the NLSS could have gotten truthful (or any) information from conflict areas.

Last, endogeneity is clearly a problem in the case of the negative correlation between violence and government economic development allocations (GRANT). Bohara *et al.* acknowledge so much when they quote evidence that the Maoists obstructed the implementation of hundreds of development projects. Do and Iyer are, once more, more forthcoming in this respect since they recognize that the effect of poverty may be endogenous to the conflict insofar as the state is likely to expend a greater effort to prevent rebel activity in richer areas or, alternatively, the opportunity costs of violent repression are lower in poorer areas. Likewise, they speculate that the effect of polarization they find may actually be due to the fact that the state is perhaps more repressive in areas where society is extremely polarized.

More generally, civil war is a deeply "endogenous" process (Kalyvas 2006), meaning that behavior, beliefs, preferences, and even identities can be altered as a result of the conflict and its violence. This is why the use of prewar lagged variables to address endogeneity concerns creates more problems than it solves. For example, Murshed and Gates rely on sociopolitical variables collected either in or before 1996, the year the war started. Their assumption is that year-to-year fluctuations in violence can be causally traced exclusively to prewar causes. However, this assumption flies in the face of evidence from many conflicts that (a) the war generates "contagion" effects independent of prewar factors, and (b) these variables (e.g. road density, human development index) change in the course of the conflict, partly as a result of the war.

Overaggregation

The turn to micro-analysis is testament to the need for disagreggation (Brubaker and Laitin 1998). It is, therefore, rather surprising to observe that micro-level studies may also suffer from overaggregation. In fact, this problem is made much more obvious precisely by the adoption of a micro-focus.

I identify two problems of overaggregation. The first one concerns the unit of analysis. All three papers adopt a district-level analysis. While Nepal's seventy-two districts provide a number that is high enough for statistical analysis, it is important to keep in mind that these are large areas averaging 1,948 square kilometers with a population of 309,000 (in 2001). Obviously such a size is likely to conceal significant internal heterogeneity. Furthermore, the decision to run the analysis exclusively at the district level is dictated less by the coding level of the independent variables (which are often collected at the community or even household levels and must be aggregated up at the district level) and more by the coding level of the dependent variable. In other words, this is an inefficient use of data dictated by the availability of an "off-the-shelf" dataset. The alternative would have been a deeper engagement with the case at hand which would have led to the collection of data at multiple levels of aggregation and, thus, allowed for a more sophisticated research design.

This brings up the second, and more serious, problem of overaggregation, that of violence. The analysis of the dynamics of violence requires at least three levels of disaggregation: (a) by actor (incumbent and insurgent violence), (b) by temporal period (e.g. monthly, yearly), and (c) by type of violence (homicides versus other types of violence; combatant versus noncombatant fatalities;[3] and selective versus indiscriminate violence).

Murshed and Gates do not disaggregate at all: they use one fatality data point per district for the entire February 1996–July 2001 period; Bohara *et al.* introduce a measure of disaggregation: they distinguish between insurgent and incumbent violence and test for three time periods. Finally, Do and Iyer go further by introducing yearly violence data for both sides and disaggregating the insurgent violence into killed and abducted.

The absence of disaggregation impacts on the analysis as can be seen by its effect when it is actually introduced: Bohara *et al.* find significant

---

[3] Bohara *et al.* (2006) point out that close to two-thirds of the total fatalities in Nepal are thought to be noncombatants.

differences in the violence produced by the two rival sides: ethnic heterogeneity reduces Maoist violence but not its state counterpart. Likewise, Do and Iyer find, among others, that poverty and literacy rates are not significantly associated with Maoist violence before 2002 but are significantly associated with state deaths in 1999; they also find that poverty explains killing but not insurgent abductions, but that literacy levels do (they speculate that insurgent violence may move from poor to wealthier areas over time). Not coincidentally, common to all three papers is the absence of any direct evidence about the belligerents: who they are, what are their goals and strategies, how they think, and so on. What allusions there are to these matters, and they are not numerous, tend to be inferred in a very indirect way from the data analysis.

All three papers fail to recognize the distinction between selective and indiscriminate violence, which is based on the level at which "guilt" (and hence, targeting) is determined. Violence is selective when targeting requires the determination of individual guilt and it is indiscriminate when targeting is based on guilt by association or collective guilt. States and rebels engage in a variable mix of selective and indiscriminate violence, primarily as a function of their degree of local knowledge (Kalyvas 2006). Note that, though indiscriminate violence is often associated with mass killing, this distinction is independent of the scale of targeting: selective violence can be massive while indiscriminate violence can be limited. The Phoenix Program in Vietnam was massive despite being selective in intent, whereas more recent violence in Kosovo was rather limited yet indiscriminate, as targeting was ascertained primarily by group membership.

The failure to disaggregate violence is deeply problematic from a theoretical perspective, as violence is an inherently *interactive* and *dynamic* process: the violence of one side impacts on the violence of the other side, while the war evolves and changes as the political actors strategize in response to evolving constraints and their rivals' strategy.

Omitted variable bias

A last problem flows from the failure to recognize the impact of territorial control on violence. I have formulated and tested a theory of selective violence (Kalyvas 2006) where the level of territorial control is the main explanatory variable, summarized as follows.

Most civil wars are fought as asymmetric or "irregular" wars – sometimes referred to as "wars without fronts." Irregular war is defined by the twin processes of segmentation and fragmentation of sovereignty: segmentation refers to the division of territory into zones that are monopolistically controlled by rival actors; while fragmentation refers to the division of territory into zones where the rivals' sovereignty overlaps. Put otherwise, civil wars are political contexts where violence is used both to challenge and to build order. The type of sovereignty or control that prevails in a given area affects the type of strategies followed by political actors. Political actors want to capture popular support ("collaboration") and deter noncollaboration ("defection"). The degree of control determines the extent of collaboration instead of the other way around, because political actors who enjoy substantial territorial control can protect civilians who live on that territory – both from their rivals and from themselves – giving civilians a strong incentive to collaborate with them, irrespective of their true or initial preferences. In this sense, collaboration is endogenous to control. In the long run, military resources, best proxied by geography, generally trump prewar political and social support in spawning control: incumbents tend to control cities, even when these cities happen to be the social, religious, or ethnic strongholds of their opponents, while the insurgents' strongholds tend to be in inaccessible rural areas, even when rural populations are opposed to them. However, the military resources that are necessary for the imposition of control are staggering and are usually lacking. The rival factions are, therefore, left with little choice but to use violence as a means to shape collaboration. The use of violence is bounded by the nature of sovereignty exercised by each political actor and, generally, must be selective rather than indiscriminate.

Political actors maximize territorial control subject to the (local) military balance of power. Territorial control in the context of irregular war requires the exclusive collaboration of individual civilians who, in turn, maximize various benefits subject to survival constraints. Irrespective of their preferences (and everything else being equal), most people prefer to collaborate with the political actor that best guarantees their survival. However, collaboration is much more uncertain in areas of fragmented sovereignty where control is incomplete. Because of its value for consolidating control, it is here that the premium on selective violence – that is, violence against defectors – is particularly steep. Selective violence, however, requires private information, which is asymmetrically distributed among political actors and civilians: only the latter may know who the *defectors* (i.e. those who collaborate with the actor's rival) are – and they have a choice: to *denounce* them or not. Put otherwise, selective violence is the result of transactions between political actors and individuals: it is *jointly* produced by them.

The likelihood of violence is a function of control. On the one hand, political actors do not want to use violence where they already enjoy high levels of control (because they do not need it) and where they have no control whatsoever (because it is counterproductive, since they are not likely to have access to the information necessary to make it selective). Instead, they want to use violence in intermediate areas, where they have incomplete control. On the other hand, individuals want to denounce only where it is safe for them to do so. This is the case in areas of full control (where political actors do not need their information) but not in areas of low control (where they are likely to face retaliation). This argument specifies the exact geographical space where violence is most likely to occur as a result of the intersection between the logics of the two sets of actors: it is where control is neither too skewed toward one side or the other, nor too balanced. It is, in other words, where the organizational demand for information meets the civilian supply of information via denunciation. Outside this space, violence is less likely: political actors may demand information but individuals will fail to supply it (or veto its application), and individuals may supply information but political actors will not need it. In short, the model predicts, rather ironically, that strategic political actors will not use violence where they need it most and, likewise, strategic individuals will fail to get rid of their enemies where they are most willing to denounce. The outcome, in other words, is suboptimal for both.

I operationalize control on a five-zone continuum, from zone 1 (total incumbent control) to zone 5 (total insurgent control). The main prediction is that the distribution of selective violence is likely to be bimodal, concentrating in zones 2 and 4. Incumbents will be most likely to resort to selective violence in areas where they exercise hegemonic, though not total control (which I call zone 2) and insurgents most likely to resort to the same type of violence in similar areas on their side (which I call zone 4). Areas of total control (zone 1 for incumbents and zone 5 for insurgents) will be largely free of violence (though not of repression). Areas of complete contestation and parity where both sides are simultaneously present in equal force (zone 3) will be free of violence. Figure 16.1 provides a graphic depiction of these predictions.

Figures 16.2 and 16.3 display the actual distribution of both selective and indiscriminate violence in the Argolid, a Greek region that experienced a civil war in 1943–1944 which I studied intensively in order to test these predictions. It is easy to note the multiple differences in the distribution of these two types of violence as well as the difficulty of distinguishing a clear pattern, at least for selective violence.

Figure 16.4 shows the observed distribution of selective violence as a function of control. Note the similarity in the shape of the distribution compared to Figure 16.1.

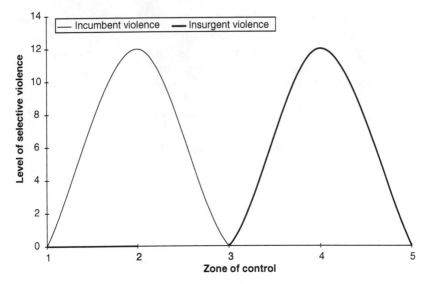

Figure 16.1 Predicted levels of selective violence as a function of
territorial control

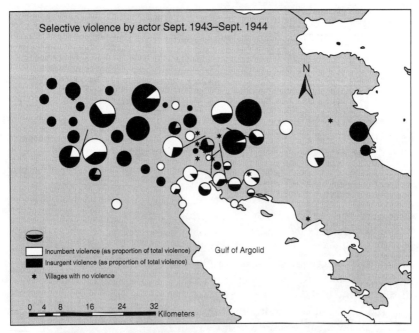

Figure 16.2 The spatial distribution of selective violence: Argolid,
Greece, 1943–1944

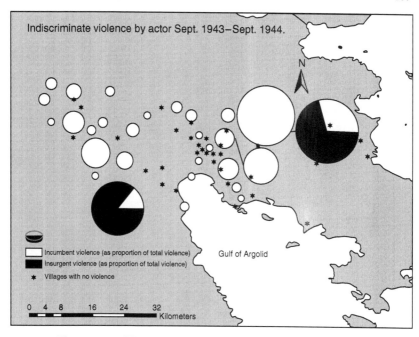

Figure 16.3 The spatial distribution of indiscriminate violence: Argolid, Greece, 1943–1944

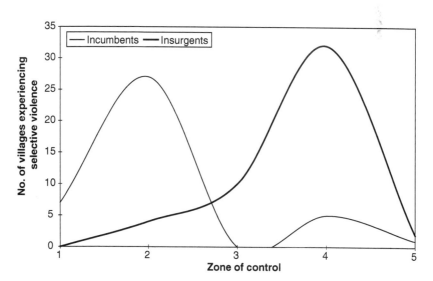

Figure 16.4 Observed levels of selective violence across control zones: Argolid, Greece, 1943–1944

Table 16.1. *Basic descriptive statistics, Argolid 1943–1944*

		No. of homicides	% of total violence	% of population
	Total violence	725		1.61
Type of violence	Selective	366	50.48	0.96
	Indiscriminate	359	49.52	0.94
Actor	Incumbents	353	48.69	0.92
	Insurgents	372	51.31	0.97
Time period	t_1	66	9.10	0.16
	t_2	295	40.69	0.77
	t_3	168	23.17	0.44
	t_4	196	27.03	0.50
Location	Plains	152	20.97	0.40
	Hills	450	62.07	1.18
	Mountains	123	16.97	0.32

Table 16.1 displays the basic descriptive statistics. Note the geographical concentration of violence: 62.07% of all homicides are located in hilly terrain, compared to 20.97% in the plains and 16.97% in the mountains. The parallels with the most robust finding of the three Nepal studies are striking.

Last, Table 16.2 includes the results of a multivariate test using these data, with selective violence as the dependent variable and a set of independent variables that includes territorial control.[4] Note that what

---

[4] These are OLS regressions estimating the *intensity* of selective violence, coded as the number of deaths per village. The model was estimated for the four time periods based on major shifts in control. The main explanatory variable is a dummy variable whose value is 1 if a village is located in zone 2 or 4. Control variables include the following: village population (as recorded in the 1940 census – logged); educational level (measured as the per-capita number of village children attending secondary school in 1937–1939), intended to capture a variety of hypothesized effects in both directions, including civilizing effects, political moderation which may reduce violence and rising expectations, or political extremism which may increase it; altitude (logged meters), intended to capture rough terrain which may have a positive effect on violence given that insurgencies are more likely to take place in such areas; distance from the closest town (logged travel minutes from the closest town in 1940), intended to capture the geographic ability of the two sides to access a particular locale and provide credible opportunities and sanctions; litigiousness (the total number of trials in the civil and penal courts of the region during the period 1935–1939, logged), intended to capture social polarization as well as the absence of social capital which should reduce violence; and a three-scale ordinal GDP proxy, intended to capture wealth and opportunity costs. See Kalyvas (2006) for more details on coding and specification.

Table 16.2. *Determinants of the intensity of violence (no. of homicides per time period), Argolid 1943–1944, OLS regressions (robust standard errors and p values in parentheses)*

Dependent variable: selective violence (number of homicides)	t1	t2	t3	t4
Control zone	1.29*	3.62***	3.28**	10.06***
2 and 4 (dummy: 1	(0.66)	(1.06)	(1.39)	(3.54)
when control zone is	(0.056)	(0.001)	(0.022)	(0.006)
2 or 4)				
Population (1940) (log)	0.24	1.28**	1.42*	1.05
	(0.22)	(0.59)	(0.73)	(0.81)
	(0.27)	(0.034)	(0.056)	(0.198)
Education level (high-	−0.11	0.37	0.38	0.52
school students per	(0.21)	(0.52)	(0.42)	(0.46)
capita)	(0.600)	(0.477)	(0.365)	(0.257)
Altitude (meters) (log)	−0.22	0.96***	0.63**	0.51
	(0.22)	(0.28)	(0.33)	(0.49)
	(0.335)	(0.001)	(0.044)	(0.298)
Distance from closest	0.36	0.36	−1.47*	0.14
town (in minutes)	(0.62)	(0.68)	(0.76)	(0.53)
(log)	(0.561)	(0.597)	(0.066)	(0.789)
Prewar conflict (court	0.11	−0.67**	−0.47	0.69
suits per capita	(0.17)	(0.33)	(0.48)	(0.43)
1935–1939) (log)	(0.513)	(0.046)	(0.334)	(0.110)
GDP proxy (interval	0.32	−0.09	−1.13**	0.61
variable; wealthiest	(0.36)	(0.42)	(0.50)	(0.46)
village = 3)	(0.379)	(0.815)	(0.028)	(0.192)
Constant	−2.09	−17.65	−3.46	−9.11
	(2.96)	(6.7)	(5.58)	(7.17)
	(0.485)	(0.011)	(0.538)	(0.209)
Observations	61	61	61	61
R-Squared	0.265	0.372	0.328	0.543
Prob > F	0.0258	0.0172	0.0062	0.1357

*p<0.10; **p<0.0.05; ***p<0.01 (two-tailed test) (p-values in parentheses)

looked like a powerful effect of geography disappears in a multivariate setting that includes a measure of territorial control.

How robust is this finding? I provide two additional pieces of evidence from two very different conflicts: Colombia and Vietnam. The impact of territorial control on the patterns of recruitment can be seen in Table 16.3 and Figure 16.5 which use data from a survey of demobilized combatants in Colombia (Arjona and Kalyvas 2006).

Table 16.3. *Recruitment as a function of control, Colombia*

		Joined the guerrillas	Joined the paramilitaries
Who ruled one year prior of joining?	Guerrillas	75.36	24.63
	Paramilitaries	2.98	97.02
	Neither	30.67	69.29
	Both	50	50

Source: Arjona and Kalyvas (2006)

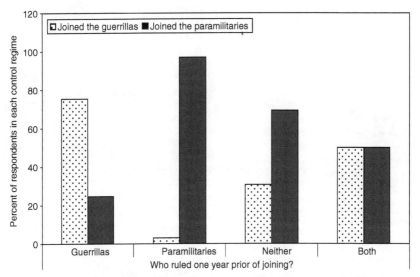

Figure 16.5 Recruitment as a function of control, Colombia

These data are based on a survey question that asks ex-combatants who had joined either the guerrillas or the paramilitaries, where they used to live one year prior to joining. Ex-combatants who lived in an area ruled by the guerrillas a year prior to joining were 50% more likely to join the guerrillas than the paramilitaries; those who lived in areas run by the paramilitaries were 95% more likely to join them as opposed to the guerrillas; those who lived in areas ruled by neither actors (i.e. primarily ruled by the state) were about 40% more likely to join the paramilitaries; and last, when control was divided between these two actors, joiners split in half. These data strongly suggest, in other words, that territorial control

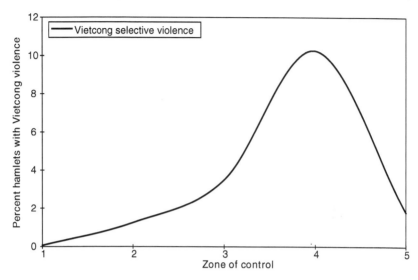

Figure 16.6 Vietcong selective violence as a function of territorial control

is clearly associated with recruitment. A multivariate test assigns causal significance to this finding (Arjona and Kalyvas 2007).

Last, Figure 16.6 is derived from an analysis of the Hamlet Evaluation System, a data-collection system initiated by the US during the Vietnam war which includes information on territorial control at the hamlet level, as well as data on Vietcong selective violence (though not state selective violence) (Kalyvas and Kocher 2006). Data from a random monthly cross-section (July 1969) covering 10,479 hamlets and measuring Vietcong selective violence across five zones of controls show a distribution very similar to what I found in the Argolid: insurgent violence is much more likely in zone 4 compared to everywhere else.

A replication

What this evidence suggests is that omitting territorial control from an analysis of violence is likely to bias the results. Rather than just assert this point, I replicate the Greek test using an overaggregated version of the variable for violence and omitting the variable for territorial control. I then compare the results to the "correct" model which includes the properly disaggregated variable for violence and the variable for territorial control.

How were these data collected in the first place? The choice of Greece was motivated by practical concerns – the ability to conduct wide-ranging research in a rural context combining archival and field components. Within Greece, I selected the prefecture (*nomós*) of Argolid, located in the northeastern part of the Peloponnese peninsula in southern Greece. This choice was dictated by the discovery of an important judicial archive that included information about most of the 725 homicides that occurred during the civil war (1943–1944) in every village of the two major counties of the Argolid – an area including sixty-one villages with a total population of 45,086 inhabitants and two towns with a population of 20,050, in 1940. In most cases I was able to reconstruct the identity of the perpetrator and the victim, the links between perpetrator and victim, the time and location of the homicide, the way it was carried out, the links between this homicide with anterior and subsequent instances of violence, and the justifications (if any) that were given or that can be inferred about it. In addition to the Argolid judicial archive, I consulted the archives of the Greek Communist Party, the Greek army, the British Foreign Office, and the (British) Special Operations Executive (SOE).[5] Beyond archival sources, I relied on tens of published and unpublished memoirs, autobiographies, and local histories as well as 116 taped interviews covering all the villages via a "snowball sampling" technique. These interviews were not restricted to "victims." I interviewed both women and men, active participants (in various capabilities: low-level and middle-level political and military cadres, soldiers, collaborators of various shade) and nonactive participants, mostly peasants. I also interviewed perpetrators, victims, their relatives, and bystanders. Finally, I talked to leftists, rightists, politically uncommitted people, as well as people who shifted political identities over time. By conducting archival and field research simultaneously, I was able to cross-check facts between different types of written sources, between individuals of different political orientation, between individuals with different war and postwar experiences, and between individuals from neighboring communities.

In short, reconstructing the process of violence in a war that took place in the 1940s required an extremely labor-intensive assemblage of multiple sources. Because of the fragmentary character of the sources, I had to proceed like an archaeologist and "gather discrete and disparate traces of the past and assemble them in order to shed light on the circumstances and background of what we otherwise can only know from a haunted

---

[5] In fact, there were SOE operatives in the Argolid during 1943–1944 whose reports complement other local sources. Last, I made limited use of German military and military justice archival material that focuses on the military situation of the Argolid.

Table 16.4. *Replications*

Model: Dependent variable	1 Totviol	2 Totviol	3 Indviol	4 Selviol	5 Incviol	6 Insviol	7 Incviol	8 Insviol	9 Indviol (t4)	10 Selviol (t4)	11 Indviol (t4)	12 Selviol (t4)
Population (log)	14.036*** [3.70]	12.799*** [3.48]	12.434** [2.6]	4.151*** [3.05]	8.026*** [2.82]	8.559** [2.46]	7.833** [2.59]	8.191** [2.28]	2.99 [1.06]	1.071 [0.94]	2.993 [1.05]	1.051 [1.30]
Education	2.699 [1.45]	2.167 [1.20]	0.723 [0.39]	1.163 [1.02]	2.048** [2.06]	−0.161 [−0.11]	1.965** [1.89]	−0.319 [−.23]	0.571 [0.78]	0.237 [0.53]	0.535 [.74]	0.522 [1.15]
Altitude (log)	5.542*** [2.76]	6.513*** [3.09]	4.049* [1.9]	2.128*** [3.35]	3.149** [2.03]	3.028** [2.33]	3.301** [2.22]	3.316** [2.31]	0.335 [0.73]	0.342 [0.58]	0.313 [.69]	0.517 [1.05]
Dist. from town (log)	4.792 [1.51]	5.399 [1.64]	7.585 [1.53]	0.161 [.12]	1.35 [0.74]	6.396* [1.74]	1.445 [.76]	6.577** [1.80]	2.726 [1.07]	0.420 [0.82]	2.761 [1.06]	0.141 [.27]
Court litigation (log)	−1.639 [−.84]	−2.464 [−1.08]	1.882 [0.82]	−1.124 [−1.34]	0.609 [0.51]	0.148 [0.09]	0.479 [.32]	−0.096 [−.05]	−0.779 [−.93]	0.376 [0.58]	−0.820 [−.93]	0.694 [1.63]
GDP	2.558 [1.07]	1.652 [0.68]	5.749 [1.6]	0.187 [.20]	1.676 [1.13]	4.26 [1.51]	1.534 [.92]	3.991 [1.31]	1.538 [1.03]	0.111 [0.22]	1.474 [1.01]	0.613 [1.32]
Mean control		−3.827 [−1.30]					−0.598 [−.33]	−1.136 [−.46]				
Disaggregated control											−1.271 [−.79]	10.068*** [2.85]
Constant	−139.038*** [−3.84]	−127.872 [−3.68]	−135.529 [−2.47]	−35.998 [−2.53]	−69.614 [−2.82]	−101.913 [−2.45]	−67.867 [−2.58]	−98.596 [−2.32]	−39.266 [−1.07]	−8.391 [−0.86]	−39.175 [−1.07]	−9.114 [−1.27]
Observations	61	61	61	61	61	61	61	61	61	61	61	61
R-Squared	0.44	0.45	0.33	0.29	0.30	0.34	0.30	0.34	0.12	0.05	0.12	0.54

Note: Robust *t* statistics are in brackets.
*Significant at 10% **Significant at 5% ***Significant at 1%

memory" (Geyer 2000, 178). At the same time, however, this type of engagement with data collection allowed me to properly disaggregate the data and code the key variable of territorial control. Though restricted to a single region, this dataset is, therefore, ideal for the purposes of comparing the results of a "correct" test to deficiently specified alternatives.

A different way of describing this exercise is as follows: suppose that I did not conduct this extensive data-collection effort, but instead stumbled upon a count of fatalities compiled by historians or a local NGO – like the authors of the three Nepal papers. What would an analysis based on such data look like?

To begin with, had I relied on historical data, it is highly likely that I would have undercounted two key variables: the level of selective violence (which turns out to reach 50.48% of all homicides) and the level of insurgent violence (which accounts for 51.31% of the fatalities). The reason is that the historical record has preserved the more visible large indiscriminate massacres rather than the individualized targeted killings. Furthermore, it has also privileged the more visible (and politically more blameworthy) violence of the incumbents rather than the violence of the insurgents. Last, I would have been completely unable to distinguish between selective and indiscriminate violence or to disaggregate violence by time period.

I estimated eleven models to fit these different scenarios which I compare to the correct model (model 12; Table 16.4). The dependent variable in model 1 (total violence or **Totviol**) is the aggregate total count of fatalities. Like the paper by Murshed and Gates (2005), it is a single indicator (for each village). This model does not include the independent variable for territorial control. Two variables are significant: altitude (like in all the Nepal models) and population. Model 2 is similar, save for the introduction of an aggregate measure of control (i.e. one that averages control over the entire 1943–1944 year). The same variables (altitude and population) remain significant and aggregate control fails to attain significance (in fact, its sign is opposite from predicted). The dependent variable in models 3 and 4 are the counts of indiscriminate and selective fatalities respectively (**Indviol** and **Selviol**) aggregated, again, by actor and time. Population and altitude remain significant in both models, but their effect goes down in model 4. Models 5 and 6 disaggregate violence by actor and focus respectively on insurgent and incumbent violence (**Insviol** and **Incviol**). Population, education, and altitude are all positively correlated with incumbent violence whereas population, altitude, and distance from the closest town are positively correlated with insurgent violence – though the statistical significance in all specifications is lower compared to the previous models.

Models 7 and 8 have the same dependent variable but introduce the aggregate measure of control which is not significant. The same variables stay significant. Last, models 9–11 are the most "disaggregated": they disaggregate violence by actor and into selective and discriminate, and also introduce temporal aggregation.[6] I omit the measure for territorial control from models 9 and 10. No variable is significant and the R-Squared collapses. A disaggregated measure for control is introduced in model 11 where the dependent variable is indiscriminate violence. No variable is significant in that model either which also has a very low R-Squared. Last, model 12 is the "correct" one. The dependent variable is selective violence disaggregated by time period but not by actor (as the theoretical prediction applies to all actors). In this model, the control variable is large and statistically significant, and the R-Squared is the highest.

Conclusion

The conclusion is straightforward. Had I relied on insufficiently disaggregated or "mis-aggregated" data and omitted a measure of territorial control, the analysis would have produced biased results. Clearly, disaggregation is essential, as is the inclusion of a measure for territorial control.

There is no doubt that collecting data at that level of disaggregation is not easy. However, the alternative is to use highly aggregated data and omit the crucial control variable with the results I have suggested. Alternatively, one could compensate for the lack of these variables in creative ways. Such an example is contained in a recent paper by Humphreys and Weinstein (2006) that uses survey data from Sierra Leone to estimate a model of civilian abuse by armed groups. Having coded no variable for control, they rely on a substitute called "dominance," which records the estimated size of a unit relative to the estimated total number of troops in the zone. This measure, however, is highly problematic as any student of insurgency and counterinsurgency would easily surmise: the ability of an armed group to control a particular locality is only partly a function of the raw numbers of combatants. Control is a function of the distribution of these troops across an area with specific geographical features, combined with the number, commitment, and distribution of civilian supporters across the same area.[7] In short, when it comes to coding territorial control there is no

[6] For simplicity, I use here one cross-section, the fourth time period (t4) which covers the period of August–September 1944.
[7] This paper also fails to distinguish between selective and indiscriminate violence. Again, lack of appropriate coding is justified by a dubious argument whereby this distinction is "blurred" (Humphreys and Weinstein 2006, 444). The entire exercise is quite

easy alternative to either direct and careful data collection using all available sources, or prior coding by the insurgents or counterinsurgents themselves, when they do leave extensive archival material behind.

To sum up, although this essay fully endorses the current "micro-dynamics of civil war" research program, it calls for a deeper engagement with cases, careful and detailed collection of fine-grained data, and thorough theorization. Unless these conditions are fulfilled, the current turn to the micro level will miss the opportunity to live up to its promise.

REFERENCES

Arjona, Ana, and Stathis N. Kalyvas. 2006. "Preliminary Results from a Survey of Demobilized Fighters in Colombia". Unpublished paper, Yale University.

——— 2007. "Rebelling Against Rebellion: Insurgent and Counterinsurgent Recruitment." Unpublished paper, Yale University.

Barron, Patrick, Kai Kaiser, and Menno Pradhan. 2004. "Local Conflict in Indonesia: Measuring Incidence and Identifying Patterns." Working paper, World Bank.

Blattman, Christopher, and Jeannie Annan. 2007. "The Consequences of Child Soldiering." Unpublished paper.

Bohara, Alok K., Neil J. Mitchell, and Mani Nepal. 2006. "Opportunity, Democracy, and the Exchange of Political Violence." *Journal of Conflict Resolution* 50 (February): 108–128.

Brass, Paul R. 1997. *Theft of an Idol: Text and Context in the Representation of Collective Violence.* Princeton University Press.

Brubaker, Rogers, and David D. Laitin. 1998. "Ethnic and Nationalist Violence." *Annual Review of Sociology* 24: 243–252.

Cederman, Lars-Erik, and Luc Girardin. 2007. "Beyond Fractionalization: Mapping Ethnicity onto Nationalist Insurgencies." *American Political Science Review* 101 (February): 173–185.

Collier, Paul, and Anke Hoeffler. 2004. "Greed and Grievance in Civil War." *Oxford Economic Papers* 56 (October): 563–595.

Cramer, Christopher. 2002. "*Homo Economicus* Goes to War: Methodological Individualism, Rational Choice, and the Political Economy of War." *World Development* 30 (November): 1845–1864.

——— 2007. *Violence in Developing Countries: War, Memory, Progress.* Bloomington: Indiana University Press.

Deininger, Klaus. 2004. "Causes and Consequences of Civil Strife: Micro-Level Evidence from Uganda." Working paper, World Bank.

Deininger, Klaus, Ana Maria Ibáñez, and Pablo Querubin. 2004. "Towards Sustainable Return Policies for the Displaced Population: Why Are Some Displaced Households More Willing to Return than Others?" Working paper, Households in Conflicts Network.

problematic as the type of abuse described in the paper is clearly of an *indiscriminate* nature, thus rendering its test of theories of *selective* violence pointless.

Do, Quy-Toan, and Lakshmi Iyer. 2007. "Poverty, Social Divisions, and Conflict in Nepal." Working paper, World Bank.

Eckstein, Harry. 1965. "On the Etiology of Internal Wars." *History and Theory* 4 (February): 133–163.

Fearon, James D., Kimuli Kasara, and David D. Laitin. 2007. "Ethnic Minority Rule and Civil War Onset." *American Political Science Review* 101 (February): 187–193.

Fearon, James D., and David D. Laitin. 2003. "Ethnicity, Insurgency, and Civil War." *American Political Science Review* 97 (February): 75–86.

Geyer, Michael. 2000. "Civitella della Chiana on 29 June 1944: The Reconstruction of a German 'Measure.'" In *War of Extermination: The German Military in World War II, 1941–1944*, ed. Hannes Heer and Klaus Naumann. New York: Berghahn Books, 175–216.

Gould, Roger V. 2003. *Collision of Wills: How Ambiguity about Social Rank Breeds Conflict.* University of Chicago Press.

Greer, Donald. 1935. *The Incidence of the Terror During the French Revolution: A Statistical Interpretation.* Cambridge, MA: Harvard University Press.

Guichaoua, Y. 2007. "Who Joins Ethnic Militias? A Survey of the Oodua People's Congress in Southwestern Nigeria." Working paper, Households in Conflicts Network.

Gutiérrez Sanín, Francisco. 2004. "Criminal Rebels? A Discussion of War and Criminality from the Colombian Experience." *Politics and Society* 32 (June): 257–285.

Hegre, Havard, and Nicholas Sambanis. 2006. "Sensitivity Analysis of Empirical Results on Civil War Onset." *Journal of Conflict Resolution* 50 (August): 508–535.

Humphreys, Macartan. 2005. "Natural Resources, Conflict, and Conflict Resolution: Uncovering the Mechanisms." *Journal of Conflict Resolution* 49 (October): 508–537.

Humphreys, Macartan, and Jeremy M. Weinstein. 2006. "Handling and Manhandling Civilians in Civil War." *American Political Science Review* 100 (August): 429–447.

Kalyvas, Stathis N. 2001. "'New' and 'Old' Civil Wars: A Valid Distinction?" *World Politics* 54 (October): 99–118.

2003. "The Ontology of 'Political Violence': Action and Identity in Civil Wars." *Perspectives on Politics* 1 (September): 475–494.

2006. *The Logic of Violence in Civil War.* Cambridge University Press.

2007. "Civil Wars." In *Handbook of Political Science*, ed. Carles Boix and Susan Stokes. Oxford University Press, 416–434.

Kalyvas, Stathis N., and Matthew Adam Kocher. 2006. "Violence and Control in Civil War: An Analysis of the Hamlet Evaluation System (HES)." Unpublished paper.

2007a. "Ethnic Cleavages and Irregular War: Iraq and Vietnam." *Politics and Society* 35 (June): 183–223.

2007b. "How Free is 'Free-Riding' in Civil Wars? Violence, Insurgency, and the Collective Action Problem." *World Politics,* 59 (January): 177–216.

Kocher, Matthew Adam. 2004. "Human Ecology and Civil War." Ph.D. thesis, University of Chicago.

Miguel, Edward, Shanker Satyanath, and Ernest Sergenti. 2004. "Economic Shocks and Civil Conflict: An Instrumental Variables Approach." *Journal of Political Economy* 112 (August): 725–753.

Montalvo, J. G., and Marta Reynal-Querol. 2005. "Ethnic Polarization, Potential Conflict and Civil War." *American Economic Review* 95 (June): 796–816.

Murshed, S. Mansoob, and Scott Gates. 2005. "Spatial-Horizontal Inequality and the Maoist Insurgency in Nepal." *Review of Development Economics* 9 (February): 121–134.

Petersen, Roger. 2001. *Resistance and Rebellion: Lessons from Eastern Europe.* Cambridge University Press.

Przeworski, Adam, Michael E. Alvarez, José Antonio Cheibub, and Fernando Limongi. 2000. *Democracy and Development.* Cambridge University Press.

Restrepo, Jorge, Michael Spagat, and Juan Fernando Vargas. 2004. "The Dynamics of the Colombian Civil Conflict: A New Data Set." *Homo Oeconomicus* 21 (February): 396–428.

Sambanis, Nicholas. 2004a. "Using Case Studies to Expand Economic Models of Civil War." *Perspectives on Politics* 2 (June): 259–279.

2004b. "What is Civil War? Conceptual and Empirical Complexities of an Operational Definition." *Journal of Conflict Resolution* 48 (December): 814–858.

Scott, James C. 1976. *Moral Economy of the Peasant: Rebellion and Subsistence in Southeast Asia.* New Haven: Yale University Press.

Skocpol, Theda. 1979. *States and Social Revolutions: A Comparative Analysis of France, Russia, and China.* Cambridge University Press.

Straus, Scott. 2006. *The Order of Genocide: Race, Power, and War in Rwanda.* Ithaca, NY: Cornell University Press.

Tarrow, Sidney. 1998. *Power in Movement: Social Movements and Contentious Politics.* Cambridge University Press.

Tilly, Charles. 1978. *From Mobilization to Revolution.* Reading, MA: Addison-Wesley.

Tong, James. 1991. *Disorder under Heaven: Collective Violence in the Ming Dynasty.* Stanford University Press.

Trejo Osorio, Guillermo. 2004. "Indigenous Insurgency: Protest, Rebellion, and the Politicization of Ethnicity in 20th Century Mexico." Ph.D. dissertation, University of Chicago.

Varshney, Ashutosh. 2002. *Ethnic Conflict and Civic Life: Hindus and Muslims in India.* New Haven: Yale University Press.

Verwimp, Philip. 2003. "Testing the Double-Genocide Thesis for Central and Southern Rwanda." *Journal of Conflict Resolution* 47 (August): 423–442.

2006. "Machetes and Firearms: The Organization of Massacres in Rwanda." *Journal of Peace Research* 43 (January): 5–22.

Viterna, Jocelyn. 2006. "Pulled, Pushed, and Persuaded: Explaining Women's Mobilization into the Salvadoran Guerrilla Army." *American Journal of Sociology* 112 (July): 1–45.

Weinstein, Jeremy M. 2007. *Inside Rebellion: The Politics of Insurgent Violence.* Cambridge University Press.

Wickham-Crowley, Timothy P. 1992. *Guerrillas and Revolution in Latin America: A Comparative Study of Insurgents and Regimes since 1956.* Princeton University Press.

Wilkinson, Steven I. 2004. *Votes and Violence: Electoral Competition and Ethnic Riots in India.* Cambridge University Press.

Wimmer, Andreas, and Brian Min. 2006. "From Empire to Nation State: Explaining Wars in the Modern World, 1816–2001." *American Sociological Review* 71 (December): 867–897.

Wood, Elisabeth Jean. 2003. *Insurgent Collective Action and Civil War in El Salvador.* Cambridge University Press.

Index

Made in the USA
Lexington, KY
03 September 2012